A Conceptual Lexicon for Classical Confucian Philosophy

SUNY series in Chinese Philosophy and Culture
Roger T. Ames, editor

A Conceptual Lexicon for
Classical Confucian Philosophy

经典儒学核心概念

Roger T. Ames
安乐哲　著

SUNY PRESS

Published by State University of New York Press, Albany

© The Commercial Press, Ltd., 2021
A Conceptual Lexicon for Classical Confucian Philosophy is published by arrangement with The Commercial Press, Ltd. Not for sale in China.

All rights reserved

Printed in the United States of America

No part of this book may be used or reproduced in any manner whatsoever without written permission. No part of this book may be stored in a retrieval system or transmitted in any form or by any means including electronic, electrostatic, magnetic tape, mechanical, photocopying, recording, or otherwise without the prior permission in writing of the publisher.

For information, contact State University of New York Press, Albany, NY
www.sunypress.edu

Library of Congress Cataloging-in-Publication Data

Names: Ames, Roger, author
Title: A conceptual lexicon for classical Confucian philosophy / Ames, Roger, author.
Description: Albany : State University of New York Press, [2022] | Includes bibliographical references and index.
Identifiers: ISBN 9781438490816 (hardcover : alk. paper) | ISBN 9781438490823 (e-book) | ISBN 9781438490809 (paperback)
Further information is available at the Library of Congress.

10 9 8 7 6 5 4 3 2 1

Table of Contents

Introduction ... vii

霸	***ba.*** "Hegemon."	001
本	***ben.*** "Root, trunk."	001
誠	***cheng.*** "Sincerity, with integrity, resolve, (co-)creativity."	011
恥	***chi.*** "A sense of shame."	015
道	***dao.*** "The proper way, way-making, ***dao***."	019
德	***de.*** "Moral virtuosity, excelling morally, virtuality."	028
惡	***e.*** "Rudeness, uncouthness, nasty, ugly, unrefined, base."	037
法	***fa.*** "Standards, norms, laws, models."	038
和	***he.*** "Optimal harmony, optimizing symbiosis."	040
幾	***ji.*** "Inchoate, incipient beginnings."	052
祭	***ji.*** "Sacrificing, sacrifice."	054
諫	***jian.*** "Remonstrating, remonstrance."	057
兼愛	***jian'ai.*** "Inclusive care, inclusive concern."	059
教	***jiao.*** "Teaching, education."	061

精神	***jingshen.*** "Spirituality, vigor, vitality, mystery."	067
敬	***jing.*** "Respecting, revering, seriousness."	069
靜	***jing.*** "Sustained equilibrium."	071
君子	***junzi.*** "Exemplary persons, ruler, prince, lord."	073
樂	***le*** (also pronounced ***yao*** when transitive). "Enjoyment, making the music of enjoyment."	079
類	***lei.*** "Categories, groupings."	082
禮	***li.*** "Ritual propriety in one's roles and relations, ritual practices, 'social grammar, rites, customs, etiquette, propriety, morals, rules of proper behavior, reverence'."	085
理	***li.*** "Patterning, coherence."	105
利	***li.*** "Benefitting, profiting, personal advantage."	111
倫	***lun.*** "Order, relation, category, class."	113
美	***mei.*** "Beautiful."	116
民	***min.*** "The common people."	118
命	***ming.*** "Commanding, ordering, command, mandate, the propensity of things, the force of circumstances."	124
明	***ming.*** "Acuity, brilliance."	128
名	***ming.*** "Naming, making a name for yourself, reputation."	132
內外	***neiwai.*** "Inner and outer, inside and outside."	136

氣	*qi.* "Vital energy, *qi.*"	141
情	*qing.* "Emotions, passions, feelings, the way things are, situation, circumstances."	155
仁	*ren.* "Consummate persons, consummate conduct."	163
儒	*ru.* "Confucianism, Ruism, scholar-teacher, literati tradition."	181
善	*shan.* "Felicity, efficacy, behaving well, auspicious conduct."	186
上帝	*shangdi.* "High god(s)."	192
神	*shen.* "Heavenly gods, ancestors, spirituality, vigor, vitality, mystery."	194
身	*shen.* "Lived, social body."	197
生	*sheng.* "Living, growing, birthing."	197
聖（人）	*sheng* or *shengren.* "Sage, sagacity."	211
慎其獨	*shenqidu.* "Internalizing and consolidating virtuosic conduct as one's habituated disposition for action, being circumspect when dwelling alone."	219
士	*shi.* "Warrior, retainer, knight, scholar-official."	223
勢	*shi.* "Purchase, momentum, configuration."	225
始	*shi.* "Fetal beginning, natal beginning, genealogical beginning."	238
恕	*shu.* "Putting oneself in the other's place, deference, empathy, dramatic rehearsal."	248

術	*shu.* "Techniques of rulership."	257
思	*si.* "Thinking, reflecting."	261
四端	*siduan.* "The four inclinations."	271
太極	*taiji.* "The furthest reach."	280
體	*ti.* "Lived body, discursive body, embodying."	283
天	*tian.* "***Tian***, conventionally 'Heaven'."	291
天命	*tianming.*	299
天志	*tianzhi.* "The purposes or intent of ***tian***."	299
體用	*tiyong.* "Reforming and functioning, trans-*form*-ing."	303
同	*tong.* "Sameness, similarity."	309
王	*wang.* "King, True King."	311
萬物	*wanwu.* "The ten thousand things, the ten thousand processes or events, the myriad things or happenings."	313
文	*wen.* "The written word, patterns, culture, refinement, King Wen."	315
文化	*wenhua.* "Culture, enculturation."	316
無	*wu.*	324
無極	*wuji.*	324
無爲	*wuwei.* "Noncoercive acting."	324
五行	*wuxing.* "Five modes of virtuosic conduct, the five phases."	330

象	***xiang.*** "Figuring, figuring out, configuring, figure, imaging, imagining, image."	339
孝	***xiao.*** "Family reverence, filial piety."	349
小人	***xiaoren.*** "Petty and mean persons."	373
孝悌	***xiaoti.*** "Family reverence and fraternal deference."	373
心	***xin.*** "Heartmind, bodyheartminding, thinking and feeling."	373
信	***xin.*** "Making good on one's word, living up to one's word."	380
性	***xing.*** "Natural human propensities."	383
虛	***xu.*** "Emptiness."	405
學	***xue.*** "Teaching and learning."	406
易	***yi.*** "Changing, exchanging, ease."	413
一	***yi.*** "One, uniqueness, continuity."	414
義	***yi.*** "Optimal appropriateness, meaning."	417
陰陽	***yinyang.*** "***Yin*** and ***yang.***"	427
勇	***yong.*** "Courage, bravery, vigor, vitality, boldness, fierceness."	433
友	***you.*** "Friend, friendship."	434
有無	***youwu.*** "Something and nothing, determinate and indeterminate, presence and absence."	438
樂	***yue.*** "Music."	446

正	*zheng.* "Proper, acting properly."	446
政	*zheng.* "Proper governing, effecting sociopolitical order."	448
正名	*zhengming.* "Using names properly."	453
知/智	*zhi.* "Living wisely, realizing, wisdom, knowing."	463
志	*zhi.*	481
直	*zhi.*	481
質	*zhi.* "Native temperament, raw stuff, basic disposition."	481
自然	*ziran.* "Self-so-ing, so-of-itself, spontaneity."	485
中	*zhong.* "Center, balance, focus, equilibrium."	487
忠	*zhong.* "Conscientiousness, doing one's utmost, loyalty."	489
中庸	*zhongyong.* "Focusing the familiar, hitting the mark in the everyday, making the ordinary extraordinary."	492
主客	*zhuke.* "Subject and object, subjectivity and objectivity."	493

Bibliography of Earlier Glossaries   494
Bibliography of Works Cited   495
Acknowledgements   506

Introduction

An Interpretive Strategy

In compiling this new *Conceptual Lexicon for Classical Confucian Philosophy*, my goal has been to try my best to take this Confucian philosophical tradition on its own terms. My concern has been that many of our new translations of these canonical texts are uncritically perpetuating the same formula for rendering key philosophical terms proffered in the earlier efforts at cultural translation. The consequence is that this now "standard" vocabulary has encouraged a sense of literalness and familiarity with an erstwhile "Chinese" philosophical vocabulary. Again, over the past several centuries these texts have in important degree been transplanted into a worldview and a commonsense not their own, and there has still been insufficient attention paid to a recovery of their own interpretive contexts that is a precondition for retaining their own integrity.

William James warns us that "We live forwards . . . but we understand backwards."[①] This same concern led William Faulkner to observe that "There is no such thing as *was*—only *is*."[②] Their important point is that we are always implicated in our experience, and thus we can never escape anachronism in our thinking about

---

[①] William James. *Pragmatism and Other Writings*. New York: Penguin, 2000, p. 98. In Lewis Carroll's *Through the Looking Glass*, the White Queen says to Alice: "It's a poor sort of memory that only works backwards."

[②] William Faulkner. *The Lion in the Garden: Interviews with William Faulkner 1926-1962*. ed. James B. Meriwether and Michael Millgate. New York: Random House, 1968, p. 258.

it. The challenge then is that if all experience is necessarily a collaboration between us and our world and is thus always in degree a reflection of our own values and interests, what strategy can we appeal to in trying to understand the conceptual cluster of concepts that are used in the organization of these canonical texts?

At the beginning of the nineteenth century, most Europeans with a few marginal if not heretical exceptions saw world culture through a biblical lens. They believed with unwavering certainty that the cosmos was only a few thousand years old, that all life on earth including humanity was descended from Noah's ark, that Christianity is the only true and consummate religion from which all other religions are derived, that human faith and piety continue to play a pivotal role in the larger cosmic order and in its divine history, that the unreason of madness was a freely chosen moral error, and that each one of us has an immortal soul which, at the risk of irrevocable damnation, will one day stand before God in judgment for our deeds done.[1] Such being the commonsense of the time, any discussion we might pursue today of the prevailing values at the beginning of the nineteenth century requires that we construct an interpretive context as a preemptive strategy for enabling us to take an earlier Europe on its own terms, and for resisting an overwriting of that period with our own, very different assumptions. If this problem of "uncommon assumptions" is a worry so close to home, how much more necessary then, is the construction of an interpretive context for our contemporary Western reading of the historically antique and culturally remote texts of classical Confucian philosophy?

Friedrich Nietzsche in his *Beyond Good and Evil* reflects upon how a specific worldview is sedimented into the very language that speaks it:

---

[1] Urs App makes just such a claim in his introductory comments to *The Birth of Orientalism*. Philadelphia: University of Pennsylvania Press, 2010, p. xiii.

The strange family resemblance of all Indian, Greek, and German philosophizing is explained easily enough. Where there is an affinity of languages, it cannot fail, owing to the common philosophy of grammar—I mean, owing to the unconscious domination and guidance by similar grammatical functions—that everything is prepared at the outset for a similar development and sequence of philosophical systems; just as the way seems barred against certain other possibilities of world-interpretation.[1]

Nietzsche is certainly not endorsing any theory of strong linguistic determinism—that is, the idea that our languages necessarily constrain us to think in certain ways. Rather, he is simply observing that natural languages and their syntax—in his example here, the Indo-European family of languages—are over time invested with a particular cultural narrative's insights into what makes the human experience meaningful. Natural languages and their structures tend to reveal the default worldviews and distilled commonsenses of the cultures they speak. Said another way, our languages "speak" us as much as we speak our languages, disposing us to entertain experience in one way as opposed to another, and prompting us to ask some questions rather than others.

Indeed, this same Nietzsche, reflecting on how languages such as French and German came to be gendered—"*la table*" and "*le soleil*"—allows that "when man gave all things a sex he thought, not that he was playing, but that he had gained a profound insight . . ."[2] In fact, the oeuvre of Nietzsche himself is an object lesson in

---

[1] Friedrich Nietzsche. *Beyond Good and Evil*. trans. W. Kaufmann. New York: Vintage, 1966, p. 20.
[2] Friedrich Nietzsche. *A Nietzsche Reader*. trans. R.J. Hollingdale. Harmondsworth: Penguin, 1977, p. 86. One wonders what in the early days of these languages would prompt the French speakers to understand the sun as masculine and the moon as feminine, while their German cousins thought the opposite.

the very problem he ponders here: that is, the tension between recalcitrant tradition on the one hand, and disruptive innovation on the other. Our languages are conservative in wanting to speak from within their own narratives, and tend to resist new ideas in proportion to the disjunction these ideas have with what has gone before. Commonsense is obstinate. Thus, when Nietzsche famously proclaims "God is dead," since his shared commonsense is heavily freighted with God, he must himself become linguistically dexterous. The object of his critique is the persistent transcendentalism and dualistic worldview that follows from it as it has become entrenched within the languages and cultural experience of the Abrahamic traditions. It is because Nietzsche is frustrated, compromised, and even betrayed by the deeply committed language in which he is attempting to give voice to his revolutionary ideas that he has little choice but to turn away from the more "literal" expository language available to him, and rely heavily upon rhetorical devices and literary tropes.

The distinguished British sinologist, Angus Graham, like Nietzsche, ascribes unique and evolving categories and conceptual structures to different cultural traditions, and in so doing, challenges the Saussurian structuralist distinction between *langue* (universal and systematic linguistic structures and rules governing all languages) and *parole* (diverse and open-ended speech acts in any of our natural languages).[1] All the same, we might borrow Saussure's distinction and take liberties with it that resists his structuralist assumptions to reinforce Graham's point. We can use *langue* (language) to contrast the evolved, theoretical, and conceptual structure of any given language system as it has been shaped by an aggregating cultural intelligence over millennia, with *parole* (speech) as the application

---

[1] Saussure uses the analogy of a chess game, where *langue* are the fixed rules that govern the game while *parole* are the actual, varied moves made by different people that come to constitute any particular game.

of this natural language in the individual utterances we make.[①] Graham and we fellow pluralists, need just such a distinction to reinforce our claim that the Chinese language has neither developed nor has available to it an indigenous concept or a term that can capture the Abrahamic notion of "God," while at the same time insisting that this same Chinese language has all of the semantic and syntactic resources it needs to give a fair and robust account of such an idea. The basic claim here is that there is no vocabulary available in our Western languages to do justice to the conceptual structure of Confucianism. At the same time, while we have committed to the impoverishing translation of *li* 禮 as "ritual," we cannot in fact "say" *li* in English, or in German either. Nonetheless we can say lots about this key Confucian notion in both European languages, and get pretty clear on what it means.

Recently, and specifically in reference to the classical Chinese language, Graham concludes that in reporting on the eventful flow of a Chinese *qi* 氣 cosmology made explicit in the first among the Confucian classics, the *Yijing* 易經 or *Book of Changes*, "the sentence structure of Classical Chinese places us in a world of process about which we must ask ... 'Whence?' and also, since it is moving, 'At what time?'"[②] What Graham is saying here is that any perceived coherence in the emergent order of things assumed in Chinese cosmology, while being expressed in abstract, theoretical terms, is

---

[①] I am "borrowing" this distinction from Saussure because I do not want to endorse any kind of structuralism that would allow for a severe separation between *langue* and *parole*. Instead I would side with the sentiments of a Zhuangzi or a Mikhail Bakhtin who would see these two dimensions of language as mutually shaping and evolving in their always dialectical relationship. Utterances gradually change the structure of language, and the changing structure of our languages orients and influences the utterances that it makes possible. For them, what we think about and how we think, are coterminous and mutually shaping.

[②] A.C. Graham. *Studies in Chinese Philosophy and Philosophical Literature*. Albany: State University of New York Press, 1990, pp. 360-411, especially p. 408.

at the same time resolutely historicist and situated, and hence has to be qualified by a location, by a particular time in its evolution, and also by its applications. For example, when understood within the context of this Confucian cosmology, Graham problematizes the translation of *renxing* 人性 as "human nature." He avers that *renxing* in describing the human experience has been conceived of as an ongoing, open-ended, and evolving process rather than as some essential and "timeless" property or some universal endowment defined by formal and final causes. Thus, beyond the question of "*What* does the term *renxing* mean?" we must also ask the other questions: "*Where* was it thought of in this way?" "*Whence* did it come to mean this?" "*How* did it serve us to think of it in this way?," and perhaps most importantly, "*Whither* is its impetus in defining who we will become?" Indeed, to appreciate the ubiquitousness of processual, gerundive thinking in this early cosmology, we might invoke a key distinction found in the *Changes*. While cosmic order and all that emerges within it has certainly been understood in general and persistent terms (*tong* 通), at the same time, it must always be qualified by the local, the specific, and the transitory process of change (*bian* 變). For Confucian cosmology, in referencing the ongoing transformation of the world around us, we must always respect the *where*, the *when*, and the *who* as specific qualifications integral to this ineluctable process. The crucial implication of Graham's insight into Confucian cosmology is that all of the rational structures that might be appealed to in expressing our understanding of the human experience—that is, whatever theories, concepts, categories, and definitions we might reference—are all ultimately made vulnerable to change by the always shifting organs and objects of their application. In the flux and flow of experience, making sense of a changing world is itself a changing process.

An entailment of the claim that early Chinese cosmology gives privilege to change is that the language that expresses the worldview and the commonsense in which the Chinese corpus is to be located is first and foremost "gerundive," a feature that requires us at times to stretch ourselves conceptually by "verbing" nouns much more frequently than is the norm for English-speakers. Chinese, like ancient Hebrew but unlike most members of the Indo-European family of languages, is more eventful than substantial in its syntactic structure, and in much of its semantics as well. It is fairly well known that apart from context, virtually every Chinese graph can be here a noun, there an adjective, verb or adverb; less well known, or at least acknowledged by most translators, is the dynamic cosmos reflected in the language itself. "Things" are less in focus than events; nouns that would abstract and objectify elements of this world are derived from and revert back to their gerundive sensibilities. Indeed, I have argued at some length that a human being in this world is better understood to be an irreducibly relational "human becoming."①

The ontological language of substance and essence tends to defy this linguistic priority of dynamic thinking, committed as it is to the primacy of "things" rather than "happenings," and to a more substantial "world" rather than a more fluid "experiencing of this world." It is a fair observation that a careful reading of the introduction included in my *Sourcebook in Classical Confucian Philosophy* and this companion *Lexicon* is made necessary by the fact that the target language of this translation—English—reflects and reinforces ontological assumptions that differ in crucial respects from the natural cosmology sedimented into the structure of the object language—classical Chinese—and hence can only imperfectly be employed to "speak" the world being referenced in these Confucian texts.

We do not at all wish to suggest that the Chinese had no notion of substantiality, or that Indo-European languages cannot well

---

① See Roger T. Ames. *Human Becomings: Theorizing Persons for Confucian Role Ethics*. Albany: State University of New York Press, 2020.

chronicle events.① Chinese toes surely hurt when stubbed on rocks, and English joggers are not seen to be performing miracles. Nevertheless, English grammar tempts us to emphasize "thingness" in a way that classical Chinese did and does not, instead providing a framing of the event being referenced. Think of a simple English sentence such as "The wind is blowing." We could never be surprised by this observation because wind cannot "do" (verb) anything *but* blow. But in fact, "wind" is made redundant in understanding that it is nothing more or less than the "blowing" itself. Rain is slightly more versatile: It can "pour;" but what does the "It" (noun) refer to in either "It is raining" or "It is pouring?" A "thing"—a subsisting agency, a subject—in our substance language is assumed as a necessary ground for action.

In the same way, while we as translators and commentators cannot easily avoid making statements such as "Master Zeng was the most *xiao* 孝 of all the disciples of Confucius," it would be more sinologically accurate, if more stilted, to say that "Master Zeng *xiao*-ed more consistently than any of his peers." And it would be even more accurate to understand Master Zeng himself as a compounding lifetime narrative of "*xiao*-ing" rather than as some discrete, constant entity. Thus, our exhortation to the reader of this *Lexicon* and the *Sourcebook* is: Think gerunds first, and try not to impose too many Western philosophically and/or religiously pregnant concepts on the text at hand. For instance, the isomorphic relationship between family and governing institutions (*jiaguotonggou* 家國同構) that is made so clear in these texts should warn the reader not to seek the sharp and dialectical distinction between private and public—the

---

① I am inclined to use "we" rather than "I" in my attempt to translate Confucian culture into the Western academy in deference to my teachers D.C. Lau, Lao Siguang, Fang Dongmei, Yang Youwei, and Angus Graham, and to the collaborators I have worked with over my career: especially David L. Hall and Henry Rosemont Jr. They are all very present in different ways in what I am trying to say.

"us" and "them"—that political theory as usually applied normally obliges us to draw, for it isn't there. Nor is there any relevance to the bulk of the other largely exclusive dualisms so historically central in the Greek-inspired narrative of philosophy and theology: mind/body, transcendent/immanent, objective/subjective, sacred/profane, individual/collective, reality/appearance, and more. In sum, before we can appreciate the many ways in which the early Confucians are truly "just like us," we must come to understand deeply the ways in which they were not.

Here as in our previous work, in seeking to revise the existing formula of translations, we want to be at once deconstructive and programmatic. That is, we begin from the concern that the popular translations of these philosophical terms in themselves often do not adequately respect the degree of difference between current ways of thinking, and the worldview in which these Chinese texts were produced. What is the most comfortable choice of language and what at first blush makes the best sense to the translator within the target language, might well be a warning signal that something that is originally *un*familiar is, at a stroke, being made familiar.

To take an example, if "principle" seems to most felicitous in translating *li* 理, particularly because of its moral connotations, we have to worry that it locates *li* squarely within classical Greek "One-behind-the-many" metaphysical thinking. L. *principium* from *princeps*—"first in time, position, or authority>prince, emperor"—introduces a notion of independent agency that might not be relevant to *li*. *Principium* is of course used to translate the Greek *arche* from *archon*—"the beginning, the ultimate underlying substance, the ultimate indemonstrable principle." Indeed, the popular understanding of principle is strongly attached to associations that in sum suggest a fixed, foundational, predetermined, and originative law. In the absence of the degree of qualification that would in fact disqualify "principle" as a useful translation of *li*, such associations have come to obscure rather than illuminate the processual worldview that predominates in Chinese cosmology. As clear evidence of this problem, influenced by an understanding of *li* as subsisting principles, many of the current interpretations of Zhu Xi have tended to subordinate an understanding of his project of self-cultivation to the recovery of a putative systematic metaphysics.

The existing formula of translations that includes *li* as "principle" has been "legitimized" by its unchallenged persistence and by its gradual insinuation into the standard Chinese-English and English-Chinese dictionaries and glosses. These dictionaries, in encouraging the uncritical assumption that this set of translations provides the student with a "literal" and thus "conservative" rendering of the terms, have become complicit in the entrenched cultural equivocation that we are attempting to address herein. Our argument is that it is in fact these now familiar, formulaic usages that are the "radical" rather than conservative interpretations. That is, to consciously or unconsciously transplant a text from its own intellectual soil and replant it in one that has a decidedly different philosophical terrain is as "radical" as it gets, tampering as it does with the very roots that have secured the text historically and culturally. A failure to conserve sufficiently the original cultural assumptions and problematic of the text is to take gross liberties with it. Indeed, it is our claim that it is our concerted effort to understand the text within its own cultural landscape, however imperfectly accomplished, that is properly conservative.

To be fair to the important new translations of the Confucian canons that have appeared over the past few generations, we must ask the question: At the end of the day, can European languages, freighted as they are with a historical commitment to substance ontology—what Jacque Derrida has called "logocentrism" and "the language of presence"—actually "speak" the processual worldview that grounds these Chinese texts? Can these canonical texts such as the *Book of Changes* and the *Expansive Learning* (*Daxue* 大學) be translated into English and still communicate the worldview that has been invested in them? And more to the point, given the project presently at hand, how does this new conceptual lexicon propose to address the challenge of trying to provide an explanation of these Chinese terms that would respect its own implicit worldview?

Complexities in the Philosophy of Culture

Are we then to understand that the generic, persistent cultural assumptions that distinguish this Confucian worldview—what we are calling "an interpretive context"—are "essential" and unchanging conditions? Of course not. We have to unload this familiar "essentialism" charge that elides the important distinction between an impoverishing orientalism and responsible generalizations, between an exclusionary relativism and an open, inclusive pluralism, between incommensurability and the mutual accommodation that provides the possibility for hybridic growth.[①]

But the need for unloading the essentialism charge against philosophers of culture is more complex. As a consequence of the challenge of new directions in historiographical thinking, over the past several decades the assumption that cultural families develop their distinctive patterns of values, norms, and practices in relative isolation from one another has become markedly less trenchant. Both historians and philosophers have come to recognize significant distortions that attend any unreflective tendencies to compartmentalize the ancient and premodern worlds according

---

[①] See my essay "Unloading the Essentialism Charge: Reflections on Methodology in Doing Philosophy of Culture." *Comparative Philosophy and Method: Contemporary Practices and Future Possibilities.* ed. Steven Burik, Robert Smid, and Ralph Weber. London: Bloomsbury Academic Press, forthcoming.

to currently prevailing spatial and conceptual divisions and their underlying (often highly political) rationales. In particular, critical assessment is now well underway regarding the degree to which persistent prejudices about metageography—especially the "myth of continents"—have shaped and continue to shape representations of history and cultural origins. The classic assertion of "independently originating" European and Asian cultures on either side of the Ural mountains, for example, is being abandoned in favor of highlighting "Eurasian" characteristics in the complex cultural genealogies of both "West" and "East."[1] Indeed, given that cultures arise interculturally, or better yet, *intra*-culturally, in wide-ranging, intimate commerce with one another over time as a borderless ecology of cultures having an inside without an outside, it would seem that no culture *can* be fully understood in isolation from others. It was for this reason that years ago, David Hall and I asked the question: Is there really more than one culture?[2] If we follow Wittgenstein with his "family resemblances" and "language games" to its logical conclusion, then given the contingencies of culture, foregoing reduction or sublation, it is the unsummed and unbounded context containing mutually incoherent and yet imbricated games that may be called "culture." The engagement between two cultures, then, is the articulation of alternative importances within a single (incoherent) complex. This understanding of culture resonates rather closely with the "focus and field" understanding of *dao* 道 as the unbounded and unsummed totality of orders as they are construed from insistently particular perspectives (*de* 德). Given the vagueness and complexity that attends such an understanding of order, one needs to make no

---

[1] See Martin W. Lewis and Karen E. Wigen. *Myth of Continents: A Critique of Metageography.* Berkeley: University of California Press, 1997.
[2] David L. Hall and Roger T. Ames. *Anticipating China: Thinking Through the Narratives of Chinese and Western Culture.* Albany: State University of New York Press, 1995, Chapter 2, "The Contingency of Culture."

final distinction among different cultures and their languages.①

Again, we must think genealogically as well as morphologically. That is, the development and growth of particular cultures certainly takes place through historical interactions among them that result either in accommodations of differences as conditions for mutual contribution, or in a competition for acknowledged superiority. But cultures change not only in adaptive response to other cultures and to political, economic, and environmental exigencies, but are also animated by an internal impulse as an expression of their own particular aspirations. Quite often, this change involves and requires envisioning ways of life distinctively other than those that are near and familiar, revealing with greater or lesser clarity what present cultural realities are not, and do not promise. Cultural change *does* occur in response to differing circumstantial realities, but it also takes place as a function of pursuing new or not-yet-actualized ideals. Said differently, ideals as "ends-in-view"—what Charles Taylor calls "hypergoods"—are also realities that live in history, and that at least in degree, have the force of directing the patterns of change.②

This recognition of the indigenous impulse has as its own corollary the insight that the histories through which cultures narrate their own origins and development are not primarily aimed at accurately depicting a closed past, but rather at disclosing arcs of change projected into open and yet more or less distinctly anticipated

---

① See David L. Hall and Roger T. Ames. *Anticipating China*. pp. 175-179.
② "Hypergoods" is a useful neologism introduced by Charles Taylor in his *Sources of the Self: The Making of the Modern Identity*. Cambridge MA: Harvard University Press, 1989, pp. 62-63:
   Most of us not only live with many goods but find that we have to rank them, and in some cases, this ranking makes one of them of supreme importance relative to the others. . . . Let me call higher-order goods of this kind "hypergoods," i.e. goods which not only are incomparably more important than others but provide the standpoint from which these must be weighed, judged, decided about.

futures. The cliché that history is written by the winners is perhaps better couched in terms of history being written to affirm that what has occurred *amounts to* a victory. At some level cultural change is inseparable from the process of both valorizing and actualizing new (or at least alternative) interpretations of the changes that have occurred. Thus, in trying to glean resources from our own past cultural narratives, we must be self-conscious of the fact that our redescriptions of these histories while certainly being informed by their past, are also being reformulated to serve our own contemporary needs and interests.

Resources for Developing a Chinese Philosophical Vocabulary

An astute Ludwig Wittgenstein insists that "the limits of our language mean the limits of our world." If this is the case, in order to take Chinese philosophy on its own terms, we will quite literally need more language. The premise then is that there is no real alternative for students of Confucian philosophy but to cultivate a nuanced familiarity with the key Chinese vocabulary itself included in this lexicon. The self-conscious strategy of this conceptual lexicon is to prepare students to read the seminal texts by going beyond simple word-for-word translation and by systematically developing their own sophisticated understanding of a cluster of the most critical Chinese philosophical terms themselves. We might take as one example, *tian* 天, conventionally translated as "Heaven." I would argue that such word-for-word translation not only fails utterly to communicate the import of this recondite term, but can in the long run be counterproductive to the extent that it encourages students in reading texts to inadvertently rely upon the usual implications of the translated term "Heaven" rather than on the range of meaning implicit in the original Chinese term itself. When students read *tian* 天 as "Heaven" rather than as *tian* 天, they are sure to read the text differently, and in all likelihood, in a way heavily freighted with Western theological assumptions.

By way of analogy, when we reflect on our best efforts in the discipline to read and teach classical Greek philosophy, many if not most of us do not have an expert knowledge of classical Greek and the original language texts. But in developing a sophisticated understanding of an extended cluster of the most important Greek philosophical terms—*logos, nomos, nous, phusis, kosmos, eidos, psyche, soma, arche, alethea*, and so on—we can with imagination, get beyond our own uncritical Cartesian assumptions and at least in degree, read these Greek texts on their own terms. In a similar way, by seeking to understand and to ultimately appropriate the key philosophical vocabulary around which the Chinese texts are structured, students will be better able to locate these canonical texts within their own Confucian intellectual and cultural assumptions. The only alternative to doing our best to take the tradition on its own terms is to participate in a further colonializing of Chinese philosophy and the truncating of its long history. We have to resist the unconscious and patently spurious assumption that this tradition's fairly recent encounter with the vocabulary of the Western academy has been its defining moment. Such an uncritical approach places the uniqueness, the heterogeneity, and the intrinsic worth of the Chinese philosophical tradition at real risk.

I and my collaborators D.C. Lau, David Hall, and Henry Rosemont Jr. in our earlier translations of several of the canonical texts have over the years compiled a rather substantial glossary of philosophical terms describing the implications and the nuanced evolution of this extended cluster of key philosophical concepts. Indeed, it is this collaboration that is again my warrant for often using a plural "we" rather than the singular "I." Robert Cummings Neville has mused upon how we as a small group of Confucians with our considerable intellectual, philosophical, and personal differences have in many ways over our shared narratives actually "become" one another—as good Confucian friends are wont to do.① Neville's point is that the sustained dividends to be reaped from enduring friendships over a lifetime are not only substantial, but indeed transformative. In this Confucian tradition, to "make" friends is quite literally to participate in the "making" of each other to the extent that it is the friendships that are most concrete, while the putative "individuals" who participate in this matrix of relationships become increasingly only an abstraction from it.

In this new conceptional lexicon, I have revised and expanded upon our earlier efforts. In addition, in order to prompt and encourage students to reference this explanatory glossary, in the companion *Sourcebook in Classical Confucian Philosophy* I have included along with the "placeholder" translations, the romanization and the Chinese characters for these key terms as, for example, "exemplary persons" (*junzi* 君子). Again, sometimes the same Chinese term in a different context is better served by a different English translation. For example, this same *junzi* in other contexts should quite properly be translated as "lord" or "prince" or "ruler." Just as our reflections on the interpretive context is a self-conscious attempt to be as cognizant as we can about our uncommon assumptions, I think it is equally important to say up front why we have translated particular terms in the way we do, and what reasons we have for abandoning some of the earlier formulations.

But let me be clear about the expectations I have for the reader of this lexicon. At the end of the day, the project here is not to replace one set of problematic translations with yet another contestable set of renderings. The goal is to encourage students to reference this glossary of key philosophical terms in their reading of the translated

---

① Robert Cummings Neville. "On the Importance of the Ames-Hall Collaboration." *Appreciating the Chinese Difference: Engaging Roger T. Ames on Methods, Issues, and Roles.* ed. Jim Behuniak. Albany: State University of New York Press, 2018.

texts with the hope that in the fullness of time they will appropriate the key Chinese terminologies themselves and make them their own—*tian* 天, *dao* 道, *ren* 仁, *yi* 義, and so on. In thus developing their own increasingly robust insight into these philosophical terms, the students will be able to carry this nuanced understanding over to inform a critical reading of other currently available translations. Ultimately for students who would understand Chinese philosophy, *tian* 天 must be understood as *tian* 天, and *dao* 道 must be *dao* 道.

The Resolutely Interpretive Nature of Translation

In describing our translation of these key terms as "self-consciously interpretive," I am not allowing in any way that we are recklessly speculative or given to license in our renderings, nor that we are willing to accept the reproach that we are any less "literal" or more "creative" than other translators. On the contrary, I would insist first that any pretense to a literal translation is not only naïve, but is itself an "objectivist" cultural prejudice of the first order. Just as each generation selects and carries over earlier thinkers to reshape them in its own image, each generation reconfigures the classical canons of world philosophy to its own needs. We too are inescapably people of a time and place. This self-consciousness then, is not to disrespect the integrity of the Chinese philosophical narrative, but to endorse one of the fundamental premises of this commentarial tradition—that is, textual meaning is irrepressibly emergent, and that, like it or not, we translators are integral to the growth of the tradition, and as such, are not passive in the process of interpretation.

At a general level, I would suggest that English as the target language carries with it such an overlay of cultural assumptions that, in the absence of "self-consciousness," the philosophical import of these Chinese terms can be seriously compromised. Further, a failure of translators to be self-conscious and to take fair account of their own Gadamerian "prejudices" with the confidence that they are relying on the existing "objective" Chinese-English dictionary—a resource that, were the truth be known, is itself heavily colored with cultural biases—is to betray their readers not once, but twice.① That is, not only have they failed to provide the "objective" reading of the terms they have promised, but they have also neglected to warn their unsuspecting reader of the cultural assumptions they have willy-nilly insinuated into their translations.

Chinese Philosophy as "Eastern Religions"

As a case in point, it has become a commonplace to acknowledge that, in the process of Western humanists attempting to make sense of the classical Chinese philosophical literature, many unannounced Western assumptions and generic characteristics have been inadvertently introduced into their understanding of these texts, and have colored the vocabulary through which this understanding has been articulated. We must allow that this tradition has often if not usually been analyzed within the framework of categories and philosophical problems not its own.

Well-intended Christian missionaries bent on saving the soul of China introduced this ancient world into the Western academy

---

① In the second part of *Truth and Method*, 2nd ed. London: Sheed and Ward, 1989, Hans-Georg Gadamer develops four key concepts central to his hermeneutics: prejudice, tradition, authority, and horizon. He uses "prejudices" not in the sense that prejudice is blind, but on the contrary, in the sense that a clear awareness of our prejudgments can facilitate rather than obstruct our understanding. That is, our assumptions can positively condition our experience. But we must always entertain these assumptions critically, being aware that the hermeneutical circle in which understanding is always situated requires that we must continually strive to be conscious of what we bring to our experience and must pursue increasingly adequate prejudgments that can inform our experience in better and more productive ways.

by appealing to the vocabulary of their universal faith, ascribing to Confucian culture most of the accouterments of an Abrahamic religion. Early on, traditional Chinese philosophical texts were translated into English and other European languages by missionaries who used a Christian vocabulary to convert these canonical texts wholesale into the liturgy of what could only be a second-rate Christianity. Indeed, over the last several centuries of cultural encounter, the vocabulary established for the translation of classical Chinese texts into Western languages has been freighted by an often-unconscious Christian framework, and the effects of this "Christianization" of Chinese texts are still very much with us. The examples of grossly inappropriate language having become the standard equivalents in the Chinese-English dictionaries that we use to perpetuate our understanding of Chinese culture are legion: "the Way" (*dao* 道), "Heaven" (*tian* 天), "benevolence" (*ren* 仁), "righteousness" (*yi* 義), "rites" or "rituals" (*li* 禮), "virtue" (*de* 德), "substance" (*ti* 體), "principle" (*li* 理), "material substance" (*qi* 氣), and so on. How can any Western student read the capitalized "Way" without thinking of Jesus's proclamation that "I am the Way, the Truth, and the Life?" How can a capitalized "Heaven" be read as anything other than a metonym for the notion of a transcendent God? Is living a life as this grandfather's granddaughter properly described as a "rite" or "ritual?" How can we reduce what is quite literally the image of cultivated, consummate human beings in all of their aspects—their cognitive, moral, aesthetic, religious, and somatic sensibilities—to a single, patently Christian virtue: "benevolence?" When and in what context would a native English speaker ever utter the word "righteousness" other than as having a religious reference?[①]

[①] The Tyndale Bible (1526) translates the Hebrew term *tzedek* occurring some 500 times in the Hebrew Bible and is conferred on those who are pleasing to God as "righteous."

Chinese philosophy understood through this existing formula of key philosophical terms has been made familiar to Western readers by first "Christianizing" it, and then more recently, by "orientalizing" it and ascribing to it a deprecating poetical-mystical-occult and religious worldview as the alter image to our logical-rational-enlightened and humanistic self-understanding. The classics of Chinese philosophy in most American and European bookstores are usually located under the rubric "Eastern Religions" between the Bibles and the New Age, and are shelved in our libraries under either "BL" as "Eastern Religions" or "PL" as literature.

Many of the more philosophically-inclined sinologists who have been involved in the recent translation of canonical Chinese works are now acknowledging that a fuller inventory of semantic matrices might be necessary for the translation of these philosophical texts, and are struggling to get beyond the default, "commonsensical" vocabularies of their own native cultural sensibilities. As a matter of fact, the recent archaeological recovery of new versions of existing philosophical texts and the discovery of many others that have been long lost, in occasioning the retranslation of many of the philosophical classics, has provided both a pretext and an opportunity for philosophers to step up and rethink our standard renderings of the philosophical vocabulary. Most importantly, it has presented us with the challenge of trying, with imagination, to take these texts on their own terms by locating and interpreting them within their own worldviews.

An Interpretive Asymmetry: Vernacular Asian Languages and the Language of Modernity

Beyond this impoverishing "Christianization" and "orientalization" of the Confucian canons that has taken place within the Western academy, there is also another kind of profound asymmetry that continues to plague our best attempts to make responsible comparisons between the Chinese and Western philosophical narratives. To state the problem simply, we have been given to relentlessly theorizing the Chinese tradition according to our Western philosophical assumptions, shoehorning Chinese concepts into categories that are not its own. We are given to pondering with some philosophical nuance: "Is Mohist utilitarianism agent-neutral or agent-relative?" But it would not occur to us to ask if Jeremy Bentham or John Stuart Mill are latter-day Mohists. Again, we are given to a penetrating debate on: "Is Confucian ethics an Aristotelian aretaic ethic or a Humean-inspired sentimentalist ethic?" But it would not occur to us to ask if Aristotle, and Hume too, are classical or early modern Confucians. Kwong-loi Shun has recently made much of this asymmetry:

> [T]here is a trend in comparative studies to approach Chinese thought from a Western philosophical perspective, by reference to frameworks, concepts, or issues found in Western philosophical discussions. This trend is seen not only in works published in the English language, but also in those published in Chinese. Conversely, in the contemporary literature, we rarely find attempts to approach Western philosophical thought by reference to frameworks, concepts, or issues found in Chinese philosophical discussions.[1]

As Shun observes, this problem is as true in the writings of contemporary East Asian intellectuals as it is of their Western counterparts, speaking as they do a vernacular language recently transformed by its encounter with a dominating Western modernity.

---

[1] Kwong-loi Shun. "Studying Confucian and Comparative Ethics: Methodological Reflections." *Journal of Chinese Philosophy* (September 2009) Vol. 36, No. 3, p. 470.

In the middle and late nineteenth century, the institutional apparatus of Western education was transplanted wholesale to reconfigure East Asian education to its very core. The institutions of European and American education—the public-school systems through to the universities with their disciplinary taxonomies and curricula—were imported in their entirety into the East Asian cultures of Japan, China, Korea, and Vietnam. First, the Meiji Japanese reformers and then the Chinese, Korean, and Vietnamese intellectuals, at once enamored of, and overwhelmed by Western modernity, created their own Sinitic equivalencies drawn largely from traditional Chinese literary resources, to appropriate and give voice to the conceptual and theoretical language of the imported Western academic culture. The vocabulary of modernity with its liberating enlightenment ideas was translated into, and transformed fundamentally, the vernacular languages of East Asia, prompting these cultures themselves, then and today, to theorize their own traditions through a largely Western conceptual structure. Scholars are deploying a largely Western conceptual structure—a Western *langue*—even while speaking their own vernacular languages—an East Asian *parole*.

The complexity and the politics of this process of synchronizing the East Asian languages with the vocabulary of Western modernity, and the role that the Chinese literary tradition served as a resource for constructing this vocabulary, has been discussed in considerable detail by Lydia H. Liu. In thinking through the impact of this newly emerging conceptual structure as it surfaced and reconfigured the discourse of modern Chinese academic literature, Liu herself probes the "*discursive construct of the Chinese modern*." "I am fascinated," says Liu.

> . . . by what has happened to the modern Chinese language, especially the written form, since its early exposure to English, modern Japanese, and other foreign languages. . . . The true object

of my theoretical interest is the *legitimation of the "modern" and the "West"* in Chinese literary discourse as well as the *ambivalence of Chinese agency* in these mediated processes of legitimation. ①

The consequences of this effort at synchronization are still with us as Western modernity continues to be the language through which East Asian traditions are conceptualized and theorized not simply abroad, but also within their own corridors of learning. Indeed, we might ask if it is true, as I.A. Richards has observed, that "Western notions are penetrating steadily into Chinese, and the Chinese scholar of the near future will not be intellectually much nearer Mencius than any Western pupil of Aristotle and Kant?"②

But perhaps Richards needs a larger picture because this is not a simple story. Just as South Asian Buddhism has been sinicized to become a distinctively Chinese Huayan, Chan, and Sanlun Buddhism and just as Marxism has been sinicized to become a kind of Chinese socialism, the Chinese appropriation of a Western modernity is also in transition. An important factor in understanding the emergence of China's own modernity is to reflect on the skewed way in which Chinese translations of the vocabulary of Western modernity, to use the language of Friedrich Schleiermacher, have been "domesticated." Although China has constructed an elaborate vocabulary to synchronize Chinese thinking with Western modernity, in its application, this language as it is being deployed has often been transformed into its own sinicized version of Western modernity rather than expressing the substance of Western modernity

---

① Lydia H. Liu. *Translingual Practice: Literature, National Culture, and Translated Modernity—China, 1900-1937*. Stanford: Stanford University Press, 1995, pp. xvi-xviii.

② I.A. Richards. *Mencius on the Mind: Experiments in Multiple Definition*. London: Kegan Paul, Trench, Trubner & Co.; New York: Harcourt, Brace, 1932, p. 9.

itself. Many of the terms created explicitly to express a Western conceptual vocabulary have, over time and unconsciously perhaps, been retrofitted to give voice to a persistent Chinese worldview.① For example, the term *pubian* 普遍 that was invented to express the Western concept of "universal" when used by Chinese scholars today to describe Confucian values has come to mean the more modest and inclusive notion of "shared" or "common values" rather than exclusive and exclusionary "universal values" as resident in the One, True God. The term *chaoyue* 超越 created to introduce the Western concept of "transcendence" that serves as the ontological ground for its persistent "reality and appearance" dualistic categories has been revised to function within the inclusive parameters of "the inseparability of *tian* and the human experience" (*tianrenheyi* 天人合一).

Lost and Found in Translation

There is another issue that needs to be addressed in these introductory pages. A rather natural question to be asked is: In our attempt to get past earlier culturally reductive readings of the Confucian philosophical vocabulary, are we not in fact just substituting one Western philosophical reading of these texts with another? Are we not rescuing the Chinese tradition from an uncritical Greek, a calculated Christian, or a more familiar Cartesian reading only to overwrite it with our own pragmatic, process assumptions?

Encountering the unsummed richness of the original texts themselves, we as interpreters are always people of a specific time and place. Such an interface in itself is a formula for inescapable

---

① I have tried to address this issue in an essay entitled "China and the Search for Its Own Modernity." *Modernities in Northeast Asia*. ed. Jun-Hyeok Kwak. New York: Routledge, forthcoming.

cultural reductionism. Certainly, our too hastily constructed interpretive strategies and overarching theories—"philosophical" or otherwise—when applied in the practice of cultural and textual translation, cannot help but put concrete detail at some considerable risk. When Robert Frost remarks that "what is lost in translation is the poetry," I think that as an artist he is quite properly concerned that the project of translation is a literary transaction that in its outcomes, at best makes a text different, and that most often, makes it less.

On the other hand, it can be argued that "wisdom" emerges analogically through establishing and aggregating patterns of truly productive correlations between what we already know and what in our intellectual adventures we would aspire to know. Such correlations are "productive" in that they serve to increase meaning, and we actually achieve a modicum of wisdom to the extent that we are able to optimize these meaningful correlations effectively in our life situations. Of course, not all analogies are equally apposite, and as we know from the experience with Chinese philosophy, poorly chosen comparisons can be a persisting source of distortion and of cultural condescension. A heavy-handed and impositional "Christian," "Heideggarian," and yes, even "Pragmatic" or "Whiteheadian" reading of Chinese philosophical terms betrays the reader by distorting both the Chinese tradition and the Western analog in the comparison. Having said this, at the end of the day we have no choice but to identify productive analogies that, with effort and imagination, can in the fullness of time be qualified and refined in such a way as to introduce culturally novel ideas into our own world to enrich our own ways of thinking and living.

Importantly, we need to be analogically retail and piecemeal rather than working in whole cloth. That is, in *Focusing the Familiar* (*Zhongyong* 中庸) the human being is celebrated as having the capacity and responsibility to be a cosmic co-creator with the heavens and the earth. In this context, we might find analogy between the key philosophical term *cheng* 誠 invoked in this text to describe such human creativity and Whitehead's concern to reinstate "creativity" as an important human value.① At the same time, we might be keenly aware that when the same Whitehead invokes the primordial nature of God and the Eternal Objects that the primordial nature of God sustains, the long shadow of Aristotelian metaphysics sets a real limit on the relevance of this dimension of Whitehead's thought for classical Chinese process cosmology.

Again, analogies can be productive of both associations and contrasts, and we can learn much from both. While Aristotelian teleology and his reliance upon logic as method might serve as points of contrast in understanding Confucian philosophical terms, his resistance to Platonic abstraction in promoting an aggregating practical wisdom does resonate productively with one of the central issues in classical Confucian moral philosophy: that is, its commitment to the cultivation of excellent habits of the heart-and-mind. In this project of cultural translation, we must pick and choose our analogies carefully—but pick and choose we must.

Reading Philosophical Texts Philosophically: The Bad News

The preparation of any new *Conceptual Lexicon for Classical Confucian Philosophy* must also take account of a recent confluence

---

① Whitehead argues that making God more primordial than creativity has made conventional theology incoherent because the existence of a perfect, transcendent God threatens the very possibility of creativity itself. There is God's perfection, and that is all. With Whitehead's challenge to conventional ways of thinking about creativity, the word "creativity" becomes an individual entry in a 1971 supplement to the *Oxford English Dictionary* with two of the three references being made to Whitehead's *Religion in the Making*.

of circumstances that is promoting a reevaluation of the classical Chinese corpus. First, we are living in exciting times. As alluded to above, a continuing series of truly dramatic archaeological digs in China are providing us with earlier versions of still extant texts that have not suffered the many corruptions unavoidable over the course of some two thousand years of transmission. Again, these same finds are also offering us access to documents that disappeared from sight millennia ago. Often, these recovered texts as they surface are requiring contemporary scholars to reassess our previous understanding of the principal philosophical terminology defining of the canonical core.

At the very least, these newly available archaeological resources have provided real incentive for the retranslation of the canonical texts. At the same time, until very recently most professional Western philosophers have had little interest in claims on the part of proponents of Chinese philosophy that there is much of philosophical significance in the texts of ancient China. Indeed, it can be argued that in the discipline of philosophy it has been geographical rather than philosophical criteria that have been invoked as reasons to exclude Chinese and other alternative philosophical traditions from proper investigation. As a consequence, texts that are profoundly "philosophical" have not been treated as such within the sanctum of professional philosophy.

The consequences of this historical omission are serious. That "philosophy" as a professional discipline has historically defined itself largely as an Anglo-European enterprise is a claim that is as true in Beijing, Tokyo, Seoul, Delhi, Nairobi, and Boston, as it is in Oxford, Frankfort, and Paris. For many reasons—certainly the asymmetry introduced by economic and political factors included among them—philosophers belonging to other traditions who go about their business within the academies outside of Europe have themselves not only acquiesced in the claim of Anglo-European philosophy to have a monopoly on their discipline, but have moreover worked assiduously to make this European narrative the mainstream curriculum in the best of their own home institutions. In this process of self-colonization, indigenous traditions of philosophy—Chinese, Japanese, Korean, South Asian, African, and American too—have been marginalized within their own terrain, while at the same time, the heirs to British Empiricism and Continental Rationalism have continued to wage their battles on foreign soil. That is, if indigenous Asian, African, and American philosophies have been largely ignored by Western philosophers, they have also been significantly relegated within their home cultures. William James was almost right when he began his 1901 Gifford lectures at Edinburgh University by admitting that "to us Americans, the experience of receiving instruction from the living voice, as well as from the books of European scholars, is very familiar. . . It seems the natural thing for us to listen whilst the Europeans talk." James is reporting on a self-understanding of the discipline of professional philosophy that is in important degree alive and well more than a century later. The only caveat offered here would be that James would have been more accurate had he included the Asian and African philosophers along with him and other Americans as the seemingly "natural" audience for European philosophy.[1]

Wilfrid Sellars has insisted that

> . . . the aim of philosophy, abstractly formulated, is to understand how things in the broadest possible sense of the term hang together in the broadest possible sense of the term.[2]

---

[1] William James. *The Varieties of Religious Experience.* Cambridge, Mass: Harvard University Press, 1985, p. 11.
[2] Wilfrid Sellars. "Philosophy and the Scientific Image of Man." *Empiricism and the Philosophy of Mind.* London: Routledge & Kegan Paul Ltd., 1963, p. 1.

If the essential occupation of professional philosophers is to identify and describe the generic traits of the human experience and to thereby locate the problems of the day within their broadest possible contexts, philosophy as a professional discipline has the unfulfilled responsibility to our academy and to our intellectual community to expand its purview and to treat the subject of philosophy in a more inclusive and capacious way. Philosophers through rigorous critique and persuasion must shoulder their share of responsibility in producing the social intelligence needed to address the pressing problems of our times, problems that are significantly different as we move from one cultural and epochal site to another. Indeed, given the complexity of our contemporary world, philosophers in our times as producers of knowledge have the responsibility to rise above ethnocentrism and counter a pernicious cultural reductionism and the misconceptions that such parochialism entails. Thus it is that the relative absence of philosophers in the interpretation of Chinese philosophy—a tradition that is the legacy of something near a quarter of the world's population—has come at a real cost in knowing the world around us.[①]

Philosophy in Revolution: The Good News

But we do not need to invoke Chinese philosophy to problematize some of the persisting assumptions within the Western narrative that have excluded Confucian philosophy from consideration as philosophy. Indeed, it is the revolution currently taking place within

---

[①] The population of China proper is over 22.5%, with China and the various diasporas making it what Lucian W. Pye has called "a civilization pretending to be a nation-state." "International Relations in Asia: Culture, Nation, and State" published by the Sigur Center for Asian Studies, July 1998, p. 9. Indeed, China is a continent rather than a country—a third more populous than Africa and almost two Europes.

the Western philosophical community, a revolution that might be described as an attempt to think process and reinstate wisdom, that provides an opening and an invitation to take Chinese philosophy more seriously. An internal critique continues to be waged within professional Western philosophy under the many banners of process philosophy, hermeneutics, post-structuralism, postmodernism, pragmatism, existentialism, neo-Marxism, deconstructionism, feminist philosophy, and so on, that takes as a shared target what Robert Solomon has called "the transcendental pretense"—idealism, rationalism, objectivism, formalism, logocentrism, essentialism, the master narrative, onto-theological thinking, "the myth of the given"—the familiar reductionistic "isms" that have emerged as putatively novel choices to allow philosophers to switch horses on the merry-go-round of systematic philosophy.

As heir to its legacy of metaphysics and epistemology, the main problematic in a Cartesian dualistic worldview is one of closure articulated in the vocabulary of 1) the quest for certainty guaranteed by clear and distinct ideas, 2) the attainment of objective truth, and 3) the reconciliation and ultimate salvation that follows from it. In place of this Cartesian philosophical language, new vocabularies of process, change, particularity, creative advance, and indeed productive vagueness are increasingly coming into vogue. These recent developments in Anglo-European philosophy have themselves begun to foreground an interpretative terminology that has some real resonance with Confucian culture.

A main problematic in the correlative cosmology we associate with process philosophy in its many varieties, is one of personal cultivation and disclosure—that is, an aestheticizing of the human experience. There is a perceived synergy in being shaped by, and in turn shaping the world around us. Novelty emerges in the interface between the force of environing natural, social, and cultural conditions, and the creative contribution we are able to make to our own contexts. One of the most interesting ramifications of the increasing popularity of process language, from the perspective of our present project, is that the stimulation offered by the need to better understand Asian sensibilities, is in fact recursive. While process vocabularies are leading to increasingly productive interpretations of the conceptual structure that informs the classical Chinese world, these process interpretations of Chinese texts in turn provide us with new lenses through which to see our own Western sensibilities. Previously ignored or misconstrued elements within our own cultural self-understanding are beginning to receive new and decidedly more coherent interpretations.

Classical Confucian cosmology subscribes to the mantra, the only kind of creativity is situated co-creativity. And, in the wake of the process thinkers such as A.N. Whitehead and John Dewey, a sustained reflection by philosophers on the alternatives to transcendentalism and the many dualisms that mark its presence that are to be found in the classical Chinese assumptions about cosmic order may pay us important philosophical dividends. The pervasive Chinese assumption about the always gerundive and emergent nature of order that underlies the key vocabulary might at this particular historical moment provide us with a salutary intervention in the Western philosophical narrative. That is, in this classical Chinese worldview there is an alternative nuanced and sophisticated processual way of thinking about cosmology that can join this ongoing internal critique of transcendentalism taking place within the professional discipline of philosophy itself. Simply put, with the present surge of interest in Whitehead and particularly the American pragmatists, these newly emerging Western versions of process philosophy as they mature within our own philosophical culture can, with profit, draw both substance and critique from a Chinese tradition that has been committed to various forms of process philosophy since the beginning of its recorded history.

The happy conclusion that may be anticipated from these recent developments is that an era in which philosophy and philosophical thought have been considered essentially Anglo-European monopolies is drawing to a close. And further, while Western philosophy—primarily British, French, and German philosophy—constituted the mainstream curriculum for the discipline of world philosophy in the twentieth century, the revolution that is taking place within the Western academy itself presages a time when the process sensibilities pervasive in the long Chinese philosophical narrative may well become increasingly relevant in finding our way forward to a more inclusive understanding of world philosophy.

A Lexicon of Key Philosophical Terms

As noted above, this present glossary is informed by the earlier work of Hall and Ames, D.C. Lau and Ames, and of Ames and Rosemont, cited in the *Bibliography*. We have attempted to provide an explanation for some of the key philosophical vocabulary and a justification for the particular translations selected for these terms. In the translations in the companion *Sourcebook in Classical Confucian Philosophy*, I have included the romanization for the key terms included herein to facilitate the cross-referencing of a recurring philosophical vocabulary. In our *Introduction* to *Focusing the Familiar: A Translation and Philosophical Interpretation of the Zhongyong*, David Hall and I invoked Whitehead's "Fallacy of the Perfect Dictionary" to challenge the wisdom of "one-for-one" equivalencies in translating philosophical terms. We introduce the notion of "linguistic clustering" as an alternative strategy that allows us to give priority to the semantic value of a term by parsing its range of meaning according to context, with the assumption that philosophical ideas are multivalent, and that the full range of meaning with a different configuration of emphasis is in play on each appearance of the term. And further, the meaning of language is itself a historical narrative. That is, the semantic value of a term and its subtle nuances of meaning are an emergent product of its specific linguistic contexts and usages over time.

We do use different English terms for the same Chinese graph when the context, in our view, requires it. *Jiao* 教, for example, is here rendered "teaching," there "instruction," and there again as "education." With *cheng* 誠, it can be translated here as "sincerity," there as "integrity," and again as "co-creativity," and when these several meanings are combined as a kind of "creative resolve." In parsing the range of meaning of a particular Chinese character with different English equivalents in different contexts I hope to encourage a contextual understanding of these polysemous terms that is historical, dynamic, allusive, and relational rather than simply referential.

We have argued consistently for a processual understanding of Chinese natural cosmology as entailing both persistence and change, and believe that such a way of thinking and living has shaped the grammar of the Chinese language and its key philosophical vocabulary. We do not deceive ourselves in thinking that in the *Sourcebook* we are proffering the final translation of these canonical texts, or that our interpretation is philosophically neutral. Indeed, eschewing claims of an impossible objectivity, we feel obliged in this *Lexicon* to make the assumptions on which our translations rest explicit, and provide our best reasons for why we have made them.

*霸 **ba.** "Hegemon." See 王 ***wang.*** "King, True King."

*本 **ben.** "Root, trunk."

In the ongoing transactional processes of associated living, cultivation of one's unique person within one's specific and often changing relations is the "root" from which a full canopy of interdependent personal bonds grows. These bonds define the various radial spheres of family lineage, neighborhood, community, village, polity, and ultimately, cosmos, with each of these mutually implicated dimensions making its own contribution to the prevailing social ethic. As the *Expansive Learning* (*Daxue* 大學) enjoins us, in the singularly important project of becoming consummate persons, personal cultivation in the relations that constitute us is fundamental, and we must thus give it our highest priority:

> 自天子以至於庶人，壹是皆以修身為本。其本亂而末治者否矣，其所厚者薄，而其所薄者厚，未之有也！
> From the emperor down to the common folk, everything is rooted in personal cultivation. There can be no healthy canopy when the roots are not properly set, and it would never do for priorities to be reversed between what should be invested with importance and what should be treated more lightly.[①]

The binomial, "roots and branches," "fundamental and incidental," "the whole course of an event from beginning to end" (*benmo* 本末) underscores the correlative and symbiotic relationship between the root and the tree. It is necessary to

---

[①] I have borrowed this translation of the title of *Daxue* rather than the familiar *Great Learning* from Jung-Yeup Kim because it captures the expansive radiality of the Confucian project as it is rehearsed in this foundational text.

understand the underlying focus-field holism here. Continuing this familiar root and branches metaphor, root and canopy must grow together, with the tree spreading its roots outward beneath the earth and simultaneously stretching its branches upward towards the sky. While the root is certainly growing the tree, the tree is also in turn growing its roots. The root and its flourishing canopy are perceived as aspects of an interactive and organic whole that grow together symbiotically, or not at all. In the same way, the aspiration to become consummate in our conduct as persons (*ren* 仁) is the expansive process of persons becoming increasingly rooted in virtuosic habits of conduct and extending themselves outward synergistically in their relations within family, community, and cosmos. Indeed, the *Record of Rites* (*Liji* 禮記) version of the *Expansive Learning* fascicle concludes the excerpt cited above by declaring that personal cultivation sets the root deeply and securely while at the same time fostering the social intelligence needed for a flourishing world. In the words of the text itself:

此謂知本，此謂知之至也。
This resolve in one's personal cultivation is called both the root and the magnitude of wisdom.[①]

Here again, the project of personal cultivation eschews exclusive means-end distinctions. The "root" and its erstwhile product, "wisdom," are perceived as an organic whole that in growing together are two ways of viewing the same phenomenon. This is just to say that the practice of personal cultivation and the wisdom that thereby comes to characterize one's conduct are aspectual abstractions from the concrete narrative of living consummately within the relations of

---

[①] *Liji* 禮記 (*Record of Rites*), *A Concordance to the* Liji. ed. D.C. Lau and Chen Fong Ching. Hong Kong: The Commercial Press, 1992, 43.1/164/30.

family, community, and cosmos.

Relationally-constituted persons are born into the broadest swath of family, community, and cosmic relations. They cannot exist exclusive of these relations, nor can they grow without them. By locating the notion of persons within the relational ecology that serves as interpretive context for these texts, we can argue that terms such as "root," "potential," "cause," and "source" that are at times taken as disjunctive and exclusive terms to be associated with some underlying cosmic teleology, have to be reconceived as referencing always multilateral, symbiotic, and reflexive processes. Such an alternative understanding of the project of civilizing experience is immediately relevant in thinking through the intergenerational, genealogical, and holographic implications of family reverence (xiao 孝) that would construe persons as radial centers within an unbounded cosmic ecology.

In the *Analects* 1.2 it says:

孝弟［悌］也者，其為仁之本與。
As for family reverence (xiao 孝) and fraternal deference (ti 悌), these are, I suspect, the root of becoming consummate in one's roles and relations (ren 仁).

Again, in the *Chinese Classic of Family Reverence,* Confucius begins by elevating xiao to be Confucianism's highest moral imperative, declaring that this "way of family reverence" is the very substance of morality and education:

子曰："夫孝，德之本也，教之所由生也。"
It is family reverence (xiao 孝) that is the root of moral virtuosity, and whence education (jiao 教) itself is born."[1]

---

[1] Henry Rosemont, Jr. and Roger T. Ames. *The Classic of Family Reverence: A Philosophical Translation of the* Xiaojing 孝經. Honolulu: University of Hawai'i Press, 2009, p. 105.

What then does it mean to take the practical activities of revering family members (*xiao* 孝) and of deferring appropriately to elders (*ti* 弟 [悌]) to be the *root* (*ben* 本) of becoming consummate in one's roles and relations (*ren* 仁)?

First of all, the association between *ren* and "family" is clear in the alternative graphic form of the character found on the bamboo strips, with *ren* being the combination "lived body" (*shen* 身) and "heartminding" (*xin* 心), where we learn from the bronze inscriptions that this notion of lived body is conceived of as a woman's pregnant body ![].① Clearly, any conception of family must begin from woman with child. Allowing that human narratives are always *in medias res* as narratives nested within narratives, *ren* as "consummate person/conduct" cannot be taken to be descriptive of the content of some essential, *ab initio* notion of "human nature." Indeed, we must resist any means-end reduction that would introduce a severe separation between "practicing" what it means to be consummate, and "becoming" consummate as a person. Getting an education and being educated have the same content. Thus, *ren* has no meaning or possibility independent of our family and community relations. Such *xiao* and *ti* activities—the various things done in being this proper son to this loving mother, in being this solicitous youth to this congenial elder—are the content of a consummate narrative (*ren*).

In a parallel way, the Confucian notion of "cultivating one's natural propensities" (*xing* 性) conventionally translated as "human nature" is better understood as in large measure referencing the narrative *content* of the life experience rather than some isolatable "nature" as the erstwhile reduplicative *source* of human conduct. Both *ren* and *xing* too are, in important measure, something that we "do" as an aesthetic achievement rather than denoting something that we

---

① Kwan Tze-wan. "Multi-function Character Database." at http://humanum.arts.cuhk.edu.hk/Lexis/lexi-mf/, 西周中期 CHANT 246.

本 ben.   005

already "are." Or perhaps said more clearly, our narratives and our persons, rather than entailing some means and end distinction, are one and the same thing.

John Dewey makes a similar point in resisting the fallacy of decontextualizing and essentializing one element within the continuity of experience, and then in the effort to overcome this *post hoc* diremption, making this element foundational and causal:

> The reality is the growth-process itself; childhood and adulthood are phases of a continuity ... The real existence is the history in its entirety, the history just as what it is. The operations of splitting it up into two parts and then having to unite them again by appeal to causative power are equally arbitrary and gratuitous.[①]

This perception of the root and the tree as a symbiotic process stands in stark contrast to thinking of, and separating off the root as some independent, single source, and has important ecological implications. What applies to the notion of "root" is also true of cognate ideas such as "potential," "source," "nature," and "cause." Such symbiotic thinking reflects the holistic cosmological assumptions that would anticipate an always situated answer to our most fundamental and perennial philosophical questions: "What is the 'source' of meaning, and how is it conveyed?" By way of contrast, in the Abrahamic traditions the answer is simple: Meaning comes from a Divine "source" beyond and independent of the human community. Yahweh or God or Allah provides us with a continuing vision of life's purpose, and each of us must return to this source when we lose our way.

For the Confucian project, on the other hand, with no appeal to

---

[①] John Dewey. *The Later Works of John Dewey* (1925-53). ed. Jo Ann Boydston. Carbondale: Southern Illinois University Press, 1985, Vol. 1, p. 210.

some independent, external principle, meaning arises *pari passu* from a vital network of meaningful relationships in the process of the intergenerational transmission and embodiment of a living civilization. Human narratives are "rooted" in their genealogical and cultural lineages, and grow therefrom. A personal commitment to achieving relational virtuosity within one's own family relationships is both the starting point and the ultimate source of personal, social, and indeed, cosmic meaning. In cultivating our own persons through aspiring to and extending robust relations as they evolve in our families and beyond, we enlarge the cosmos by adding meaning to it, and in turn, this increasingly meaningful cosmos provides an increasingly fertile context for the project of our own personal cultivation.

The important adjustment in thinking that a narrative understanding of persons requires that we must avoid what Dewey has called the philosophical fallacy: the abstracting of one element out of the continuing process of experience, reifying it, and then making this second order "principle" first order by claiming that it is antecedent, causal, and determinative. Dewey references this fallacy specifically with reference to the notion of "good:"

> There is no morality in my ethics, i.e., there is no apart morality. Good conduct (once conduct is defined as activity which is an end to itself) seems to me a pleonasm. Conduct, full activity, is the good. ... Now the usual idea of the Good seems to be an abstraction which has been frozen. It denotes full activity, but then it [is] abstracted and put over by itself and then frozen in its isolated form apart from the content of specific activities which first gave it meaning.[1]

---

[1] *The Correspondence of John Dewey, 1871-2007 (I-IV)*, Electronic Edition, Vol. 1, 1871-1918, 1891.03.14 (00453), John Dewey to Thomas Davidson.

We are guilty of this fallacy of "pleonasm" or redundancy when the notion of "potential" as cause, root, source, or nature is reduced to some antecedent teleological principle that is then reduplicated in the process of growth. In the *Mencius* and other canonical Confucian texts, the familiar appeal to the horticultural and husbanding metaphors—knowing the "root"—is often construed as reinforcing the idea that specific plants and animals grow to become what they essentially are: They simply actualize their inherent potential. But what makes horticulture and husbanding apposite analogies for relationally constituted "human becomings" is in fact the acute dependence of farming and raising animals upon a contrived environment and upon concentrated human effort. Without sustained intervention, most seeds far from becoming what they "are," become anything and everything else. Without the benefit of intensive intervention and cultivation on behalf of what we think they will "naturally" become, most acorns become squirrels, most corn becomes cows, most eggs become omelets, and most apples become compost. The "root" or "seed" of anything and what it will become is as much a function of the contingencies of circumstances as it is of the initial conditions from which it "begins."

This same fallacy of "pleonasm" or redundancy is apparent in our familiar use of the notion of "source." The conventional understanding of "source" is that it is the point of origin exclusive of what is derived from that point. Geographically, the source of the Yangtze River is the Himalayas. When we introduce the idea of efficient cause, the source becomes something analytically independent of the product that causes, creates, and initiates. It is a maker from which whatever is made, is derived. "*Dao* 道" is often described as a "source" and yet the exclusive understanding of "source" as efficient cause has no relevance to *dao*. *Dao*, far from standing independent of the world we experience, is in fact the unsummed totality of all that is happening. *Dao* is the process of the world in its entirety. To understand the notion of *dao* as "source" we might cite the *Daodejing* 25 that states: 道法自然 "*Dao* emulates what is spontaneously so of itself." The energy of growth and transformation resides within the world itself, wherein the entire field of what is happening is implicated in each relationally constituted event, just as each event is adumbrated in the totality. Acknowledging the cosmological postulate of "the inseparability of one and many" (*yiduobufenguan* 一多不分觀), *dao* and the myriad happenings (*wanwu* 萬物) are two aspectual, nonanalytical ways of looking at the same phenomenon.

Bringing this rather abstract reflection to bear on how we are to understand "human nature" as the "root" or "source" of what we become as humans, we would have to allow that human nature is a provisional generalization made with respect to the totality of human lives as they have been lived within their natural and social relations. The contingency in the ongoing process of what humans have become is no less relevant to this notion of source than where they have come from. The source is the collaborative nature of relations themselves *and* what is produced in this collaboration. In becoming human as in making friends, there is no separation between maker and made, between means and end, between cause and effect, between source and product.

Of course, the identities of persons are certainly rooted in their thick native beginnings within the environing relationships of family and community which, as a received and thus retrospective inheritance integral to who they are, needs to be both nurtured and protected from loss or injury. And the conduct of such persons is certainly guided by the normative generalizations that a cultural tradition has best remembered in its customs and institutions. But such identities and the realization of their highest aspirations only emerge prospectively in the process of these initial relationships achieving thick resolution as they are cultivated, grown, and consummated over their particular lifetimes, and as the normative generalizations are continually being retheorized to refine its practices. Their potential far from being an antecedent given, in fact emerges most significantly in the always transactional events that in sum constitute lives lived in the world.

Again, the "potential" for becoming human is not some causal "beginning" or teleological "end"—that is, some inborn, essential potential exclusive of context and family relations, or some potential that is actualized as the ineluctable process of growth toward some predetermined ideal. To begin with, in this Chinese natural cosmology, there are no such deracinated, individual persons who could possibly be described as living outside of the context of family relations. Persons do not live their lives inside their skins; they exist in their associations, and only in their associations. And since persons in their nested, narratives-within-narratives are constituted by these evolving, eventful relations, the "potential" of persons and their achieved identities in fact emerge *pari passu* from out of the specific, contingent transactions of their lives. Thus, the best sense we can make of "potential" here is that while it certainly has a retrospective reference to native conditions within an evolving narrative, rather than being understood as wholly antecedent as a set of given, defining factors, such potential is most significantly prospective and contingent, evolving and compounding within the ever-changing ebb and flow of circumstances. Rather than being generic or universal, such potential is unique to the career of this specific, self-aware and relational person; and rather than existing simply as an inherent and defining endowment, the full measure of such potential can only be known *post hoc* after the unfolding of the particular narrative, a shared narrative that usually continues long beyond the putative demise of specific persons.①

There is the fallacy of redundancy in taking human nature as causal in the sense that it reduplicates itself in action—the idea that our conduct is *ren* because we are potentially *ren*. Rather habits of moral conduct and native conditions should be understood as symbiotic and mutually determining. When we ask: Which comes first, the chicken or the egg? we have to allow that they come together or not at all. From the perspective of classical Western metaphysics, we might say that Chinese cosmology shaves with Ockham's razor not once, but twice. Chinese cosmology does not appeal to the notion of a transcendent and independent God as the source of the world, but begins from what is happening in the autogenerative world itself (*ziranerran* 自然而然). And Chinese cosmology does not appeal to an independent nature or soul as the source of human conduct, but begins from a phenomenology of what unfolds and aggregates as moral habits within human conduct itself.

What makes our human propensities most profoundly variable is the quality of the families and cultures into which we are born. If the family is a morally strong, thriving association of significant persons within a mature culture, much is available for investment in and growth for the incipient person. If the family is barren and troubled within only a thinly cultured environment, it is a more difficult road for the emerging person. But even when the legendary Shun is

---

① For Dewey too, "potentialities cannot be known till after the interactions have occurred. There are at a given time unactualized potentialities in an individual because and in as far as there are in existence other things with which it has not as yet interacted." *Later Works*, Vol. 14, p. 109. Lincoln is not Lincoln independent of the circumstances of history, nor are the circumstances of history the making of Lincoln. Indeed, Lincoln is a collaboration between person and circumstances expressed as thick habits of conduct. "The idea that potentialities are inherent and fixed by relation to a predetermined end was a product of a highly restricted state of technology." Dewey, *Later Works*, Vol. 14, p. 110.

born into the family of the morally deficient Blind Man, the model of Emperor Yao is still available as part of a rich cultural resource that enables Shun through the assiduous cultivation of habits of conduct to become a sage himself. Shun's circumstances are a fair demonstration that there are cultural assets available for everyone to draw upon in aspiring to become sagely in their conduct.

The basic significance of the mantra, "the continuity between the numinous and the human" (*tianrenheyi* 天人合一) that is invoked to describe the Confucian religious sensibility is making this same point about potential. It is the person nourished by culture who becomes consummately human, and it is the life of the consummate human who contributes to the cultural resources that make a consummate humanity possible. Potentiality emerges in these collaborations between aspiring persons and an inspired world.

Turning to causality as yet another way of conceiving of "root," given the constitutive nature of relations, causality is not some agency outside and prior to the perceived configuration of things happening—some independent "first cause"—but rather a function of the creative and thus causal nature of the relations themselves. The originally militarist notion of causality captured in the term *shi* 勢 comes immediately to mind. *Shi* describes the always particular and inclusive manifold of spatial, temporal, and existential factors as they unfold in an emerging situation. *Shi* is a calculus of differentials in configuration, momentum, timing, terrain, morale, equipment, logistics, and so on.

*誠 **cheng***. "Sincerity, with integrity, resolve, (co-) creativity."

Beginning with the *Shuowen* as the earliest lexicon, in the traditional dictionaries *cheng* 誠 and "living up to one's word" (*xin* 信) are frequently glossed by appeal each other. *Xin* 信

denotes the situational rather than agency-centered combination of perceived "credibility" and the concomitant "trust" that such credibility inspires; it describes a situation in which its participants conduct themselves sincerely and honestly with mutual regard. *Cheng* is thus the ground of *an integrative and creative process* of becoming consummately human. It is not "being whole," but the process of "becoming whole" within the multilateral relations that constitute one's natural, social, and cultural environments.

This cluster of three alternative yet overlapping translations—"sincerity, with integrity, and creativity"—receives support etymologically from the fact that the "creative" sense of the graph *cheng* 誠 is reflected in its cognate *cheng* 成—"consummating, completing, finishing, bringing to fruition"—that together with the "speech" classifier as "discoursing" (*yan* 言) makes up the character. This etymology suggests the cultivation of a fiduciary network achieved through the various modalities of communicating effectively with one another. Thus "sincerity" as "the absence of duplicity" necessary as ground for cultivating relations, "integrity" as "a consummating wholeness" that comes from such cultivation, and "creativity" as the process leading to the achievement of such wholeness, can within different contexts all be viable translations.

In our translations, we certainly concur with the familiar renderings for *cheng*, but have also introduced "creativity" as an additional dimension of meaning for this term when it appears as a central cosmological idea found initially in the *Mencius* and then elaborated upon in some detail in *Focusing the Familiar* (*Zhongyong* 中庸). The appropriateness of using "creativity" as a translation for *cheng* lies in acknowledging the process assumptions underlying the classical Confucian worldview. In a cosmology of ever-changing events, "integrity" is not simply conserving what one already is, but further suggests the active process of bringing one's relationships into focus in a consummatory way to achieve optimum meaningfulness in these relations. Reflection upon *cheng* is revealing of a sense of relational growth. Integrity thus understood is not just "being" one, but "becoming one" with other participants in one's family and community. The cultivation of these trusting relationships entails integrity not only in the sense of the persistent particularity of persons, but also in the integrative sense of becoming one together in their concrete, social relationships. Under such circumstances, "integrity" is not simply retaining what you "have" or being who you "are;" it is what you "do" and "become" in *integrating* effectively with family and community. And "sincerity" then connotes the subjective form of feeling on the basis of which this creative process proceeds. That is, it suggests the mood or emotional tone that promotes successful integration.

This inseparability of integration and creativity is reinforced explicitly in the notion of *ren* 仁, the correlative, consummatory notion of "persons" in which the realization of oneself and other persons are mutuality entailing. And the spontaneous emergence of significance in these relationships is the very meaning of this collaborative personal creativity. Indeed, the prefix "co-" is made redundant by the fact that it is *only* this kind of situated co-creativity—at once cognitive and affective, aesthetic and intensely religious—that can legitimately be called "creativity." Or stated negatively, in this cosmology as interpretive context, there is no such thing as *creatio ex nihilo*—creativity without context.

The parsing of *cheng* principally as "creativity" rather than "sincerity" or "integrity" in some contexts brings attention to the centrality of human participation in cosmic creativity as an axis in the tradition broadly, and as the main theme of *Focusing the Familiar* in particular. When we couple Confucius's introduction of the neologism *zhongyong* 中庸—"focusing the familiar," "hitting the mark in the everyday"—with the Mencian elevation of the human feeling of 誠 *cheng* as a cosmic force, we can then parse *cheng* further as a modality of "resolve and commitment" in this creative process. The collateral role of a distinctly human creativity within its large cosmic context is described in the *Mencius* 4A12:

> Creative resolve is the proper way of *tian* (誠者，天之道也); applying this creative resolve is the proper way of becoming human (誠之者，人之道也).

There is a passage in *Focusing the Familiar* 20 seemingly inspired by if not borrowed directly from this Mencian innovation:

> 誠者，天之道也；誠之者，人之道也。誠者不勉而中，不思而得，從容中道，聖人也。誠之者，擇善而固執之者也。
>
> Creative resolve is the way-making of *tian*; applying this creative resolve is the way-making of becoming human. Such resolve is achieving equilibrium and coalescence without coercion; it is succeeding without reflection. Freely and easily traveling at the center of way-making—this is the sage. Resolve is selecting what is efficacious and holding on to it firmly.

This process of cosmic co-creativity is then elaborated upon and described perhaps most clearly and powerfully in *Zhongyong* 25 and the chapters that follow from it.

In the *Mencius* and these middle passages of *Focusing the Familiar*, *cheng* is a human sentiment that has been elevated and projected onto the cosmos to describe the process of procreation itself, making the resolve of intense human feelings not only integral to its operations, but a source of the world's boundless capacity for growth.

The meaning of *cheng* is extended from the familiar personal attitude of sincerity and integrity to describe the cosmic process of worldmaking in which the sages (*shengren* 聖人) play a key role as co-creators. The discursive element *yan* included in the graph of *cheng* suggests that creativity involves a dynamic, discursive, and transactional partnership between the living human world and its natural, social, and cultural contexts, achieving consummation through effective communication in family and community, and productive transactions between the human and the natural world. *Focusing the Familiar* goes on to identify optimum human creativity with sagacity. Cosmic creativity is influenced dramatically by the virtuosic contributions of this highest level of humanity: the sages (*shengren*) who are able to orchestrate the communal discourse and coordinate it with the heavens and the earth to achieve a cosmic flourishing.

*恥 *chi.* "A sense of shame."

The classical Confucian canons reflect the always transactional nature of this Confucian philosophy as a "face" or "shame" culture. "Face" itself as a discursive social phenomenon is performed in our roles in "giving face," "saving face," and "losing face," where the effects of such conduct are both felt and seen. This sense of shame is a reflection of a cultivated and critical self-awareness integral to consummate conduct (*ren*) in our roles and relations. This wholeness and integrative nature of the moral experience means that a socially responsive "sense of shame" (*chi* 恥) is of high value in the Confucian culture; after all, it is a robust sense of shame that is the clearest evidence of one's commitment to the family and community nexus. Shame is such a powerful expression of moral awareness that when properly nurtured, it can become a galvanizing value that promotes social and political solidarity, and can enable the community to be inclusive of difference, and to become self-regulating.

Confucius himself as he is portrayed in the canonical literature has a much-developed sense of shame, and the feelings of belonging that accompanies it. Shamelessness by contrast is poison in the well, unleashing aberrant individuals to roam freely and to act arbitrarily without reference to the roles and relations that would properly secure them within their families and community. Such selfish and morally stunted individuals erode the communal solidarity on which the moral life depends.

The Confucian canonical texts give primacy to the thick notion of "achieving propriety in one's lived roles and relations" (*li* 禮) as its primary criteria for moral judgment that must take the relevant, specific interests of all parties into account (*yi* 義). And while Confucians certainly regard abstractions such as the rule of law and the application of punishments as necessary social institutions, at the same time they construe recourse to law as an unfortunate although sometimes necessary intervention and a clear admission of communal failure. We read a classic statement of these priorities in the *Analects* 2.3:

> 道之以政，齊之以刑，民免而無恥；道之以德，齊之以禮，有恥且格。
> If you lead the people with policy and effect social order with punishments, they will avoid wrongdoing, but will not develop an appropriate sense of shame. If you lead the people by modeling virtuosity in your conduct (*de* 德) and effect social order by encouraging propriety in roles and relations (*li* 禮), the people will not only develop a sense of shame (*chi* 恥), but will also order themselves.

It is the moral virtuosity displayed in the role modeling of rulers, the proper functioning of familial and social roles, and the commensurate sense of shame that develops within ritually choreographed family and community relations, that serve as a basis for critical assessment. While the dynamics of *li*-structured family lineages provide a concrete normative pattern of relations for a thriving community, abstract precepts such as the application of laws or policies, or the attendant threat of punishment, are at best only secondary injunctions.

Certainly, in a world disciplined by the pursuit of a "ritualized propriety" (li 禮), the formal and institutionalized aspects that structure conduct have an indispensable role in theorizing our practices. But the aesthetic dimension is also integral to this holistic understanding of human conduct in which all aspects of the life experience have more or less relevance, and thus have some value for determining a worthwhile outcome. There is an important role for elegance and moral artistry in Confucian ethics. Indeed, an inclusive and holistic Confucian role ethics can be distinguished from the more formalized and thus reductionistic principled-based ethical theories by referencing how in this Confucian moral vision, the particular, the informal, and the contextualizing aspects of experience, far from being ignored or marginalized, in fact take on a central role in optimizing the outcomes of always particular human activities.

Since morality itself is nothing more than those modalities of acting that conduce to the enhancement of relations, any kind of conduct that has a disintegrative effect on the fabric of family or community is perceived as fundamentally immoral. Lifestyle takes on crucial import when we consider the corrosive consequences on the community of those who live lives without style. Carelessness becomes of major concern when we have to worry about those who could care less. And ignorance in the sense of ignoring others and their needs, far from being detached or neutral, is in fact to inflict a violence upon the persons of our friends and neighbors. Graciousness, on the other hand, has gravity when we reflect on the relevance that charm and deportment have for an overall sense of fittingness and propriety. Morality is much more than formal correctness, emerging as it does importantly from poise and demeanor in our discursive transactions with others.

Whatever persons are and whatever putative "individuals" might or might not be, they cannot be the separate and isolated things without reference to past and current relations that our retrospective thoughts might assume they are. Persons are not present at birth, but are emergent in the relations that constitute them from this initial stage, shaping and being shaped in their roles and relations. As they become increasingly social, they also become increasingly reflective and self-conscious through communicating in the families and communities in which they live, and in which the production of the erstwhile "self-" within a distinctively human self-consciousness is arguably in imitation of their more primary social interactions. That is, persons have discursive relations with others, and under such influence and with reference to such a discursive model, they then gradually come to be reflective and engage in introspective conversation with themselves. In *Analects* 4.17:

子曰："見賢思齊焉，見不賢而內自省也。"
The Master said, "When you meet persons who are truly worthy, think to stand shoulder to shoulder with them; on meeting persons who are otherwise, look inward and examine yourself."

Gilbert Ryle in *The Concept of Mind*, seems to be making a similar point regarding the social origins of our self-awareness:

The trick of talking to oneself in silence is acquired neither quickly nor without effort; and it is a necessary condition of our acquiring it that we should have previously learned to talk intelligently aloud and have heard and understood other people doing so.[1]

We might further observe that there is a direct correlation between

---

[1] See Gilbert Ryle. *The Concept of Mind*. New York: Routledge, 2009, p. 16. I am indebted to Kevin J. Turner for having pointed this out to me.

the quality of one's critical self-awareness together with the sense of shame that attends it on the one hand, and moral conduct that might be deemed consummatory on the other. We might recall Hannah Arendt's seemingly mild indictment of the genocidal monster Adolf Eichmann as being "thoughtless;" it was her considered view that Eichmann lacked the critical self-awareness to see the world from another's point of view. In Confucianism, not "I think therefore I am," but rather "through communicating I am becoming a critically self-conscious 'we.'" This always collaborative, discursive process of becoming persons is why the language of roles is so powerful in expressing what is indeed a robust, narrative notion of agency.

*道　*dao.* "The proper way, way-making, *dao.*"

Conventionally translated "the Way," *dao* is probably the most pervasive and widely recognized idea in Chinese philosophy. This term has both a cosmological and moral significance that are really two aspects of the same thing. The signature of the Confucian tradition is a commitment to an aesthetic holism that requires that we strive to take all of the conditions in the human experience into account in making determinations about the totality of any particular effect. This sense of wholeness is captured and expressed in the language of *dao* 道 where this term takes us beyond any partial grasp of a situation to reference a comprehensive understanding of how, from a particular perspective, "everything comes together" to produce the event, including the penumbra of latent possibilities implicated within the process. This comprehensiveness in understanding is alluded to in Tang Junyi's cosmological proposition of *yiduobufenguan* 一多不分觀 which is a claim that "knowing" requires both comprehending the oneness of a situation (its continuity, its uniqueness, its vectoral direction) and its multiplicity (its relationally constituted field of particulars, its multivalence, its polysemic meanings). In contrast to Aristotle's logic of knowing as an analytic grasping of the essence of something, what-it-means-to-be-a-thing-of-this-kind, Confucian knowing requires a full inventory of the particular conditions relevant to any particular situation.

Again, *dao* like the word "life" is holistic and inclusive—the totality of all that is. This cosmic understanding of *dao* is more prominent in the Daoist literature, but it is also a suppressed assumption in the Confucian texts. We might remember a passage in *Daodejing* 25 that helps in bringing some clarity to this cosmic meaning in describing *dao* as 獨立而不改, a phrase that has almost uniformly been translated into English as some variation on "standing alone it does not change" (Legge, Waley, Karlgren, Lau, LaFarge, Henricks, Feng and English, Wu). Yet we must ask what could it mean to assert that *dao* "does not change" in the "eventful" world of classical Chinese philosophy in which the *Book of Changes* makes explicit the shared cosmology? We must allow that change is so real in fact that it is expressed in many different ways, with *gai* 改 being only one among them. On reflection, the specific kind of change referenced by *gai* is to alter or correct or reform or improve upon X on the basis of some external and independent standard or model Y. In our version of the *Daodejing*, we have translated this line as "standing alone as all there is, it does not suffer alteration."[①] The virtue of translating *gai* as "alteration" is that it introduces the

---

[①] See Roger T. Ames and David L. Hall. *A Philosophical Translation of the Daodejing: Making This Life Significant*. New York: Ballantine, 2003, p. 115. Fukunaga Mitsuji has also avoided this equivocation in offering the *kanbun* reading of *aratamezu* "is not reformed, revised." His modern Japanese translation is the passive-causative *kaerarezu*: "is not made to change." Fukunaga Mitsuji 福永光司 (trans.) *Roshi* 老子. Tokyo: Asahi Shinbunsha, 1968, pp. 143-145. The contemporary comparativist Gu Zhengkun in his translation has the same insight, translating the phrase simply as "it relies on nothing." Gu Zhengkun 辜正坤. (trans.) *The Book of Tao and Teh*. Peking: China Foreign Translation Press, 2006, p. 69.

notion of "alterity" to dismiss the possibility that there is something other than *dao*. The meaning here is not that *dao* "does not change," but being the *sui generis* and autopoietic totality of everything that is, *dao* is not open to alteration by appeal to something other than itself; it cannot be changed by something else. The Wang Bi commentary observes that *dao* has no counterpart—that is, there is nothing beyond it. And as we read further on in this same *Daodejing* chapter, one thing might emulate another: "human beings emulate the earth, the earth emulates the heavens." But when it comes to *dao*, 道法自然 "*dao* emulates what is spontaneously so-of-itself." Since *dao* is an inside without an outside, change can only come from within its own ecology, and it does so spontaneously and of itself.

The specific characteristics of Chinese philosophy arise because a dominant cosmological factor in the tradition, now and then, has been the priority of two differing patterns of change—alternation (*yi* 易) and transformation (*hua* 化)—that become normative in the aspiration after virtuosity (*de* 德) in the vital "zoetology" of "birth, life, growth" (*sheng* 生) as "the art of living." These modalities of productive change stand in contrast to the classical Greek substance ontology as "the science of being" that focuses on one pattern of change—causation—with its opposite being the unchanging, the real, the eternal, the True. In the processual cosmology of the Confucian tradition that does not appeal to some permanent and unchanging substratum with its formal and final causality, *dao* speaks to the wholeness and unboundedness of vital experience as it unfolds, while its dyadic correlate *de* 德 reflects its commitment to particularity. That is, the wholeness of experience is always entertained and engaged from one particular perspective or another; each focus construes its field of the unsummed totality from its own unique point of view.

Etymologically, the character *dao* 道 is constructed of two elements "walking," (*chuo* 辵 stylized as 辶) and hence, "passing over," "going over," "leading through" (on foot), and "head" (*shou* 首)—hair and head together—and therefore "foremost." In the *Shuowen* lexicon, it is defined as "the roadway that is walked, a thoroughfare." It is significant that the character for *dao* found on the bronzes is not simply a road—"the Way" as it is conventionally translated. *Dao* is reflexive, including within it a clear graphic representation of persons composed of the human and head (*shou* 首) complete with a full head of hair found as on the oracle bones and on the bronzes.① Simply put, *dao* is not *the* Way or *His* Way, but is rather the making of *our* way together, both ancestors and progeny, both whence and whither, as we intentionally and self-consciously forge ahead and strive to be true in our way-making. We might reflect on what seem to be certain suppressed "focus and field" premises in the cosmological and normative language of "virtuosity" (*de* 德) that make it a specifically human attainment: that is, the achieved quality of coalescence between cultivated persons (*de* 德) and their worlds (*dao* 道) in our project of becoming consummately human.

Importantly, this shared road and its trajectory has been constructed by those progenitors who have come before us. But far from them bequeathing a finished and predetermined way, it requires of us our full and deliberate participation in laying the connector to the next generation. The ancestors have provided the coordinates in their passing on of the cultural legacy (*daotong* 道統), but the responsibility of each and every generation is to "broaden the way" (*hongdao* 弘道) for their own time and place, and to provide the generations that succeed them the benefit of their own extension of this living cultural tradition. For Confucians, the road signs for a "proper" *dao* are to be found in the ritualized living (*li* 禮) that by definition differs from laws and abstract principles by requiring

---

① See Kwan, "Database," 西周晚期 CHANT 4469, 甲骨文合集 CHANT 3501C, and 西周中期 CHANT 2813.

personalization and reauthorization across generations. It is a historicist and revisionist way of life transmitted through emulation and appropriation rather than through compliance with unchanging verities. As *Zhuangzi* says, "The path is made in the walking 道行之而成." *Dao* means both to lead along a path, and to be led along it.

The parts of speech that order Western languages—nouns, verbs, adjectives and adverbs—encourage us to divide up the world in a culturally specific manner. Under the influence of these grammatical determinants, we are inclined to separate things from actions, attributes from modalities, where from when, and when from what. However, given the fluidity between time, space and matter assumed in classical Confucian cosmology, these familiar categories do not govern the way in which the world is divided. Time, space, and matter are simply explanatory language used to describe different aspects of the same experience. Thus, the categories used to define a Confucian world must be seen as crossing the borders of time, space, and matter. *Dao* is both "what is" (things and their attributes) and "how things are" (actions and their modalities). *Dao* has as much to do with the subjects of knowing and their quality of understanding as it does with the object of knowledge and its attributes. There are no clear lines between things and events, and hence we cannot separate "the Way" as *what* from this way as *how*. And *dao* is always episodic: a vital series of events seeking their own consummation.

Given that the word "world" as *w(e)oruld* (Old English) is etymologically derived from a Germanic compound of *wer* ("man") and *eld* ("age"), it means quite explicitly, "the age or the life of man." This reference to the specifically human sojourn is a warrant for translating *dao* as "world-making" to the extent that as a family- rather than a God-centered cosmogony, cosmic order is a full collaboration between persons and world. In the absence of the strong teleology and idealism of the classical Greeks, there is a contrapuntal relationship between persons and world, that encourages an understanding of *dao* as both way-making and world-making.

The *shou* "head" component has the suggestion of "leading" in the sense of "giving a heading." Thus, the character is primarily gerundive, processional, and dynamic: "a leading forth." Taking the gerundive *dao* as primary, its several derived meanings emerge rather naturally: "leading through," and hence, "road, path, way, method, art, teachings; to explain, to tell, doctrines." At the most fundamental level, *dao* denotes the active project of "moving ahead in the world," of "forging a way forward," of "road building." Hence, the neologism that we sometimes use, "way-making." By extension, *dao* comes to connote a pathway that has been made, and hence can be traveled. It is because of this more passive connotation that *dao* is most often nominalized by translating it as "way," or more problematically—is "nouned" once and for all as "the Way."

In the human world, this *dao* cosmology becomes evident in the focus on personal cultivation as the way of producing meaningful relations. Its distance from classical Western metaphysical thinking lies in the contrast between forging one's shared way in the world rather than questing after apodictic knowledge and its truth, the contrast between becoming a co-creator with the heavens and the earth rather than discovering what is objectively real. As Confucius made clear in the *Analects* 15.29, "It is persons that broaden the proper way (*dao*), not the way that broadens persons 人能弘道，非道弘人." Put another way, we might say that the contrast lies in an emphasis on the Confucian pursuit of a practical wisdom and the virtuosity it inspires rather than on the ambitious Greek search for the knowledge of some universal and unchanging reality.

Moral action in service to a thriving community requires the pursuit of such holistic understanding. In ethics we are inclined to assume that being moral has something to do with "according with what is right" or "being good," as though the notions of "right and wrong" and "good and bad" are available to us by appeal to some pre-existing standard: a pre-existing principle (causal) or some pre-existing ideal defined in the language of virtues (teleological). From the Confucian perspective, however, in the stead of pre-existing norms we discover a phenomenology of experience that serves as a resource for determining what it would mean to act in such a way as to enhance our relations. That is, we have to ask: What will make this situation as it is comprised of these particular relations and their possibilities better, and what will make this situation worse? Confucian ethics takes the substance of morality to be nothing more or less than positive growth in the constitutive relations of any particular situation. This understanding of morality is captured in the binomial *daode* 道德 that is used to express "morality" in the vernacular language: that is, the most productive coalescence between the particular and the totality, between this focus and its field.

In surveying the range of meaning invested in *dao* as it unfolds in the tradition, we can identify at least three overlapping and mutually entailing semantic dimensions that might have relevance in any particular passage. First, there is the primary "momentum" sense of the vital *dao* as an unfolding disposition or propensity. It is in this sense that *dao* (like John Dewey's use of the term "experience") is to be understood as a generic idea such as "life" or "climate" or "culture" or "history" that resists resolution into familiar dualisms such as "subject/object," "self/world," "form/function," "agency/action," and so on. With respect to the human world, *dao* (or *rendao* 人道) is simply the sea of our lived experience as human beings, with its cadence, continuities, and disjunctions. There is an ineluctable force of circumstances at play in this lived experience that at once accounts for the persistence and regularity of our daily lives, and also provides the context and the possibility for the sometimes delicious and sometimes poignant novelty that honeycombs experience. In fact, it is the richness and depth of one's experience that allows for the most productive shaping of what is novel within it.

Secondly, human beings have a proactive role in making our way forward in the world. *Dao* certainly connotes the continuing disposition of experience that gives us context. There is a palpable glacial weight to experience as it inches ahead. But this unfolding process is also underdetermined, allowing for our own creative participation and influence upon the course it will take. Making our way forward includes making productive adjustments in the direction of our lived experience by manipulating the more fluid and indeterminate opportunities that this experience presents. In the still "inchoate (*ji* 幾)" circumstances we can find the "trigger (*ji* 機)" that allows us to nudge the unfolding world in one direction as opposed to another. *Dao* as such is not only "way," but also "way-making," a forging of an always new way forward.

Dao as way-making is decidedly gerundive. It is *dao* 導: the leading-forth, the guiding, and the shaping of experience from which we are able to educe our shared future. In the process of personal cultivation, it is the achieved intensity and extensiveness of one's relations that determines the degree of one's influence. We find cosmological metaphors such as the "swinging gateway" (*tianmen* 天門) that captures "the opening out and closing up" of experience—its ineluctable presencing and consummating. *Dao* at a given time and place spontaneously "opens out" to provide creativity a space to make its "entrance," qualifying the processive nature of *dao* with the immediacy and specificity of the creative act. In contrast to a use of spontaneity that might suggest either mechanically uncaused or random action, spontaneity here means the productive spontaneity made possible by the personal cultivation of the artist. And it is personal cultivation in optimum degree that culminates in the contribution of "utmost sagacity (*zhisheng* 至聖)" itself to cosmic way-making.

In the case of the *Analects*, for example, the central "image" around which the text is constructed is the life of Confucius treading

道 *dao.*

a path until at age seventy he 從心所欲，不踰矩 "could give heart-and-mind free rein without overstepping the boundaries." A careful reading of the *Analects* reveals that much of the vocabulary or "words" used to present Confucius's philosophical insights is specific "way" imagery. Consider the cluster of terms that bring this image into focus, beginning with *dao* 道 as "way-making:" the proper path we are forging straight ahead on together. And walking this path is *de* 德 (悳) as "virtuosity:" persons moving virtuosically straight ahead on the proper path together. The "way" language is ubiquitous: *you* 由: "going out from," *qi* 齊: "standing shoulder to shoulder = ordering," *men* 門: "gate," *zhi* 之: "going to," *ji* 及: "reaching," *ju* 居: "residing," *chu* 處: "dwelling," *lin* 臨: "looking out over," *guo* 過: "overstepping," *wei* 違: "going against, deviating from," *da* 達: "getting through = understanding thoroughly," *zhi* 直: "going straight," *shi* 逝: "passing," *ji* 濟: "fording a stream," *shu* 述: "following the proper way," *xiu* 修: "repairing, constructing, clearing," *yuan* 遠: "distancing," *jin* 近: "coming close," *yi* 遺: "leaving behind," *ji* 跡: "leaving tracks," *jin* 進: "moving ahead," *tui* 退: "retiring," *tu* 徒: "followers = disciples," *yu* 迂: "straying," *xi* 徙: "moving to," and so on.

Much of the *Analects* is given over to the image of following the path that Confucius, having embodied the cultural tradition as his own, has marked out for himself and his protégés: going out and walking the path, moving ahead on it, extending it, clearing it, going against it, quitting it, sinking into confusion over it, confronting obstructions along it, finding company upon it, taking one's place on it, dwelling or lodging along it, having the strength to continue the journey along it, driving a carriage on it, and so on. When the ever-modest Confucius describes his own project he says 述而不作 "following the proper way, I do not forge new paths." But in fact, he is always doing both.

The most familiar yet derivative "pathway" sense of *dao* is a *post hoc* combination of its more primary meanings: the dynamic disposing of experience and our creative way-making that goes on within it. As a "way" that has been laid, *dao* is stipulated and defined. This is the objectified use of *dao* that would allow for the familiar demonstrative translation as "the *dao*." But to thus nominalize and conceptualize *dao* betrays its fluidity, reflexivity, and openness to the future, and if given priority, this way of thinking about *dao* is the first step to inadvertently overwriting a process sensibility with substance assumptions. We can neither step outside *dao* nor arrest its always changing disposition. Even when we reflect on a temporally prior "way"—the way of Confucius, for example—we must allow that our present vantage point involves us reflexively in our interpretation and reauthorization of it, making Confucius both dynamic and corporate rather than simply referential and antiquarian. As the oft-cited opening passage of the *Daodejing* itself cautions, we cannot do justice to the throbbing complexity of our always personal experience by anything we have to say about it.

德　de. "Moral virtuosity, excelling morally, virtuality."

On the oracle bones, "excelling morally" (*de* 德) conventionally rendered nominally as "virtue" or "excellence," appears as 㣧. Reminiscent of the character *dao*, it combines the graphs "a small step, a path" (*chi* 彳) and "going straight ahead" (*zhi* 直), suggesting as it does persons walking deliberately forward focused on the road ahead, and having both the physical and the moral connotations of being "straight" and "true."[①] On the bronze inscriptions, the heartmind (*xin* 心) is added as an additional element in the graph for *de* 悳, underscoring the intentionality and self-awareness required to direct the life experience to optimum effect as we extend our way

---

① 殷墟文字甲編 2304.

in the world.①

Reinforcing this understanding of *de* as a kind of "*de*-making" or "conatus"—as the purposeful effort of persons striving forward to make the most of their life's experience—is the fact that in several of the recently recovered bamboo texts, the character *de* 德 is written using its graphic variant, 悳. This graphic alternative has the heartmind radical *xin* 心 placed beneath the character *zhi* 直 that means "upright," "true," and "going straight ahead." There is clearly a cognate relationship between these variants for *de* as 德 and 悳 on one hand, and the character *zhi* 直 meaning "going straight ahead" on the other. According to the reconstructed archaic language, the characters *de* and *zhi* were markedly similar in pronunciation, with *zhi* in the variant graph 悳 being the phonetic as well as having semantic reference.

When we parse this notion of forging "straight ahead" on life's path, and reflect upon the normative qualities of action that would follow from such resolve, we find a glossary of related terms: true, direct, proper, candid, authentic, rightly positioned, immediate, timely, main, undiluted, deliberate, judicious, decisive, effective, resolute, intense, upright, and so on. Such deliberate, judicious, and disciplined conduct is in sum the meaning of "moral virtuosity" itself. That is, *de* is being true and resolute in optimizing all of those available resources that would allow us to find the most productive way forward in our world-making together.

When we locate this notion of *de* within the early Confucian cosmology where the cosmos is not more or less than the unsummed totality of the myriad things (*wanwu* 萬物) as they come to accommodate one another, our world of experience is *kosmoi* rather than *kosmos*, a "pluriverse" rather than a universe, without any single order being privileged above all others, and with each thing

---

① See Kwan, "Database," 西周早期 CHANT 2837.

having its own distinctive trajectory. In the early philosophical literature, *de* has this strong cosmological sense, connoting the insistent particularity of things, and most often, of human beings. It is for this reason that *de* is conventionally translated as "virtue," or "power," or "potency," suggesting a prospective momentum, or to use a Heideggerian term, *dasein* in the sense of a "presencing," a "being-here" within its own field of experience. *De* is most often but not exclusively positive, and because it is the human being more than any other phenomenon that has a penchant for growth and refinement, it is most often but not exclusively used to describe the acquired excellence of human beings and the attendant influence such achievement brings with it.

This early Confucian cosmology with the priority it invests in vital relationality begins from the uniqueness of the relationally-constituted particular, *de* 德. Given the intrinsic and constitutive relatedness of particulars in this process conception of existence, *de* is the achieved virtuosity of any particular focus within the totality of things. *Dao* and *de* are thus related as field and focus respectively. The particular focus of persons establishes their always unique identities, and the totality as a noncoherent sum of all possible orders, is adumbrated in each one of them. This insistent particularity is focal in the sense that it is a convergence of the field of all of the constitutive relations that collaborate in sponsoring and animating it. *De* 德 in being defined paronomastically as *de* 得 "getting, gaining" reflects the fact that the reach and influence of any particular—its excellence, virtuosity, virtuality, or potency—is a function of its deference to everything else and the quality of coalescence it is able to achieve in its constitutive relationships with them as they come to constitute it as a unique particular.

De is thus "holographic," meaning that each element among the totality of things contains and expresses the totality in some adumbrated form, with the greater degree of resolution achieved by any particular focus expressing a greater degree of significance for itself and for the totality. It is the quality of coalescence in this open-ended focus-field relationship describable in the language of optimizing symbiosis (*he* 和) and creative resolve (*cheng* 誠) that is doing the work of teleology in the classical Greek scheme of things. Distinguished persons constituted as they are by a web of robust relationships focus the world in profoundly meaningful ways. By contrast, small persons who are deficient and defused in their relations are neither intensive nor extensive in the resolution they express.

In a holographic cosmology, a *this* always entails a *that*. *This* focus always has *that* field implicated within it, and *this* field is always construed from either *that* particular focus or another. With *dao* and *de* as unbounded field and focal center respectively, there is an immediate graphic resonace between the field of *dao* as an open-ended way that is continuously being extended, and its dyadic correlate, the focal *de*, that denotes the insistent particularity of self-conscious human "becomings" as they live deliberately. Of course, the optimal coalescence between particular persons and the road they are forging together is reflected in the meaning that emerges from the combination of these two terms as the binomial *daode* 道德 which in the modern language has conventionally come to be translated as "moral, morality."

But this expression *daode* has ancient provenance, and early on was used to express the human virtuosity achieved when, through focus and resolution, we achieve an optimizing symbiosis within our field of experience. The main theme of the canonical *Daodejing* 道德經, for example, is captured in the various *wu*-forms—*wuwei* 無為 (non-coercive acting), *wuzhi* 無知 (unprincipled knowing), *wuyu* 無欲 (objectless desiring), *wushi* 無事 (non-interfering governing), and so on—as defining of the optimum, most productive coalescence that can be achieved between self-conscious persons and their world. In its field-focus, holographic cosmology, the *Daodejing* is dedicated to an exposition of how persons can be most effective in bringing their perspectival fields into resolute focus. It is this process of focusing *de* that, for the human being, is productive of cognitive, moral, aesthetic, and spiritual meaning. For this reason we were inspired to translate the title of this text, revised according to the order found in the recent archaeological digs as the *Dedaojing* 德道經—literally "the classic of this *de* and its *dao*"—as "*Making This Life Significant.*" The *Daodejing*, recognizing the meaning-creating and meaning-disclosing power of cultivated human beings, emphasizes the way in which this personal articulation extends beyond the human community to appreciate the cosmos itself. Those with the "highest virtuosity" (*shangde* 上德) as human paragons have cosmological significance in maximizing the symbiotic relationship between the human experience and the cosmic environment within which that drama unfolds.

The earliest literature that we associate with Confucius is anything but speculative (*wuyi* 毋意), tending to focus his concerns on the ordinary human experience, where *de* more nearly suggests a cultivated, personal "moral virtuosity." *De* is what we can truly *do* and *become* if in living wisely we "realize" (*zhi* 知) satisfying personal lives as members of a flourishing community. The extension of one's *de* in the world entails both an act of intending and the attraction of the deference and support necessary to effect what is intended. As artists, as teachers, as communal leaders, persons are able to collaborate in their natural, social and cultural environments and disclose the possibilities of these environments for a flourishing family and community. Particular persons are thus configurations of patterns of deference within a community and world, where the direction and volition of the contextualizing "others" are implicated in their own identities. To the extent that persons achieve a consensus in their activities, and these same activities remain free of coercion, their *de* becomes a kind of relational autonomy.

Among the Confucian canons, *Focusing the Familiar* can perhaps be read as a response to the more explicit cosmological speculation found in the Daoist texts. It extends the resolutely human-centered focus of the *Analects* to take as its main theme the capacity and responsibility of cultivated persons to stand as full partners in the production of cosmic harmony. In the Confucian tradition specifically, the cultivation of *de* is pursued through a person's full participation in the ritualized community, where achieved excellence in the roles and relationships that come to constitute a human narrative makes this person an object of deference for other members of the family and community. It is the extension of and participation in established patterns of deference that comes to constitute a shared world of cultural values. It is in this way that across time and space, a corporate and evolving Confucius has served each generation in perpetuating a shared Confucian identity.

There is also a political dimension to this idea of *de* that reflects its cosmic focus-field meaning. When referenced within the political realm, *de* describes the most productive relationship between a ruler and the people. To the extent that the ruler reaches out to become coextensive with the prevailing cultural propensities of the people, the ruler embodies and expresses the values of the community. To the extent that the ruler becomes culturally coextensive with the community through the patterns of deference that superior leadership elicits, the people come to share in the ruler's values and moral insights and are won over to them. In this context, *de* has a range of meanings that reflects the priority of situation over agency, including both giving and getting. That is, *de* is both the "beneficence" extended to the people by the ruler in response to their perceived worth, and the deference and "gratitude" of a people expressed in response to the largesse of a worthy ruler. *De* is a fiduciary configuration inclusive of both benefactor and beneficiary achieved through productive, noncoercive communal relations.

Because *de* is what we accrue through a life of service to others, Confucius in *Analects* 12.21 defines the accumulation of excellence (*chongde* 崇德) explicitly as 先事後得，非崇德與 "Getting only after having given of oneself—is this not the accumulating of excellence?" The getting comes in the giving. It is for this reason we must be careful not to give priority to agency in understanding *de*, thereby making the ruler and people exclusive categories, and making the ruler active and the people passive.① To the extent that the *de* of the people is implicated in the ruler's *de*, the ruler's potency is enhanced, becoming the wind that bends the grass (12.19), the North Star around which the other stars circumambulate (2.1), and the maker and transmitter of a compounding cultural legacy to which succeeding generations both continue to subscribe and contribute (7.1, 3.14). It is in this sense that the emperor as a focus of productive relations *is* the empire. *De* is the character or ethos of the polity as a whole as it is embodied in the ruler. On this basis, we might suggest "virtuality" in its archaic sense of "having inherent virtue or power to produce effects" as another possible translation of *de*.

The conventional translation of *de* is "virtue," and there is certainly some overlap between *de* and the Greek notion of *arête*. Both entail purpose and discipline directed at becoming singularly effective in

---

① May Sim. *Remastering Morals with Aristotle and Confucius*. Cambridge: Cambridge University Press, 2007, p. 17 for example, makes the ruler and people exclusive when she states:
> Confucius so completely embeds moral principle in customary norms and the model persons embodying and exhibiting them that he hangs all his political hopes on rule by an exemplary individual who inspires others to virtue.

But if we recall Analects 2.3, Confucius on the contrary is relying upon the achieved capacity of the people to order themselves through a sense of shame and belonging. See also:
> The Yi and Di barbarian tribes with rulers are not as viable as the various Chinese states without them. 夷狄之有君，不如諸夏之亡也。(3.5)

what one does. In both cases, education and cultivation are integral to this process. While Plato does stipulate *aretēs* as separate virtues such as temperance, courage, wisdom, and justice, it is because they all share a single essence that there is a unity among them. Again, while *de* and *aretē* have broad application as a kind of potency, they both have a strong moral connotation. *De* can be given a general characterization, but given the primacy of vital relationality and the focus-field relationship between *de* and *dao*, *de* are resolutely unique instances of moral conduct from which such generalizations can be made. That is, like "consummate conduct" (*ren* 仁), *de* can be generalized from particular instances—we can certainly speak of a "human moral virtuosity" (*rende* 人德)—but such a generalization has its beginnings in the conduct of particular exemplars.

Along with some similarities between *aretē* and *de*, there also seem to be important differences. Although the notion of *aretē* itself as it appears in the classical Greek thinkers is anything but clear, there does seem to be a strong sense of teleology that would distinguish it from *de*. *Aretēs* in Plato are defined as having an *eidos* where each instance of conduct that demonstrates a particular virtue has some self-same, identical characteristic. It is for this reason that in the works of Plato, such virtues are taken to be the subject of formal definition that in turn becomes the object of our knowledge about them. There is an innate potential for excellence in things, and in the striving to realize such a human potential, we find a way of life.

While for Aristotle, *aretē* as a mean between extremes requires rational calculation, *de* in the Confucian canons seems closely tied to moral imperatives such as family reverence (*xiao* 孝). In the first chapter of the *Classic of Family Reverence* (*Xiaojing* 孝經) we read that 夫孝者德之本也 "it is family reverence that is the root of moral virtuosity (*de* 德) ". *De* goes beyond rational calculation as an achieved ritual propriety in our roles and relations (*li* 禮) that is expressed through consummate conduct (*ren* 仁) and an optimizing appropriateness (*yi* 義) in what we do.

Perhaps the most important difference between *arête* and *de* is that the two traditions begin from fundamentally different conceptions of what it means to be a person: teleologically-informed, discrete human beings on the one hand, and human becomings whose identities emerge in the assiduous cultivation of personal relations. Plato gives temporal and logical priority to the innately virtuous human "being," and then treats the subsequent process of social and political transformation as a secondary, epiphenomenal affair in which a given virtuous nature is actualized in practice. For Aristotle, individuated subjects stand ontologically independent of their actions, making of *arête* those cultivated character traits that belong to individuals and inform their conduct. *De* on the other hand, belongs to a tradition grounded in a gerundive understanding of persons as events, where persons are radically situated within a matrix of relations. *De* thus describes the virtuosic quality of those inclusive, transactional activities themselves within their continuing narratives.

John Dewey in abjuring what he calls "*the* philosophical fallacy" alerts us to our inveterate habit of decontextualizing and essentializing one element within the continuity of experience, and then in our best efforts to overcome this *post hoc* diremption, of then construing this same element as being both foundational and causal. "Virtue" is a concrete example of this habit. As we achieve a certain virtuosity in the process of our ongoing conduct, we abstract something called "virtue" out of the complexity of this continuing experience, and then make this abstraction antecedent to and causal of the process itself. For Dewey,

> ...the reality is the growth-process itself... The real existence is the history in its entirety, the history just as what it is. The operations of splitting it up into two parts and then having to unite them again

by appeal to causative power are equally arbitrary and gratuitous.①

The classical Greeks give us a substance ontology grounded in "being *qua* being" or "being *per se*" (*to on he on*) that guarantees a permanent and unchanging subject as the substratum for the human experience. With the combination of *eidos* and *telos* as the formal and final cause of independent things such as persons, this "sub-stance" necessarily persists through change. This kind of foundational and causal thinking is precisely what Dewey is referencing in his concern about *the* philosophical fallacy.

*惡 *e.* "Rudeness, uncouthness, nasty, ugly, unrefined, base."

Although *e* 惡 has conventionally been translated as "evil," we need to worry about avoiding the Manichean dualism that is introduced by reifying and hypostasizing what is instead a fundamental failure to achieve productive relations. The *Shuowen* lexicon defines *e* as *guo* 過: "going beyond, transgressing, excess," and thus by extension, "a fault." It is a negative: a failure to stay on course and hit the mark due to actions that exhibit a lack of refinement. It is a failure to achieve and sustain a desirable standard of conduct.

E is taken as the dyadic opposite of *shan* 善 that references the gregarious activity of achieving felicity in our relations and thus making them "meaningful" in "relating" to each other through effective communication. *Shan* as "good" is thus not in the first instance a quality or character trait or antecedent principle, but is rather a cultivated, aesthetic way of behaving that in making the most of a situation has felicitous consequences. If *shan* is the

---

① Dewey, *Later Works*, Vol. 1, p. 210.

product of our prosocial inclinations, *e* is the stunted outcome of our pathologies, and the depraved consequences that follow from it. *E* like *shan* is a way of behaving, but far from being felicitous, is as a consequence of untoward actions, a gross failing to make the most of our conditions, social and otherwise. With this sense of aesthetic conduct being primary, *e* is failing to realize the creative possibilities of a situation because of rudeness, uncouthness, boorishness, or vulgarity. This fundamentally aesthetic meaning of *e* as "ugly," "nasty," "unrefined," and "base" is evident in its being used on occasion as the dyadic opposite of "beautiful" (*mei* 美).

The functional equivalent of "evil" in the Confucian tradition is waste—the outcome of a failure of application and imagination. It is a possibility in human relations that because of disintegrative behaviors, they lay fallow and fail to produce meaning: a rudeness and brutishness that produces a depraved dysfunctionality in family and community. A cognate of *e* is *wu* 誣: deceiving through slander and accusing falsely as good examples of the kind of callous behavior that undermines communal solidarity and trust. Aesthetic failure frequently entails fraudulence—proffering a fake that pretends to be something it is not. And anything that is lacking in integrity inevitably becomes a source of disintegration.

*法 *fa.* "Standards, norms, laws, models."

Fa refers to both the objects of compliance, and also the emulating of such models of order, suggesting the priority of situation over specific agency. It anticipates the Buddhist usage of *fa* as *dharma*: both things and the proper order of things. Since this Confucian cosmology begins from the uniqueness of the particular, in social and political philosophy modeling role "models" does much of the work of obeying abstract principles and laws. To emulate a model requires an appropriate analogical projection between particular persons in their always unique situations, and the particular models they would emulate. Confucius for example does not provide categorical imperatives for right conduct nor does he appeal to some moral law as a regulative ideal. Rather he himself serves as a specific model of a mode of conduct that can be emulated analogically by succeeding generations across the centuries to the extent that the remembered pronouncements and chronicled events of his life can be applied productively to always novel situations. What is being recommended is a way of behaving—being resolute (*cheng* 誠), cherishing learning (*haoxue* 好學), striving to be consummate (*ren* 仁) and optimally appropriate in one's roles and relations (*yi* 義), and so on. The Confucian canons do not provide a catechism for right conduct, but offer the reader an album of anecdotes, snapshots, and laconic sayings that provide an inspiring vocabulary for personal cultivation.

The term *xing* 刑 as "penal law" appears in the Confucian texts as a subset of *fa* in its sense of rule by appeal to promulgated laws. This conception of externally imposed regulations stands in immediate contrast to the organization of the community brought about through a shared aspiration to an achieved propriety in one's roles and relations (*li* 禮). Given that for Confucius, appeal to law is an admission of communal failure, it follows that his ideal society would be one in which the application of law is unnecessary (*Analects* 12.13). But we must be careful not to overstate the case. There can be no question Confucius advocated for a social and political order that is achieved through a process of education, suasion, and example, and that aspires to be self-ordering. This did not prevent the eminently practical Confucius from assigning penal law a place in his political thought as an unfortunate but necessary backstop to remove the recalcitrant and to ward off any descent into social chaos.

For Confucius, appeal to law as a means of ordering society was fundamentally dehumanizing. Litigation from the perspective of a defendant is extrinsic and coercive. Because the use of law to effect order does not require the active participation of those most affected by it, it can have little transforming or refining influence on the people. On the contrary, because it is fundamentally restrictive and imposed, it constitutes a real limitation in their possibilities for person-making. In the employment of ritual action (*li* 禮) to effect order, on the other hand, these *li* and the people who perform them are mutually determining and refining. *Li* permits and in fact encourages an emergent communal harmony that is expressive of the needs and interests of the people in their diversity and insistent particularity. The society in its reliance upon *li* maximizes the possibilities for a qualitative self-regulating harmony, and pursues an overlapping consensus in thinking rather than uniformity of thought. Where ritual action fails, however, law simply serves as a means to prevent decline into social discord, and to thus guarantee the stability provided by the more effective and enduring methods of ritual action to again be applied. In this vision of social order, the harmony that can be achieved through ritual action is an end in itself, whereas the imposed order achieved through law has only a functional and instrumental value as a temporary means to a higher end.

When this term was appropriated by the philosophical lineage that has come to be called the Legalists (*fajia* 法家), it was invested with strongly external, objective meaning, and celebrated as a promulgated set of standards that required compliance from everyone, including the ruler himself.

*和   *he.* "Optimal harmony, optimizing symbiosis."

He is conventionally translated as "harmony." The etymology of the standard character is culinary, combining the graphs for "millet" (*he* 禾) and "mouth" (*kou* 口). Throughout the early corpus, the preparation of food is appealed to as a gloss on this sense of elegant, integrative harmony. Although harmony entails the art of combining and blending two or more foodstuffs so that they mutually enhance one another without losing their distinctive flavors, the appreciation of harmony begins from the aesthetic experience of the dish as a coherent whole. That is, harmony is expressed as each particular ingredient with its own particular characteristics discloses the taste of the dish as a whole. Each of the ingredients is a unique perspective on a dish that can only be experienced from one perspective or another. It is the always perspectival and thus local nature of harmony that makes it both unique and underdetermined. The local nature of harmony means that an always situated creativity is dependent upon reading and responding effectively to still indeterminate, initial conditions (*ji* 幾). Harmony does not overcome the indeterminate or chaotic; rather it is achieved through the space and generosity that the indeterminateness provides.

Needless to say, harmony applies no less to the musical than to the culinary arts, with "instruments of the orchestra" and "voices of the chorus" replacing "ingredients" that combine to form an aesthetically satisfying whole while each element yet retains its uniqueness. Harmony so considered entails both the insistent "integrity" of the particular ingredient and their "integration" into some larger whole. Signatory of this harmony is the persistence of the particular ingredients and the aesthetic and cosmetic nature of the harmony—an elegant order that emerges out of the collaboration of intrinsically related details in such a way as to make the most of the unique contribution of each one. Harmony is achieved when their differences are activated to make a difference.

This Confucian understanding of achieved "harmony" is not simply the mutual accommodation of difference that would attenuate dissonance, but more importantly, it references the creative and productive consequences of coordinating such differences to optimum, superlative effect: that is, the achievement of a human and cosmic "musicality." The composition of the earlier, more complex graph for "optimal harmony" (*he* 和) found on the oracle bones is ▨ and on the bronzes is ▨. This character is composed of a *yue* 龠 wind instrument constructed out of reed pipes, with "growing grain" (*he* 禾) as the phonetic element, alluding to the playing of music as one metaphorical way of understanding this particular, highly aesthetic sense of harmony.①

One important vocabulary cluster that gives expression to Confucian role ethics in the canonical texts is the aspiration to "an optimizing harmony" (*he* 和) through an "achieved propriety" (*li* 禮) in the "embodied living" (*ti* 體) within one's roles and relations. Perhaps the best way of understanding the dynamics of "family reverence" (*xiao* 孝) as the prime moral imperative in the process of intergenerational transmission, is to appeal to these two cognate characters—*li* 禮 as "embodied living" and *ti* 體 as "lived body"—that would speak to the physical, cultural, and narrative continuities within an enduring family and cultural lineage. These two terms *li* and *ti* are further informed qualitatively by the aspiration to an optimizing "harmony" (*he* 和) we find pervasive in Confucian cosmology. While this term *he* is conventionally translated simply as "harmony," it is perhaps better understood as the aspiration to optimize the creative possibilities of any particular situation—in the case of Confucian ethics, the roles as they are lived in family and community.

Although we find that "optimizing harmony" (*he*) is a generic idea with wide application in all human activities from the kitchen to the cosmos, what needs to be emphasized here is the Confucian assumption that when such an aspiration has reference to human

---

① Kwan, "Database," 甲骨文合集 CHANT 1490 and 戰國早期 CHANT 17 respectively. The early twentieth century reformer, Lu Xun 魯迅, in describing Sima Qian's *Record of the Grand Historian* appealed to just such hyperbolic terms, calling this great work "the historians' most perfect song."

flourishing specifically, the harmony must necessarily be mediated through familial roles and relations for it to be robust, genuine, and enduring. It is the family that is the ultimate source and the indispensable ground of an achieved propriety (*li* 禮) in all of our roles and relations. As it is asserted in the *Analects* 1.12:

> 禮之用，和為貴。先王之道斯為美，小大由之。有所不行，知和而和，不以禮節之，亦不可行也。
>
> An optimizing harmony (*he* 和) is the most valuable function of achieving propriety in our roles and relations (*li* 禮). In the ways of the Former Kings, the sustaining of this quality of harmony through achieving propriety in their roles and relations made them elegant, and was a guiding standard in all things large and small. But when things are not going well, to realize harmony just for its own sake without regulating the situation through an achieved propriety in roles and relations, will not work.[①]

Morality so understood describes a generative quality of conduct that makes familial bonds stronger and thicker and more enduring. Without being properly negotiated through our roles and relations, however, actions that simply eliminate dissonance can be meaningless or worse. That is, a putative "harmony" that is achieved by imposing external mechanisms and constraints as a means of enforcing order—the application of laws, policies, or rules—is dehumanizing to the extent that such "harmony" precludes personal confirmation and participation.

The pursuit of the superlative in our conduct is explained by medical anthropologist Zhang Yanhua in the following terms:

> Harmony defined here is related to the Chinese sense of *du* 度

[①] See also 12.1 and 12.15.

(degree, extent, position) ... In other words, in a dynamic interactive environment, harmony is brought about when each particular unfolds itself in its unique way and to an appropriate *du* such that "each shines more brilliantly in the other's company" (*xiangdeyizhang* 相得益彰).①

The goal of healthy living is a lived equilibrium in which we avoid both excess and insufficiency in our giving and getting, in our doing and undergoing, in our shaping and being shaped. We are only able to get the most out of the ecology of the human experience by achieving full measure (*du* 度) in both the particularities and the scope of our transactional activities.

An optimizing harmony, understood in these Confucian terms, serves the ultimate goal of aestheticizing the human experience. This aesthetic dimension—the need for elegance and moral artistry in ethics—is integral to this holistic understanding of human conduct in which all aspects of the life experience have more or less relevance, and thus have some value for determining a worthwhile outcome. It is because the moral vision of Confucian role ethics is holistic, and is concerned with coordinating the contribution of each aspect of experience in achieving the totality of the effect that the normative language to which it appeals, and the sense of order to which it aspires, is in the Whiteheadian sense, fundamentally aesthetic.②

Allowing for the consummatory nature of experience in its beginnings and endings, we can draw commonalities and contrasts between this Confucian notion of superlative "harmony" (*he* 和) that seeks to optimize the possibilities of "lived body" (*ti* 體) and

---

① Zhang Yanhua. *Transforming Emotions with Chinese Medicine: An Ethnographic Account from Contemporary China.* Albany: State University of New York Press, 2007, p. 51.
② A.N. Whitehead. *Modes of Thought.* New York: Macmillan, 1938, Chapter 3.

"embodied living" (*li* 禮) within the Confucian process cosmology, and the strong sense of teleology that has motive force in a substance ontology with its historical roots in ancient Greece. Both harmony and teleology have an important albeit-different function in explaining the organization, the evolution, and the completion of events within the human experience. Greek teleology gives impetus and direction to a cosmos informed by an overarching, predetermined design. Such teleology, with its formal and final causes directing the actualization of order to a given end, is linear and front-loaded in the sense of being in important degree determined in advance. By contrast, the Confucian idea of an achieved "optimal harmony" within its own process cosmology has no presumed beginning or predetermined and final end. Moreover, it is ever emergent in the sense of focusing on the capacity and responsibility of the most exemplary of human beings to make the most of the possibilities that arise in their continuing present. This being said, the pursuit of such harmony does much of the work of teleology as a determining factor in the flourishing and consummation of the human experience. This optimizing harmony, resourcing the historical past as its reservoir for analogy and projection, draws upon human resolve and imagination to forge an always new way forward. Our human capacity for design, purpose, and direction assumed in this Confucian sense of harmony gives us a vital and prominent role in the evolution of an emergent and always provisional cosmic order.

There is an alternative understanding of "harmony" as it functions within the teleological interpretation of cosmic order that in favoring *ratio* over *oratio* tends to be reductionistic in the Whiteheadian sense of a "rational" or "rationalized" order. Such an order is established through a process of "tuning" Y to X as opposed to allowing for the mutually "attuning" and accommodation of X and Y. That is, the antecedently determined goal disciplines the evolution of the many according to the one privileged order, making the details that collaborate to constitute the cosmic order relevant only to the extent that they contribute to its completion. To give an example of such a rational order, the construction of a triangle needs three points to complete it, where such points can alternatively be coins, cabbages, or Caledonians, and where such obvious and interesting differences among these three "points" (collectors, cultivars, and kilts) have no relevance or value for the desired order. The concrete many are reduced to an abstract, reduplicated one as they are disciplined and rationalized to constitute a single-ordered world. Moving from the triangle to some grand, Divine design, the *kosmoi* as many, are rationalized to become a *kosmos*, and the *pluri*-verse as many, are rationalized to become a "*uni*-verse."

The Confucian optimizing harmony is an example of the Whiteheadian holistic and inclusive "aesthetic order" in the sense that everything without remainder is relevant to the achieved totality of the effect. Because each unique thing conduces to the flourishing of every other unique thing, order has to be conceived of in terms of *equity* or *parity* among things as the heightened realization of their dynamically shared well-being. And the *diversity* to be aspired to in this sense of order is the full appreciation of the creative possibilities of any situation through the conserving and coordinating of those differences that make each ingredient unique, and as unique, uniquely relevant.[1]

---

[1] I am using "equity" here in the Aristotelian sense of serving as a corrective on the notion of universality that is necessary in respect of the particularity of things. In the *Nicomachean Ethics*, Book 5, Aristotle observes that "the equitable is just, but not the legally just but a correction of legal justice. The reason is that all law is universal but about some things it is not possible to make a universal statement which will be correct.... And it is none the less correct; for the error is not in the law nor in the legislator but in the nature of the thing, since the matter of practical affairs is of this kind from the start." *Complete Works* 1137b11-20. Peter Hershock makes much of this superlative, aesthetic sense of order as the Buddhist *kusala* conduct in his monograph, *Valuing Diversity: Buddhist Reflection on Realizing a More Equitable Global Future*. Albany: State University of New York Press, 2012.

Perhaps the most prominent example in the Confucian tradition that illustrates the centrality of this aesthetic, superlative sense of "harmony" (*he* 和) is role that the institution of family occupies as the governing and pervasive cultural metaphor. Family—a model of order that when optimally functional is one and many at the same time—is that powerful social nexus to which members are most inclined to invest themselves utterly and without remainder. That is, persons as required are inclined to give their families their time, their fortunes, their body parts, and even their lives. Confucian philosophy promotes this institution of family with its primary moral imperative of "family reverence" (*xiao* 孝) as its governing cosmological trope as a deliberate strategy to maximize the creative possibilities available within all of the human activities as they are rooted in family and extend outward socially, politically, and religiously from this resilient core. Importantly, such a commitment to family, far from entailing self-sacrifice or self-abnegation, requires the full expression of personal worth, and thus becomes that context in which one can most effectively pursue personal realization.

One signature of Confucian political philosophy is the assumed isomorphism between family and state (*jiaguotonggou* 家國同構). In the *Classic of Family Reverence*, an optimizing harmony is the quality of life attained among the people that is brought about through their emulation of cultural heroes and exemplary persons in their community. *Xiao* or family reverence also defines the relationship between the ruler—the father and mother of the people—and the people as his extended family. But the analogy works in both directions. That is, to effect proper familial relationships is to participate in governing at its most fundamental level. Politics are local. It is for this reason that in *Analects* 2.21 when Confucius is asked by a mean-spirited contemporary why he does not serve in the government, he replies:

"《書》云：'孝乎惟孝、友于兄弟，施於有政。'是亦為政，奚其為為政？"

The *Book of Documents* says: "It all lies in family reverence (*xiao* 孝). Being filial to your parents and finding fraternity with your brothers (*ti* 悌) is in fact carrying out the work of governing." In doing these things I am participating in governing. Why must I be employed in government?

In the *Classic of Family Reverence* 2, it is on this basis that the method the emperor appeals to in nurturing family feeling within his population broadly is a display of sincere deference to his own parents:

愛親者，不敢惡於人；敬親者，不敢慢於人。愛敬盡於事親，而德教加於百姓，刑於四海。蓋天子之孝也。

The Emperor who loves (*ai* 愛) his own parents would not presume to hate the parents of others; he who respects (*jing* 敬) his own parents would not presume to be rude to the parents of others. With love and respect being fully expressed in this service to parents, such conduct will educate and transform (*dejiao* 德教) the common people, serving as exemplary in all corners of the world. Such, then, is the family reverence of the Emperor.

Confucian role ethics is a radial way of thinking about the moral life, with human feelings grounded as they are in a familial center and then extended outward by cosmic way-makers to "family" the world in which we live. The Eastern Han dynasty philosopher, Wang Chong 王充, summarizes the fundamental value that this Confucian tradition has traditionally invested in the institution of family as its strategy for the pursuit of optimal harmony in the following terms:

聖人以天下為家，不別遠近，不殊內外……聖人舉事求其宜適也……賢聖家天下。

Sages take the whole world as their family without distinction of near or far, of domestic or foreign . . . In their undertakings, the sages seek what is optimally appropriate . . . The most sagacious among us would "family" the whole world.①

In many of the texts associated with Confucius, this sense of an optimizing harmony is celebrated as the highest cultural achievement. Herein harmony is distinguished from mere agreement by defining it in terms of eliciting the optimum contribution of each particular to its context. *Focusing the Familiar* (*Zhongyong* 中庸), the fourth among Zhu Xi's *Four Books*, has been celebrated across the centuries in this tradition as the highest statement of the Confucian vision of the moral life. In *Focusing the Familiar* the meaning of this Confucian sense of harmony (*he* 和) is further stipulated by its association with "focus" or "equilibrium" (*zhong* 中) as bringing into "focus" (*zhong* 中) "the familiar affairs of the day" (*yong* 庸). This seminal text appeals directly to this superlative sense of "harmony" in its own iteration of the holistic and aspirational Confucian project of optimizing familial, political, and cosmic relations.

Our warrant for translating the title of the text, "*zhongyong* 中庸", as *Focusing the Familiar*, is the fact that "familiar" and "family" share the same etymological root: L. *familiaris* "domestic, private, belonging to a family, of a household." A close reflection on *Focusing the Familiar* here will help us bring this important aspiration for optimizing the human experience into clearer focus. The Confucian ethic of roles as an alternative to rule-based ethics begins from its recognition of the native human capacity to collaborate creatively

---

① 王充, 論衡 16.7-8. Li Chenyang in "The Confucian Ideal of Harmony," *Philosophy East and West* 56, No. 4 (October) pp. 596-598 argues that this Confucian concept of harmony is fully consonant with value pluralism and hence has worldwide applicability. See his more recent *The Confucian Philosophy of Harmony*, New York: Routledge, 2015.

with our environments in pursuit of a consummatory, aesthetic end. As the *locus classicus* among the Confucian canons in celebrating human beings as having both the office and the responsibility to be full co-creators with the heavens and the earth, *Focusing the Familiar* opens with the oft-cited passage:

> 天命之謂性，率性之謂道，修道之謂教。
> What *tian* commands is called our native human propensities; acting upon these propensities is called way-making; advancing this way is called education.①

One possible reading of this opening line that comes to mind when the text is located within its own historical context would be to interpret it dialectically as a Confucian argument against the Mohist camp, a philosophical lineage that constituted a pervasive and powerful polemical force during this pre-Qin period. A Mohist interpretation of this line would have construed the relationship between *tian* and the human being in a decidedly more conservative, "theistic" direction by suggesting that "Heaven" (*tian* 天) largely imposes its natural and moral order on the human world from without (*wai* 外).②

The Confucians in arguing here against the Mohist assertion that cosmic order is divinely imposed upon the human world, are not simply advancing the claim that human beings have an active role to play in the production of cosmic order. Indeed, the Confucians go on to insist that, in this aspiration to live inspired lives, human

---

① Roger T. Ames and David L. Hall. *Focusing the Familiar: A Translation and Philosophical Commentary on the* Zhongyong. Honolulu: University of Hawaii Press, 2001, p. 89.

② This Mohist claim that moral order is ultimately derived from an external source is the basis of a frequently encountered debate in the Confucian texts, with the *Mencius* being perhaps the clearest case in point. See for example, the *Mencius* 6A chapter.

beings contribute in an intense and inimitable way to the refulgent spirituality of the cosmos. Moreover, this spirituality far from being singular in purpose as might be implied by the Mohist notion of "the purposes of 'Heaven'" (*tianzhi* 天志), is multivalent, pluralistic, and inclusive.① The myriad things obey no single unifying principle, but achieve their harmony and their diversity through resourcing the interpenetrating differences that obtain among them to make a difference for each one of them. Stated more simply, according to this text, the Confucian vision of the moral life is enhanced and all things in the world flourish when powerful human feelings achieve coalescence in their relations with their environing others, and are orchestrated together with them into a productive, optimal harmony—an optimizing symbiosis.

In many ways, the structure of *Focusing the Familiar* serves as an object lesson in a Confucian cosmology that requires of its human co-creators the production of added significance, and in so doing, the expansion of the cosmic order. It exhorts its readers to exercise their capacity of *ars contextualis*—"the art of contextualizing"—to strive with imagination to take full advantage of both the indeterminate energy that honeycombs the determinate world, and the profound

---

① To be clear, I would argue that the erstwhile "external" standard of the Mohist is a publicly determined and implemented objective norm, and while certainly conservative and impositional, it still remains as one possible extreme within the assumed framework of a correlative relationship between *tian* and the human world. That is, the "purposes of *tian*" are negotiated and function within the parameters of "the continuity and inseparability of the human and the cosmic orders" (*tianrenheyi* 天人合一) in which this relationship is collateral and of mutual influence. As such, as a putatively objective standard, it is of a fundamentally different quality of "objectivity" than that derived from the dualistic, two-world order we would associate with the conventional Abrahamic notion of the perfection, and thus the aseity or self-sufficiency, of an independent, transcendent God. We might draw a contrast between a Greek impartial and reductionistic objectivity that excludes all partiality with a Mohist holistic objectivity that achieves its objectivity by striving to be inclusive of all partiality.

differences always unique human beings have in their relations with those things present-to-hand.

The "aspectual" notions of "achieved propriety in one's roles and relations" (*li* 禮), "embodied living within one's roles and relations" (*ti* 體), and the aspiration to "an optimizing harmony" (*he* 和) provide the framework for the highest statement of the Confucian project. Without appeal to any strong sense of cosmic teleology, this Confucian project requires a fundamentally different, open-ended and provisional language. We must think processually, collaboratively, and creatively to exercise ourselves as relational human "becomings" who have some real responsibility for cosmic way-making rather than as ready-made human "beings" who are disposed to actualizing some given human potential within a linear and teleologically-driven historiography.

*幾　*ji.* "Inchoate, incipient beginnings."

Classical Chinese cosmology is a celebration of the birth and growth of the world around us, with what might be called the zoetology (*shengshenglun* 生生論) of "birthing, living, and growing" as "the art of living" being the functional equivalent of "science of being" in classical Greek ontology. In the absence of essences to individuate things and teleology to guide their growth, things and events have inchoate, tenuous beginnings that are part of a vital ecology that is at once autogenerative and available as a resource for further enhancement. Such beginnings are always nested and embedded rather than discrete, and although they are still indeterminate, they are animated by the vital relations that give them context, and that will come to constitute them. As they gradually become determinate, they will be both one and many at the same time: *yiduobufen* (一多不分).

The omnipresent feature that underscores the contingent

nature of any emerging order—human or otherwise—is its underdeterminacy. That is, there is an indeterminate aspect (*ji* 幾) entailed by the uniqueness of each participant that qualifies order, making any pattern of order novel and site-specific, irreversible, reflexive, and in degree, unpredictable. Taking persons as an example, all human beings might be similar enough to justify certain generalizations, yet each person is at the same time a unique, *one* of a kind. It is this uniqueness of each person that serves the complexity of the human experience, and that precludes the possibility of any logarithmic understanding of human conduct, keeping the definition of humanity an open-ended and ongoing proposition.

Ji then is a term that connotes the yet indeterminate beginnings of things—throbbing with life, potent, promising, yet still amorphous. Again, *ji* as it appears in the literature is frequently associated with the highest order of human beings—the sages and exemplary persons—because their responsive intervention must occur at the intersection between the determinate and the as-yet-indeterminate, between what already is, and what with their benign influence, will become. The wisdom associated with the sages (*shengren* 聖人) and exemplary persons (*junzi* 君子) is the ability to read the process of life at this inchoate level and to anticipate, with the intervention of their own guiding hand, the gradual and coordinated emergence of a flourishing world.

In the "Great Commentary" A10 of the *Book of Changes* we read:

夫《易》，聖人之所以極深而研幾也。唯深也，故能通天下之志；唯幾也，故能成天下之務。

The *Changes* is the sage's means of probing what is profound to its very limits, and examining thoroughly what is still incipient (*ji* 幾). It is only through having reached such depths that the sages can discern the purposes of the world; it is only through the incipient that they can consummate the business of the world.

And again, in the "Great Commentary" B5:

知幾其神乎……幾者動之微，吉之先見者也，君子見幾而作，不俟終日。

Understanding the incipient (*ji* 幾) gives insight into the mysteries of the world (*shen* 神) . . . The incipient is a hint of movement from which one can see in advance impending fortune. Exemplary persons having seen the incipient are aroused to action without waiting a single day to see what transpires.

*祭 *ji.* "Sacrificing, sacrifice."

On the oracle bones the character for *ji* is 𝍣 and on the bronzes is 𝍤,① in both cases a pictograph of a hand grasping sacrificial meat with the several dots representing drops of blood as an offering for the spirits. The later addition of *shi* 示 is an image of the sacrificial tablet of the ancestors or spirits to whom the offering is being made. Animal sacrifice is fundamental in this Confucian "zoetology" or "art of living" in that the solemn liberating of the life of the sacrificial animal and the sharing of the meat is itself the sanctification and celebration of life itself. It would seem that such regularized discursive practices are replete with personal, social, political, and religious meaning. The centrality of ancestors in the sacrifices, for example, speaks to the continuity of a shared genealogical identity at every level. The importance of this custom is reflected in the fact that the complex writing system with some five thousand characters we have recovered from the oracle bones had its origins in these same practices, and was then used in the compilation of the canonical texts that set the root for the continuing growth of the civilization.

---

① Kwan, "Database," CHANT 甲骨文編 and 春秋晚期 CHANT 245.

As pointed out by Zhou Yiqun, some twenty percent of the *Book of Songs*, is devoted to remembering such ancestral sacrifices and the banquets that followed.①

The *Analects* 20.1 in describing the priorities needed for effective governance, ascribes importance to four areas of responsibility: 民、食、喪、祭 the common people, food, mourning, and sacrifice. Again in 10.21, it states that Confucius 朋友之饋，雖車馬，非祭肉，不拜 "would not kowtow on receiving gifts from friends, even those as lavish as a horse or a carriage, with the sole exception of sacrificial meat."

The responsibility of continuing sacrificial practices to ancestors has high value in an aristocratic tradition that takes "family reverence" (*xiao* 孝) as it is expressed through intergenerational transmission of the cultural legacy as its prime moral imperative. Throughout the Confucian texts, sacrifice as a sign of deference and respect to ancestors and the cultural heroes who have come before is taken as an integral aspect of the "ritual propriety" (*li* 禮) that undergirds the continuity of the civilization itself. The graph for other key philosophical terms such as "optimizing appropriateness" (*yi* 義) is constituted by a sacrificial sheep (*yang* 羊) and the dagger-ax (*ge* 戈) that is used to dispatch and bleed it for the ceremony. Again the same character *yi* is itself cognate with *yi* 儀 meaning the ceremonial decorum, as well as with the animal of a pure color prepared for the sacrifice (*xi* 犧).

From earliest times, sacrifice was a communal affair that through the proper exercise of ritual propriety reflected the proper social hierarchies and protocols. There is a continuity between role of the ritual priest, the first in the descent group, and the head of state as they reside in the same person. In an extended passage in *Focusing the Familiar* 19, Confucius rehearses a detailed account of how such

---

① Zhou Yiqun. *Festivals, Feasts, and Gender Relations in Ancient China and Greece*. Cambridge: Cambridge University Press, 2010, p. 104.

practices were used by the former sage-kings to establish and reinforce a structure of deference and refinement in society, and promote a religious sense of worth and belonging among their peoples:

> 子曰："武王、周公，其達孝矣乎！夫孝者：善繼人之志，善述人之事者也。春、秋修其祖廟，陳其宗器，設其裳衣，薦其時食。宗廟之禮，所以序昭穆也；序爵，所以辨貴賤也；序事，所以辨賢也；旅酬下為上，所以逮賤也；燕毛，所以序齒也。踐其位，行其禮，奏其樂，敬其所尊，愛其所親，事死如事生，事亡如事存，孝之至也。"

The Master said: "King Wu and the Duke of Zhou—there indeed were two thoroughly filial exemplars (*xiao* 孝)! Family reverence (*xiao* 孝) means being good at continuing the purposes of one's predecessors and at maintaining their ways. In the proper season, they made repairs to the ancestral temple, laid out the sacrificial vessels of their ancestors, exhibited the robes used in funerary observances, and sacrificed from the newly harvested crops. They used ritual propriety (*li* 禮) in the ancestral temple as their way of arranging the tablets of the departed generations appropriately on the left and right sides of the temple; they deferred to the titles of office as their way of recognizing degrees of nobility; they used the sequence of the services as their way of distinguishing those most worthy; they used the drinking pledges in which inferiors toast superiors as their way of reaching down to include the lowliest, and they took into consideration the color of the hair as their way of seating participants according to their seniority. Taking up the places of their forbearers, carrying out their ritual observances (*li* 禮), playing their music (*yue* 樂), showing respect to those whom they esteemed, extending their affections to those of whom they were fond, serving the dead as though they were living, and serving those who are long departed as though they were still here—this then is family reverence at its utmost."

This same important passage concludes by echoing the claim in *Analects* 3.11, that those who really knew how to explain the highest of these sacrifices could rule the empire as easily as watching something being turned over in the palm of their hand:

"宗廟之禮，所以祀乎其先也。明乎郊社之禮、禘嘗之義，治國其如示諸掌乎！"

"Ritual observances performed in the ancestral temple are ways of making sacrifices to one's forbearers. For one who has a clear understanding of the sacrificial observances to the heavens and the earth, and the various ceremonies such as the Grand *di* sacrifice and the autumnal *chang* sacrifice performed in the ancestral temple, the governing of the empire is as turning something over in the palm of one's hand."

*諫   ***jian***. "Remonstrating, remonstrance." See also 孝 ***xiao*** "Family reverence, filial piety."

A key to understanding critical engagement in the Confucian world is the important distinction between an emphasis on dispute that assumes two exclusive, competing perspectives we would associate with Greek dialectics, and the idea of remonstrance as an inclusive mode of persuasion—what Xunzi calls "the art of accommodation" (*jianshu* 兼術)—that assumes a shared commitment to a common goal we would identify with the Confucian tradition.[1] Such a distinction is echoed in two very

---

[1] See A.S. Cua. *Ethical Argumentation: A Study in Hsün Tzu's Moral Epistemology*. Honolulu: University of Hawaii Press, 1985, pp. 8-10. Also, Geoffrey Lloyd and Nathan Sivin. *The Way and the Word: Science and Medicine in Early China and Greece*. New Haven: Yale University Press, 2002, pp. 180-187.

different meanings of the term of "protest." The first usage is to take exception to something ("I protest against the war"), while the second is to affirm with solemnity ("I protest my innocence"). The first sense of protest is dialectical and agonistic—I seek to displace the opposite and thus "opposing" point of view with my own. The guiding assumption is that the positions are exclusive—one is right, the other wrong. The second sense of protest assumes a shared concern and seeks to persuade the other with the quality of my sincerity in the recommendation I am making for our common end.

Both dialectical and remonstrative modes of engagement are attempts to advance and improve an existing situation. The former dialogical mode is more purely rational and assertive, based upon a sense of external relations that allows each disputant to maintain their own integrity and a sense of equality. The latter appeal to suasion is more rhetorical and exhortative, assuming intrinsic relations that locate the differences among mutually accommodating family members, or other groups, who although hierarchically related, are all concerned to sustain the shared integrity of the family or group to which they belong, rather than just the integrity of its individual members. What is at stake in this distinction is the fact that, as Peter Hershock avers, "something that is good for each of us, considered individually, may not be good for all of us."[1]

The *Classic of Family Reverence* follows the *Analects* and other classical Confucian texts in advocating remonstrance rather than dialectical engagement as the primary and most appropriate method of resolving differences. As stated emphatically in Chapter 15, the hierarchically subordinate persons in family and in government not only have a right to remonstrate, in fact they have a stern obligation to do so. Such often seemingly impertinent and yet sincere exhortation is in the interests of everyone concerned. Said another way, blind

---

[1] Peter D. Hershock, *Valuing Diversity*, p. 133.

obedience, far from serving the value of family reverence (*xiao* 孝), frequently offends against it.

There are several conditions of remonstrance that must not be overlooked. First, the putative goal is behavioral change, and to this end, concerns must be expressed with the utmost tact and respect if they are to be effective. Excessive candor can easily be heard as insulting and offensive, replacing as it does the expected deference with disrespect. Secondly, the sincerity with which the admonishment is proffered is the key to its persuasiveness. There is a world of difference between real concern and rebuke, between honest counsel and impudence. Thirdly, remonstrance is not an option, but an obligation. And to do less is to fail in a solemn and sacred duty. It is only obedience and remonstrance in tandem and in proper measure that constitute the substance of "doing one's best" as a family member and political loyalty (*zhong* 忠) as a minister. Fourthly, remonstrance has its limits and can only be taken so far. There is a point at which the remonstrator must relent: Remonstrating parties must not simply assume that their judgment is better than that of their parent or elder or ruler. As we see in *Analects* 4.18:

> 子曰："事父母幾諫。見志不從，又敬不違，勞而不怨。"
> The Master said, "In serving your father and mother, remonstrate with them gently. On seeing that they do not heed your suggestions, remain respectful and do not act contrary. Although concerned, voice no resentment."

兼愛 *jian'ai.* "Inclusive care, inclusive concern."

This Mohist tenet has conventionally been translated as "universal love," but such an interpretation introduces unfortunate biblical associations with *agape,* the universal and unconditional love that originates with God. Angus Graham suggests "Concern for Everyone," rejecting "universal love" because

> ... it is both too vague (*chien* [*jian*] implies 'for each' rather than 'for all') and too warm (the Mohist *ai* is an unemotional will to benefit people and dislike of harming them). The Mohists were dour people whose ears were open to the demands of justice rather than to the appeal of love.①

While the Mohist sentiment does seem to be something other than love in any strong sense of the term, it is probably because the Mohists as an early form of socialism speak in terms of benefit for all of the world and about concern over the welfare of everyone as a population rather than as individuals. This sense of inclusiveness is consistent with the later Mohist canons in which there is an important distinction made between the "unit" or "one" (*ti* 體), and the "complex" or "many" (*jian* 兼) to which it belongs, or stated more concretely, some exclusive "thing" and its inclusive grouping.② This distinction, far from providing a principle of individuation by producing simples, makes the point that within an ecological cosmology, any fixed and final sense of individuation—of "thing"—is problematic.

The difference between concern over an inclusive population as opposed to each and every person is clarified by Peter Hershock who makes the observation: "something that is good for each of us,

---

① A.C. Graham. *Disputers of the Tao: Philosophical Argument in Ancient China.* La Salle, IL: Open Court, 1989, p. 41.
② See A.C. Graham. *Later Mohist Logic, Ethics and Science.* Hong Kong: The Chinese University Press, 1978, p. 265.

considered individually, may not be good for all of us."[1] We live in a world of gross income disparity wherein the guarantee of certain individual freedoms such as property, for example, that seems to be good for each of us individually, is in fact working for the benefit of an elite and privileged few. For those of us like the Mohists who are committed to the primacy of social and distributive justice, we must confront the fact that this property right for the elite is being purchased at the expense of substantial justice for an increasing number of the world's peoples.

The argument of the Mohists against the Confucians is that their aristocratic extravagance depletes finite resources needed to secure subsistence for the non-elite, and come at the cost of the general welfare of the people as a whole. The historical context of endless warfare is significant in the rather thin definition Mohists have of what constitutes benefit for all of the world.

*教　*jiao.* "Teaching, education."

Jiao 教 is most often translated as "teaching," "learning," "education," "instruction," but originally means "teaching and learning." We begin by accepting the commonplace that personal cultivation is certainly the root of the Confucian philosophy of education. But I would also observe that any root not been properly

---

[1] Hershock, *Valuing Diversity*, p. 133. Hershock is making the point that while comparative equality and individual autonomy guarantees that difference can only be variations among basically similar people (variety), the pursuit of relational equity and an achieved diversity allows for the continuing diversification of qualities and propensities that grow our differences into resources for mutual enrichment (diversity). The Mohists by contrast are not interested in the diversity that emerges from activating differences, but rather in the more pedestrian and anti-elitest notion of making sure that everyone has a share in the material well-being guaranteed by the state.

set and that is lacking a fertile context will soon wither and die. To continue this metaphor, Confucian education must be understood as a process that is "radically" embedded in and grows within the roles and relations that constitute us as persons in the fertile context of our families and communities. The close link between education and Confucian morality lies in the fact that they are both grounded in growth in our roles and relations. Education and morality so conceived is not instrumental as a means to some desired end, but is a process that is an end in itself. We get educated to live intelligent lives, and become moral to act morally. These same themes of situatedness and vital relationality, are revealing of the correlative, "*yinyang*" nature of teaching and learning as two mutually-implicated and non-analytic ways of describing the same holistic process of learning. Education is the full complement of learning from which the categories of teaching and learning are simply abstractions. And at the end of the day, the role of teacher provides us the opportunity to be the most advanced among the learners.

The value of "family reverence" (*xiao* 孝) that serves this tradition as its governing moral imperative sets the ultimate goal of Confucian education. The perceived immediate relationship between education and social order arises from the fact that the end of education is nothing less than the transformative growth of the people through the intergenerational embodiment and transmission of the living cultural tradition. Indeed, education is the internalization of a continuing cultural legacy that enables the people to transform their ordinary lives and to make them extraordinary, and that ideally allows the people to become self-ordering.

The etymology of the Chinese term argues for the placement of the process of education squarely within the family context. The graph for "family reverence" (*xiao* 孝) itself is constituted by "elder (*lao* 老)" and "younger (*zi* 子)," and the graph for "education" (*jiao* 教) adds to the character *xiao* the "branch" radical (*zhi* 支),

suggesting that the younger generation is rooted in and grows from the root and trunk of the generations that have come before. Importantly the character *jiao* underscores the centrality of familial reverence in the actual content and goal of proper education, just as the cognate relationship it has with the character "emulating" (*xiao* 效) emphasizes the modeling role that the elder generation has for its progeny. The *Shuowen* lexicon captures these associations in defining *jiao* as 上所施下所效也 "that which those above disseminate and those below emulate" in the transmission of the tradition from one generation to the next.

The *Classic of Family Reverence* has at its center the notion that all education is simply an extension of family feeling. The Emperor loves his parents and extends that same affection to his people as sincere concern for their well-being; the son respects his father, and extends that same respect to his sovereign as loyalty. Thus, education that transforms and secures the human experience is naturalized as the extension of family reverence (*xiao* 孝) to the entire world. Morality in the Confucian tradition is growth in relations, and it is because the purpose of education too is to promote growth and extension that it always has a strong moral aspect.

The *Classic of Family Reverence* 7 defines the ultimate goal of both education and consummate governance as nothing less than "the transformation of the people" (*huamin* 化民) through the moral imperative of family reverence (*xiao* 孝):

先王見教之可以化民也，是故先之以博愛，而民莫遺其親；陳之［以］德義，而民興行；先之以敬讓，而民不爭；導之以禮樂，而民和睦；示之以好惡，而民知禁。《詩》云："赫赫師尹，民具爾瞻。"

The former kings saw that their teachings were able to transform the people (*huamin*). Thus, setting their own example of magnanimity before the people, none of the people would neglect their parents;

demonstrating excellence and appropriateness in their own actions, the people were inspired to conduct themselves accordingly; setting their own example of respect and reverence before the people, the people did not contend among themselves; guiding the people with ritual propriety and music, the people found harmony and accord with each other; showing the people what they deemed acceptable and unacceptable, the people understood what was proscribed. The *Book of Songs* says, "Illustrious Grand Tutor Yin, the people all look up to you." ①

The vocabulary surrounding this central notion of "family reverence" as the substance of education provides concrete guidelines for moral conduct by acknowledging the practical, situated, interpenetrating, and dispositional nature of all goods, values, and virtues. While we do have a compelling sense of how to act as mothers to our sons and uncles to our nieces, including acting courageously to defend them and treating them justly, we must struggle to find our way when we try to act on "courage" or "justice" as abstract virtues. In seeking directives for moral conduct, the ambiguity that invariably attends our practical understanding of complex family relations is somewhat offset when we attempt to identify, stipulate, and apply moral principles that, while seeming to be more straightforward, are in actual deployment anything but clear.

Again, the etymology of the English word "education" is helpful in articulating the Confucian notion of *jiao*. The word "education" has two principal roots—L. *educare* and *educere*. The first root means "cultivating, rearing, bringing up," while the second means "educing, evoking, leading forth, drawing out." *Educare* resonates

---

① Cf. *Analects* 2.3. *Book of Songs* 191. Cf. James Legge. *The Chinese Classics*, 5 volumes. Hong Kong: University of Hong Kong Press, 1960 rep, Vol. IV, p. 309 and Bernhard Karlgren. *The Book of Odes: Chinese Text, Transcription and Translation*. Stockholm: The Museum of Far Eastern Antiquities, 1950, p. 133.

with the sense of education as rationally ordered, generic guidance; it is the logical and more systematic mode of education that we associate with transmission of cognitive understanding. Education in a "discipline" (L. *disciplina* meaning "instruction and training" from the root *discere* "to learn") requires discipline: a knowledge of its history, its key figures and their stories, its theories and terminologies. There is much that is common and rote in laying a solid foundation. The customary, habitual, and ritualistic aspect of education as *educare* leans toward indoctrination and enculturation.

On the other hand, *educere* suggests the more creative, personal, and expansive understanding of education. The evocative sense of *educere* resonates with the articulation of one's inner genius and feelings (*qing* 情) through novel and imaginative elaborations of one's own mode of personal cultivation. Education so construed is a transactional, collaborative process including teaching and learning that entails both continuity and creativity in the growth of both *this* able teacher and *that* able student.

Since family feeling is fundamental to the human experience, the process of education is most effectively accomplished through a process of modeling and emulation both within the family and within the polity. It requires both *educare*—a labored transmission of knowledge from elders to the young—and *educere*—the spontaneous and natural way in which parental affection and parental reverence "educe" and reinforce each other within the family, and by extension, within the state. Indeed, the *Classic of Family Reverence* 2 underscores the role of emulation in education, claiming: 德教加於百姓，刑於四海 "such moral edification (*dejiao* 德教) will transform the common people and will serve as exemplary in all corners of the world."

By identifying education primarily with improving upon and extending the proper way forward, the Confucian texts are invested in both the foundational and the creative aspects of education. To say that the function of education is not primarily that of transmission and training but of evocation would be misleading because the more conservative *educare* also has a key if not even primary role to play in passing on the details of the rich cultural heritage from one generation to the next. Indeed, the balance necessary between the *educere* and *educare* functions of education is captured in *Focusing the Familiar* 21:

> 自誠明，謂之性；自明誠，謂之教。誠則明矣，明則誠矣。唯天下至誠，為能盡其性……可以贊天地之化育，則可以與天地參矣。
> Understanding born of creative resolve (*cheng* 誠) is what we call the expression of our natural human propensities (*xing* 性); creative resolve born of understanding is what we call learning (*jiao* 教). Where there is creative resolve, there is understanding; where there is understanding, creative resolve. Only those of utmost resolve in the world are able to make the most of their human propensities (*xing* 性) ... and only if they can assist in the transforming and nourishing activities of heaven and earth can human beings take their place as members of this triad.

Grasping the gist of this passage requires some sensitivity to the complexity of the central terms and of their relationships. *Creative resolve* (*cheng* 誠) as the spontaneous expression of our natural propensities is a responsiveness to the world that leads to secure an *understanding* of it. In this context, "understanding" means primarily deferring to and appropriating the "*what*" of what is being learned (*educare*). The compounding process continues, however, as creative resolve emerges again, prompted as it is by an imaginative projection that takes us beyond our existing *understanding* of the world. Such learning requires imagination, and thinking and feeling outside the box. "Understanding" in this new context is the extension of the content of experience acquired through learning (*educare*) as a creative leap that allows for the contrapuntal collaboration with the heavens and the earth to produce new meaning (*educere*).

*精神 *jingshen.* "Spirituality, vigor, vitality, mystery." See also 神 *shen*. "Heavenly gods, ancestors, spirituality, vigor, vitality, mystery."

With the Confucian focus-field conception of persons, we might use the familiar language of *jingshen* 精神 to capture the perceived isomorphism between the intensity and resolution of one's focus and the enhanced extension of one's field. The binomial *jingshen* as it is used in the modern language is usually translated as "spirit, vigor, vitality, drive, full of life." Separately, the character *jing* 精 conventionally translated as "essence," is not some ontological essence to be contrasted with accidents or attributes, but is the concentrated, quintessential source of personal vitality, both physical and intellectual that is both inherited from parents and acquired from various forms of nourishment. *Jing* is the sap of life, the potency of semen (*jingye* 精液), a tangible, life-giving energy as it is felt self-consciously within one's actions. And *shen* 神, conventionally translated as "spirit," is not the spiritual as opposed to the corporeal, but is this same *jing* vitality as it extends, courses through, and pervades the functional life activities of the mind and the body as a whole. *Shen* is the mystery of how we become "great souled" in our expansive and inspired living. As the *Book of Changes* describes this amorphous energy: 陰陽不測之謂神 "That which cannot be fathomed through effecting a *yinyang* contrast and correlation is what is meant by the truly mysterious (*shen* 神)."[1]

Zhang Yanhua insists that the vocabulary used for both the formal and the vital aspects of life must be understood as resolutely

---

[1] *Book of Changes* "Great Commentary" A5.

situated and transactional:

> Although *jingshen* 精神 is translated in English as "mind" or "spirit," it is very much part of *shenti*. . . . Primary *jing* provides the basis for the process of transforming the energy distilled from food and is enriched and strengthened by "acquired *jing*." Chinese medical theories view *jing* and *qi* 氣 (air, breath, vital energy) as the same life-giving energy. When it is concentrated, it is *jing*; when it is dispersed it turns into *qi*. If *jing* is the nurturing aspect of this energy, *qi* is the active configurational aspect of the same energy. . . . If *jing* and *qi* are the basis of life, then *shen* 神 is the manifestation of that life. . . . In other words, *shen* is the phenomenon of life activity itself.[①]

The flow of life energy requires coordination and direction. The heart-mind (*xin* 心) provides the directive force negotiated in and guided by the efficacious possibilities inherent in the particular circumstances. In the human experience,

> . . . *xin* is a system of functioning that forms a continuous process of being or becoming a person, involving the physiological, psychological, and sociological. . . What is particular about this process-centered heart-mind physiology is . . . the commitment to an unobstructed process of transformation in accordance with a given social context and natural environment.[②]

[①] Zhang Yanhua, *Transforming Emotions*, pp. 37-38.
[②] Zhang Yanhua, *Transforming Emotions*, p. 41.

*敬 *jing.* "Respecting, revering, seriousness."

Jing connotes respect for other people broadly: a focused regard for others with the seriousness and solemnity that follow from it. The *Shuowen* lexicon defines *jing* as "solemn" (*su* 肅). In the bronze inscriptions, it is frequently associated with sacrifice, and it would seem to connote the seriousness necessary to bring such solemn affairs to their proper conclusion. It is in this sense that it can be rendered "revering" or "reverence" with the connotation of fear and awe directed at persons seen as one's superiors.

What is key to our understanding of the notion of respect is considering how it is "taught," and how it reflexively benefits those persons who extend such respect to the senior members of their own families and communities. In *Analects* 14.42, it says of exemplary persons (*junzi* 君子): 脩己以敬 "cultivating themselves they earn respect." These exemplars modeled a respectful attitude for the people by respecting their own family elders, and demonstrated to the people that personal growth, refinement, and pleasure is to be found in such deference. This way of teaching is not only respecting one's seniors, but also respecting the capacity of those people to willingly do what is most appropriate (*yi* 義). The emphasis on the transformative effect of the role model in proper governance is made explicit in the *Classic of Family Reverence* 7 where we read:

先王見教之可以化民也，是故先之以博愛，而民莫遺其親；陳之[以]德義，而民興行；先之以敬讓，而民不爭；導之以禮樂，而民和睦；示之以好惡，而民知禁。

The Former Kings saw that their teachings (*jiao* 教) were able to transform the people. Thus, setting their own example of magnanimity (*bo'ai* 博愛) before the people, none of the people would neglect their parents; demonstrating excellence (*de* 德) and appropriateness (*yi* 義) in their own actions, the people were inspired to conduct themselves accordingly; setting their own example of respect (*jing* 敬) and deference before the people, the people did not contend among themselves; guiding the people with ritual propriety (*li* 禮) and music (*yue* 樂), the people found harmony (*he* 和) and accord with each other; showing the people what they deemed acceptable and unacceptable, the people understood what was proscribed.

The Former Kings did not teach respect by demanding it from the people. Indeed, respect to be respect must be willingly conferred on one person by another. This notion of leading by example and transforming the people through their own willing participation in a self-regulating communal order is fundamental in Confucianism. The *Analects* provides many examples of the contrast between the imposition of a minimally effective top-down order that applies a coercive strategy for compliance, and effecting an enduring bottom-up, participatory order that depends up the people being transformed through a cultivated sense of shame, and by taking ownership of their community (1.2, 1.9, 2.3, 6.30, 8.2, 8.19, 12.1, 13.2, 13.3, 13.4).

Even more strongly put, in reporting on the effectiveness of teaching through exemplary modeling, the Master said:

"無為而治者，其舜也與？夫何為哉，恭己正南面而已矣。"
"If anyone could be said to have effected proper order while remaining non-coercive, surely it was Shun. What did he do? He simply assumed an air of deference and faced due south." (15.5)

Such passages give us a Confucian version of "non-coercive" governing (*wuwei* 無為) through winning over the people to participate of their own accord in a ritually constituted community. Important here is that in such non-coercive governance, Shun far from standing independent of the people, has the people and their achievement of self-governance implicated within his own person.

If we think of the "binding tightly" that constitutes a Confucian family-centered religiousness as the combination of a willing deference to others and a full sense of one's own cultivated self-disclosure within that context, we might find an important link between *shu* 恕 as the willing "deference" to accommodate the needs and desires of others, and *jing* 敬 as the regard shown to, and the "respect" conferred upon others. We find this attitude captured explicitly in one of the most powerful passages of the *Analects* 12.2: 出門如見大賓，使民如承大祭 "In your public life, behave as though you are receiving honored guests; employ the common people as though you are overseeing a great sacrifice."

*靜 *jing.* "Sustained equilibrium."

The notion of *jing*, with stillness or tranquility often used to characterize this posture, must be located within the process cosmology that gives classical Confucianism its interpretive context. It must be understood as an "aspectual" rather than an analytic term. Far from being passivity or quietism, *jing* is the ongoing, dynamic attainment of equilibrium that requires constant monitoring and adjustment within the flow of experience. It is important to remember that all correlative pairs such as "agitation and tranquility" (*dongjing* 動靜) are aspectual and entail their opposites in the sense that *dong* is "agitation-within-tranquility" and *jing* is "tranquility-within-agitation." Thus, tranquility (*jing* 靜) when achieved stands in a dominant relationship in its partnership with agitation (*dong* 動); it does not negate or exclude its opposite. Indeed, it is the collaboration between tranquility and agitation that produces and sustains equilibrium—a kind of centeredness and balance while always in motion.

This same qualification of process cosmology as the interpretive context has to be brought to bear on other familiar dyadic pairs that might otherwise mislead us. For example, "emptiness" (*xu* 虛) in the dyad "fullness and emptiness" (*shixu* 實虛) is not the "nothingness" of a vacuum or void, but the achieved and sustained "emptiness-within-fullness," and "fullness" being "fullness-within-emptiness." "Clarity" (*qing* 清) in "clarity and turbidity" (*qingzhuo* 清濁) is not transparency or lucidity, but a sustained "clarity-within-turbidity," and so on.

Tang Junyi takes this correlative conceptual structure to be a defining feature of early Confucian cosmology with his postulate, "the notion that there is a continuity and inseparability that obtains between determinacy and indeterminacy, motion and equilibrium, and all other such correlative binomials" (*he youwu dongjing guan* 合有無動靜觀).① To take "determinacy" and "indeterminacy" (*youwu* 有無) as an example, these terms are a nonanalytic, explanatory vocabulary of "aspects" that we must appeal to in giving a fair account of the ceaseless emergence of any of the things and events that come to constitute the continuing human experience. Persons, for example, are determinate (*you* 有) and can thus be recognized by a persistent physical form and pattern of intellectual engagement. At the same time, they are profoundly indeterminate (*wu* 無) as vital and unpredictable innovators and makers of novel meaning as they cultivate the creative possibilities of relationships in the world. And such an ineluctable process of continuing transformation requires a gerundive, explanatory language such as "forming" (*ti* 體) and "functioning" (*yong* 用) to report on the mutuality of structure and performance as the world turns.

Rather than being driven by any kind of a necessary, deterministic teleology, the *Book of Changes* cosmology allows for the possibility of significant human collaboration in a contingent and negotiated optimizing symbiosis (*he* 和) expressed as equilibrium. This is

---

① Tang Junyi 唐君毅. *Complete Works* 唐君毅全集. Taipei: Xuesheng Shuju, 1991, Vol. 11, pp. 11-16.

but to say that human flourishing is the consequence of our best attempts to make the most out of the creative possibilities of the human experience. The omnipresent feature that underscores the contingent nature of any emerging order—human or otherwise—is its underdeterminacy. That is, there is an indeterminate aspect (*ji* 幾) entailed by the uniqueness of each participant that qualifies order, making any pattern of order novel and site-specific, irreversible, reflexive, and in degree, unpredictable. The penumbra of indeterminacy that honeycombs an always provisional cosmic order means that the erstwhile forms and functions that define the events of our lives are mutually entailing. All form is constantly undergoing adjustment to maintain functional equilibrium, and is vulnerable to and ultimately outrun by the process itself. At the same time, all functioning is shaped, refined, and made more efficient by evolving formal structures, and is constantly being reformed to meet changing demands. There is nothing and thus no one that does not give way to the process of trans-*form*-ation.

*君子   *junzi.* "Exemplary persons, ruler, prince, lord."

The *Shuowen* lexicon defines *jun* 君 paronomastically with the rhyming *zun* 尊 meaning first "honoring" and "holding in high esteem," and then derivatively "of high rank." In other early sources collected in the *Shuowen* commentaries, *jun* is again defined paronomastically by its cognate, *qun* 群 meaning "gathering," with the implication that the *junzi* is the exemplary person to whom the community repairs. The *Shuowen* further identifies *jun* 君 as a "combined meaning" graph (*huiyi* 會意), isolating the etymonic elements of *yin* 尹, "managing, ordering, regulating," and *kou* 口, "the mouth," and suggesting that they both have semantic reference. The inference is that *junzi*, through their various modes of effective communication, become exemplary models for the community and thus have agency in bringing about and sustaining sociopolitical order. To summarize the etymological data of *junzi*, it provides us with the following associations: (1) noble rank and status, (2) a term of respect, (3) persons whose cultivation and refinement is such that they serve as a model of order and attract the emulation of their communities, and (4) persons whose personal sense of order is extended to a wider social context through political responsibility and engagement.

It is because the *junzi* has this sociopolitical reference, and most often indicates models available within the community for other persons to emulate that we translate this term "exemplary person." Other translations are "superior man" (Legge), "gentleman" (Lau, Leys, Huang, Brooks, Slingerland), noble man (Schwartz, Goldin), and several others. While rendering *junzi* as "gentleman" seems most popular, it is to impose on it a decidedly masculine reading of the term that is not marked in *junzi* itself. One motivation for this translation, of course, is because most scholars wish to point out the patriarchal hierarchy within the aristocracy of ancient China, and "gentleman" does this. And again, making it singular as "gentleman" is also an extrapolation that is not indicated by the characters themselves, and yet prompts "he" and "him" as the pronominal form when it refers back to *junzi* as its antecedent. Consequently, while the resultant sexist translation "gentleman" appears straightforward enough, such a connotation is altogether absent in the original term. (And there is at least some evidence that women could be regarded as having some of the same qualities of the *junzi* at the time of, or shortly after, the composition of the *Analects*.)[1]

---

[1] See "Administration of Family." *Early China's Empires: A Re-appraisal*. ed. Michael Nylan and Michael Loewe. Cambridge: Cambridge University Press, 2010. See also Lisa Raphals. "A Woman Who Understood the Rites." *Confucius and the Analects: New Essays*. ed. Bryan Van Norden. New York: Oxford University Press, 2002. See also Raphals. *Sharing the Light: Representations of Women and Virtue in Early China*. Albany: State University of New York Press, 1998.

It is often observed that in the literature prior to Confucius, the expression *junzi* as a diminutive form of *jun* meaning "child of *jun*" was a political category denoting nobility of birth, blood, and rank, with no necessary reference to nobility of character. In this context, it would be best to translate it as "ruler" or "lord." It is demonstrably the case that with Confucius, this category that had originally indicated social and political status was appropriated and revised to express the correlative relationship between political responsibility and moral growth. That is, the cultivation of one's person necessarily requires active participation both in the family and in the sociopolitical order, not simply in service to others, but as that forum in which the compassion and concern that is integral to one's own personal refinement can be expressed. It is inconceivable that full personal growth and disclosure could be achieved in the absence of social and political responsibility. Said another way, one does not first become a *junzi* and then enter the arena of social and political life; rather, one can only *become* a *junzi* through responsiveness to the social and political obligations that emerge in communal living.

In the *Analects*, the term *junzi* is consistently invoked as a model of conduct for the edification of Confucius's students, appearing almost as many times as his signature neologism, "consummate person/conduct" (*ren* 仁). For Confucius, these exemplars in achieving this moral status have traveled a goodly distance along the way, and have lived a goodly number of roles. Benefactors to many, they are still the beneficiary of others like themselves. While they are still capable of anger in the presence of inappropriateness and concomitant injustice, they are in their persons calm and composed. They know many rituals and much music, and perform all of their functions not only with felicity (*shan* 善), but also with grace, dignity, and beauty. They are certainly filial toward their parents and elders, but are now expansive in their compass, taking "all under *tian*" as their provenance. While being real enough to still be capable of the occasional lapse in their otherwise exemplary behavior (14.6, 17.23, 19.21), they are resolutely proper in the conduct of their roles—conduct that is not contrived, but rather that seems effortless, spontaneous, and creative. There is, in sum, a very strong aesthetic dimension to the ways in which they live their lives. Reauthorizing the values of ritual propriety in everything they do, they are respected among their contemporaries as authors of the proper way of humankind.

Exemplary persons (*junzi* 君子) are throughout the texts frequently contrasted with *xiaoren* 小人—literally "small," and thus "petty and mean" persons. This contrast would suggest that becoming exemplary in one's personal conduct is the result of continuing articulation and extension. In fact, morally achieved persons exhibit growth to the extent that they are on occasion referred to as "grand persons" (*daren* 大人) and "developed persons" (*chengren* 成人), and are depicted in paintings and other representations relative to others as being larger than life. In the repeated contrast between "small persons" (*xiaoren* 小人) and "exemplary persons" (*junzi* 君子) ubiquitous throughout the *Analects*, such small persons are not only socially and morally stunted individuals, but in their selfish conduct, they are also a continuing source of communal divisiveness and distress. Small persons are properly described as "small" in the sense that they are aberrantly discrete "individuals" who, having failed to participate in the family and community life necessary to grow themselves self-consciously as persons, are stunted and devoid of meaningful relations.

In the *Classic of Family Reverence* or *Xiaojing*, exemplary persons have responsibilities both as positive models and as negative censors. That is, transformative education is effected in families and community by the emulation inspired by these exemplary models, and on their own part, by the unrelenting introspection needed for their personal improvement. This same bi-directional and symbiotic dynamic is at work in the relationship between these exemplars and their rulers, where "doing their utmost" or loyalty (*zhong* 忠) requires that they actively promote what they find commendable in the conduct of their sovereign while at the same time through a process of vigilant remonstrance (*jian* 諫) taking steps to remedy what cannot be condoned.

Exemplary persons have a prominent role in *Focusing the Familiar* or the *Zhongyong*, and are in fact defined as those who are able to "*zhongyong*" 中庸: that is, those who are able to hit the mark in what they do, and to thus "focus and bring resolution to the familiar affairs of the day." In *Focusing the Familiar* 12, 君子之道費而隱 the way of exemplary persons is described as being "both broad and hidden," a correlative pairing of seemingly contradictory terms reminiscent of the *Daodejing*. Their way is broad in the sense that, having its beginnings in the routine lives of ordinary people, there is much about it that is apparent to even the most ordinary of men and women. It is obvious and easy. On the other hand, 及其至也，雖聖人亦有所不能焉 in its subtlety and complexity it is described as being "so lofty and demanding that at its furthest limits even the sages cannot fathom it all":

> 故君子語大，天下莫能載焉；語小，天下莫能破焉。
> Thus, were exemplary persons to discourse on the profundity of their way, there is nothing in the empire that could bear its weight; were they to discourse on its subtlety, there is nothing in the empire that could further refine it.

The final chapter of *Focusing the Familiar*, in a series of passages taken from the *Book of Songs* it sheds some light on a seemingly paradoxical claim made about exemplary persons in the opening passage of this text:

君子戒慎乎其所不睹，恐懼乎其所不聞。莫見乎隱，莫顯乎微。

... exemplary persons are so concerned about what is not seen, and so anxious about what is not heard. There is nothing more present than what is imminent, and nothing more manifest than what is inchoate.

The *Book of Songs* citations, in appealing again to contrastive correlative pairings, describes the way of exemplary persons as near yet distant, subtle yet conspicuous, awesome yet unintimidating. It is in this sense that the model of exemplary persons, as the middle ground between the ordinary and the extraordinary, anticipates and is implicated in, the emergence of the most exalted category of personal cultivation, the sage (*shengren* 聖人).

There are several terms in these Confucian texts that the Master and sometimes his disciples use with approbation to identify persons as human ideals, the most important among them being "scholar-officials" (*shi* 士), "consummate persons" (*renzhe* 仁者), "exemplary persons" (*junzi* 君子), and sages (*shengren* 聖人). When we ask what is the relationship that obtains among these different designations, it is clear that the sages are the highest. In 16.8 we learn that exemplary persons 畏聖人之言 "stand in awe of the words of sages" and again in 6:30: 如有博施於民而能濟眾……何事於仁，必也聖乎 "as to those who confer benefits on, and lend assistance to everyone ... why stop at consummate persons? They are indeed sages." In 19.12: 有始有卒者，其惟聖人乎 not even exemplary persons, "but sages alone can walk this path every step from start to finish." In the *Analects* and elsewhere it is the sage that is the loftiest human goal, standing above all other categories in having cosmic and epochal implications.

Confucius seems to be training his students to serve in the practical social and political role of "scholar-official" (*shi* 士). The *shi* are described as having assumed the heavy burden and embarked upon the long road of striving to become consummate in their conduct (8.7). Again, the *shi* are never tutored in the proper behavior and demeanor due their parents, children, or other relatives, but are consistently being instructed both positively and negatively on how to serve their communities. Exemplary persons (*junzi* 君子) are described in the text, not instructed; that is, exemplary persons *are* while scholar officials *do*. If this reading of the text is warranted, it would seem that the major goal toward which the apprenticed *shi* are striving is to become exemplary persons by becoming consummate in their conduct. They share with the *junzi* the focus of social and political engagement and responsibility, but have only just begun their journey.

*樂 *le* (also pronounced *yao* when transitive). "Enjoyment, making the music of enjoyment."

The character *le* on the oracle bones is a depiction of a stringed musical instrument made of wood ¥, with the *bai* 白 element meaning to pluck the strings being added to the graph in the early Zhou bronzes ▒.① Hence the character does not mean simply "music," but the *making* of music for the enjoyment of others. *Le, yao* is "*en*-joyment:" that is, a rejoicing in the musicality of the human experience that can be shared by all. Resonance with the etymology of the term "enjoy" is instructive. With *en-* being "making" and L. *gaudere* "rejoicing in," there is the strong causative sense of producing those conditions for a shared rejoicing within the fiduciary relationships of family, community, and cosmos, and as such, the production of both moral and religious meaning. Such enjoyment is

---

① Kwan, "Database," 甲骨文合集, CHANT 3166 and 春秋晚期 CHANT 233 respectively.

a communal flourishing achieved through the deepening of robust personal bonds, where the meaning that is created becomes the very character of the community itself, its *ethos*. Such enjoyment becomes a profound sense of felt worth and belonging of truly religious proportions that is not vitiated by the vicissitudes of a human life; even in the most unfortunate of circumstances, *le* is an underlying feeling of depth, stability, and contentment.

The religious implications of *le* arise from the kind of spirituality that emerges as members of a flourishing community are able to cultivate their unique individuality through participation in its shared practices, and to make their personal contribution to the whole. Religion thus understood is the combination of personal distinctiveness as it is activated in producing a shared well-being for all. As such, Confucian religiousness is the flowering of the communicating family and community, wherein an aspiring and thus an inspired people, becomes a spiritual people.

Much is made of the fact that the same character pronounced differently is used to mean "enjoyment" (*le, yao* 樂) and "music" (*yue* 樂), but the fact that this graph references the same basic idea parsed differently should not be lost. The playing of music is an obvious source of shared enjoyment that has competition perhaps only with food as being the most essential prerequisite where and whenever human beings gather together. Hence, there is a pervasive truth that in the shared events punctuating the most important moments within the human experience, music and food usually come together. But it works the other way around as well. That is, shared enjoyment also confers on human practices their musicality. In *Mencius* 1B1, for example, we have an earlier version of Nietzsche's popular maxim, "Evil men sing no songs." People will truly celebrate the music (*yue* 樂) of the court if they are enjoying (*le* 樂) life under the benign rule of a True King; on the other hand, they will resent the music bitterly if they attribute their dire straits to the court's misrule. Indeed, the music associated with a despised ruler will not rise to the level of being music, and will be only dissonance in their ears. The complex relationship between Wagner and Nazism immediately comes to mind. Again, *le* is cognate with "medicinal remedies" (*yao* 藥), suggesting that both the enjoyment of music and the music of enjoyment have therapeutic and restorative qualities.

On the assumption that ritual propriety (*li* 禮) and music (*yue* 樂) have a collateral function in strengthening relationships and producing harmony within the community, in the classical corpus they are taken as a dyadic pair. Not only do they collaborate as they inform the human experience in being symbiotic and synergistic practices, together they provide the structure and rhythm of the cosmic order. In the "Record of Music" chapter of the *Record of Rites* (*Liji* 禮记), it states:

樂者，天地之和也；禮者，天地之序也。和故百物皆化；序故群物皆別。樂由天作，禮以地制。過制則亂，過作則暴。明於天地，然後能興禮樂也。

Music is the harmony of the heavens and the earth; ritual propriety is their order. It is because things are all harmonious that they transform; it is because they have their proper order that all things have their distinctiveness. Music is initiated in the heavens, and ritual propriety is regulated by the earth. Too much regulation is chaos; too much innovation is mayhem. It is only through an intelligent understanding of the workings of the heavens and the earth that ritual propriety and music are able to thrive.

Enjoyment (*le* 樂) speaks to the pervasive assumption in the Confucian tradition that the most important thing in a human life is the quality of the relationships which locate one within family and community as roles that come to constitute one's continuing identity. In the *Analects*, for example, the contexts in which *le* appears are invariably relational. *Le* is associated with friendship (1.1, 16.5), consummate conduct (4.2), efficacious knowing and social intelligence (6.20, 23), and full participation in ritualized roles and relationships (16.5). As such, *le* is that moral and religious satisfaction inspired by the vital and enduring relationships that locate and define us within our life-world. At the same time, *le* is disassociated from wealth (1.15, 6.11, 7.16) and sensual enjoyment (16.5), not because prosperity or sensuality are in themselves necessarily harmful, but because they can lead to conflicted habits of the heart that are socially corrosive and disintegrating. In fact, Confucius is explicit in claiming that material well-being can be unproblematic for a community where the flourishing of all of its members is made possible by the quality of the life they forge together (1.15).

*類　*lei.* "Categories, groupings." See also 倫 *lun.* "Order, relation, category, class," 理 *li.* "Patterning, coherence," and 象 *xiang.* "Figuring, figuring out, configuring, figure, imaging, imagining, image."

Lei is defined in the *Shuowen* classical lexicon as meaning 種類相似 "a designation for the similarity that obtains between and among things" so that as a verb it means "resembling." As such, it is translated variously as "class, group, kind, category, type, species," and more. However, "categories" or perhaps better, "groupings" in this cosmology, rather than being constituted by appeal to some putative essential, shared characteristic owned by each member of a species or genera, are constructed analogically on the basis of a perceived functional similarity or association that obtains among unique particulars.

In Aristotle's unchanging hierarchical order, a particular individual thing—Socrates—has a primary substance as a composite being that tells us most clearly what it is to be Socrates: the immanent formal cause (*eidos*) as it is embodied in matter. The reduplicated *eidos* makes Socrates a member of an immutable species, a "human being," and a genera, "animal" can be predicated of him. The categories "human being" and "animal" constitute Socrates's secondary substance, with the species having a greater claim on being substance than the genera because it is closer to the particular and thus tells us more about Socrates. Of course, this assumption about *eidos*, the hypostatized subject of definition that becomes an immutable species, introduces the notion of strict identity as the intelligible essence that is fundamental for Aristotelian logic and epistemology.

In the Confucian process cosmology, things in their relations are continuous with one another, and thus are interdependent and always conditions for each other. Indeed, in this cosmology, the starting point is the uniqueness of each particular. As it states in *Focusing the Familiar* (*Zhongyong* 中庸) 26:

> 天地之道可壹言而盡也：其為物不貳，則其生物不測。
>
> The way-making of the heavens and the earth can be captured in one phrase: Since things and events are never duplicated, their issue is unfathomable.

In the absence of teleological assumptions that introduce fixed formal and final causes, there is both the vital propensity and the inertia of existing circumstances. Within these circumstances, there is the ongoing process of correlation and negotiation that is productive of an emergent order. We investigate the *li* 理 or patterns of things in the practical world in order to uncover relations and to discover resonances among things that make our correlations and categorizations possible.

In this alternative notion of classification, order is thus situational, and things can either be associated or not under the prevailing conditions (*tongleibulei* 同類不類). *Lei* has to do with perceived resonant relations or connections between two changing things rather than with some shared specific or generic quality that would make them members of a third fixed category. A.S. Cua is sensitive to this basic meaning of *lei* when he states that "a *lei* is formed by way of comparison or analogy between similarities and differences."① The technical term for the construction of such groupings is "analogical projection" (*tuilei* 推類). A.S. Cua is concerned that the central role of retrospective history in the Confucian analogical reasoning process be fully appreciated because it is this historicist appeal that makes the exercise of Confucian rationality both concrete and contingent. Cua states:

> The Confucian emphasis on the role of historical knowledge, given the backward-looking character of analogical projection, is a useful reminder that any piece of ethical reasoning, if it is to claim interpersonal significance, though itself occasioned by a present perplexity, must have some contact with the cultural-historical experience of the people. It is in culture and history that an analogical projection finds its anchorage and not in rules and principles of *a priori* ratiocination. In this basic way, the prospective significance of analogical projection is rooted in retrospective ethical thinking.②

For the Confucian, the functional approximation of what we would regard as valid reasoning involves the discovery and articulation of appropriate and efficacious historical instances of reasonableness. "Reasoning" (*li* 理) and historical analogy are inseparable. On the

---

① A.S. Cua, *Ethical Argumentation*, p. 55.
② A.S. Cua, *Ethical Argumentation*, pp. 96-97. See also pp. 56-61.

one hand, *li* that involves the mapping out of patterns can only operate on the basis of assumed classifications (*lei* 類); on the other hand, it is the mapping operation of *li*, including and excluding on the basis of perceived similarities and differences, that established classifications (*lei* 類) in the first place.①

Interestingly, while Aristotle would interpret inclusion in a category as being descriptive as a matter of objective fact, in Confucianism such inclusion is also normative. A child is praised for being filial (*xiao* 孝) or criticized for being unfilial (*buxiao* 不肖)—literally, "being unlike, not resembling the parents." It is assumed that "resembling" conduces to a productive relationship, while failing to do so is disintegrative. It is for this reason that *lei* as "measuring up" is also defined normatively as "efficacious" (*shan* 善).

*禮 **li.** "Ritual propriety in one's roles and relations, ritual practices, 'social grammar, rites, customs, etiquette, propriety, morals, rules of proper behavior, reverence'."

Properly contextualized, each of these English terms can render this complex idea of *li* on occasion. In classical Chinese, however, the character *li* carries *all* of these meanings on every occasion of its use with the particular context determining the emphasis and how it should be parsed. The compound character is an ideograph connoting the performance and presentation of sacrifices (*shi* 示) to the primarily ancestral spirits at an altar to them (*li* 豊), suggesting the profound religious significance of this term. It is defined in the *Shuowen* paronomastically (homophonic in the ancient pronunciation) as *lü* 履, meaning "treading a path," and hence "conduct, behavior"—that is, "how to conduct oneself in service to

---

① A.S. Cua, *Ethical Argumentation*, p. 54.

the spirits in order to bring about good fortune." The character *li* 禮 is further cognate with the graph for "body" (*ti* 體), underscoring both the somatic dimension of ritual propriety and its formal and regulatory aspects.

What recommends the translation of *li* as "propriety" is that along with other words such as "appropriate," "proper," and "property," it is derived etymologically from the Latin, *proprius* with its core meaning of "making something one's own." The substance and depth of *li*, unlike formal regulations, is dependent upon a continuing process of personalization—that is, it is the aspiration to make the unique role of this particular daughter in her relationship with this particular father, something moving and magical. What makes ritual profoundly different from law or rule is this sustained effort to embody and perpetuate the tradition and its institutions through one's lived roles and relations, and to make them one's own.

The holistic, process cosmology that gives these Confucian texts their interpretive context is an inside without an outside. It is an ecological and organic way of thinking that locates all activity *in medias res*, and makes it reflexive, always turning back upon itself. The Latin *proprius*, "making something one's own," gives us a cognate series of just such reflexive expressions that are useful in translating key Confucian philosophical terms to capture this sense of participation and personalization: *yi* 義 is not "righteousness" as compliance with some external divine directive, but rather is an optimal "appropriateness" in this particular communal context as "a sense of what is fitting for all concerned including oneself." *Zheng* 正 is not merely "rectification" or "correct conduct" as an appeal to some external standard, but "proper conduct" as it can best be determined by serving the interests of all persons within a particular context. *Zheng* 政 is not simply "government" but taking personal responsibility for "governing properly." And *li* 禮 is not just "what is ritually appropriate in one's roles and relations," but "*personally doing* what is ritually appropriate" in such relations. As Confucius observes in *Analects* 3.12:

祭如在，祭神如神在。子曰："吾不與祭，如不祭。"
The expression "sacrifice as though present" is taken to mean "sacrifice to the spirits as though the spirits are present." But the Master said: "If I myself do not participate in the sacrifice, it is as though I have not sacrificed at all."

As a footnote to this understanding of *li* as "making something one's own," we have to allow that one important factor that is integral to the quality of our understanding of these Confucian canons is our own lived experience. Theoretical explanation and cognitive insights cannot do all of the work of making the function of *li* clear to the apprentice. The expository limits of these canonical texts lie in their tacit assumption that readers will invoke their own life experience to inform and amplify the themes under discussion. And at the same time, the ultimate expectation of these documents is that they will not only provide their readers with cognitive clarity when it comes to reflection on moral issues, but further and more importantly, do nothing less than transform their always unique persons into morally competent human actors (*jiaohua* 教化).①

Again, the concern for achieving ritual propriety in one's own roles and relations works in complex ways to promote order and elegance in the communal living of irreducibly relational persons.

---

① I.A. Richards in his *Mencius on the Mind*, pp. 6 and 49, for example, allows that the seeming ambiguity that we register in reflecting upon the Mencian conception of "native human propensities" (*xing* 性) arises from the assumption of the text that the reader's own experience as a human being can be called upon to fill in the existential details needed to bring clearer definition to this idea. Such an assumption stands in contrast to the early Greek expectation that formal definitions rising above and excluding subjective opinion is the source of truth.

Michael Ing in his monograph, *The Dysfunction of Ritual in Early Confucianism*, introduces the important caveat that while this Confucian ethic of ritual in contrast to the integrity provided by fixed "rule" and "law" brings with it a degree of flexibility, adjustment, and innovation, at the same time it is also a source of moral ambiguity and a personal vulnerability that can have both positive and negative consequences for the Confucian project of personal cultivation.[1]

Throughout the classical Confucian canons, "propriety in one's roles and relations" (*li* 禮) and "making music" (*yue* 樂) are treated as a complementary dyadic pair, *liyue* (禮樂). For Confucius, language, ritual, and music are all formal media in which selves grow. They are sources of meaning as well as the structures that organize and transmit it. The distinguishing characteristic of music that is immediately relevant to "making something one's own" is that it is the formative medium perhaps least dependent upon reference. Philosopher Susanne Langer observes:

> Music . . . is preeminently non-representative even in its classical productions, its highest attainments. It exhibits pure form not as an embellishment, but as its very essence; we can take it in its flower . . . and have practically nothing but tonal structure before us: no scene, no object, no fact.[2]

---

[1] Michael David Kaulana Ing. *The Dysfunction of Ritual in Early Confucianism.* Oxford: Oxford University Press, 2012.

[2] Susanne Langer. *Philosophy in a New Key.* Cambridge, MA: Harvard University Press, 1951, p. 209. At the same time, Langer departs radically from Confucius in her unwillingness to acknowledge the performative if not transformative power of music. She states unequivocally:
> Music does not ordinarily influence behavior. . . . On the whole, the behavior of concert audiences after even the most thrilling performances makes the traditional magical influence of music on human actions very dubious. Its somatic effects are transient, and its moral hangovers or uplifts seem to be negligible. (p. 212).

In music, indeed, we move towards the highest level of communication insofar as meaning is lodged both in the particular tones themselves and in their structural relatedness. Music does not represent; it presents. And to the extent that it is independent of objective reference, it is receptive to and expressive of the concrete particular. While language references types of things, classes of items, ontological particulars cannot be referenced. They must be alluded to, hinted at, suggested. Music has that allusive, suggestive power precisely to the degree that it is free of logical reference.

The "Great Preface" to the *Book of Songs* (*Shijing Daxu*《詩經·大序》) sequences a diminution in the degree of reference as the medium of feelings moves from the generality of the spoken word to the particularity of one's song and dance:

> 情動於中而形於言，言之不足，故嗟歎之，嗟歎之不足，故詠歌之，詠歌之不足，不知手之舞之足之蹈之也。
>
> Feelings that move one inwardly are expressed in words, but when the words are deemed inadequate, they are given voice in sighs and exclamations. But when these utterances are deemed inadequate, they are put to music and song. When again music and song prove inadequate, unknowingly the hands dance them and the feet tap them out.

While feelings expressed through the words written on an obligatory Hallmark birthday card tend to be public and impersonal, those same gross sentiments when expressed by lovers in their own poetry, song, and dance are highly personal, revealing of their innermost emotions.

Going back to the high culture of the Shang dynasty, formally prescribed rites and rituals were performed at stipulated times to reinforce the political and religious status of the royal participants within the extended family lineages, and to punctuate the seasons of the life at court. For that group of officials responsible for the casting of the bronzes and for the choreography of the court functions that made use of them, "ritual propriety" (*li* 禮) meant quite literally knowing one's place in the formalities and thus knowing where to stand. The graph for *li* 禮 is found on the oracle bones as ▧ and on the bronzes as ▧, a pictograph with two pieces of jade in a ritual vessel depicting a sacrificial offering made at the court to seek the blessings and good fortune from its ancestral lineage.① Originally ritual performances were formal and narrowly defined religious procedures enacted by the ruling classes and their entourage to fortify their relationship with both nature and the other world. These rituals were often constituted in imitation of perceptible cosmic rhythms as a means of strengthening the coordination of the human, natural, and spiritual environments, and were used to reinforce a sense of human participation in the regular operations of the cosmos.

If bronze production can tell the story of the Shang dynasty historically, economically, religiously, and politically, it is the evolution and broad dissemination of this notion of "observing ritual propriety" (*li* 禮) as a widespread cultural value that provides a window on the millennial-long narrative of the Zhou dynasty. First, the increasingly wide-spread propagation and performance of a kind of institutionalized propriety within the society broadly took place during the Zhou dynasty. Gradually over the ensuing centuries these ritual activities were extended outwards from the ruler himself to the community, and with this expanding reach, accrued an increasingly important significance for social and political order. In these amplified ritual observances, participants would have their proper status and place, their *wei* 位. If persons did not understand

---

① Kwan, "Database," 甲骨文合集 CHANT 2809 and 西周早期 CHANT 6015 respectively.

the details and spirit of the ritual procedures, they would quite literally not know where to stand (*li* 立) or what to do. Thus it is that the term "stance" or "standing" (*li* 立) found on the oracle bones 癶 and on the bamboo strip manuscripts 立 is closely associated with "rank, position, status" (*wei* 位) 位.① In Confucius's account of his own personal growth in *Analects* 2.4, he states that

吾十有五而志于學，三十而立.
... by fifteen I had set my purposes on learning, and by thirty I had taken my stance (*li* 立)...

Confucius is here referring to taking a stand on his commitment to the assiduous effort needed to fund his continuing project of personal cultivation. Importantly, throughout the *Analects*, these physical and spatial terminologies are closely linked to the pervasive, governing metaphor of the text: "advancing resolutely on the proper way" (*dao* 道). It is repeatedly stated that it is "ritual propriety" (*li* 禮)—"rites," "ceremony," "etiquette," "decorum," "manners"—that enables persons to determine, consolidate, and display virtuosity in the relational transactions of their daily lives. Indeed, education in its broadest sense was learning where to stand and what to say.

In *Analects* 16.13, Confucius counsels his own son on precisely this understanding of education:

陳亢問於伯魚曰："子亦有異聞乎？" 對曰："未也。嘗獨立，鯉趨而過庭。曰：'學詩乎？' 對曰：'未也。''不學詩，無以言。' 鯉退而學詩。他日又獨立，鯉趨而過庭。曰：'學禮乎？' 對曰：'未也。''不學禮，無以立。' 鯉退而學禮。"

---

① For a fuller description of this extension of *li* to the population broadly, see Robert M. Gimello. "The Civil Status of *li* in Classical Confucianism." *Philosophy East and West*. No. 22 (1972), pp. 203-211.

> Chen Gang asked Boyu, the son of Confucius: "Have you been given any kind of special instruction?"
> "No," he replied, "but once my father was standing alone, and as I was hastening across the courtyard, he asked me, 'Have you been studying the *Book of Songs*?' I replied, 'Not yet,' to which he remarked, 'If you do not study the *Songs*, you will be at a loss as to what to say.' I deferentially took my leave and am now studying the *Songs*.
> On another occasion, my father was again standing alone, and as I was hastening across the courtyard, he asked me, 'Have you been studying the *Book of Rituals*?' I replied, 'Not yet,' to which he remarked, 'If you do not study the *Rituals*, you will be at a loss as to where to stand.' I deferentially took my leave and am now studying the *Rituals*."

But not everyone, not even Confucius's rather unremarkable son, can "live" *li* in an equally felicitous way. It is ultimately the quality of particular persons as it is registered in the virtuosity of their roles and relations and expressed in the meaning and the musicality of the ritually aestheticized life that is the substance of *li*.

We have chosen to translate *li* with variations on "aspiring to propriety in one's roles and relations." Again, this rendering is a considered choice. On the formal side, *li* are those meaning-invested familial and social roles, relationships, and institutions which facilitate communication, and which foster a sense of community. The compass is broad including all formal conduct, from table manners to patterns of greeting and leave-taking to graduations, weddings, funerals, from gestures of deference to ancestral sacrifices; all of these, and more, are *li*. They are a social grammar that provides each member with a defined place and status within the family, community, and polity. *Li* are evolving life forms transmitted from generation to generation as repositories of meaning, enabling the youth to appropriate persisting values, and in the process of reauthorizing them for their generation, to revise them and make them appropriate to their own particular situations.

Perhaps the greatest obstacle to understanding what *li* means in the aristocratic world of Confucius is thinking that since "ritual" is a familiar dimension of our own world, we fully understand what it entails. "Ritual" in contemporary English usage references formal ceremonies, and can even be pejorative, suggesting as it often does compliance with hollow and hence meaningless social conventions. A careful reading of the Confucian literature, however, uncovers a way of life carefully choreographed down to appropriate facial expressions and physical gestures, a world in which a life is a performance requiring enormous attention to detail. Importantly, this *li*-constituted performance begins from the insight that personal refinement is only possible through the discipline provided by formalized roles and behaviors. Form without creative personalization is coercive and dehumanizing law; creative personal expression without form is randomness at best, and license at worst. It is only with the appropriate combination of form and functional personalization (*tiyong* 體用) that behavior within family and community can be self-regulating and increasingly refined.

Although an achieved propriety in one's roles and relations clearly has a formal and redundant structure, still the preponderant significance of these activities in defining family and communal life lies in those informal, personal, and particular aspects that conduce to and are necessary for real meaningful experience. These *li* have a profoundly somatic dimension where the social, vital body is often more effective than spoken language in communicating the deference necessary to strengthen the bonds among those participating in the various life forms. The body is the vital and existential site of learning and the conveyance of what is learned that has both a subjective and objective dimension to it. The *li* also have an important affective aspect wherein feelings suffuse and fortify all of our relational activities, providing the communal fabric a tensile strength that resists the tensions and ruptures which inevitably attend associated living. Pursuing refinement through the performance of *li* must be understood in light of the uniqueness of each participant engaged in the profoundly aesthetic project of becoming this exceptional and always inimitable person. *Li* is again a process of personal articulation—the growth and disclosure of an elegant disposition, an attitude, a posture, a signature style, and ultimately, a persistent and singular identity.

With respect to Confucius himself, *li* is a resolutely personal performance revealing his worth to both himself and to his community. It is a public discourse through which he is able to compose and reveal himself qualitatively as a unique individual, a whole person, doing what he does for the benefit of everyone, including himself. Importantly, there is no respite. *Li* requires unrelenting attention to every detail of what Confucius does at every moment he is doing it, from the drama of the high court to the posture he assumes in going to sleep, from the reception of different guests to the proper way to comport himself when alone, from how he behaves in formal dining situations to appropriate impromptu gestures when encountering friends.

In our reading of the *Analects*, there is a tendency to give short shrift to the middle books 9-11 as a series of intimate portraits depicting the historical person, Confucius. If such personal information is considered at all, we are inclined to pass over it quickly as insufficiently philosophical to be relevant to the Confucian project. But in fact, in overlooking these personal details, we are in danger of missing the real substance of Confucius's moral vision. We must not lose sight of the fact that Confucian role ethics ultimately and invariably has to do with specific persons in their particular situations. While laws and formal institutions can certainly serve as important guidelines, it is ultimately analogy and correlation with family members, role models, and cultural heroes that has the greatest motive force in promoting a commitment to personal cultivation and the flourishing community that follows from it. This being the case, the deferential yet authoritative life habits of Confucius himself and the emulation of this specific role model over succeeding generations is nothing less than an object lesson in understanding the real workings of role ethics. From these passages, it should be clear that propriety in our roles and relations does not reduce to generic, formally prescribed "rites" and "rituals" performed at stipulated times to announce status and to punctuate the seasons of our lives. The *li*—the realization and expression of propriety through our roles and relations—are more, much more than such performances.

One compelling image we have of Confucius from *Analects* 10.19 is the self-conscious display he makes of his dedication to official duties even from his sick bed:

疾，君視之，東首，加朝服，拖紳。
When ill, and his lord came to see him, Confucius reclined with his head facing east, and had his court robes draped over him with his sash drawn.[①]

Indeed, these many, seemingly random snapshots of Confucius reveal an image of a person aspiring in the conduct of the largely routine events of his daily life to express a quality of relational virtuosity that is sufficiently robust to transform and indeed to

---

[①] The bed for the master of the house was usually on the western side of the southern window. When one's lord would visit, the lord would approach by ascending the stairs from the east. The eastern stairs is the place of the "host," but since the lord himself is the proper host of the entire country, he would ascend and descend from these same eastern steps.

enchant the ordinary affairs of his life.

One way to distinguish the inclusive and holistic Confucian role ethics from more formalized and thus reductionistic principle-based ethical theories is to give an account of how in this Confucian moral vision, the particular, the informal, and the contextualizing aspects of experience, far from being discounted or marginalized, in fact take on a central importance as those resources that can be drawn upon to maximize the productive outcome of always particular human activities. This aesthetic dimension—the need for elegance and moral artistry in ethics—is integral to this holistic understanding of human conduct in which all aspects of the life experience have more or less relevance, and thus have some value for determining a worthwhile outcome. It is because the moral vision of Confucian role ethics is concerned with coordinating the contribution of each aspect of experience in achieving the totality of the effect that the normative language to which it appeals, and the sense of order to which it aspires, is in the Whiteheadian sense, fundamentally aesthetic.[①] The effect itself is most often characterized in these texts in the language of authenticity or duplicity rather than by appeal to the rationalizing language of right and wrong, or good and evil. There is a perceived, inseparable relationship between elegance and morality, and conversely, between baseness and immorality. On being asking about family reverence (xiao 孝), for example, Confucius would insist that this moral imperative cannot be satisfied by some set of formally prescribed, reduplicative activities that would resolve to a binary right or wrong, but rather is dependent upon the specific attitude expressed as the actions are being carried out. In *Analects* 2.8 Confucius observes:

色難。有事弟子服其勞，有酒食先生饌，曾是以為孝乎？

[①] A.N. Whitehead, *Modes of Thought*, Chapter 3.

Family reverence (*xiao* 孝) lies primarily in showing the proper countenance. As for the young contributing their energies when there is work to be done, and deferring to their elders when there is wine and food to be had—how can merely doing such things be considered being properly filial?

In thus defining family reverence (*xiao* 孝), Confucius is not concerned that parents are provided with food and shelter—we do as much for our domestic animals (*Analects* 2.7). The substance of family reverence lies in the "face" (*se* 色) one brings to filial responsibility—the bounce in one's step, the cheerful heart, the goodwill with which one conducts the otherwise rather ordinary business of caring for aging parents. It is the unrelenting attention to one's roles and relationships in every moment of the day rather than simply formal gestures that is defining of ritual propriety.

This ethics of proper responsiveness is elaborated upon in great detail in these middle books of the *Analects* 10.24-26 wherein the life habits of Confucius are displayed as a model for the ages:

寢不尸，居不容。見齊衰者，雖狎，必變。見冕者與瞽者，雖褻，必以貌。凶服者式之。式負版者。有盛饌，必變色而作。迅雷風烈，必變。升車，必正立執綏。車中，不內顧，不疾言，不親指。

In sleeping, he did not assume the posture of a corpse, and when at home alone, he did not kneel in a formal posture as though he were entertaining guests. On encountering someone in mourning dress, even those with whom he was on intimate terms, he would always assume a solemn visage. On coming across someone wearing a ceremonial cap or someone who is blind, even though they were persons of frequent acquaintance, he would invariably pay his respects. On meeting up with a person in mourner's attire, he would lean forward on the crossbeam of his carriage. He would do the same on encountering an official with state census records on his back. On being presented with a sumptuous table, he would always take on a solemn demeanor and rise to his feet. On experiencing a sudden clap of thunder or fierce winds, he would change his countenance ... In mounting his carriage, he would always stand upright and grasp the cord. While riding in the carriage, he would not turn his head to look inward, speak hastily, or point at things.

This detailed portrait of Confucius rehearses a succession of images that are revealing of his unrelenting attention to proper countenance and a quality of responsiveness to particular circumstances. It discloses a pattern of proper conduct on the part of this particular human being in the particular circumstances of his life. And at the end of this series in 10.27, the text then naturalizes these ritualized behaviors by ascribing just such a responsive pattern of conduct to the animal world:

色斯舉矣，翔而後集。曰："山梁雌雉，時哉！時哉！" 子路共之，三嗅而作。

Sensing their approach, the bird took to flight, and soared about them before alighting. The Master said, "Look at that hen-pheasant on the mountain bridge—What timing! What timing!" Zilu clasped his hands together and saluted the bird, which flapping its wings three times, took to the air once again.

For us, there is ostensibly a distinction to be made between being boorish and being immoral. For Confucius, however, there are simply varying degrees of inappropriate, demeaning, and hurtful behavior along a continuum on which a failure in personal responsiveness is not just bad manners, but fully a lapse in moral responsibility. Since morality itself is nothing more than those modalities of acting that conduce to the enhancement of relations, any kind of conduct that has a disintegrative effect on the fabric of family or community is perceived as fundamentally immoral. Lifestyle takes on crucial import when we consider the corrosive consequences on the community of those who live lives without style. Carelessness becomes of major concern when we have to worry about those who couldn't care less. And ignorance in the sense of ignoring others and their needs far from being detached or neutral, is in fact to inflict a violence upon the persons of our friends and neighbors.[1]

Graciousness, on the other hand, has gravity when we reflect on the relevance that charm and deportment have for an overall sense of fittingness and propriety. Morality is much more than formal correctness, emerging as it does importantly from poise and demeanor in our discursive transactions with others. The *Analects*, for example, reflects the always transactional nature of this Confucian philosophy as a "face" or "shame" culture. On the informal and uniquely personal side, full participation in a ritually-constituted community requires the personalization of prevailing customs, institutions, and values. What makes ritual profoundly different from law or rule is this process of making the tradition one's own, and in the process of doing so, developing the quality of self-consciousness that makes the community self-regulating.

As we have seen, for Confucius ritual practices are not simply a given: standards of appropriateness sedimented within a cultural tradition that shapes its participants. They have both a personal and a creative dimension. What distinguishes ritual from law as a source of order is that ritual action not only informs participants of what is proper, but is also performed by them in a way that expresses their own uniqueness. Rituals are formal structures that are personalized and reformulated to accommodate the uniqueness and the quality of each participant, enabling them to reform the community from their own inimitable perspective, and to leave their mark on the

---

[1] Vrinda Dalmiya, "Linguistic Erasures." *Peace Review*, 10 (4), 1998.

tradition. Where ritual practices are conduits of meaning to be appropriated by each succeeding generation, they are also a reservoir that accumulates additional meaning from the intergenerational connector (*dao* 道) as it is being constructed and extended by each generation. Ritual action is a necessary condition for Confucius's vision of social harmony because, by definition, it not only permits of, but actually requires personalization. For Confucius, a formal ceremony without personal commitment is a hollow, meaningless and even antisocial parody of what should be a source of social cohesion and enjoyment. Community thus defined through the meaningfulness of its members is programmatic and open-ended: it exists neither as an immediate reality nor as a fixed ideal. It is rather an aesthetic achievement, contingent upon the particular players and their moral imagination. Further, this demand of ritual action for personal signature, while promising to make the most of available diversity, means also that the achieved community will in some important respect always be "local" or "parochial," conditioned as it must be by the aspirations and the imagination of its cultural leaders and the circumstances of its particular time and place.

Are the differences between this understanding of Confucius's notion of ritual practices (*li* 禮) and that of Xunzi significant? In formulating his own theory of ritual practices, Xunzi begins from several premises that are covered in the passages selected below. A value-neutral, amoral natural force (*tian* 天) gives rise to human beings whose native condition is basically an aggregate of base desires. Given that humankind by definition all share the same desires and aversions, and that cumulative demand outweighs supply, the state of nature is chaotic. Human beings do not have the option of avoiding contest by withdrawing and living a solitary life because of the pressure of their own desires, and of the division of labor needed to best satisfy them (chapters 10 and 19). To resolve and preclude further social strife, the ancient sage-kings established conventions governing status and conduct that guaranteed an orderly distribution of goods. These conventions are the *li*, and being more contrived (*wei* 偽) than natural, are an important component in the content of Xunzi's vision of the moral life. Further, the fact that these conventions for conduct were formulated by sages in high antiquity at some considerable distance from the specific concerns of Xunzi's world is mitigated by Xunzi's conviction in the constancy of both the human condition and its context:

君子位尊而志恭，心小而道大；所聽視者近，而所聞見者遠。是何邪？則操術然也。故千人萬人之情，一人之情也。天地始者，今日是也。百王之道，後王是也。君子審後王之道，而論百王之前，若端拜而議。推禮義之統，分是非之分，總天下之要，治海內之眾，若使一人。

Exemplary persons although having an exalted status are respectful in their purposes, recognizing that their own thoughts and feelings are minor while the proper way is grand. But how is it that what they look at and listen to are near at hand, but what they are able to see and hear is so remote? It is because they have a firm grasp on how to parse experience. It is thus they see that the condition of all humans is the same as any one of them, that the beginnings of the cosmos are still very much with us, and that the proper way of all kings is the same as the most recent kings. Exemplary persons survey the proper way of the recent kings to pronounce on that of the kings of old as though, with hands raised in salute, they are expressing an opinion in court. As simple as looking at the situation of a single person, they discern the mainstay of ritual action and moral principle, grasp the distinction between right and wrong, have a synoptic view of what is essential in the world, and bring proper order to the multitude.

The passage cited here lends itself to two very different

interpretations. One strong reading of sameness relies upon the concept of strict identity, and thus would eliminate any notion of change, and would thus deny any meaningful sense of history by asserting that from earliest times to the present, we basically have the same world and everything that is in it. Every person is identical with every other. The weaker reading would appeal to the *Book of Changes* postulate of "continuity in change" (*biantong* 變通), and argue that the sameness is a continuity in identity in a cosmology where one is many, many one (*yiduobufen* 一多不分). This same cosmology with its primacy of vital relationality is thus holographic, where the entire cosmic field resides within each focal detail. What recommends this second interpretation over the first is that in assuming a holistic, processual cosmology, it has the virtue of allowing Xunzi to be read within his own interpretive context.

Xunzi's attitude toward the tradition is at obvious variance with that of Confucius. Confucius would know the present by a careful examination of the past, but Xunzi seems to recommend the converse. For Confucius, one not only understands the contours of the present situation by appeal to the relief and detail of historical models, but further can best address a future course of action by analogy with the past (2.11). It is particular historical persons and events rather than abstract principles that are most helpful in charting a course. Xunzi, on the other hand, says repeatedly the 古今一也 "the ancient and the present are one" and 類不悖，雖久同理 "since classes of things do not contradict themselves, even though distant in time, they share in the same pattern."

With specific reference to ritual practices, Xunzi describes the *li* as markers on the proper way:

百王之無變，足以為道貫。一廢一起，應之以貫，理貫不亂……水行者表深，表不明則陷。治民者表道，表不明則亂。禮者，表也。

We can take what the myriad kings did not change to serve as the connector that persists in the proper way. In the vicissitudes of life, respond to things with this one conjunctive thread, for where it sets the pattern there will be no disorder.... Watermen mark the depths, for where these markers are not clear, people will drown. To bring proper order to the common people, set markers on the proper way, for where these markers are not clear, there will be disorder. Ritual practices are just such markers.

For Xunzi, 夫道者體常而盡變 "as for this proper way, it embodies constancy and is the sum of all change." His complaint against his Confucian predecessors such as Zisizi and Mencius is that they have only a partial knowledge and have thus failed to grasp the underlying unity provided by the proper way: 略法先王而不知其統 "they model themselves on the Former Kings only superficially but do not understand what unites them." Xunzi's way of talking about the proper way contrasts rather sharply with the cumulative *dao* of the *Analects*, where 人能弘道非道弘人 "it is persons who broaden the proper way, not the converse" (15.29).

For Confucius, the *li* are meaning-invested and meaning-disclosing actions that are ultimately derived from the personal sense and expression of appropriateness (*yi* 義). It is this grounding in personal appropriateness that makes *li* irreducibly participatory and makes the achievement of social harmony a "bottom-up" communal responsibility. Confucius in the *Analects* says explicitly that *yi* does not reduce to right and wrong or some generic principle (4.10).

Xunzi, on the other hand, has departed from this Confucian understanding to an extent that has escaped the notice of few commentators. In fact, Xunzi explicitly assimilates *yi* to *li* to form a binomial expression *liyi* 禮儀 in some 85 instances, more than one third of the occurrences of *li* in the text, with the effect of subordinating *yi* to *li* and thus, in important degree, externalizing *li* as public norms. That there is this tendency for *yi* to be externalized and made generic at the expense of its specific reference to individual instances of appropriateness is reflected in the rendering of *yi* in the current *Xunzi* English translations as "justice," "just principles," "moral law," "moral principles," and "standards of righteousness."

The ramifications for *li* that are introduced by these altered implications of *yi* are profound. The diminished importance of personal participation in the actual production of social harmony transforms *li* into a largely external, closed, and "top-down" set of prescriptions that dictates a regulatory order for society. Using Xunzi's own metaphors, the *li* are a plumbline, a pair of scales, a compass and set square, all of which can be applied to people to bring them to rule. *Li* are a templet against which the people can be steamed and pressed into shape, can be whetted on a grindstone and brought to form:

故枸木必將待檃栝、烝矯然後直；鈍金必將待礱厲然後利；今人之性惡，必將待師法然後正，得禮義然後治。

Thus it is that warped wood can only be straightened by being steamed and bent into shape in a pressframe; blunt metal can only be sharpened by being whetted on a grindstone. And since the natural propensities of human beings are base, they can only be made proper through their teachers and set norms and can only be properly ordered through ritual practices and moral principles.

There are several other signals in the *Xunzi* of the movement toward a more generic and objective conception of ritual practices. This perception is reinforced by the emergence of *li* 理—generally rendered "principle" or "reason"—as a central concept in Xunzi and the appeal to it for authority as a rationalizing of both ritual practices (*li* 禮) and morality (*yi* 義). There is the increasingly exalted status of the ruler to the extent that the issue of order versus chaos becomes focused in the effectiveness of the ruler at the top. As Hsiao Kung-chuan (Xiao Gongquan 蕭公權) observes, the emphasis in Confucius and Mencius was on the moral quality of the ruler while the Legalist thinkers stressed the ruler's status and the power that issued from it.[①] In Xunzi as a latter day Confucian and the teacher to Legalists such as Han Feizi and Li Si, there is real concern for both moral quality and the exercise of power. Xunzi with his idiosyncratic interpretation of the baseness of native human propensities is much more inclined to rely on fear and awe in addition to deference as the best way to keep the people in line. The appropriation of "political purchase" (*shi* 勢) from the Militarists and Legalists and the retrofitting of it as a Confucian concept together with the development of the "hegemon" (*ba* 霸) as an acceptable albeit inferior alternative to sagely government are both indications of this inclination in Xunzi.

*理　*li.* "Patterning, coherence." See also 類 ***lei.*** "Categories, groupings," 倫 ***lun.*** "Order, relation, category, class," and 象 ***xiang.*** "Figuring, figuring out, configuring, figure, imaging, imagining, image."

We want to give an account of how the conventional translations of *li* as either "reason" or "principle" while foregrounding our own philosophical importances, pay the unacceptable penalty of concealing precisely those meanings that are most essential to an appreciation of its differences. In its earliest occurrences, *li* is both verbal and nominal: "ordering and order," "patterning and pattern," "marking and markings." Actually, in its earliest reference in the

---

[①] Hsiao Kung-chuan. *A History of Chinese Political Thought.* trans. F. Mote. Princeton: Princeton University Press, 1979, Vol. 1, p. 205.

Book of Songs 210, *li* refers to the Sage-king Yu dividing up land into cultivated fields in a way consistent with the natural topography. It refers to the pathways that give pattern to the agricultural landscape and permit access to the fields under cultivation. The *Shuowen* lexicon and its commentaries state that *li* 理 is composed of the *yu* 玉 signific meaning "jade," and the *li* 里 phonetic from which it takes its pronunciation. It suggests that *li* in referring to the cutting and polishing of jade into ornaments and vessels (marking), and the unique veins and striations within the jade (markings), are its most basic meanings. Significantly, the dressing of jade requires craftsmen to conform their creative expression to those possibilities resident in the natural striations of the stone. The best lapidary is the one whose art maximizes the richest possibilities of the stone itself.

The most familiar translation of *li* within Western translations is "principle," with alternatives being "reasoning, rationale" (Cua), "coherence" (Peterson), and "organism" (Needham). Needham's use of the term "organism" is inappropriate if understood in the standard Aristotelian sense that defines the organic in terms of activity conditioned by specific teleological ends. This characterization leads to classifications of ends or aims that would then undergird a taxonomic organization of "natural kinds."

The most familiar use of *li* in the classical literature is to indicate the inherent formal and structural patterns in things and events, and their intelligibility. In expressing this notion of coherence and intelligibility, no severe distinction is made between nature and nurture, between "natural" coherence (*tianli* 天理 or *daoli* 道理) and "cultural" coherence (*wenli* 文理 and *daoli* 道理). Just as nature and culture are embraced within the notion *dao*, so each is integral to *li*. The expressions of *dao*, *wen*, and *li* all overlap in evoking a sense of pattern and markings.

Li is the fabric of order and regularity immanent in the dynamic process of experience, and hence is frequently rendered "reasoning" or "reason." However, *li* in defining order confounds the familiar distinction between rational faculty and the underlying principles it searches out. *Li* has neither an exclusively subjective nor objective reference: the modern Chinese expression *wulixue* 物理學 that translates "physics" is "investigating the patterns of things and events," while the term for "psychology" is *xinlixue* 心理學: "investigating the patterns of the heartmind." Again, *li* does not entail the distinction between the intelligible and the sensible worlds that has had such prominence in Western philosophy after Plato. The absence of effective notions of transcendence suggests that there can be no efficacious appeal to objective reason. The *li* of both heartmind and of things and events are immanent in the phenomena themselves.

Another condition of *li* that separates it rather distinctly from our common understanding of "principle" and that produces some consternation is that *li* is at once one and many. In his analysis of *li*, Allen Wittenborn notes:

> The problem ... is whether *li* is a unity, or a multiplicity. It cannot be both. If it were then our entire way of thinking, our complete thought processes and forms of reasoning would have to be seriously reconsidered, and probably discarded.①

This is precisely the point. As Willard Peterson observes, *li* is the coherence of any "member of a set, all the members of a set, or the set as a whole."② This description reflects both the uniqueness of each particular and the continuities that obtain among them.

---

① Allen Wittenborn. "*Li* Revisited and Other Explorations." *The Bulletin of Sung-Yuan Studies* 17 (1981), p. 42.
② Willard J. Peterson. "Another Look at *Li*." *The Bulletin of Sung-Yuan Studies* 18 (1986), p. 18.

A similar point is made by A.C. Cua, who expresses his reservations about "principle" as the conventional translation of *li* because "principle"

> ... is often used as a context-independent notion that can be employed as referring to a basis for justifying particular moral rules or notions.... For Confucians, duty and obligation are tied to the roles and positions of persons in the community.[①]

The translation of *li* as "principle" has created some confusion in the minds of Western interpreters of Chinese philosophy, many of whom just assume that *li* like "principle" must at some level be transcendent. After all, *principium* is the Latin equivalent of Gk. *arche*: an originative and determinative principle. But *li* is what establishes the ethos of a given community. As such *li* can never be considered as independent of context. There are no transcendent *li*. *Li*, as a "making sense of things," cannot be understood as the process of seeking out principles as the determining sources of order, or of discovering essential categories inclusive of particular things. It is, rather, an activity that constructs categories (*lei* 類) analogically, and then traces, again by analogical means, correlated details that manifest patterns of relationships immanent within things and events. This sort of reasoning depends upon noninferential access to enlarged and deepened patternings. Inclusion or exclusion of items within a "category" is not associated with set-theoretical notions of logical "types" or "classes." The sortings are analogical, not logical. This understanding of "reason" and "reasoning" is one more implication of the fact that the Confucian tradition has not appealed to a substance ontology as the answer to why things exist.

When the Confucian texts turn to cosmological issues of the sort

---

[①] A.C. Cua, *Ethical Argumentation*, pp. 22-23.

that require an understanding of the basic categories that make up the world as we know it, we must proceed with caution. While it is true that Confucian philosophers ask about things, they do not ask about "categories" or "kinds" in any manner that would suggest that things have "formal essences" or constitute "natural kinds." The principal reason Confucian thinkers are not apt to ask after the *logos* of the cosmos is that they have not embraced an operative sense of the world as a *uni*verse, as a cosmos, as a single, coherent whole. Their sense of the pattern or coherence of the world (*li* 理) is instead a radically situated notion. In fact, the Confucian understanding of "cosmos" as *wanwu* 萬物 (literally, "the ten thousand things") means that, strictly speaking, Confucian philosophers have no fixed concept of "cosmos" insofar as that notion entails either a coherent, single-ordered world or a congeries of entities with essential features or essential modes of connectedness. The Confucians are therefore primarily "acosmotic" thinkers. *Li* has application to particular things, to convenient groupings of things, and to the world in its unsummed totality. When we use the term "cosmology" in relationship to these early texts, it is simply meant to distinguish a way of thinking about how the world hangs together most productively from the ontological quest to achieve certainty by knowing what is really real.

In the absence of teleological guidance, there is only an ongoing process of correlation and negotiation. One investigates *li* in order to uncover patterns that relate things, and to discover resonances among things that make correlations and categorization possible. The nature of classification (*lei* 類) in this world is juxtaposition through some presumed similarity. As Joseph Needham has pointed out, "things influence one another not by acts of mechanical causation, but by a kind of 'inductance'."[1] Things are continuous

---

[1] Joseph Needham. *Science and Civilisation in China*, Vol. II. Cambridge: Cambridge University Press, 1956, p. 280.

with one another, and thus are interdependent conditions for each other. In a tradition that develops from the assumption that existence is a dynamic process that begins from "life" (*sheng* 生) itself, the causes of things are resident in themselves as their conditions, and the project of giving reasons for things or events requires a tracing or mapping out of the conditions that sponsor them.

Perhaps the closest correlate to our typical understanding of "reason" or "reasoning" is to be found in "figuring out the pattern of things." In general, to think or act in accord with such patterns (*heli* 合理) is to be reasonable or rational or coherent, and entails an awareness of those constitutive relationships that condition each thing, and that, through patterns of correlation, make the world meaningful and intelligible. All things evidence a degree of coherence as their claim to uniqueness and complexity, as well as in their claim to continuity with the rest of their world.

Li constitutes an aesthetic coherence in the sense that it begins from the uniqueness of any particular as a condition of individuation, and is at the same time a basis for continuity through various forms of collaboration between the given particular and other particulars with which, by virtue of similarity or productivity or contiguity, it can be correlated. It is this collaboration that provides a ground for the various modes of analogical relationship that are the closest approximation of "reasoning" available in this cosmology.

In contrast to reasoning as the process of uncovering essences of which particulars are instances, *li* involves tracing out correlated details forming the pattern of relationships that obtain among things and events. Confucian thinking has as its goal a comprehensive and unobstructed awareness of interdependent conditions and their latent, vague possibilities, where the meaning and value of each element is a function of the particular network of relationships that constitute it. Such "reasoning" permits noninferential access to concrete detail and nuance. For example, one may appeal to the categories of correlative "kinds" (*lei* 類) to organize and explain items in the world. The correlations one pursues among the welter of concrete details foregrounds similarities among them. Inclusion or exclusion in any particular "kind" is a function of analogical activities rather than logical operations dependent upon a notion of strict identity or non-contradiction. Such correlations are meant to provide a sense of continuity and regularity in the world, and are more or less effective as coherent orders to the extent that some juxtapositions tend to maximize difference, diversity, and opportunity, and hence are more productive of meaningful harmony than others.

Li is both descriptive and normative. It also suggests how things ought to be. This prescriptive aspect of *li*, however, does not appeal to any order beyond that which is available by analogy to historical models. Ideals reside in history. In this sense, *li* is not "metaphysical" and must be distinguished from assertions about some a priori structure or transcendent aim. Said another way, in the absence of being as the ground of all things, the act of understanding and articulating the way of the world—*daoli* 道理 (a grasp of the patternings of the ways of things)—is nonanalytic and has explanatory rather than ontological reference. It does not identify an essential reality that can be separated from appearances, but rather provides access to the world by correlating the way we think about our experience and the determinate nature of the world in which that experience is entertained.

*利　*li.* "Benefitting, profiting, personal advantage." See also 義 *yi.* "Optimal appropriateness, meaning."

In modern Chinese there is a familiar distinction between other-regarding altruistic conduct (*lita* 利他) and selfish conduct (*liji* 利己) that reflects the basically positive meaning of *li* 利 as "benefitting" and a derived pejorative connotation of simply benefitting oneself.

In its positive sense, *li* frequently occurs as the rhyming antithesis of "harm or injury" (*hai* 害), and means to be of benefit. A familiar Confucian political precept, for example, is "benefitting the people" (*limin* 利民). The concept that the people are the root of government was established early in the tradition to become the foundation of its political philosophy. Rather than political leadership determining the occupation of the people, it is the collective realization of the welfare of the people that should determine the disposition and concerns of government. While the notion of government for the people is certainly a feature of pre-Qin Confucian thinkers, it was by no means their exclusive property. Early on it was absorbed and elaborated upon by the Mohists until it became a central principle of their political thought.

In its pejorative sense, *li* is frequently contrasted with "appropriateness" (*yi* 義)—that is, dedication to the furtherance of one's exclusive private interests as opposed to an effort to exert one's moral sense to do what is right for everyone in each unique situation. This contrast is familiar in the early Confucian literature with passages such as *Analects* 4.16:

> 子曰："君子喻於義，小人喻於利。"
> The Master said, "Exemplary persons (*junzi* 君子) understand what is most appropriate (*yi* 義); petty persons understand what is of personal advantage (*li* 利)."

The *Mencius* famously opens with Mencius in conversation with King Hui of Liang in which *li* as the exclusive benefit of the ruling classes is contrasted with the kind of consummate conduct (*ren* 仁) and appropriateness (*yi* 義) that allows for enjoyment to be shared with the people broadly:

> 孟子見梁惠王。王曰："叟不遠千里而來，亦將有以利吾國乎？"

孟子對曰：" 王何必曰利？亦有仁義而已矣。王曰 ' 何以利吾國'？……"

Mencius had an interview with King Hui of Liang. "You sir have come a considerable distance to see me." said the King. "What counsel then do you have that will be of benefit to my state?" "Why is it necessary to speak of 'benefit' (*li* 利)?" replied Mencius. "I only have counsel on consummate conduct (*ren* 仁) and optimal appropriateness (*yi* 義), and nothing more. Why would the King ask me: 'What counsel do you have that will be of benefit to my state'?..."

*倫 **lun.** "Order, relation, category, class." See also 理 *li.* "Patterning, coherence," 類 **lei.** "Categories, groupings," and 象 **xiang.** "Figuring, figuring out, configuring, figure, imaging, imagining, image."

Confucianism is grounded in the everyday lives of the people, and has as its source of animation the natural deference that is ubiquitous in family living. For Confucianism, the meaning and value of family relations is not just as they serve as the primary ground of social and political order; family relations have cosmological and religious implications as well. Family bonds properly observed are the point of departure for understanding that we each have moral responsibility for an expanding web of relations that, reaching far beyond our own localized selves, has cosmic consequences.

The family is conceived of as the center of all order extending outward from our persons to cosmos, and as we have seen in the *Expansive Learning*, all meaning ripples out in concentric circles that begins from personal cultivation within family, and then returns again to nourish this primary source. In fact, this same image emerges when we ask after the meaning of personal "roles" (*lun* 倫) or "the living of one's roles and relations" as this process is understood in the classical Chinese language. The character *lun* 倫 is one of a cluster of immediately cognate terms that offer various ways of characterizing radial order. We might begin from the notion of "a wheel, or taking turns" (*lun* 輪). And the notion of "bonding" in our roles is reinforced by cognates such as "selecting out" (*lun* 掄) and "twisting a cord, the woof" (*lun* 綸). This cluster of terms all share in their association of developing and strengthening a functional pattern of relations and of achieving a desired order. But the dynamic, articulate, and discursive aspects of living our roles are perhaps best captured in cognates such as "conversing, conversation" (*lun* 論), "rippling, ripples" (*lun* 淪), and the root character, "turning over in one's mind, thoughts, ordering, achieving coherence" (*lun* 侖). Indeed, this root character *lun* 侖 dates back to the oracle bones, and is constructed from an "opened mouth" and "an orderly bundle of bamboo written strips," 冊 suggesting a coherent exposition that elicits from and brings coherence to a particular written document.[①]

When we bring the various associations of this cluster of characters together, the insight gleaned is that the perceived source of growing proper "relations" is fundamentally discursive: an aggregating "relating to" and "giving an account of oneself" within the compass of one's roles that are defining first of family, and then by extension, the community at large. Simply put, a thriving, family-based community emerges from continuing familial patterns of effective communication. Said another way, "speaking" our family roles in the broadest sense of living them is the ground of coherence and order within the human experience. Family roles as a strategy for getting the most out of relations is thus an

---

① Kwan, "Database," 甲骨續存 1.477.

inspiration for order more broadly construed—social, political, and cosmic order. We might say that Confucianism is nothing more than a sustained attempt to "family" the lived human experience. For Confucian philosophy, it is through discursive living in a communicating family and community that we are able to enchant the ordinary, to ritualize the routine, to invigorate the familiar, to inspire the customary habits of life, and ultimately, to commune spiritually in the common and the everyday.

It should be noted that we need the term "role" in the English expression "Confucian role ethics" to make clear the difference this gerundive notion of person has from other ethical traditions. But "role" is actually redundant when we turn to the Chinese language. That is, "role" is already presupposed in the Chinese translation of the term "ethics" itself as *lunlixue* 倫理學, with *lunli* 倫理 meaning specifically "the quality achieved in the patterns of human roles and relations." Again, *lun* 倫 is not only used descriptively to mean roles such as "king" or "husband," but also has qualitative implications as "exemplary or ignoble" or "caring or indolent" respectively.[①]

An interesting footnote here is that this same term *lun* also means "category" and "class," suggesting that in this cosmology the construction of theoretical discriminations such as "categories" and "classifications" are a function of analogical correlations among things. Such a functional method of organizing experience stands in stark contrast to the classical Greek tradition in which categories are established through the positing of some assumed essence or self-same and reduplicative, identical characteristic—that is, some

---

① See Lydia Liu, *Translingual Practices*, p. 316 for the Han dynasty sources of this term *lunli*. Although *lunlixue* as a translation of "ethics" is a late nineteenth century term invented to synchronize the East Asian traditions with the language of Western modernity, the binomial expression *lunli* itself dates back millennia to Han dynasty sources.

eidos—shared among members of particular *genus* or *species*.① In this Confucian cosmology, categories of things broadly including humans beings are to be constructed by correlating what they *do* in the various roles they perform in relation to one another rather than by some ontological reference to what they *are*.

美 mei. "Beautiful."

On the oracle bones, the character *mei* 美 written as 𦮃 depicts a human being with head ornamentation, sometimes understood as a feathers-and-hair headdress, and sometimes as jewelry made from animal horns.② This graph *mei* 美, often translated as "beauty," is in fact much better rendered "beautiful," where the semantic difference lies in our culturally specific tendency to understand "beauty" as some given and essential quality something "has." "Beautiful" on the other hand is the description of a particular thing or event that is being referred to within its specific context. As Joseph Needham has observed with respect to early Chinese cosmology:

> Things behaved in particular ways . . . because their position in the ever-moving cyclical universe was such . . . If they did not behave in those particular ways they would lose their relational

---

① The later Wittgenstein is making a similar point with respect to language when he insists that words are not defined by core meanings present in all uses of that word. Rather, we should approach words historically and contextually, mapping them through "a complicated network of similarities, overlapping and criss-crossing." Ludwig Wittgenstein. *Philosophical Investigations (PI).* ed. G.E.M. Anscombe and R. Rhees. trans. G.E.M. Anscombe. Oxford: Blackwell,1953, Sec. 66. Wittgenstein surrenders his earlier concern for certainty and exactness and fixed boundaries when he introduces the expressions "family resemblances" and "language games"—that is, when he appeals to similarities and associations rather than strict identity and formal definitions in language usage.

② Kwan, "Database," 甲骨文合集 CHANT 0210.

position in the whole (which made them what they were), and turn into something other than themselves. They were thus parts in existential dependence upon the whole world-organism.[1]

Things are what they are because of where they are, and are thus inseparable from their narrative contexts. Needham here is echoing Tang Junyi's cosmological postulate, "One is many, many one" (*yiduobufen* 一多不分) as it insists that the identity of all things is a function of their particular context.

And as the *Zhuangzi* observes, different contexts produce different "beautifuls":

猨，猵狙以為雌，麋與鹿交，鰌與魚游。毛嬙、麗姬，人之所美也，魚見之深入，鳥見之高飛，麋鹿見之決驟。四者孰知天下之正色哉？

A gorilla will take a female ape as his mate, an elk will mount his doe, and fish will frolic about with other fish. Mao Qiang and Lady Li were eyed as great beauties by the gentlemen, but when fish see these ladies they dive into the deep, when birds see them they soar into the skies, and when deer see them they bolt for their lives. Who among these four animals knows what is the right source of arousal?

Indeed, it is because this same term *mei* 美 can be attached to so many different things and situations that it can be parsed to mean every kind of "beautiful" (*meili* 美麗, *duomei* 多美), "fine" (*meihao* 美好), "handsome" (*jianmei* 健美), "exquisite" (*youmei* 優美), "elegant" (*jingmei* 精美), "dainty" (*jiaomei* 嬌美), "pretty" (*junmei* 俊美, *meimao* 美貌), "pleasing" (*meiguan* 美觀), "improving" (*meirong* 美容), "happy" (*meiman* 美滿), "aesthetic" (*meigan* 美感, *shenmei* 審美), "majestic" (*huamei* 華美),

---

[1] See Needham, *Science and Civilisation*, Vol. II, pp. 280-281.

"magnificent" (*zhuangmei* 壯美), "moral excellence" (*meide* 美德), "splendid" (*meimiao* 美妙), "gorgeous" (*xiumei* 秀美), "charming" (*meise* 美色), "perfect" (*wanmei* 完美, *chunmei* 純美), "scenic" (*meijing* 美景), "mellow" (*chunmei* 醇美), "good reputation" (*meiyu* 美譽, *meiming* 美名), "poignant" (*qimei* 凄美), "fertile" (*feimei* 肥美), "delicious" (*meishi* 美食), "tasty" (*xianmei* 鮮美), "voluptuous" (*meiyan* 美艷), "lush" (*weimei* 味美), "scrumptious" (*bianmei* 便美), "delicate" (*meiwei* 美味, *roumei* 柔美), "sweet" (*tianmei* 甜美), "praise" (*zanmei* 讚美), "kindnesses" (*meiyi* 美意), "laudatory" (*meicheng* 美稱), "quiet and happy" (*tianmei* 恬美), "embellish" (*meihua* 美化), "smug" (*choumei* 臭美). Again *mei* can be further stretched poetically to describe "springtime beautiful" (*chunmei* 春美), "the beautiful rains" (*meiyu* 美雨), and importantly, "the finest of wines" (*meijiu* 美酒).

*民 *min*. "The common people."

The character for *min* 民, conventionally translated as "common people" appears as 🈂 on the oracle bones, and is interpreted by Guo Moruo 郭沫若 as the eye being pierced with a sharp object to make the person blind.[①] It is taken as the original form of the character for "blind" (*mang* 盲), where blindness was the mark of slaves who were being used for human sacrifice. On the bronzes during the Zhou dynasty, it appears as 🈂 where in most instances, the eye is missing its pupil.[②] By the time of these early Zhou inscriptions, and on the later Warring States texts written on bamboo strips, the term *min* had already come to refer to the common people.

The character *min* 民 seems to carry with it a range of negative connotations derived from its earliest history. The graph is the root

---

[①] Kwan, "Database," 合集 20231.
[②] Kwan, "Database," 西周早期 CHANT 2837.

of a field of cognate characters that share the primitive meaning of "blindness." For example, *min* 泯 means "troubled, confused, disorderly;" *hun* 昏 "dusk, darkness, benighted, blinded;" *men* 惛 "dark in the mind, obtuse." Another cognate, *min* 珉 is "jade," but it is an abundantly available serpentine stone or pseudo-jade that Confucius says is distained by exemplary persons as being counterfeit. For Confucius, it is not that jade is more precious than other stones because it is rarer than them, but rather that the special characteristics of real jade resonate with the qualities defining of highly cultivated persons.①

Dong Zhongshu defines the common people (*min* 民) paronomastically as "closed eyed" people (*ming* 瞑) who need to be awakened through learning:

民之號，取之瞑也。使性而已善，則何故以瞑為號？……性有似目，目臥幽而瞑，待覺而後見……譬如瞑者待覺，教之然後善。

The term we use to refer to the "common people" (*min* 民) is taken from the word "closed eyes" (*ming* 瞑). If in their natural propensities (*xing* 性) the common people are already good (*shan* 善), how could we use "closed eyes" as their term of reference? ... The natural propensities are similar to the eye. When the eye is asleep, it is closed, and must be awakened before it can see.... Just as the closed eye needs to be awakened, the common people need to be instructed before they can become good.②

The distinction between the common people (*min* 民) and "persons" (*ren* 人) we find in the *Analects* and other classical texts has

---

① *Hsün Tzu [Xunzi]*, Harvard-Yenching Institute Sinological Series, Supplement 22, Peking: Harvard-Yenching Institute, 1950, 105/30/7.
② Dong Zhongshu 董仲舒. *Luxuriant Dew of the Spring and Autumn Annals*《春秋繁露・深察名號》Chapter 35.

been the focus of some debate. The question is framed as whether or not this is a conscious class distinction between the common people (*min* 民) who have no right to office, and the upper classes (*ren* 人) who do have political status and privilege. While a first response might be the worry that this might be a recently imported distinction contrived to serve Marxist ideas about class contradictions, D.C. Lau, himself a conservative interpreter of Confucian texts, allows that this distinction has a certain plausibility. At the same time, Lau is quick to point out that the seemingly unsystematic use of these terms in the *Analects* goes a long way toward blunting the force of the contrast.①

Following Lau, we believe that a credible case can be made for a perhaps blurred yet still significant contrast in this aristocratic culture between the amorphous, indeterminate mass of common people (*min* 民), in themselves having little by way of distinguishing character or structure, and particular persons. The distinction, however, as we would understand it revealed in the *Analects* at least, is importantly a matter of culture and education rather than birth and social or political status. Confucius's egalitarian attitude toward education is captured in his claim in *Analects* 15.39: 有教無類 "I teach (*jiao* 教) everyone, regardless of class distinctions or other such discriminations." His favorite student Yan Hui was a pauper. For Confucius, persons are not entitled to political participation because they are born into an exclusive class, but instead become distinguished as a consequence of personal cultivation and the sociopolitical contribution they are able to make that follows from it. Becoming distinctive as a person is something done; an achievement rather than a given.

For Confucius, what makes people common lies at the unfortunate convergence of lack of opportunity, of capacity, and

---

① Confucius. *The Analects* (*Lunyu*). trans. D.C. Lau. Hong Kong: Chinese University Press, 1983, pp. xxxiv-xxxvi.

of application, with emphasis being placed on the latter two. In *Analects* 16.9 he declares that as for

困而不學，民斯為下矣。
The common people who will not learn even when vexed with difficulties—they are at the bottom of the heap.

In 8.9 Confucius again expresses real reservations about the capacity and the application of the common people to the important matter of becoming exemplary human beings:

民可使由之，不可使知之。
The common people can be induced to travel along the proper way, but they cannot be made to understand or realize it.

Again in 6.29, he characterizes the conduct of the common people as lacking in virtuosity:

中庸之為德也，其至矣乎！民鮮久矣。
The virtuosity (*de* 德) required to bring the familiar affairs of the day into proper focus is of the highest order. That it is rare among the common people is an old story.

The low status of the common people is clear in the *Analects* where they are frequently contrasted with "those above" (*shang* 上) who are their superiors and who are to be followed and emulated (13.4, 14.41, 19.19). Perhaps Confucius's most devastating critique of the common people is in 17.16 in which he facetiously criticizes the common people of his time, saying obliquely that, while the people of old certainly had their faults, the common people of today have taken this unfortunate condition to new heights.

Lau is clearly right in claiming that Confucius as he is portrayed in the *Analects* has a decidedly low opinion of the amorphous "masses" (*min* 民) who stand in sharp contrast to persons such as his students who are striving through assiduous personal cultivation to distinguish themselves in the world (*ren* 人). But letting Lau speak for himself:

> Confucius may not have had too high opinion of the intellectual and moral capacities of the common people, but it is emphatically not true that he played down their importance in the scheme of things. Perhaps, it is precisely because the people are incapable of securing their own welfare unaided that the ruler's supreme duty is to work on their behalf in bringing about what is good for them.[①]

The concept that the common people are the root of the state (*minben* 民本) is a position that appears relatively early in the development of Confucian political philosophy, with the position of the ruler being defined in terms of his obligations and responsibilities to his people. *Mencius* 5A5 is repeating a passage from the "Great Oath" in the *Book of Documents* when it declares:

> 天視自我民視，天聽自我民聽。
> *Tian* sees as the common people see; *tian* hears as the common people hear.

This traditional idea of "benefitting the people" (*limin* 利民) was absorbed into the Confucian doctrine at its inception to become the foundation of its political philosophy. The ruler is successful to the degree that he is able to advance the welfare of the people. This Confucian emphasis on the interests of the people is demonstrated by a survey of the representative classical texts.

[①] Confucius, *The Analects* (*Lunyu*), trans. D.C. Lau, p. xxxv.

In 20.2 Confucius when asked what kind of person can be given the reins of government, responds:

因民之所利而利之，斯不亦惠而不費乎？
Give the common people those benefits that will really benefit them—is this not being generous without being extravagant?

Again in 15.25 he says that

斯民也，三代之所以直道而行也。
It was because of the common people that the Three Ages of the Xia, Shang, and Zhou were able to continue steadfastly on the proper way.

In *Mencius* 4B16 we read:

孟子曰："以善服人者，未有能服人者也；以善養人，然後能服天下。天下不心服而王者，未之有也。"
Mencius said, "There was never a ruler who was able to win the allegiance of the people with good deeds alone. It is only when he uses such good deeds to serve their welfare that he is able to win over the empire. There has never been a True King who ruled the empire without winning the hearts of the people.

Again, in *Xunzi* 26/9/21 in the "Regulations of a True King" it states:

傳曰："君者、舟也，庶人者、水也；水則載舟，水則覆舟。"此之謂也。故君人者，欲安、則莫若平政愛民矣。
There is a traditional saying: "The ruler is the boat and his people are the water; while the water can float the boat, it can also capsize it." This is my point. If the ruler is looking for security, there is nothing better than governing fairly and loving the common people.

A familiar Confucian metaphor for the relationship between the ruler and his people is that of parent and child, the welfare of the child being the parents' most vital concern. The *Expansive Learning* cites the *Book of Songs*:

> "樂只君子，民之父母。"民之所好好之，民之所惡惡之，此之謂民之父母。
>
> "How the ruler rejoices! He is the father and mother of the common people." What the common people like, he likes; what they dislike, he dislikes. This is what it means to be father and mother to the common people.

A standard reading of this Confucian concern for the common people is that as a model of governance, it is "government of and for the people," but has no role for "government by the people." But perhaps this is too simple. The Hegelian caricature of oriental despotism where order is unilaterally imposed by the emperor from above is a perception of the Chinese conception of governance that still continues to have real currency today. The perceived isomorphism between family and state suggests that the correlation between the ideal family and sociopolitical order is to be found in the prime moral imperative of "family reverence" (*xiao* 孝) and in the aspiration to achieve and sustain a quality of ritual propriety in the roles and relations (*li* 禮) that constitute these institutions. We need a better understanding of the role of ritual propriety (*li* 禮) in effecting sociopolitical order as it establishes and sustains a broad social consensus on shared Confucian values.

*命　**ming.** "Commanding, ordering, command, mandate, the propensity of things, the force of circumstances."

Etymologically, the *Shuowen* lexicon analyzes the graph into its two components, *ling* 令 "commanding," and *kou* 口 "mouth," defining *ming* 命 as *shi* 使 "causing something to happen." There are numerous examples in the early literature of *ling* and *ming* being used interchangeably, suggesting that the fundamental idea represented by *ming* is "commanding," "causing to happen." Adding the mouth radical means that, when understood practically, the basic idea is "causing something to happen through effective communication."

The mouth radical as a symbol of the causal force of effective communication is an association shared with many of the other core concepts in the Confucian philosophical vocabulary: *zhi* 知 "knowing, realizing," *junzi* 君子 "exemplary persons," *he* 和 "superlative harmony," *shu* 恕 "deference," *xin* 信 "making good on one's word," *cheng* 誠 "sincerity, resolve, creativity," and so on. Significantly, *ming* 命 is similar in pronunciation to *ming* 名 "naming," and is on occasion used interchangeably with this character. This association with "naming" suggests both the power of language to command a world into being, and the high value of making a name for oneself through sociopolitical participation that would command the admiration and respect of others.

At some point, and quite understandably, *ming* came to designate those specific conditions that define a person's existence in the world: one's lifespan, one's social and economic status, one's physical health—not only one's "lot" in life, but one's life itself. It is in this sense that *ming* refers to the propensity of things, the force of circumstances. In any case, *ming* identifies those factors in a life over which human beings seem to have the least control. With the basic meaning of *ming* as "commanding," by extension it is often and perhaps unfortunately translated as "Fate" or "Destiny." Such an understanding of *ming* takes a person's lot within the ineluctable propensity of circumstances and makes it predetermined and irrevocable. While there are indeed circumstances over which humankind has minimal control, the nature of all relations is that they are in some degree collateral. Fate overdetermines *ming* as the unilateral prophetic and inexorable doom of the gods.

As early as the Zhou dynasty, the concept *tianming* 天命 "the mandate or command of *tian*" emerged as a condition for the ruler's continuance in office, and thus as a claim to political legitimacy. In the early corpus, this "command" of *tian*, far from being arbitrary or unilateral, is situational and collateral, being described as contingent upon and responsive to the virtuosity (*de* 德) of the ruling authority. *Tian's* command is invested in the person who has won over the people and who thus "commands" their allegiance. This allows us to understand *tianming* in a fiduciary sense. When a credible ruler commands the respect and confidence of his people expressed through their deference to his leadership, such a ruler is given cosmic sanction within this moral cosmology. Of course, this principle of legitimacy also works the other way around, serving as a warrant for rebellion against tyranny and a sanctified justification for the victor in a regicide to have overthrown the previous despotic ruler.

Tang Junyi in his survey of the early philosophical literature discerns the collaterality of *ming*, concluding that

> ... the term *"ming"* represents the interrelationship or mutual relatedness of Heaven (*tian* 天) and man. . . . [W]e can say that it exists neither externally in Heaven only, nor internally in man only; it exists, rather, in the mutuality of Heaven and man, i.e. in their mutual influence and response, their mutual giving and receiving.[①]

Given Tang's definition of *ming*, it might be compared in some

---

[①] T'ang Chun-I. "The T'ien Ming (Heavenly Ordinance) in Pre-Ch'in China." *Philosophy East and West* 11 (1962), p. 195.

ways to the alternative, holistic understanding of *ziran* 自然 causality captured in the complex notion of *shi* 勢, "conditions and circumstances." Both *ming* and *shi* describe a vital calculus of existing conditions—physical, moral, environmental—that constitute the matrix of relations collaborating to sponsor any given thing or event. This same alternative understanding of a holistic causality is expressed in *Mencius* 5A6:

皆天也，非人之所能為也。莫之為而為者，天也；莫之致而至者，命也。
All such things were brought about by *tian*; they are not things that human beings are able to do. Things that are done when there is no one who does them are the workings of *tian*; things that have no conveyance and yet arrive any way are the workings of *ming*.

Both *tian* and *ming* describe the complex ecological understanding of causality and agency in which anything has implicated within it the entire organic ecology, and is thus the product of everything else rather than of any specific, isolatable agency.

To translate *ming* as "Fate" or "Destiny," and to make proper nouns of these terms strongly hints at transcendence in which some principle, power, or agency independent of human beings legislates at least certain aspects of their existence. To cast *tianming* as an external, objectively existing moral imperative is to challenge the fundamental collateral and collaborative relationship expressed by the binomial, *tianren* 天人 itself: "the inseparability and mutuality of *tian* and human beings" captured in the mantra, *tianrenheyi* 天人合一. Absent a cosmogonic act on the part of some transcendent source of meaning and value, *ming* is a negotiation within the limitations and possibilities of one's conditioning environs that eventuates in the creation of one's world. Such environing conditions are neither predetermined nor inexorable, and inasmuch as human beings in Confucian philosophy are conceived of as meaning-makers and an important creative force in the cosmos, existing conditions and specifically one's own circumstance are in greater or lesser degree alterable through one's own participation.

We might speculate on the relationship between *tianming* and *ming* is the following way. Rehearsing the cosmology made explicit in the *Book of Changes*, we are introduced to human beings called exemplary persons (*junzi* 君子) and sages (*shengren* 聖人) who have high personal resolution and the influence that follows from it. Such persons have insight into the workings of the cosmos, and have established a strongly collaborative relationship with such forces in adapting them to the welfare of their fellow human beings. The greater the resolution and intensity in the foci of persons, the greater is their awareness of the role they can play in shaping the conditions of their lives, their *ming*. And conversely, the less intensely focused persons are, the greater their sense of the weight of *ming* as determining conditions over which they seem to exercise little control. Confucius himself is a good example of someone who is portrayed as profoundly frustrated by the circumstances of his time, but is also seen as the case of a singularly exemplary person who rose above his circumstances to change the world. Indeed, when in the fullness of time the people defer to the sage's values and virtuosity, the sage "speaks" for the world.

*明   *ming*. "Acuity, brilliance."

This graph appears on the oracle bones as ⊙⟍, and among several different explanations for the pictographic character, comprised as it is of "sun" and "moon," it captures the moment at which the sun has begun its ascent and the moon has yet to set; hence, optimal illumination.[①] Just as with the English word "bright," *ming* too

---

[①]   Kwan, "Database," 甲骨文合集 CHANT 1154C.

means both "well-illumined" and "intelligent." By extension, *ming* also means "acuity, brilliance, enlightened action." It is not through some internal struggle of reason against the passions but through "acuity" (*ming* 明)—a mirroring of the things of the world as they evolve in their interdependent relations with us—that we reach a state in which nothing among all of the myriad "goings-on" in the world will be able to agitate our heartminds. In other words, we defer to and accommodate those others who contextualize us, establishing a frictionless equilibrium that, through the cultivation of productive relationships, allows us to become one together with them. Such cultivated spontaneous action is a mirroring process. As such, it is action that accommodates the other to whom one is responding. It takes the other on its own terms. Such spontaneity requires us to recognize the continuity between oneself and the other, and to respond to it in such a way that one's own actions promote the well-being both of oneself and of the other. Such activity far from leading to imitation or replication, is the precondition for coordination and complementarity. This is the process of becoming consummate as persons (*ren* 仁) as it is advocated first in the *Analects* and then other early texts. It is this state of achieved equilibrium that is most conducive to not only symbiotic but also synergistic growth and productivity.

But this same process cosmology is the interpretive context for the earliest Daoist philosophers as well who challenge the classical Confucian thinkers to understand this primacy of vital relationality in a broader and more inclusive way, leading Confucian philosophy itself as it evolves to become more cosmic: witness texts such as *Focusing the Familiar* and the *Classic of Family Reverence*. The mirroring activity associated with Daoism is a form of activity that allows things to be themselves both in their transitoriness and in their particularity. It is the things themselves as individual events, and the orders construed from their particular perspectives, that are reflected in the mirroring process. The Daoist sages in the *Huainanzi* are described in precisely such terms:

故聖若鏡，不將不迎，應而不藏，故萬化而無傷。
Sages are like mirrors—
They neither go out to meet things nor see them off,
And respond to things without storing anything up.
Hence in a myriad of transformations they go unscathed.[①]

And again, the *Huainanzi* elaborates upon the objectivity of mirroring:

夫鏡水之與形接也，不設智故，而方圓曲直弗能逃也。
It is because the mirroring water does not in anticipating its encounter with shapes equip itself with cleverness and presuppositions that it cannot but reflect them as they really are: square, round, bent, straight.[②]

Rules of thumb, habits of action, customs, fixed standards, methodologies, stipulated concepts, categories, commandments, principles, laws of nature, all require us "to go out to meet things" and "to see them off." Having stored up past experience and prioritized things in terms of values and standards, we anticipate, recall, and celebrate a world patterned by such discriminations. Sages, however, "respond to things without storing anything up," and mirror the world at the moment without overwriting it either with the conditions of a world passed away, or by anticipation of a world yet to come.

There is this alternative notion of "objectivity" to be found in

---

[①] *A Concordance to the Huainanzi.* ed. D.C. Lau and Cheng Fong Ching. Hong Kong: The Commercial Press, 1992, 6/51/15.

[②] *A Concordance to the Huainanzi,* 1/2/13.

making an effort to mirror things as they are and in so doing, to take them on their own terms as our "guests" (*ke* 客). This mirroring attitude enables one to respect as many perspectives on a situation as are relevant to its understanding without overwriting the concerns of others with one's own needs and importances.

In the *Classic of Family Reverence*, *ming* serves as a link between the human and the natural world. It states: 昔者明王事父孝，故事天明 "of old the enlightened kings (*mingwang* 明王) served their fathers with familial reverence, and in doing so, served the heavens (*tian* 天) with their acuity" (16). That is, in enabling the people to take the 則天之明 "illumination (*ming* 明) of the heavens as their model" (7), these enlightened rulers were not only able to bring order to the human experience but also, through ancestral sacrifices conducted in the Hall of Brilliance (*mingtang* 明堂) (9), were able to coordinate the human landscape that 天下和平 "was peaceful and free of strife," with the natural landscape, so that 災害不生，禍亂不作 "natural disasters did not occur, and man-made calamities were averted" (8).

There are certain cosmological presuppositions sedimented into the classical Chinese language itself that give priority to situation over agency. That is, in this process cosmology in which our vital relationality cannot be separated from our uniqueness as persons, the language tends to describe relationally-constituted situations such as "teaching and learning" rather than the actions of separate and specific agents either teaching or learning. Here we see that *ming* 明 means "brilliance" transactionally as both the brilliance of something and the penetrating perspicacity of the person who perceives this brilliance fully. And the language is replete with just such examples. In each case, given that agency within this kind of associated conduct is always in varying degrees bilateral, the language that describes situations suggests that, rather than ascribing an individuality to actions, we must also accommodate a more inclusive sense of relational agency.

*名 **ming.** "Naming, making a name for yourself, reputation." See also 正名 **zhengming.** "Using names properly."

On the oracle bones, the graph appears as ㅂ), and is explained by Xu Shen in his *Shuowen* lexicon as persons on encountering each other in the darkness of the night announcing their names to facilitate identification and recognition.①

One narrow but important meaning of *ming* in classical Confucianism is "making a name for yourself." In the *Analects* 15.20, for example, we read:

子曰："君子疾沒世而名不稱焉。"

The Master said, "Exemplary persons (*junzi* 君子) despise the thought of ending their days without having established a name."

The point here is not to commend a crass desire for fame and fortune for its own sake, but rather to express the resolute commitment of exemplary persons to make an enduring contribution to their family and community. Young people are entitled to respect because of the potential they have to make a difference, and older people to only distain if they fail to do so. In *Analects* 9.23, Confucius insists that

後生可畏，焉知來者之不如今也？四十、五十而無聞焉，斯亦不足畏也已。

The young should be held in high esteem. After all, how do we know that those yet to come will not surpass our contemporaries? It is

---

① Kwan, "Database," 甲骨文合集 CHANT 1155.

only when one reaches forty or fifty years of age and yet has done nothing of note that we should withhold our esteem.

Herein Confucius in celebrating youth and condemning those who have not made good use of their time clearly dispels the unwarranted assumption that age devoid of accomplishment is in itself deserving of deference.

The *Classic of Family Reverence* 14 underscores the local and developmental nature of the aspiration for recognition, beginning here and going there:

是以行成於內，而名立於後世矣。
Thus, when one is successful in what one does at home, a name is established that will be passed on to posterity.

In the Confucian tradition, persons do not *perform* roles and *have* relations; in fact, they are constituted by these roles and relations. A person *is* a daughter, and a friend, and a teacher—and nothing else besides. And such persons become "individuated" and "distinguished" by achieving a quality of behavior that eventuates in patterns of deference among family and friends. Indeed, as it states in the opening chapter of the *Classic of Family Reverence*, becoming consummately filial requires:

立身行道，揚名於後世，以顯父母，孝之終也。
... distinguishing yourself and walking the proper way (*dao* 道) of the world; raising your name high for posterity and thereby bringing esteem to your father and mother—it is in these things that familial reverence finds its consummation.

But beyond this narrow sense of "making a name for yourself," there is a broader and crucially important use of "naming" that is revealing of the underlying cosmology that serves this tradition as its interpretive context. In Confucianism, with the emphasis on history, ancestor reverence, intergenerational transmission, and continuing cultural identity, there is traditionally a powerful sense of genealogical continuity where the progeny is to be understood as the foregrounding of this particular person in a continuing lineage. One's family surname (*xing* 姓) is the first and continuing source of identity, while one's given name (*ming* 名) within the course of one's lifetime is complemented by a proliferation of assumed style names (*zi* 字), sobriquets (*hao* 號), and a web of specific family designations such as "uncle number two" (*ershu* 二叔) and "auntie number three" (*sanshen* 三姉), with a series of professional titles such as "teacher" (*laoshi* 老師) and "director" (*zhuren* 主任), and then, when all is said and done, with a usually celebratory posthumous title (*shi* 謚). Each of these different names, as the roles one lives within a complex narrative, reflects one's unique contribution to the meaning of family and community.

This serial sequencing of names is most revealing of the many events that come to constitute a personal narrative. The person we know today as "Sun Yat-sen," for example, has the genealogical name of Sun Deming 孫德明, locating him in the web of the Sun family by sharing the second character *de* with both his brother Sun Mei and his other relatives of the same generation. Born in the Guangdong village of Cuiheng 翠亨, Sun arrives in Hawaii at age thirteen and is known to his family and community by his intimate "nursing name," Sun Dixiang 孫帝象, a name that means "the god's image" to remember and celebrate the local Cuiheng village deity, the "God of the North" (*beidi* 北帝). This infant name in its Cantonese pronunciation, Tai Tseong, is found on the ledger of the Punahou School he attended, but because English lacks the Cantonese phoneme "tseong," the name was rendered "Tai Chu," and he was likely called the same by his teachers and classmates. When he is later baptized as a Christian in Hong Kong at age seventeen, he takes the name Sun Rixin 孫日新 "daily renewing," an expression that is an allusion to the *Book of Changes*. In the same year a mentor gives him the name Sun Yixian 孫逸仙, "liberated immortal" (pronounced "Yat-sen" in Cantonese), and from then on this becomes his formal name within the English-speaking world. In any official Chinese documents, however, and in his calligraphy as well, he uses his "big name" (大名), Sun Wen 孫文 as "Sun the cultured." And along the way, he assumes the courtesy name (字), Sun Zaizhi 孫載之, taken from the familiar expression introduced by Zhou Dunyi, "culture is how way-making is conveyed" 文以載道, as a play on his "big name" "cultured" (*wen* 文). In addition to the Zhongshan county in Guangdong province, every major city in China today remembers Sun Yat-sen with their "Zhongshan" (中山) parks and "Zhongshan" main streets, and Guangzhou has its Zhongshan University 中山大學. But where did this name come from? Sun Zhongshan 孫中山, and more often "Dr." Sun Zhongshan 孫中山先生, is taken from his Japanese alias "Nakayama Shō" 中山樵. Sun used this Japanese name while hiding from agents and spies enlisted by the Qing Court who dogged him relentlessly in Japan and around the world as he schemed to foment a revolution that would ultimately topple the Qing dynasty. And finally, in death, Sun Yat-sen has come to be known affectionately by a grateful China as *guofu* 國父 ("the father of our nation") locating this cosmopolitan figure squarely within the continuing genealogy of the Chinese people.

Sun Yat-sen's many names tell his complex story. Philosophically speaking, "meaning" as "sense," or "making sense" of something, requires that we acknowledge the narrative function of language wherein the social and political context is always integral to the meaning of what is being said. The application of such correlative pragmatics that relate persons to the events of their lives and that amplify the meaning of these episodes is not only retrospective but also importantly prospective and programmatic as well, constantly being deployed to anticipate new situations and to extend our complex, continuous, and evolving narratives.

*内外 *neiwai*. "Inner and outer, inside and outside." See also 心 *xin*. "Heartmind, bodyheartminding, thinking and feeling."

In the Confucian conception of persons, the distinctions between the related notions of "inner and outer" (*neiwai* 内外) and "subjectivity and objectivity" (*zhuke* 主客) far from being dualistic, are a matter of aspect rather than exclusivity, a matter of degree rather than kind. As correlative *yinyang* categories, they are complementary, and can only be understood in terms of each other. In the project of seeking optimum coalescence with the content of our various environments, achieving what is optimally fitting in these relations (*yi* 宜) speaks to objectivity, while self-consciously finding and disposing ourselves in the most appropriate way in these same relations (*yi* 義) is our subjectivity.[1]

The focus-field notion of whole persons assumed in this Confucian cosmology stands in contrast to our familiar realist-derived conception of a private inner domain and a shared outer world. Charles Hartshorne problematizes our commonsense understanding of our ostensive "inner" and "outer" worlds by elaborating on what A.N. Whitehead calls the fallacy of simple location that would place persons "outside"

---

[1] In *Focusing the Familiar* 20, "what is optimally appropriate" (*yi* 義)—that is, what is the source of moral growth—has been defined paronomastically as "what is most fitting" (*yi* 宜) in any particular situation, providing a warrant for reading this character here as what is optimally appropriate as a source of moral as well as phenomenal significance. See Roger T. Ames and David L. Hall. *Focusing the Familiar: A Translation and Philosophical Interpretation of the Zhongyong*. Honolulu: University of Hawaii Press, 2001, p. 101.

and independent of each other by. As an alternative, Hartshorne offers us his version of an interpenetrating, focus-field conception of persons:

> [A]s Whitehead has most clearly seen—individuals generally are not simply outside each other (the fallacy of "simple location") but in each other, and God's inclusion of all things is merely the extreme or super-case of the social relativity or mutual immanence of individuals.①

Hartshorne is posing the question: If we are not externally related in standing "outside" of each other, what then is the nature of our relationship to one another? And in his answer, he insists on the holographic and mutual implicating and interpenetrating understanding of persons in their relations with others. Each of us is a crowd.

The focus-field understanding of relationally-constituted persons is a Confucian answer to the same question. And in its response, it begins from an ecology of internal, constitutive relations. We begin as cells in an organism, evolve as increasingly self-conscious organisms within an ecology, and then become increasingly aware of ourselves as centered ecologies within an unbounded and unsummed galaxy of ecologies.

To make this point, we might recall *Mencius* 7A4 that expresses this "inner-outer" dynamic in a focus-field and holographic way:

孟子曰："萬物皆備於我矣。反身而誠，樂莫大焉。強恕而行，求仁莫近焉。"

Mencius said, "Is there any enjoyment greater than, with the

---

① Charles Hartshorne. *A History of Philosophical Systems*. New York: Philosophical Library, 1950, p. 443.

myriad things of the world all implicated here in me, to turn personally inward and to thus find resolution with these things? Is there any way of seeking to become consummate in my person more immediate than making every effort to act empathetically by deferring to the interests of others?"

In this passage, we see first that becoming consummate as a human being is a holographic process. There is a symbiosis between self-consciously consolidating my relations within the focus of my own personal identity, and deferentially expanding the field of relevance of this focal identity outward; between self-consciously bringing these same relations into meaningful resolution (*cheng* 誠), and deferring to and finding the optimally appropriate fit in the expanding circle of empathetic relations that converge to constitute myself (*shu* 恕). The foregrounding backgrounding shift here is between existential growth in one's self-critical awareness and deference to one's world, between foregrounding either the self-conscious resolution of one's insistent particularity (*de* 德) or the quality of one's life's narrative as it contributes to the unsummed narratives of the totality (*dao* 道). From the former perspective, my unique identity is foregrounded as I examine the existential quality of the coalescence I have achieved with my environing others and what they have come to mean as integral to who I am becoming. And in the latter, the extended field of my world is foregrounded as it is construed and brought into meaningful resolution from my own unique perspective. The quality of resolution in my own identity determines the extent to which I have influence in the world, and the extent to which this world is a better one because of me. In this way, not only are the myriad happenings of the world all implicated here in me, but perhaps more importantly, these same events are made increasingly meaningful by virtue of my capacity to give full resolution to my connectivity with them in my own person.

Focusing the Familiar 25 describes this symbiosis between inner and outer, where the deepening of the relations between inner and outer is the correlation between becoming increasingly self-consciously consummate in our always relational activities, and the wisdom such conduct inspires in the world around us:

> 誠者非自成己而已也，所以成物也。成己，仁也；成物，知也。性之德也，合外內之道也，故時措之宜也。
>
> But resolve is not simply the self-consummating of one's own person; it is what consummates everything. Completing oneself is achieving virtuosity in one's roles and relations (*ren* 仁); completing all things is advancing wisdom in the world (*zhi* 知). Such is the virtuosity achieved in one's natural propensities and the way-making that integrates what is more internal and what is more external. Thus, when and wherever one applies this virtuosity, it is fitting.

This focus-field model requires a gestalt shift in our understanding of persons in which their particular identities and the unsummed totality—their foregrounded, always uniquely self-conscious foci and their overlapping fields—are two holographic and thus mutually entailing ways of perceiving the same phenomenon. Just as each unique note as it is played within the context of a symphony requires an awareness that this note has implicated within it the entire performance and must be evaluated accordingly, so each focal event—that is the identity expressed through each self-conscious moment in a person's life—has implicated within it this person's entire, unbounded, narrative field.

To take just one among these dualisms as an example, our commonsense prompts us to read subject and object as being dualistic terms that are exclusive of each other. But when we reflect on the Chinese understanding of such distinctions, they have a coterminous relationship as correlative, aspectual categories in which each term is interdependent with and understood in terms of its dyadic relationship with the other. Reflecting on the "objective" and "subjective" dualism inherited out of the Greek tradition as the historical background of our commonsense, the assumption is that "objectivity" with its "impartiality" is the presumptive source of fact and truth. Objectivity not only stands exclusive of "subjectivity," but indeed effectively negates it as being partial, and offering us nothing more than a plethora of obfuscating opinions. *Episteme* excludes *doxa*. But in the translation of "subjective" and "objective" into the Chinese language as *zhuke* 主客—literally as "host" and "guest" respectively—these two terms stand in an interdependent *yinyang* 陰陽 relationship where the first term is immediately implicated in and can only be understood in its relation with the second. For this process cosmology, there is nothing and no one that can stand independent of its context as either purely objective or purely subjective. Given the wholeness of experience, everything and anything can only be subjective or objective as a matter of degree. Within this Confucian worldview, objectivity and subjectivity are mutually entailing as "the inseparability of one and many" (*yiduobufen* 一多不分), and impartiality is achieved not by excluding subjectivity, but by giving it full register. It is the inclusion of and collaboration among all of the competing perspectives that are the substance of objectivity—the one that emerges from the many.

What this means for heartmind (*xin* 心) of course, is that erstwhile inner and outer domains are irreducibly reflexive, with the objective world always being experienced from one self-conscious perspective or another, and with the subjective world always having the objective world adumbrated within it. With heartmind (*xin* 心), all of these many aspectual distinctions, rather than serving to separate and isolate different components within the "bodyheartminding" experience and thereby fragment the activities that are defining of it, instead reflect the interdependence and interpenetration of the matrix of myriad aspects that function together to constitute the complex human narrative.

*氣 **qi.** "Vital energy, *qi.*" See also 生 **sheng.** "Living, growing, birthing," and 勢 **shi.** "Purchase, momentum, configuration."

The ancient form of this character was *qi* 气 and then the *mi* 米 radical was added at some later time as a phonetic. *Qi* first appears on the Shang oracle bones and on the Zhou bronze inscriptions as a hieroglyph with three horizontal lines ☰. Even though the three lines were usually shorter and somewhat more fluid than the character for the number "three" ☰ (*san* 三), it was still too similar, and as a consequence the top and bottom lines became curved over time as a mark of differentiation. The *Shuowen* lexicon explains *qi* as a pictographic character and defines it as "cloud *qi*" (*yunqi* 雲氣), depicting as it does multiple layers of ascending and descending vapors. This dynamic, functional aspect of *qi*—the image of the ascending and descending of vapors—is integral to an understanding of the vitality of this key element in the early natural cosmology. While "being *per se*" is the basis of classical Greek ontology, the idea of "living" and "growing" (*sheng* 生) understood both existentially and prescriptively is the starting point of what we might call classical Chinese "zoetology" or "the art of living." One way to think of *qi* is that, in the ongoing process of transformation, it is the combination of this existential life-force and its constantly changing, autogenerative configurations (*shi* 勢).

Qi properly understood provides insight into how in this world of interpenetrating events, the myriad things are constantly transforming and being transformed in their relations to each other. The familiar translation as "material force" unfortunately introduces a form/matter, sentient/insentient dualism that has little relevance for this cosmology. Various neologisms have been offered as a translation of *qi*: "vital energy," "ether," "hylozoistic vapors," "psychophysical stuff." Wing-tsit Chan renders it "vital force." It is significant that this term has such importance in understanding early Chinese cosmology and is so resistant to the assumptions that ground substance ontology, that it has come into European languages without being translated, and is referred to simply as "*qi*" (or as "*ki*" in its Japanese pronunciation).

Kwong-loi Shun in the preamble to his discussion of the references to *qi* found in the *Mencius*, rehearses passages from the classical anthologies of historical stories, the *Zuozhuan* 左傳 and the *Guoyu* 國語, that expound upon *qi* as the vital energies making up and animating the natural world around us.[1] Although the systematized and elaborate *yinyang wuxing* 陰陽五行 "five phases" cosmology does not appear explicitly until Han dynasty sources, the idea that the world and its evolving phenomena are defined in terms of *qi* is already widely attested in the late 4th C. and early 3rd C. BCE in the *Daodejing*, the *Zhuangzi*, and the *Mencius* as well as in other early historical sources. In the cosmological speculations of the Han dynasty, *qi* came to be understood as how things congeal and disperse, and was characterized in terms of the active and passive dynamics of *qian* 乾 and *kun* 坤, and *yang* 陽 and *yin* 陰. In the several discourses in which Mencius himself invokes the language of *qi*, he is not, as suggested by some commentators, waxing mystical.[2]

---

[1] Kwong-loi Shun. *Mencius and Early Chinese Thought*. Stanford: Stanford University Press, 1997, pp. 67-68.

[2] Chad Hansen, in *A Daoist Theory of Chinese Thought*, Hong Kong: Oxford University Press, 1994, p. 175, is not alone among scholars who would describe Mencius on *qi* as a "moral mysticism."

On the contrary, Mencius is simply making explicit the commonsense of his own time and place in Warring States China. Indeed, to make sense of the *qi* worldview in our own times, we might consider it the classical Chinese analog of the now largely unconscious quantitative, genetic, and atomistic assumptions that began for Western culture in classical Greek ontology, and that continue to inform our own commonsense.

A contemporary yet problematic interpretation of *qi* found in both the Chinese and Western philosophical literature is that it is a "substance monism" familiar to us in classical Greek ontology, where all things are differentiated as a manifestation of *qi*, but unified as being grounded in a permanent, primordial, and single substance like the Greek *ouisia* (being essence). *Qi* has to be distinguished from either "basic matter" or "animating vapors" in that it will not be resolved into any kind of substance-attribute, form-matter, spiritual-material, or thing-stuff dichotomy. *Qi* is at once the *whatness* of things and also their dynamic life force. It is both the formal yet always transforming determinacy of things, their structure (*ti* 體), and what they do to and for each other in their functional relations (*yong* 用).

It is a commonplace in classical Western interpretations of the vital and spiritual character of things to appeal to a physical and spiritual dichotomy, assuming that the animating principle is distinguishable from the things it animates. But in this underlying Confucian cosmology, there are no erstwhile "things" to be animated; there is only the vital energizing field and the synergy of the ongoing focal transformations that are taking place within it.

In understanding *qi*, we must respect the underlying cosmological postulate, "the many are one, the one many" (*yiduobufenguan* 一多不分觀). *Qi* is both the multiplicity of distinctive events as well as the continuity that obtains among them. The energy of ceaseless transformation is inherent in the events of this world's narrative, where all things are in various degree energized and animated. *Qi* is both the animating energy and what is animated, where these are two nonanalytic aspects of one and the same reality—two ways of looking at the same thing. A corollary to this holistic notion of "invigorated world-ing" is the absence of any final boundary between the sentient and insentient, animate and inanimate, living and lifeless.

In thinking through *qi* then, we must begin from the wholeness and transitory nature of experience. Tang Junyi reports on the eventful and fluid nature of this process cosmology, and the absence of any appeal to a foundation and causal substance:

> In the minds of Chinese people, the cosmos has always been nothing more than a continuous stream, a kind of flow; all of the things and events of the cosmos are just a continuing process. And beyond this process there is not some other fixed substratum that supports it.[①]

The energy of transformation resides within the world itself, and is expressed in what *Zhuangzi* calls the perpetual "transforming together with things and events" (*wuhua* 物化). *Qi* is this understanding of the continuing unfolding of unique events in a focus-field process of cosmic change that early on became a kind of commonsense or worldview implicitly assumed in the texts of this period.

In reflecting on how *qi* functions, we might invoke process philosopher A.N. Whitehead who himself challenges and dismisses our own commonsense idea of "things" and their "simple location." Indeed, for Whitehead the very assumption that there is a world comprised of deracinated "individuals" who are perceiving a

---

① Tang Junyi, *Complete Works* Vol. 11, p. 9: "中國人心目中之宇宙恒只為一種流行，一種動態；一切宇宙中之事物均只為一種過程，此過程以外別無固定之體以為其支持者（substratum）。"

world of discrete "things" wherein all such persons and things are defined by external relations that obtain among them is a prime and prominent example of what he calls the "fallacy of simple location." This misstep in our thinking in nothing other than the familiar and yet fallacious assumption that isolating, decontextualizing, and analyzing "things" as simple particulars is the best way to understand the content of our experience. Whitehead rejects a world of "objects" as being mere retrospective, second order abstractions from our continuous experience, and argues the fundamental realities of both experience and nature itself are best understood as irreducibly extended, transitory, and interdependent events. For Whitehead, with respect to persons, the notion of the discrete individual is a specific and persistent example of what he calls the "fallacy of misplaced concreteness." This second fallacy is closely related to regarding abstracted entities presumed to have a simple location as being "more real" than their "transitivity," that is, more real than their field of dynamic, extended relations and all of the untidy transitions and conjunctions that constitute the genuine content of any event in the human experience.[①]

In reporting on the early Chinese alternative to metaphysical realism and the commonsense of substance ontology that projects a mind-independent world of discrete "things," Joseph Needham characterizes the Chinese cosmology in the following terms:

> The key-word in Chinese thought is *Order* and above all *Pattern* (and if I may whisper it for the first time, *Organism*). The symbolic correlations or correspondences all formed part of one colossal pattern. Things behaved in particular ways not necessarily because of prior actions or impulsions of other things, but because their position in the ever-moving cyclical universe was such that they

---

[①] Whitehead. *Modes of Thought*. New York: MacMillan, 1938, p. 137.

were endowed with intrinsic natures which made their behaviour inevitable for them. If they did not behave in those particular ways they would lose their relational position in the whole (which made them what they were), and turn into something other than themselves. They were thus parts in existential dependence upon the whole world-organism. And they reacted upon one another not so much by mechanical impulsion or causation as by a kind of mysterious resonance.①

In this cosmology, instead of positing a world of discrete and independent "things" each occupying a particular place, it is an alternative world in which interdependent and interpenetrating events defined by their contextualizing relations are "taking place."

Qi as energizing field is expressed as the unique and always changing focus of every "thing" that comes to constitute our experience. The resolute uniqueness of these always situated "things" precludes the existence of forms or ideas or categories or principles or inviolate species that provide a ground for a doctrine of natural kinds. Thus, "things" begin from their uniqueness, and are sorted, grouped, and generalized (*tuilei* 推類) as they are associated with each other by perceived qualitative resonances and analogies derived from specific conditions. Discriminations are made in terms of observed and conventional classifications associated with diurnal and seasonal changes, directions, deities, colors, tastes, sounds, numbers, smells, body parts, and so forth. Such dynamic, relational discriminations and mutually informing correlations, far from being final in any sense, are described by Needham as processive and diffusive "patterns simultaneously appearing in a vast field of force, the dynamic structure of which we do not yet understand."②

---

① Needham, *Science and Civilisation*, Vol. II, pp. 280-281.
② Needham, *Science and Civilisation*, Vol. II, p. 291.

As Needham goes on to report, it is the aggregation and application of these productive correlations that enables us to act effectively:

> The sum of wisdom consisted in adding to the number of intuited analogical correspondences in the repertory of correlations.[①]

To take an example of such associated thinking, an understanding of the correlation between emotions and physical well-being provides us with a wisdom that takes us beyond hypochondria as an adequate explanation of depression to a functional awareness of the centrality of feeling in the quality of one's health.

The division of the world not into kinds, but into correlative "*yinyang*" qualities is implicit in the natural cosmology of a proto-Chinese worldview that can be documented as far back as the Shang dynasty. As Wing-tsit Chan has pointed out, the interdependence and inseparability of structure (or formation) and function characteristic of this correlative *qi* cosmology—or more simply put, what things are "becoming" and what they are "doing"—is implicit in the correlative *yinyang* vocabulary of the early texts. Such associations are persistent in the tradition, and over the centuries become an explanatory vocabulary expressed in a proliferation of correlative pairings such as "reforming and functioning" (*tiyong* 體用), "knowing (or realizing) and doing" (*zhixing* 知行), and so on.[②]

In *Daodejing* 42 we read:

萬物負陰而抱陽，沖氣以為和。
Everything carries *yin* on its shoulders and *yang* in its arms
And blends these vital energies (*qi* 氣) together to make them

---

[①] Needham, *Science and Civilisation*, Vol. II, p. 290.
[②] Wing-tsit Chan. *A Source Book in Chinese Philosophy*. Princeton. Princeton University Press, 1963, p. 141.

harmonious (*he* 和).

All things are constituted of contrastive relations that can be made most productive—that is, healthy and robust—through the application of a nuanced imagination and the process of correlation that such insight inspires. In the classical Daoistic literature we have sources such as the meditative "Inward Training" (*neiye* 內業) chapter of the *Guanzi* 管子 that elaborate upon this "harmonizing" with techniques of correct posture, diet, and breath control aimed at bringing the internal landscape into harmony with its external conditions, thereby enabling the practitioner to achieve health and long life.

Needham draws on Marcel Granet to provide what is a vivid description of the unfamiliar cosmological vision we need as our interpretive context for understanding this vocabulary, alerting us not only to what this cosmology is, but perhaps more importantly, to what it is not:

> Social and world order rested, not on an ideal of authority, but on a conception of rotational responsibility. The Tao [*dao*] was the all-inclusive name for this order, an efficacious sum-total, a reactive neural medium; it was not a creator, for nothing is created in the world, and the world was not created. . . . Chinese ideals involved neither God nor Law. The uncreated universal organism, whose every part, by a compulsion internal to itself and arising out of its own nature, willingly performed its functions in the cyclical recurrences of the whole, was mirrored in human society by a universal ideal of mutual good understanding, a supple regime of interdependences and solidarities which could never be based on unconditional ordinances, in other words, on laws.[1]

---

[1] Needham, *Science and Civilisation in China*, Vol. II, p. 290.

In thus identifying an underlying correlation between the functioning of the natural cosmology and the human values that must guide the emergence of a coordinated and collaborative sociopolitical order, Needham is reporting on the irreducibly moral nature of this *qi* cosmology. There is a perceived coincidence among the notions of life, growth, morality, and education. Tang Junyi finds the moral aspect of this cosmology to be made explicit in the language of the *Book of Changes*:

> *The Commentary on the Book of Changes* holds that the whole existential process in the universe is a process of generation and evolution through intercourse. And the generation and evolution of a thing are themselves activities of positive values, and exhibit a moral character. Hence, this natural universe is still a universe filled with moral values, no matter whether the human mind has achieved self-consciousness or not and whether the human spirit has any part in it or not.[①]

Needham offers his explanation of *dao* as "the universal uncreated organism" that is also often described as the "source" of all things. In asserting that it "was not a creator, for nothing is created in the world, and the world was not created," Needham means that this cosmology brings with it an alternative understanding of creativity. That is, creativity is "self-so-ing" (*ziran* 自然) as an autopoietic force that animates the world. This kind of "co-creativity" is the continuing *in situ* or "situated" increase in growth and meaning that would defy any *ex nihilo* separation between creator and creature.

[①] Tang Junyi."Chang Tsai's Theory of Mind and Its Metaphysical Basis". 唐君毅全集 (*The Complete Works of Tang Junyi*) Vol. 29. Beijing: Jiuzhou Press, 2016, p. 170. This English translation was originally published under the title 張橫渠之心性論及其形上學之根據 in 東方文化 *Journal of Oriental Studies*, I, No. I (January 1954).

The furniture of the world is not created in the sense of emerging out of nothing, and it does not suffer annihilation in the sense of returning to nothing. *Dao* and the myriad things (*wanwu* 萬物), rather than referencing distinct, separate realities, are two aspectual ways of looking at the same always-transforming phenomenal world and our continuing vital experience within it.

Granet appeals to this language of "aspect" to express the way in which erstwhile "things" are in fact dynamic matrices of productive relations that constitute continuous, extended events:

> Instead of observing successions of phenomena, the Chinese registered alternations of aspects. If two aspects seemed to them to be connected, it was not by means of a cause and effect relationship, but rather "paired" like the obverse and converse of something, or to use a metaphor from the *Book of Changes*, like echo and sound, or shadow and light.[①]

Granet is here reflecting on the resonant tensile "pairings" among the dynamic alternations of aspect defining of all events. There is the synoptic tension expressed as *yinyang* (陰陽), and then "field" and "focus" (*daode* 道德), "determinacy" and "indeterminacy" (*youwu* 有無), "change" and "continuity" (*biantong* 變通), "the heavens" and "the earth" (*tiandi* 天地), "the world" and "the human experience" (*tianren* 天人), "forming" and "functioning" (*tiyong* 體用), "the social grammar" and its "musicality" (*liyue* 禮樂), "heartminding" and "spirituality" (*xinshen* 心神), "intensity" and "extensiveness" (*jingshen* 精神), "the lived body" and "heartminding" (*shenxin* 身心), "the consummatory" and "the optimally appropriate" (*renyi* 仁義), and so on. To take "determinacy" and "indeterminacy" (*youwu* 有無) as one example, these terms are a nonanalytic,

---

[①] Cited in Needham, *Science and Civilisation*, Vol. II, pp. 290-291.

explanatory vocabulary of "aspects" that we must appeal to in giving a fair account of the ceaseless emergence of any of the things and events that come to constitute the continuing human experience. The embodied definition and intelligibility of persons is one way of perceiving them; their vitality, creativity, and unpredictability is another. And we cannot separate out such aspectual distinctions analytically. Such an ineluctable process of transformation requires a gerundive, explanatory language such as "forming" (*ti* 體) and "functioning" (*yong* 用) to report on the mutuality of structure and performance as the world turns.

In understanding what Needham means here by "rotational responsibility" with each thing having "a compulsion internal to itself," we will have to recall the doctrine of internal relations and the alternative, holistic "causality" it entails. In this classical cosmology, the animating and transforming *qi* 氣 is conceptualized in terms of what in modern parlance we might call a "vital energy field" in which "things" are sometimes more and sometimes less persistent focal events with constantly changing horizons within this field. Having arisen, these intertwined, interpenetrating "events" in all of their diversity continue in the fullness of time to transform into other things. The vital field is not only pervasive as a condition of all things, but consistent with Needham's description of this field as "a reactive neural medium," it is also the "neural," existential medium through which all situated things emerge in their transactional relations to constitute what they are becoming. There is neither animating *qi* without structuring form, nor form without vital *qi*. There is no objective world without an existential, subjective experience of it.

The focus-field cosmology that Granet and Needham are ascribing to this Chinese worldview, and the aspectual language needed to give it voice are revealing of what Needham is referring to as "the universal uncreated organism" with "its own causality and its own logic." With respect to causality then, given the vital, internal, and constitutive nature of the relations that underlies the focus-field holography, causality does not reference some agency outside and temporally prior to the perceived configuration of the things that are happening, but rather speaks to the creative, interdependent, and causal nature of the vital relations themselves. We can select one of the philosophical canons—*Daodejing* 51—that in drawing upon the *Great Commentary* cosmology might serve us as a test case. This example illustrates how an understanding of the holographic cosmology described by Granet and Needham above is necessary to produce an interpretation of this text sufficiently robust to do justice to the alternative causality and logic it assumes:

> 道生之，德畜之，物形之，勢成之。是以萬物莫不尊道而貴德。道之尊，德之貴，夫莫之命常自然。
> Way-making (*dao* 道) brings all things to life,
> Their virtuosity (*de* 德) provides them with nourishment,
> Environing things shape them,
> And their contextualizing circumstances (*shi* 勢) usher them to completion.
> It is thus that all things revere way-making and esteem virtuosity.
> As for this reverence and esteem,
> It just arises spontaneously without anything decreeing it to be so.

This text describes how the quality of deference expressed within the lived ecology of things is the source of their moral character; their "virtuosity" (*de* 德) is their "getting and gaining" (*de* 得) as they grow and coalesce in their relations with other things. Putative "things" are shared horizons, and thus are only convenient abstractions from persistent and continuous matrices of interdependent relations. And these relations do not terminate anywhere, but reach out to the furthest limits of the cosmos. Any particular "thing" or situation emerges at the pleasure of every other situation, and is thus at once a cause and an effect. If we understand relationality as first order reality and all individual actors as abstractions, then we must understand the term *ziran* 自然 or autogenerative "self-so-ing" as it appears here as the backgrounding and foregrounding relationship between particular focus and unbounded field. *Ziran* means that the "self" (*zi* 自) in the "self-so-ing" process has two aspects. It is first an expression of the uniqueness of each insistent particular. And secondly, this particularity is inclusive of all of the extended relations of a thing or event as this manifold of relations conspires and gives life to the presencing of a unique conatus (*ran* 然) that makes anything insistently so. The pervasive reverence and esteem for way-making and the virtuosity it engenders emerges spontaneously among things as they are shaped by their environments and as they are ushered by the propensity of circumstances to their fruition. Beyond the process itself there is no invisible hand that makes it so.

Tang Junyi tries to capture the flux and flow of unique events within the operations of this generative *qi* cosmology in the following terms:

> Each so-called thing is but a process of beginning and ending, extension and contraction. It is generated through the intercourse of preceding things, and therefore, unless there is transformation of preceding things, a thing will not be brought into existence. Now that this thing is here, it is in turn in intercourse with other things and engaged in activity. And were it not for the spirituality, i.e., extension, character in the thing, it could not have produced any activity. Since the generation of a thing depends on the transformation of preceding things, there must be a difference between the thing generated and the preceding things. On the other hand, since this thing is a successor and continuation of the preceding things, there

must also be a degree of unity between them.①

Tang uses his own person to describe this interpenetrating, holographic cosmology in which all things including our physical bodies penetrate into everything else, and everything else is adumbrated in each of our embodied persons:

> The form-matter of my body is not a constant thing but is always in a process of transformation and intercourse with other things. The process of transformation means the process of transmutation of the thing, and intercourse with other things means penetration into them. Hence, the nature by which I am constituted to be I is actually my power of transcending myself and taking unto myself things and persons that used to be other than I. And the form-matter that has become the form-matter of my body is also that which is constantly being formed by the condensation of cosmic ether and constantly being dissolved and diffused back into the cosmic ether. Therefore, I can never hold that there is an I or my body existing separately from other things in the universe; neither can I say that my nature is merely to conserve and maintain my material body; on the contrary, I should say that my nature is to enter into intercourse with all things in the universe, and by the void nature of the mind it is to perceive all, prehend all, regarding other persons and things as myself, and it is universally to bestow our emotions and wills to all things with which we have intercourse.②

Qi is an image that, like water, is deliberate and provocative, defying Plato's project of knowing things through formal definition, and resisting any of the Aristotelian categories that have come to

---

① Tang Junyi, "Chang Tsai's Theory of Mind and Its Metaphysical Basis," p. 169.
② Tang Junyi, "Chang Tsai's Theory of Mind and Its Metaphysical Basis," p. 173.

structure and discipline our language and our thinking. That is, *qi* is at once one and many. When it accumulates and coagulates, it can have a formal coherence by taking on a shape inspired by its context that is persistent and yet changing too. Axiologically, *qi* is again both noble and base. It is conceived of through the analogy of water, where water is life-giving and purifying, irrigating our world and cleansing our bodies and spirits. At the same time, water is destructive and contaminating, working its way down through the bowels and into the sewers to offend against polite human sensibilities. Similarly, the most refined spiritual aspects of the most refined things such as human beings are constituted by the most refined *qi*, while the baser more physical aspects of the same human being is of a baser *qi*. And just as water can be a "thing" (water) and an "action" (to water) and an "attribute" (moist) and a "modality" (cascading) all at the same time, so too *qi* will not be resolved into categories that would separate forming from functioning, or subject from object. That is, water is not simply an objective phenomenon, but constitutes our own life and vitality that allows us to grow the world around us from within it.

*情 *qing.* "Emotions, passions, feelings, the way things are, situation, circumstances."

One significant contribution that has emerged from the ongoing archaeological finds in contemporary China has been the reinstatement of *qing* as a central philosophical concept in the formative pre-Qin texts. After the death of Confucius himself, the Zisizi-Mengzi lineage (*simengpai* 思孟派) that we associate with Confucius's grandson Zisizi 子思子 and Mencius develops an epistemology of concrete feelings that then becomes fundamental to the evolving Confucian tradition. This is an epistemology of affect in the prospective and performative sense of not just passively cognizing the world, but of "realizing" and thus "making real" a desired world. As a consequence of these newly recovered texts, scholars have had to rethink our more cognitive, conceptual, and theoretical interpretations of the early Confucian canons to be sure that we have given the affective dimension of personal cultivation and its effects sufficient consideration.

The importance of *qing* becomes elevated in the evolution of Confucianism because of the perceived role that properly focused human feeling is assumed to have on an emerging cosmic order. *Focusing the Familiar* appeals directly to "superlative harmony" and "equilibrium" in its own iteration of the holistic and aspirational Confucian project of coordinating human actions with their environments, where the achieved quality of the human experience is understood as having immediate and dramatic repercussions for the world around us. The opening passage of *Focusing the Familiar* traces cosmic flourishing back to the achieved harmony of human feelings:

> 喜怒哀樂之未發, 謂之中; 發而皆中節, 謂之和; 中也者, 天下之大本也; 和也者, 天下之達道也。致中和, 天地位焉, 萬物育焉。
> The condition when the feelings of pleasure and anger, grief and enjoyment have yet to arise is called a nascent equilibrium (*zhong* 中); having arisen, that these feelings are then coordinated and brought into proper measure is called superlative harmony (*he* 和). This notion of equilibrium is the great root of the world; superlative harmony then is the advancing of the proper way (*dadao* 達道) in the world. When equilibrium and focus are sustained and harmony is fully realized, the heavens and earth maintain their proper places and all things flourish in the world.

This passage begins from a description of our initial human conditions—those latent, native but as yet unexpressed feelings—that provide us with the affective resources for engaging the world effectively. It is because we are able to cultivate ourselves as responsive, feeling creatures that we have the capacity to become a truly transformative force that shapes and heightens the meaning of the ceaseless process of procreation. The notion of "feelings" here has to be read as a more holistic, capacious, and inclusive human responsiveness that has the potential to generate growth in meaning and to aestheticize the human experience and everything in it. As David Wong and others have argued, we do not find the Greek separation of emotions and reason and somaticity in these classical Confucian texts, or any assumed tension among these capacities that might follow from such a disjunction.①

Our feelings in this broad, cosmic sense seek their satisfaction by pursuing a productive continuity within the contours of the concrete world as we actually come to embody it. But such feelings can only become a powerful resource when they are properly cultivated to achieve both a deep coalescence (*zhongjie* 中節) and a superlative symbiosis (*he* 和) in these expansive relations. It is the personal resolution (*cheng* 誠) needed to be cosmic co-creators with the heavens and the earth that makes the human being an essential player in the flourishing of our world. And it is only through deepening and achieving proper measure (*du* 度) in the correlative "human and cosmic" relationship (*tianrenheyi* 天人合一) as one of the collaborating three powers (*sancai* 三才)—the heavens, the earth, and the human being—that exemplary persons can make their profound contribution to cosmic meaning. Such clear resolution and the human sagacity it produces is the very source out of which the flourishing world order emerges, and as such, adds additional

---

① David B. Wong. "Is There a Distinction Between Reason and Emotion in Mencius?". *Philosophy East and West* 41. No. 1 (1991), p. 31. Myeong-seok Kim disputes Wong's claim in her subsequent essay, "Is There No Distinction Between Reason and Emotion in *Mengzi*?". *Philosophy East and West* 64 (2014), No. 1.

momentum to the life force that guides the cosmos on its proper course. And there is a human return on this contribution. In having risen to the level of co-creators, our unique sense of felt worth and belonging is the substance of real religious experience, and gives *Focusing the Familiar* as the highest statement of the Confucian project its profound religious significance.

The name of Zisizi has loomed large in its association with the recent archaeological finds, and we have come to associate five philosophical terms with his contribution: *tian* 天 (conventionally translated as "Heaven"), "command" (*ming* 命) "human propensities" (*xing* 性), "feelings" (*qing* 情), and "heartmind" (*xin* 心). In the opening line of this same *Focusing the Familiar* chapter, we encounter three of these five terms: *tian* 天 (conventionally translated as "Heaven"), *ming* 命 ("commands"), and *xing* 性 ("native human propensities"):

> 天命之謂性，率性之謂道，修道之謂教。
> What *tian* (*tian* 天) commands (*ming* 命) is called our native human propensities (*xing* 性); acting upon these propensities is called way-making; advancing this way is called education.

An argument can be made that even though the additional two terms of the Zisizi vocabulary—"feelings" (*qing* 情) and "heartmind" (*xin* 心)—do not appear in the first chapter explicitly, they are implicit in what is being said about the intimate role that human feelings have in cosmic flourishing. That is, the semantic content if not the two remaining Zisizi terms themselves—the "feelings" (*qing* 情) of "pleasure and anger, grief and enjoyment" (*xinuaile* 喜怒哀樂) that animate and empower the human "heartmind" (*xin* 心)—are also referenced here, with these surrogates making up the full complement of the five key terms. It is later in the text that human feelings as expressed through the term *cheng* 誠—"sincerity, honesty, integrity, resolve"—are elevated to cosmic proportions as the capacity and responsibility human beings have through the expression of commitment and resolve to serve as a co-creative force in shaping the cosmos.

Stated more simply, when exemplary persons orchestrate human feelings into a productive harmony, the Confucian vision of the moral cosmos is advanced, and all things in the world flourish within it. What needs to be emphasized here is that the cosmic reach and influence of human feelings necessarily begins at home in the family. The Confucian assumption is that such human flourishing must be mediated through the intensity of familial roles and relations for it to become genuinely meaningful. It is the family that is the ultimate source and indispensable ground of an achieved propriety (*li* 禮) in all of our roles and relations.

In Confucian philosophy, the function of ritual propriety (*li* 禮) is to effect personal, social, and political order through constantly reauthorizing the concrete family feelings evoked in the appropriate performance of our roles and relationships. In the *Classic of Family Reverence*, the generic term *qing* does not occur explicitly, and yet the vocabulary of this text is profoundly affective, referencing love (*ai* 愛), family affection (*qin* 親), respect (*jing* 敬), rejoicing (*le* 樂), pleasure (*yue* 悅), and so on. An argument might be made that the role of these feelings rooted in family relations is so fundamental, in fact, that they must be parsed specifically because a generic term is perhaps too gross to do them justice. Zhang Yanhua appeals to "an aesthetics of relationships" in her attempt to take full cognizance of the powerful emotional dimension of family flourishing seen as essential to the project of intergenerational continuity and the sense of belonging:

> The cultural aesthetics of *renhe* 人和 (harmonious interpersonal relationships) finds its full expression in Chinese family ethics that guide the way the family members care for and interact with each

other according to their places within the family. The harmonious family also includes a vertical dimension. This concern for harmonious family relationships extends to the deceased members of the family, that is, the spiritual world... This is also related to the Chinese sensibility of *tong* 通 (connection and flowing)... For the Chinese, harmony presupposes a healthy process of connecting and extending.①

In addition to the vertical, diachronic concern for ancestors that reinforces the continuity of family lineage across time, there is an important horizontal, synchronic dimension of interdependent family relations that expands outward through the vital role of friendship as the radiality of the Confucian project. As Zhang Yanhua reports:

It is also important that the cultural aesthetics of *renhe* (harmonious interpersonal relations) extend beyond one's immediate circle of family members and relatives through extensive networks of "human emotions" (*renqing* 人情) created and maintained diligently by all forms of social exchanges, of gifts, labor, services, respect, and so on.②

Again, *qing* as "feelings" is important in understanding the radically contextualized and perspectival nature of creativity itself. Because persons are constituted by their relationships, and because these same relations are made increasingly significant by bringing them into greater focus and resolution, the subjective form of feeling in their creative interactions—that is, their commitment and sincerity (*cheng* 誠)—serves as the concrete ground in the co-

---

① Zhang Yanhua, *Transforming Emotions*, p. 50.
② Zhang Yanhua, *Transforming Emotions*, p. 50.

creative process of cosmic growth. It is because affect is a necessary condition for growth that it has a central role in the Confucian philosophical vocabulary.

In addition to "feelings," *qing* seems to have a second important meaning in these classical texts as "what things genuinely are," "the actual situation." This eliding of the distinction between actuality and feelings that would vitiate the fact and value dichotomy is still present in the modern language with terms such as *qingkuang* 情況 and *shiqing* 事情 meaning "the actual situation," "affairs, matters, business," and *ganqing* 感情 meaning "feelings, emotions." Angus Graham understands this distinction as having evolved chronologically. He surveys the early texts to argue that *qing* in the pre-Han literature means "what something really is" and then only later comes to mean "affect." Indeed, in making his argument he goes so far as to draw an analogy between this earlier meaning of "what something genuinely is" and Aristotelian ontology:

> *Ch'ing* [*qing* 情] in such contexts approximates very closely to the Aristotelian "essence," as may be seen when it is used in definitions; although we cannot regularly translate the word by "essence" without bringing in misleading Western associations with the verb "to be," there seems to be no serious objection to translating *ch'ing yü* [*qingyu* 情欲] by "essential desires."①

Graham's textual evidence in making his case, especially in his citing of Xunzi, is less than compelling. And again, he offers no explanation for how the term transforms in its meaning. Perhaps a better way of explaining this distinction would be to make the argument that there is no severe distinction to be made in the first place. Human feelings in the broadest sense found in the early texts are after all

---

① A.C. Graham, *Studies in Chinese Philosophy and Philosophical Literature*, p. 63.

what is most genuine about people—feelings are their facticity, what they actually are and do.

Qing is often found in the philosophical literature in tandem with the term "natural propensities" (*xing* 性) as *xingqing* 性情, and seems to mean "what things are in the circumstances." In the first chapter of *Focusing the Familiar* cited above the activation of human feelings to achieve equilibrium and superlative harmony is correlated with the Confucian understanding of how we are to best cultivate and educate our "natural propensities" (*xing* 性). There is something of evolving "disposition" and continuing "concrete affective response" in the association between *xing* and *qing* respectively, where something's natural growth and its response to its circumstances are really two aspects of the same thing. Or said another way, what something is in itself includes what it is becoming reflexively in its relations to its environing conditions. Tang Junyi describes *xing* in precisely such terms:

> Anything's natural tendencies are expressed in the quality of its interactions with other things and events. "Natural tendencies" or "life force" then entailing spontaneity and transformation have nothing to do with necessity. . . The emergence of any particular phenomenon is a function of the interaction between its prior conditions and other things and events as external influences. So how something interacts with other things and events and the form of this interaction is not determined by the thing in itself. . . Thus the basic "nature" of anything includes this transformability in response to whatever it encounters.[1]

---

[1] Tang Junyi, *Complete Works*, Vol. 4 pp. 98-100: 物之性表現於與他物感通之德量。性或生理，乃自由原則，生化原則，而非必然原則……蓋任一事象之生起，必由以前之物與其他之交感，以爲其外緣。而一物與他物之如何交感或交感之形式，則非由任一物之本身所決定……因而一物之性之本身，即包含一隨所感而變化之性。

*仁　**ren.** "Consummate persons, consummate conduct."

A starting point in trying to find an adequate vocabulary to bring sufficient clarity to Confucian role ethics is to reflect upon the stubborn ambiguity that attends this term *ren* 仁 as it occurs, and is then developed as a defining philosophical idea in the *Analects of Confucius*. Of course, the character *ren* 仁 does appear as early as in the Zhou bronzes ▨ in which the graph is composed with "corpse body" (*shi* 尸) as an alternative way of writing "person" (*ren* 人), coupled with the number two (*er* 二).① From the context in which it is used we can discern that *ren* in its earliest form means "love" or "kindness." While there are several earlier occurrences of *ren* in the literature, *ren* only accrues substantial philosophical import with its development as a key term of art in the *Analects*.

The character *ren* is also found on the Guodian bamboo strips (c. 300 BCE), where one version of the graph is similar to its modern form ▨.② Different from but still consistent with this overt sense of relationality is an alternative graphic form of *ren* found on these same strips ▨ that combines "lived-body" (*shen* 身) with the graph for "heartmind" (*xin* 心) inscribed beneath it.③ This second way of writing *ren* seems to lose the important connotation of "relationality" that in the standard form is made obvious as it is composed of the number "two" (*er* 二). However, seldom remarked upon but in this context of considerable importance is the fact that the graph for "lived-body" (*shen* 身) in its pre-stylized form is depicted as the body of a pregnant woman ▨.④ Composed of a woman's pregnant body and the heartmind or "feelings" signific, this version of *ren* points

---

① Kwan, "Database," 中山王鼎 284.
② Kwan, "Database," 馬王堆五十二病方 230.
③ Kwan, "Database," 上博竹書五君子為豊 1.
④ Kwan, "Database," 西周晚期 CHANT 63.

to perhaps the most intimate form of human relationality: that is, the symbiotic feelings felt by a mother with child, and those felt by a child within its mother's womb. In this warm world of amniotic fluid, synergetic exchange is effected between woman and child, and through osmotic and hydrostatic forces, the woman is transformed into her child's mother and the child into her mother's daughter or his mother's son. In understanding *ren* by reference to the inextricable and even sacred bonds formed between mother and child in this most intimate relationship, we are also given some insight into the profound religious import of *ren*. Such visceral family feelings might begin at home, but when they are extended radially into all of our roles and personal relationships, from our professional associates out to the commonest of acquaintances, such attentiveness to *ren* has the power to elevate what was mere associated living into a veritable sacrament. In *Analects* 12.2 when Zhonggong asks Confucius about consummate conduct (*ren* 仁), Confucius replies that 出門如見大賓，使民如承大祭 in your public life, you should "behave as though you are receiving honored guests" and should "employ the common people as though you are overseeing a great sacrifice."

There is an alternative explanation of the character *ren* 仁 we might derive from the bronze inscriptions. What appears to be the number "two" (*er* 二) is in fact an early form of "above, to ascend" (*shang* 上) that was also written with just two lines.① Such a reading would highlight the ascent and growing distinction one achieves in becoming *ren*: 仁者樂山 . . . 仁者靜 . . . 仁者壽 "those consummate in their conduct enjoy mountains, . . . are still, . . . [and] are long-enduring" (*Analects* 6.23; see also 2.1 and 17.3).

The reason the *Analects* is the first and primary reference for this philosophical definition of *ren* is because the term has come to be

---

① Bernhard Karlgren. *Grammata Serica Recensa*. Taipei: SMC Publishing Inc., 1996, p. 191. Kwan, "Database," 西周晚期 CHANT 112.

associated most closely with the person of Confucius. The fact that Confucius is asked so often what he means by *ren* would suggest that he is inventing a neologism in using this otherwise obscure term for his own purposes, and that those in conversation with him are not comfortable in their understanding of it. Confucius's creative investment of new meaning in *ren* is borne out when its unexceptional usage in the earlier texts is compared to over a hundred occurrences in the *Analects* in more than ten percent of its passages: that is, some 58 of the 499 sections.

Given that *ren* as it is developed in the *Analects* denotes the qualitative transformation of a *particular* person, it is made further ambiguous because it must be understood relative to the specific concrete conditions of that person. There is no formula, no ideal. Like a work of art, it is a process of disclosure rather than closure, resisting fixed definition and replication. We find that insight into the nature of consummate conduct is provided first in modal terms: that is, in the way, manner, or mode something is done rather than by stipulating any specific actions themselves. Indeed, such modalities are resistant to general prescription in defining the substance of exemplary conduct, and are often brought into focus by an appeal to specific historical episodes and concrete exemplars.

Ren has conventionally been translated as "benevolence," sometimes as "goodness," and "humanity," and occasionally as "human-heartedness." While "benevolence" is most familiar and thus might seem a comfortable choice for rendering *ren* into English, there are several reasons for resisting this translation. First, *ren* is the entire, irreducibly social person: 仁者人也. *Ren* is the cultivated cognitive, aesthetic, moral, and religious sensibilities of entire persons as these cultivated qualities are best expressed in their ritualized roles and relationships. *Ren* does not reference individual persons independent of family relations, but rather describes those specific persons who emerge from the cultivated relationality of these particular family roles. From the very beginning, *ren* has been closely aligned with achieving ritual propriety first in family roles and then by extension, in those relations that locate persons in their communities. As *Analects* 12.1 declares, 克己復禮爲仁 "The disciplining of one's person and the refinement made possible by aspiring to propriety in one's roles and relations is the substance of becoming consummate."

This social dimension of *ren* is central. *Ren* is a "field of selves," the sum of significant relationships that comes to constitute one as a resolutely intra-subjective person. *Ren* is not only intellectual, but affective and physical as well: one's expressed feelings and passions, one's posture and comportment, gestures and bodily communication. Hence, translating *ren* as "benevolence" is to "psychologize" it in a tradition that has had no appeal to the patently Greek notion of *psyche* in its efforts to explain the human experience. "Benevolence" impoverishes *ren* by isolating one out of many moral dispositions at the expense of so much more that comes together in the complex project of becoming human.

Another important reason for resisting "benevolence" as a translation is that in the English language this word has strong Christian connotations. "Benevolence" was a translation introduced by the nineteenth-century missionary and Oxford sinologist, James Legge, in his self-conscious and concerted effort to synchronize his Confucianism vocabulary with the eighteenth-century Presbyterian theologian, Bishop Joseph Butler.① In translating *tian* 天 as

---

① James Legge (1815-1897) is the great nineteenth century Scottish translator of the Chinese classics on whose broad shoulders twentieth-century sinology and beyond has been built. He was a missionary in the field, and as such, appealed self-consciously to the theology of Joseph Butler (1692-1752) in the vocabulary he selected as equivalencies for Chinese terms, and in his interpretation of the tradition broadly. In his translation of the *Mencius*, for example, he wonders aloud why Mencius did not just use "God" instead of the ambiguous (*Continued on next page*)

"Heaven," *dao* 道 as "the Way," *yi* 義 as "righteousness," *li* 禮 as "ritual," *ren* 仁 as "benevolence," and so on, Legge's Confucianism was converted to Christianity and thus became increasingly familiar to his Christian audience. Over the last four centuries of cultural encounter, and especially with the enormous influence that Legge's translations have had as the standard point of reference within the Western academy, the vocabulary established for the translation of classical Chinese texts into Western languages has thus been freighted with a patently Christian frame of meaning. Indeed, with the canons of Confucian philosophy being shelved under the "religion" and "literature" subsections in the Library of Congress classification system, and being found under an "Eastern Religions" rubric in the book stores, the effects of this "Christianization" of Chinese texts are still very much with us.

Again, "humanity" or "humaneness" has recently become a familiar translation, but this term would suggest a shared, essential condition of being human owned by all members of the species: their *humanitas*. But *ren* does not come so easily. *Ren* is something done, an aesthetic project, a hard-won accomplishment. The human being is not something we *are*; it is something that we *do*, and become, and either we do it together or not at all. Not a singular "human *being*," but interdependent "human *becomings*" might be a better way to understand and express the processional, emergent, and irreducibly social nature of what it means to become *ren*. *Ren* is not an essential endowed potential, but what one is able to make of oneself given the interface between one's initial conditions and one's natural, social,

---

(*Continued from previous page*) term, *tian*, and concludes that Mencius's understanding of a benevolent human nature is almost precisely the same as that of the anti-Hobbesian theologian Butler in his *Sermons on Human Nature*. James Legge (trans.), *The Chinese Classics*, Vol. 2, p. 448, note 1. For a substantial account of Legge's journey, see Norman J. Girardot. *The Victorian Translation of China: James Legge's Oriental Pilgrimage*. Berkeley: University of California Press, 2002.

and cultural environments. Certainly, the human being as a focus of constitutive relationships has an initial disposition, a co-creative capacity to be purposeful and expressive in those relations (*Analects* 17.2). But *ren* is foremost the sustained process of growing these relationships into a person who lives a life as a vital, robust, and healthy participant in the discursive human community. This aesthetic dimension—the need for elegance and moral artistry in ethics—is integral to this holistic *ren* understanding of human conduct in which all aspects of the life experience have more or less relevance, and thus have some value for determining a worthwhile outcome.

Confucius is able to make much out of the discursive implications of *ren*. For him, there is intimate association between careful attention to what one says (*ren* 認) and the cultivation of consummate conduct (*ren* 仁). Indeed, the central Confucian moral sensibility of aspiring to become consummate in one's roles and relations (*ren* 仁) is defined unambiguously as "speaking with circumspection" (*ren* 訒): "consummate persons are circumspect in what they say 仁者，其言也訒 (12.3). Defining terms paronomastically by invoking a combination of such semantic and phonetic associations is a familiar characteristic of the early philosophical literature broadly, and of the *Analects* specifically. There is much to be made of the claim in this passage that, for Confucius, not only are "saying" and "doing" inseparable, but further, the more difficult the task at hand, the more care we must exercise in the use of our language: "When things are difficult to accomplish, how can you be but circumspect in what you have to say?" 為之難，言之得無訒乎？ Consider for example, the demands of diplomacy, both personal and political. It is the centrality of effective communication as the source of growth in relations that leads us to the paronomastic ground of making meaning: that is, the Confucian application of a productive and persuasive reservoir of correlations.[①]

We might say that for Confucius, becoming *ren* is at once the easiest and the most difficult thing to accomplish. Confucius is committed to the inseparability of knowing and doing, of living consummately and the quality of conduct that provides demonstration of this personal standard. Just as we might say that no one can be deemed consummate until they authenticate such a characterization in practice, we must also say that as soon as someone is acting consummately, they have a claim on being deemed consummate. Since *ren* requires a commitment to a regimen of unrelenting personal cultivation, as soon as anyone embarks on this project, they are on their way.

On the other hand, Confucius is most reluctant to ascribe the *ren* quality of conduct to anyone, including himself (7.34). In the entire *Analects*, two persons—the ancient statesman Guan Zhong (14.16, 14.17) and Confucius's student Yan Hui (perhaps only after his early demise)—are accorded such a characterization. But even so, the attribution to Guan Zhong is qualified in both instances by two students, Zilu and Zigong, asking how Guan Zhong's conduct could possibly warrant such a description. And with Yan Hui too, he is deemed remarkable not for having become *ren*, but for being able to sustain this high standard for extended periods of time longer than other students. It would seem that for Confucius, *ren* is a never-to-be realized vision of someone optimizing the possibilities of associated living in the human experience. At the same time, for a Confucius who repeatedly underscores the wisdom of avoiding unnecessary personal danger, he is still persuaded that truly moral persons live their lives in a way that gives priority over everything

---

[①] See my "Paronomasia: A Confucian Way of Making Meaning." *Confucius Now: Contemporary Encounters with Confucius.* ed. David Jones. La Salle, IL: Open Court, 2008.

else to this aspiration to become consummate in one's conduct, including life itself. Under circumstances that demand it, such persons will happily embrace death rather than compromise their integrity (15.9).

Henry Rosemont and I used the term "authoritative person or conduct" as a translation of *ren* in our English version of the *Analects* as a considered choice. It is a somewhat novel expression, as was *ren* itself, and like *ren* in the *Analects*, it has over time often prompted a similar desire for clarification from our students and colleagues. "Authoritative" entails the "authority" that persons come to represent in community by becoming *ren*, embodying in themselves the values and customs of the continuing tradition through aspiring to a ritual propriety in their roles and relations (*li* 禮). The prominence and visibility of authoritative persons is captured in the metaphor of the mountain (6.23): majestic, stately, spiritual, an enduring landmark and a source of their moral bearings for the local culture and community.

At the same time, the way of becoming human (*dao* 道) is not a given; it falls upon authoritative persons to be "road-builders," participants in "authoring" the living culture for their own place and time (15.29) and thus serving as a beacon for others on the same path. Aspiring to ritual propriety (*li* 禮) is, by definition, a process of internalization—"making the tradition one's own"—requiring personalization of the roles and relationships that locate persons within their families and communities.

The stark contrast between a top-down and impositional "authoritarian" order when compared with the bottom-up, deferential sense of "authoritative" role models drawing deferential aspirants into their orbit is also salutary. Authoritative persons are models to whom others, recognizing the accomplishment, gladly and without coercion defer, and whose values they go on to appropriate in the construction of their own personhood. Confucius is explicit in expressing his concern about authoritative relations becoming oppressively authoritarian, and about the possibility of a ritualized community constituted by patterns of deference surrendering its non-coercive structure to externally imposed the rule of law (2.3).

More recently, we decided to use "consummate persons/conduct in roles and relations" as our translation of *ren*. This surrender is both a response to a general disaffection on the part of our readers and students for the neologism "authoritative person/conduct," and as a concrete illustration that alternative English translations stand as a distant second in our efforts to persuade students of Chinese philosophy to learn and appropriate the original Chinese terminology itself. Again, this consummate persons/conduct is a deliberate choice. "Consummate" has the virtue of using the collective and intensive prefix "*com-*," denoting the sense of "together, jointly" that does justice to the irreducible relationality of *ren*. In addition, "consummate" has many of the implications that we have ascribed to "authoritative" above. "*Summa*" is a form of "completion" that suggests a sense of disclosure more than closure, a process of gestation, maturation, and fruition more than the actualization of some given potential, the announcement of a novel achievement more than the replication of something already accomplished, and a recognition of the highest and uppermost quality that, rising above expectations, sets a new norm.

When we ask after the meaning of *ren* as it appears in the Confucian canons, it seems that this evolving and complex notion will not give itself up immediately to the "What is *ren*?" question so often asked of it. When we reflect on *ren* as it is used in the *Analects* as a way of "saying" role ethics, we must acknowledge that the meaning of *ren* is different for different people in different contexts. For example, in the *Analects* it is recorded that, Yan Hui, puzzled by Confucius's frequent use of his *ren* neologism, asks after its meaning:

"Yan Hui inquired about *ren*." In comparing the Master's answer to Yan Hui with the responses he gives to precisely the same question when it is asked by equally nonplussed Zhonggong, Sima Niu, Fan Chi, and Zigong in other passages, we might begin by reflecting on the question form being used—the interrogative term itself.[1] That is, rather than uncritically assuming that Confucius's protégés are asking "What is *ren*?" and are thus expecting a generic answer, we might infer that they are instead asking "How given my narrative do I as this particular person become *ren*?" It is for this reason the Master has a very different answer for each of them to the extent that, when the "same" Fan Chi on a second occasion repeats his question about *ren*, he gets a very different answer.

Indeed, in trying to find some clarity on *ren*, we must ask if it is indeed one perhaps cardinal virtue among many as suggested by the conventional translations as "benevolence," "love," "altruism," "humaneness," and "humanity"? Or is it a "general virtue"—Confucianism's supreme moral principle or *summum bonum*? Or, as suggested by Wing-tsit Chan 陳榮捷 long ago, is it both of these and much more?[2] Or, rather than thinking in terms of individuals and their virtues, do we need a more holistic, narrative understanding of *ren* as proposed by Alex McLeod who would construe it primarily as the moral property of communities, and only derivatively, as an individual property?[3] Or is it, as Karyn Lai would argue, all that in sum makes up an exemplary human life?[4]

---

[1] Yan Hui 12.1: 顏淵問仁. Zhonggong 12.2, Sima Niu 12.3, Fan Chi 12.22 and 13.19, and Zigong 15.10.

[2] Wing-tsit Chan. "The Evolution of the Concept *Jen*." *Philosophy East and West* 4 No. 1 (January 1955), pp. 295-319.

[3] Alex McLeod. "*Ren* as a Communal Property in the *Analects*." *Philosophy East and West* 62 No. 4 (October 2012), pp. 505-528.

[4] Karyn Lai. "*Ren* 仁: An Exemplary Life." *Dao Companion to the Analects*. ed. Amy Olberding. Dordrecht: Springer, 2014.

This profound ambiguity is compounded by the fact that, in the more than one hundred instances in which *ren* appears in the *Analects*, there seems to be a persistent eliding if not erasure of a set of familiar, rather useful distinctions guaranteed at least in part by the grammar and inflections of English and other European languages. These distinctions include the distinguishing of an inner self from an outer world, agents from their actions, selves from others, individual dispositions from communal properties, means from ends, mind from body, a person's character from the whole person, virtuous character traits from those actions that follow from them, psychological dispositions from the behaviors that are informed by them, specific virtuosic actions from an entire exemplary life, the abstract concept itself from the concrete narrative from which it is derived, specific instances of conduct from higher-order generalizations made about them, and many more. What seems clear from a close reading of our texts is that on different occasions and in different contexts, *ren* can be parsed as referencing any and all of these aspects of moral conduct. The question is: What is the status then of these many functional, often convenient distinctions in parsing the broad spectrum of meaning we associate with *ren*?

Most if not all of this list of overlapping linguistic distinctions that would break up the continuity of personal experience are meaningful for English speakers because of the commonsense realist and intellectualist penchant freighted in this language for first internalizing the mind as belonging to individual persons, and then separating such individual subjects from a putatively mind-independent world. In so doing, persons are separated from each other as discrete individuals, and then again are separated as individual agents with specific character traits from what they do. The function of these familiar and often severe distinctions, serving as they do a perceived need for clarity and precision, is to abstract and isolate one or more aspects of persons from the unity of their concrete experience. As we see with Aristotle's *Categories*, this isolating of things is a habit of thinking that has deep roots in the commitment to a substance ontology in the Western philosophical narrative and the philosophy of grammar that follows from it. Indeed it has been my continuing worry that such a fragmenting of persons and their conduct is a persistent and uncritical assumption being made by those who would argue that Confucianism offers a virtue ethics with Chinese characteristics: that is, those who would first assume that the classical Greek notion of *arête* is sufficiently analogous with, and thus can be treated as an equivalency for the Confucian term, *de* 德, and hence that the core ethical terminology in early Confucian ethical writings can by extension be comfortably rendered into an aretaic vocabulary.

But as we witness with this term *ren*, the *Analects* in fact seems to eschew any severe distinction between persons and their worlds, between any particular person and other individuals, and between persons and their conduct. No one can become consummate in their conduct (*ren* 仁) by isolating themselves from their world, by withdrawing from their interactions with other people, or by performing some generic and reduplicative *ren* action. Given that none of these distinctions have any finality, perhaps the aspectual language captured in the expression "forming and functioning" (*tiyong* 體用) can be helpful in organizing the many dyadic distinctions that can be drawn out of the narrative contexts within which *ren* is used. *Ren* parsed as an abstract virtue or character trait, for example, might seem to fall on the more determinative "formal" (*ti* 體) side, while *ren* as a specific virtuosic activity would seem to be more vital and thus be more "functional" (*yong* 用). The problem with making such distinctions, however, is that if they are taken as more than a convenience, they can vitiate the focus-field holography wherein the entire narrative is implicated in each impulse and each aspect of a person's life. That is, our relational virtuosity is fully implicated in the glowing complexion of our physicalities, the possibilities of our outer worlds are fully implicated in our achieved subjective identities, each act of kindness is fully implicated in the exemplary narrative of a consummate person, and so on. What recommends this holistic focus-field language as a way of understanding *ren* is that it requires full contextualization, where the meaning of any particular action within any particular situation can only be evaluated by reference to the entire narrative.

It is a commonplace that the standardized character for *ren* 仁 in being composed of "person" (*ren* 人) and the number "two" (*er* 二) is semantically revealing in locating the discursive process of becoming consummately human within our relations with, and our relating to, other persons. Such an etymological analysis underscores the Confucian assumption that one cannot become a person by oneself—we are, from our inchoate beginnings, irreducibly social: narratives nested within narratives. Herbert Fingarette has famously stated the matter rather concisely: "For Confucius, unless there are at least two human beings, there can be no human beings."[①] We have seen above that this "duplicity" or "twoness" in the prestylized graph is represented in several different ways. "Duplicity" from the Latin *duplicare* means first "twofold, having two parts," and then only by extension, something being other than it purports to be. It is in this sense that "duplicity" has come to connote deceit. Such an inference is particularly compelling in the Western philosophical narrative informed by a substance ontology and its principle of non-contradiction that defines particular things as having an essential individual integrity. What then are the implications of this "duplicity"

[①] Herbert Fingarette. "The Music of Humanity in the *Conversations of Confucius*." *Journal of Chinese Philosophy* 10 (1983), p. 217.

or "twoness" that attends the project of becoming consummate in one's conduct as a person (ren 仁)?

First, we must acknowledge the primacy of vital relationality that, in taking context as reflexively integral to the identity of the things contextualized, makes all things including human persons uniquely one and focally many at the same time. Nothing and no one does anything by itself. Said another way, in this holographic cosmology anything is what it is at the pleasure of everything else. The agency and actions of a son are not the conduct of some discrete person. Rather, implicated in such eventful "son" activity is not only the parenting of his parents but the living on of the distinctive physical qualities and the cultural and ethical values of his remotest of progenitorial ancestors. Much of who and what this son is, is determined by the others with whom he interacts, just as his efforts determine in part who his parents are, and indeed, who his ancestors are as well. At least one significant dimension of our personhood, of our identity, is in important measure conferred upon us by others, just as we make our contribution in the conferring of identities upon them.

As corollary to this primacy of vital relationality, the "twoness" recalls the assertion in *Focusing the Familiar* 26 that every happening in the cosmos is indelibly and uniquely one of a kind:

天地之道，可一言而盡也：其為物不貳，則其生物不測。
The way of heaven and earth can be fully captured in one phrase: Since things and events are never duplicated, their proliferation is unfathomable.

This is not a claim merely for the uniqueness of each thing, but is a statement that precludes any severe discreteness and independence among them. In speaking of the way of the heavens and the earth, in addition to affirming the unreduplicated nature of particularity, this

仁 *ren*.   177

passage is also acknowledging the continuity all things have with each other. This means that erstwhile "things" are both one and two at the same time. There is always duplicity in identity formation, with the "integrity" of human becomings best being understood as the continuing reflexive "integration" of two-becoming-one: persons who are always one and two at the same time.

Again, this duplicity or "twoness" has direct reference to how persons actually become consummate. Confucius describes this process explicitly: 能近取譬，可謂仁之方也已 "correlating one's conduct with those near at hand can be said to be the method of becoming consummate in one's conduct" (6.30). Such an understanding of the continuing and open-ended shaping of personal identity stands in stark contrast to the "oneness" of essentialist, substance models in which a person actualizes an already present, innate potential. This Confucian resolve to seek out optimally appropriate coordination with others in shaping their own emergent identities is closely related to the practice of "deference and dramatic rehearsal" (*shu* 恕) as simply another way of describing this correlative method for become *ren*.

Another implication of this duplicity or "twoness" is that terms such as *ren* are aspectual, and have immediately implicated in them the full cluster of terms that are integral to becoming consummate in one's conduct. The fact, for example, that throughout the *Analects*, *ren* and *zhi* 知 ("living wisely," "knowing," "realizing," "wisdom") repeatedly appear in tandem suggests that wisdom and morality are interpenetrating and co-terminus: that consummatory conduct transforms mere knowledge into living wisely, and that living wisely is itself an expression of moral competence. Similarly, the collateral relationship between *ren* and *yi* 義 ("being optimally appropriate," "being meaningful") reflects the reflexivity, inclusiveness, and optimal growth in the meaning of one's relations with others that occurs with consummate conduct. Again, the persistent association between *ren* and *li* 禮 locates the project of becoming consummate squarely within family and community. When these ritualized relations are fully realized they take on the sacred quality of a family-centered religiousness.

If there is one term that captures the spirit of the Confucian tradition, it is perhaps the "deference" that makes one into two. The fabric of the Confucian family and community is constituted by the always mutual patterns of persons deferring to each other in the roles of teacher and student, of daughter and neighbor, of neighbor and shopkeeper (*li* 禮). The need to act in a way that is inclusive of the interests of all concerned (*yi* 義) means of course that grandmothers must defer to their grandsons, as well as the other way around. The intergenerational transmission of the living culture captured in the character for "family reverence"—*xiao* 孝 as the combination of *lao* 老 + *zi* 子, "elders" + "juniors"—requires that each generation be prospectively and retrospectively one and two at the same time. It requires deference by each generation to what has come before, and to what will follow.

Such "twoness" is also a factor in the need for those who would be consummate in their conduct to imaginatively adapt the inspiration of their mentors to shape their own project of becoming uniquely who they want to be. The "duplicity" in the term "role" itself reflects the qualitative distance between role models and those who are inspired by them, and who seek in their own persons to achieve a comparable standard. In this Confucian tradition, deference to exemplary persons available from within the historical narrative do much of the work of abstract "principles" in serving as guides for proper conduct, but differs from the principle-based model in that the project of habituating consummate conduct by reference to role models must always be a uniquely personal undertaking. That is, consummate conduct (*ren* 仁), far from being reduplicated actions or generic virtues, is always a unique achievement by particular persons under particular circumstances. We can and should properly be inspired by our role models—our ancestors, cultural heroes, and teachers included—but consummate conduct does not brook replication. In *Analects* 15.36 Confucius says explicitly:

當仁，不讓於師。
In striving to be consummate in your conduct (*ren* 仁), do not defer even to your teacher.

One criticism directed at the term "role" in role ethics is that "playing a role" introduces a certain distance between "actors" themselves and the roles or "characters" they play. But we might use this same insight, again taking duplicity in its original sense, to appreciate the necessary distance there must be between protégés and their mentors, where it is incumbent upon the students to seize upon whatever inspiration they can find in their intimate relationships with their teachers, and adapt this stimulation in whatever direction will best serve the nourishing of their own personal growth. There is deference to our teachers in the sense of being inspired by them, but there is also deference to the particularities that are defining of each and every situation and the persons involved. It should further be noted that mentors too are themselves created by patterns of deference. That is, mentors can only become mentors by virtue of the deference accorded them from those whom they inspire.

And again, we can appeal to this "twoness" as an explanation of the evolution of human self-consciousness in the positive sense of a keen and deepening self-awareness. Whatever persons are and whatever putative "individuals" might or might not be, they cannot be the separate and spatially isolated things without any reference to either their past or current relations that our retrospective imaginations might assume they are. Persons are not present at birth, but are emergent in the growth of the relations that constitute them from this initial stage. They become increasingly self-conscious through the patterns of communication in the families and communities in which they live. The production of an erstwhile "self-" within the distinctively human sense of self-consciousness is arguably in imitation of their more primary social associations and interactions. That is, persons have discursive relations with others, and under such influence and with reference to just such a model, they then gradually come to engage in a continuing conversation with themselves.① Self-awareness intensifies as persons come to see themselves from the perspective of others, and then gradually internalize this external perspective as integral to their own identity as a sense of shame.

We might observe that there is a direct correlation between the quality of self-consciousness and the sense of shame it inspires on the one hand, and conduct that might be deemed consummatory on the other. Consummatory persons act upon a deep and abiding awareness of how they are perceived by others, and the high expectations others have of them. Conversely, the shameless conduct of aberrant individuals reflects a lack of the kind of awareness that connects one's own conduct to the narratives of others. "Petty persons" (*xiaoren* 小人) who are a major persona in the *Analects* are stunted not only in their relations with others, but also in their degree of self-consciousness. In Confucianism, the mantra is not "I think therefore I am." Rather it is both "through communicating we

---

① I am buoyed by having had it pointed out to me by Kevin J. Turner that Gilbert Ryle seems to have come to the same conclusion:
The trick of talking to oneself in silence is acquired neither quickly nor without effort; and it is a necessary condition of our acquiring it that we should have previously learned to talk intelligently aloud and have heard and understood other people doing so.
See *The Concept of Mind*, New York: Routledge, 2009, p. 16.

are becoming together" as well as "through communicating I am also becoming increasingly self-aware." This always collaborative, discursive process of becoming persons is why the language of roles is so powerful in expressing what is indeed a more robust, narrative notion of agency.

*儒　*ru.* "Confucianism, Ruism, scholar-teacher, literati tradition."

The *Shuowen* lexicon defines this term *ru* 儒 paronomastically as *rou* 柔 meaning "gentle, mild, soft, yielding," followed by 術士之偁 "the designation for a scholar-teacher." The etymology of the character *ru* 儒 itself is cognate with the graphs *ru* 臑 as "pliant, soft," *ru* 孺 as "child, weak, mild," and "weak, timid" (*nuo* 懦), fairly describing a class of "gentle" literate people who emerged and flourished as early as the Shang dynasty (1600–1046 BCE) at least thirty generations before Confucius. In several of the early classics, it carries this same meaning of scholar-teacher, and in some philosophical texts, becomes a proper name describing the lineage of scholars associated with the philosopher Confucius. The earliest occurrence of this term *ru* in our extant corpus is found in a single passage of the *Analects* 6.13:

> 子謂子夏曰："女為君子儒，無為小人儒。"
> The Master remarked to Zixia, "You want to become the kind of *ru* literatus who is exemplary in conduct, not the kind that is a petty person."

It is thus that the early philosopher and teacher, Kongfuzi 孔夫子, Latinized as "Confucius," lends his name to the English (but not to the Chinese) expression of this tradition called "Confucianism."① Confucius was certainly a flesh-and-blood historical person who lived, taught, and died some twenty-five centuries ago, consolidating in his own time a formidable legacy of wisdom that has been passed down and applied through the ages to shape the character of an entire Sinitic culture and beyond. In and of itself, the profoundly personal model of Confucius remembered by his protégés through those intimate snapshots of his life collected in the middle chapters of the *Analects* and other canonical texts, has its own value and meaning. But then, as cited above, Confucius reportedly said of himself that most of what he had to offer his students had ancient roots, and that he was one who was inclined to follow the established path rather than strike out in new directions.② In *Analects* 7.1 he describes himself as a cultural transmitter rather than an innovator who has inherited the substance of his philosophy from the legacy of the Zhou dynasty and earlier:

子曰："述而不作，信而好古，竊比於我老彭。"
The Master said, "Following the proper way, I do not forge new paths; with confidence, I cherish the ancients—in these respects I

---

① Tim Barrett in "Chinese Religion in English Guise: The History of an Illusion," *Modern Asian Studies*, 39.3, (2005), pp. 518 has identified Sir John Francis Davis (1795-1890), the second governor of Hong Kong, as the first person on record to have used the word "Confucianism." See Davis, *The Chinese: A General Description of the Empire of China and Its Inhabitants*, London: Charles Knight & Co., 1836, p. 45. It is perhaps interesting that just as with the term "Confucianism" as a decidedly Western intervention into Chinese culture, the mountain peak in Hong Kong that remembers Davis as Mount Davis in English still continues to be known in Chinese by its own name, "Star-scrapper Peak" (*Moxingling* 摩星嶺). See also Nicolas Standaert, "The Jesuits Did NOT Manufacture 'Confucianism'," *East Asian Science, Technology and Medicine*, 16, (1999), pp. 115-32 for a detailed discussion of the *ru* tradition and its questionable interpretation as "Confucianism" that absolves the Jesuits of this problematic equation.

② *Analects* 7.1.

am comparable to Old Peng."

In *Analects* 3.14, Confucius sees himself as self-consciously continuing a tradition that reaches back into the second millennia BCE:

周監於二代，郁郁乎文哉！吾從周。
The Zhou dynasty looked back to the Xia and Shang dynasties. Such a wealth of culture! I follow the Zhou.[①]

In fact, appreciating his modesty in demurring on the status of innovator, we have sufficient evidence to comfortably assert that Confucius was both a transmitter and an innovator. But most interestingly, a porous yet enduring "Confucianism" thus understood predates the historical figure of Confucius himself. Indeed, it is perhaps for this reason that in the Chinese language itself, the tradition is identified with the *ru* 儒 literati class who over the centuries provided the culture with its evolving "literati learning" (*ruxue* 儒學). And consistent with Confucius's own premises, this legacy called *ruxue*—the always porous core of an aggregating Chinese culture—is both vital and corporate. That is, Confucianism has been appropriated, commented upon, reinterpreted, and reauthorized by each of some eighty generations of Chinese scholars and intellectuals after Confucius that across the ages have contributed their own best thoughts to this "literati learning" as a continuous, living tradition.

It is these exemplars as role models who, in every age and over the eons, have enabled their progeny to intensify the human experience with the elegance and refinement of Confucian culture in its most noble sense. There is thus a parallel between the function of *xiao* 孝 that references the intergenerational embodiment and

---

[①] See also *Analects* 8.20.

transmission of family lineages broadly, and of *rujia* 儒家 as the literati (*wenren* 文人) or lettered "family lineage" that functions as literally an additional important strand of family within the family lineages. The *ru* family describes one elite stratum in the population responsible for embodying and transmitting the high literary tradition from one generation to the next. And it is the role of this elite class of literati exemplars that perpetuate the persistent yet always transforming social, political, and ethical orthodoxy of this cultural core—what is called the *daotong* 道統.

The point I want to make here is that what we call "Confucianism" and conventionally interpret as a particular doctrine or stipulated set of values is first and foremost a continuing sociopolitical class of literati whose role within the family lineage has and continues to be the embodiment and perpetuation of the living cultural tradition—a tradition that reflects markedly different content in different epochs as it continues to travel across the generations. One way of interpreting the role of this *ru* literary class is to rehearse its narrative as it emerges as an elite social stratum in the Shang dynasty. These early *ru* of the Shang began in earnest to aestheticize urban life lived within their social and political institutions, a story that can be told through the casting of mass quantities of exquisite bronze vessels that are today displayed in museums around the world as emblematic of ancient Chinese culture. Much can be learned about this literati class by going back and relocating these bronze artifacts within their own historical context—thus retrieving their original iconic status and function.

From these bronzes, we learn much about the lives of the Shang people who established a profoundly "aestheticized" way of being in a world that had begun with the production and institutionalization of ritual vessels by an elite group of literati at the Shang court. The bronzes tell an economic, political, and religious story about this early Shang culture. This same social class can be associated with the development of a program of religio-political practices (*li* 禮) of which the bronzes were a part—an elaborate social grammar that reinforced the status of the highest stratum of the population. The Zhou dynasty (1056?–256 BCE) that followed the Shang initially was comprised of a federation of tribal peoples who over time conquered the Shang but who also perpetuated its high culture. The Shang religio-political ceremonies provided the ground and the impetus for the extension of this evolving pattern of ritual life-forms and institutions (*li* 禮) to the population more broadly during the extended Zhou dynasty. The role of the *ru* literati class over these ensuing centuries was to serve as the embodiment of this constantly evolving, complex notion of *li* that in the fullness of time was to become the heart and blood of Confucian philosophy. The point is well made that *ruxue* as "literati learning" is a living, corporate tradition with deep roots in the tradition that cannot be reduced to any one historical person. It is not "Confucianism." At the same time, the man Confucius has become a cultural paragon who has more than lived up to his own exhortation that everyone ought to aspire to become an "exemplary literatus" (*junziru* 君子儒).

And it is this same lettered class including the scholars and intellectuals still at work today that continue to thrive and perpetuate the tradition some eighty generations after Confucius's death. This gentry class of intellectuals—across the ages, and in different ways at different times—has continued a shared and evolving culture corpus that has been extended by always "new" Confucians, and then reauthorized in each succeeding generation. And the *ru*, far from being doctrinaire advocates of some specific dogma, have at different times across the centuries reflected different values and embraced an ever-evolving range of ideas and cultural practices. While there has certainly been a continuing, self-conscious identity over the centuries, there are also importantly different degrees of innovation and creative advance that have occurred with the passing of each generation. Taking this literati learning as a resilient indigenous impulse—what we might call a cultural commonsense—we might define Confucianism as the always changing yet still persistent cultural core of the Chinese population itself, and then by extension and in different degree, of the very different and yet sinitically inspired cultures of Korea, Japan, and Vietnam.

*善 **shan.** "Felicity, efficacy, behaving well, auspicious conduct."

The *Shuowen* lexicon defines *shan* as "auspicious" (*ji* 吉), as synonymous with what is "optimally appropriate" (*yi* 義), and as "fine, beautiful, good" (*mei* 美), underscoring the aesthetic and thus holistic connotations of *shan*. The character *shan*, conventionally translated "good," contains two significant elements. The "sheep" (*yang* 羊) radical is associated with "sacrifice" and, as found in other similarly constructed characters such as "appropriate" (*yi* 義) and "beautiful" (*mei* 美), the sheep suggests "auspiciousness" (*xiang* 祥). The second element on the bottom is the "mouth" (*kou* 口) which in the archaic versions of the character was originally two "speech" (*yan* 言) radicals. Like many of the classical Chinese philosophical terms that contain the "mouth" and "speech" elements, it would seem that such auspiciousness is the product of effective communication.

This discursive source of *shan* is made evident in the graph as it is found on the bronzes and in the small seal script 羊 where it is indeed written with at least two and occasionally three "speech" (*yan* 言) radicals, prompting philosopher-philologist Kwan Tze-wan 關子尹 to suggest that

> ... this kind of repetition might reflect the fact that when the ancients talked about *shan* they were not referring to "good" in itself, but "good" as it obtains in the relations among people. Thus,

putting the auspicious sheep and multiple speech components together gives us the meaning of two persons speaking face-to-face with warmth and fondness.①

Although *shan* is conventionally translated as "good," such a rendering has the disadvantage of essentializing and hypostasizing a notion that is fundamentally relational and processual. That is, *shan* is a radically contextualized, discursive activity that is productive of welcome outcomes. "Good" is in the first instance "good with," "good to," "good in," "good for," "good at," and thereby only derivatively and abstractly, "good." It is first and foremost a compounding "felicity" or "efficacy" in one's relationships that in the fullness of time can be abstracted from one's habits of conduct to be a summary description of that person. Indeed, *shan* is most concretely imputed to the narrative rather than the person, the shared, efficacious path one's life is taking in one's relations with others (*zhishan zhi dao* 至善之道) as it stands in contrast to the paths of those who are less so.

A.C. Graham disputes the assumption that moral terms such as *shan* are the kind of generic "constants" (*chang* 常) we would associate with Greek notions of virtues, values, or principles. James Behuniak cites a passage from the *Book of Documents* that would reinforce Graham's claim:

德無常師，主善為師。善無常主，協于克一。
Virtuosity has no constant model; it is oriented toward what is good. What is good has no constant orientation; it accords with what is adequate to the single instance.②

---

① Kwan, "Database," 西周晚期 CHANT 704. 凡此種種，可能反映古代談《善》都不指獨善，而指人際關係中的善，故羊、詰合起來意會二人好言相向(關子尹)。
② James Behuniak, Jr. *Mencius on Becoming Human*. Albany: State University of New York Press, 2005, p. 55, citing Legge, *Chinese Classics* Vol. 3, pp. 217-218.

There is no one standard that can be appealed to to authenticate virtuosic conduct; rather, it is an orientation in what we do, and even as an orientation, it involves nonfungible activities that cannot be replicated. In making this point, Graham invokes a distinction between virtue traits and conduct, insisting that *shan* must be understood "not as a quality but as a way of behaving."[①] It is not some qualitatively superior action or a character trait derived from a prior and higher virtue of "goodness" that inheres "in" a person, or some general principle of "goodness" that informs and supervenes on an action as it is "done" by a person. The Confucian notion of "good" (*shan* 善), rather than referencing some antecedent, generic "virtue," actually means first and foremost a quantum of "moral growth" achieved through effective communication in one's roles and relations. "Good" in this sense of moral growth begins from discursive activities within a continuing narrative and only then can serve as a description of persons or their actions. *Shan* is the gregarious activity of growing our relations and making them "meaningful" by "relating" to each other effectively.

We can glean insight into how the process of becoming felicitous in our conduct (*shan* 善) evolves from what the *Mencius* calls our incipient "four inclinations" (*siduan* 四端)—that is, what Mencius generalizes as the native, constitutive conditions of the human experience and that he identifies with the inchoate heartmind (*xin* 心). The *Mencius* 2A6 provides a clear statement of how these four inclinations stir us to pro-social moral conduct:

恻隐之心，仁之端也；羞恶之心，义之端也；辞让之心，礼之端也；是非之心，智之端也。人之有是四端也，犹其有四体也。

Our heartmind in feeling pity at perceived suffering disposes it toward consummate conduct in our roles and relations; our

---

① A.C. Graham, *Disputers of the Tao*, p. 424.

heartmind in feeling shame at perceived crudeness disposes it toward appropriate conduct in our roles and relations; our heartmind in its feelings of modesty and deference disposes it toward propriety in our roles and relations; our heartmind in feeling a sense of approval and disapproval disposes it toward wisdom in our roles and relations. Persons have these four inclinations (*siduan* 四端) just as they have their four limbs.

Commenting on this passage, Graham observes that the analogy between cultivating our four inclinations and nourishing our bodies is an apposite one:

> It is essential to Mencius' case that although moral education is indispensable it is, like the feeding of the body, the nourishing of a spontaneous process. . . . A man becomes bad, not because the incipient impulses are missing from his constitution, but because he neglects and starves them.[①]

Graham underscores the analogy here linking physical (as opposed to metaphysical) growth and moral refinement. In both cases such growth occurs because of the natural conditions defining of the situated organism and the effort that is being invested in the cultivation of these conditions. And the terms "constitution" and "incipient impulses" used here to describe these natural conditions are important because *Mencius* 4B12 is referencing the native pro-social inclinations we have within our relations as human beings:

孟子曰:"大人者，不失其赤子之心者也。"
Mencius said, "Great persons are those who do not lose the heartmind of the newborn babe."

[①] A.C. Graham, *Disputers of the Tao*, pp. 126, 129.

We must resist an expository reading of this passage that might essentialize and reify some "original" heartmind here; it is perhaps better to understand Mencius as simply making a point about the pro-social orientation of the infant. Activating the native inclinations of the relationally-constituted infant is a necessary condition upon which the project of ultimately becoming exemplary in our persons depends. Mencius's description of incipient "inclinations" not only defines the "constitution" of the infant in terms of these same organic relations, but further introduces the radically embedded newborn babe as the locus of the growth that ensues from acting on these "inclinations". That is, the newborn babe begins *in medias res* as an inchoate narrative nested within the larger pattern of the more mature narratives of family and community.

The growth of infants born into the concrete matrix of the family and communal relations of a mature culture can be captured both descriptively and prescriptively by an appeal to the intense socializing impulses of these constitutive bonds that propel them towards efficacy in their conduct (*shan* 善). The *Mencius* 2A6 uses the metaphors of a run-away fire and surging water to emphasize the precipitous nature of this moral growth:

> 凡有四端於我者，知皆擴而充之矣，若火之始然，泉之始達。苟能充之，足以保四海；苟不充之，不足以事父母。
>
> Now acknowledging that these four inclinations are defining of us, the process of realizing the development and fruition of them is like a fire beginning to blaze or a spring of water beginning to gush forth. Persons who are able to bring them fully to fruition can vouchsafe everyone within the four seas; persons unable to do so cannot even be of service to their own parents.

Graham comments here that this inexorable progression of moral growth is motivated by the agreeable feelings we derive from it:

The process once launched accelerates, like fire catching, because we discover the pleasure of it.[①]

For this infant, the four inclinations that anticipate moral growth are the thick, irreducibly biological, familial, social, and cultural conditions that are defining of it. These discursive bonds are thus by nature resolutely relational and inclusive, and a source of rapid moral articulation (shan 善) as they become increasingly robust. As suggested above, shan as "good" in the sense of moral growth, to use Charles Taylor's felicitous expression, begins with "webs of interlocution" within the continuing narrative. It is only from this continuing discursive process that "good" can be abstracted as a summary description of persons or their actions. Said simply, newborns as concrete facts are constituted by the relations that define them, and as they follow the discursive promptings within the matrix of these relations, they grow their various roles into their emerging personal identities. Infants in these relations are animated and projective, and develop their inflected and reflexive sense of themselves within the expansive intrasubjective roles and relations that come to constitute them.

Importantly, it is the radial, constitutive, and transactional nature of relations themselves and their propensity to produce meaning that first locates newborns within an inchoate habitude, and thus disposes them to positive moral growth (shan 善). Given their irreducibly relational nature, infants conceived of as a discrete and separate "individual" are nothing more than a retrospective abstraction from this same manifold of relations. And further, the erstwhile "goodness" (shan 善) of infants, far from being some innate and isolatable endowment, is the product of the vital disposition and orientation they have toward social growth. Shan refers to the

---

[①] A.C. Graham, *Disputers of the Tao*, p. 126.

outcome of the semiotic processes and symbolic competencies that continue to shape them as human "becomings."

In the translation, we have struggled to retain this relational sense of *shan*, translating it on occasion as "felicity" or "efficacy." This understanding of *shan*, like "appropriateness" (*yi* 義), highlights the fundamentally aesthetic nature of classical Confucianism, where the common good is achieved in the productive relationships of a thriving community. The habitudes of persons and the ethos of the community is an ongoing aesthetic achievement.

*上帝   ***shangdi.*** "High god(s)." See also 祭 ***ji.*** "Sacrificing, sacrifice."

The term *di* 帝 is usually associated with Shang dynasty religiousness, although its meaning is speculative and in degree uncertain. It occurs on the oracle bones as ![], on the bronzes as ![], and on the silk and bamboo manuscripts as ![].①

The literary theorist Wang Guowei 王國維 interprets this character as an early depiction of the stem of a flower or fruit *di* 蒂, and thus as a phonetic loan character. The philologist Xu Zhongshu 徐中舒 reads it as a ceremonial pyre on which to make sacrifices, and by extension, as the earlier graphic form for what came to be designated as the grand *di* sacrifice 禘. Another interpretation is that the character was initially a representation of the tied bundles of wood for a pyre, and later was extended to reference the several objects of the sacrifice, *shangdi* 上帝 (the high god(s)), *tiandi* 天帝 (the god of the heavens), *hedi* 河帝 (the god of the river). By the time of the bronze inscriptions, the character is used for both the god(s) *shangdi* and also for the human ruler as *huangdi* 皇帝. The

---

① Kwan, "Database," 甲骨文合集 CHANT 1132, 商代 CHANT 5413, 馬王堆老子甲本 101 respectively.

porousness of the boundary between rulers of the human world, ancestors, and divinity reflects a culture heavily committed to sacrifice and ancestor reverence. Consistent with this looseness in the distinction between gods and humankind, the *Shuowen* lexicon defines *di* 帝 as a designation for the monarch who rules the world, and *di* 禘 as the grand sacrifice to the gods held every five years. We also know that the term *di* 帝 was used frequently as a posthumous title for the Shang dynasty kings.

John Major alludes to this fluidity between the human space and that of the divine in his attempt to provide an appropriate equivalent for this term *di* in his translations of the Chinese canons into the English language:

> I translate *di* [帝] as "thearch"—a felicitous word first used, I believe, by Edward Schafer—when it refers to specific personage such as the Supreme Thearch (*shangdi* [上帝]) or the Yellow Thearch (*huangdi* [黃帝]), or to idealized rulers ("emperors"). Thearch captures well the character of ancient Chinese thought wherein divinities might be (simultaneously and without internal contradiction) high gods, mythical/divine rulers, or deified royal ancestors: beings of enormous import, straddling the numinous and the mundane.[①]

In *Focusing the Familiar* 19, the *di* sacrifice is closely associated with ancestor reverence:

"宗廟之禮，所以祀乎其先也。明乎郊社之禮、禘嘗之義，治國其如示諸掌乎！"

"Ritual observances performed in the ancestral temple are ways

---

[①] John Major. *Heaven and Earth in Early Han Thought: Chapters Three, Four, and Five of the Huainanzi*. Albany: State University of New York Press, 1993, p. 18.

of making sacrifices to one's forbearers. For one who has a clear understanding of the sacrificial observances to the heavens and the earth, and the various ceremonies such as the Grand *di* sacrifice and the autumnal *chang* sacrifice performed in the ancestral temple, the governing of the empire is as easy as turning something over in the palm of one's hand."

We learn in the *Analects* 3.11 that Confucius too had a great reverence for this *di* sacrifice, and uses similar language in describing its efficacy:

或問禘之說。子曰："不知也。知其說者之於天下也，其如示諸斯乎！" 指其掌。

Someone asked the Master for an explanation of the *di* imperial ancestral sacrifice, and he replied: "I don't have one. Anyone who did know how to explain it could rule the empire as easily as turning something over here." And he pointed to the palm of his hand.

*神 **shen.** "Heavenly gods, ancestors, spirituality, vigor, vitality, mystery."

Shen as it appears on the bronze inscriptions is [image], and is interpreted as a flash of "lightning" from above.[1] The character consists of the radical *shi* 示 meaning "offering, displaying" and *shen* 申 meaning "extending, stretching," suggesting a capacity to extend meaning in the world. It is often translated as "spirits" or "gods," and has a range of meanings the scope of which reveals a perceived continuity in Confucian cosmology between the worlds of the numinous or divine, the ancestors, and the inspired human experience. In the *Shuowen* lexicon, it states that the heavenly

---

[1] Kwan, "Database," 西周中期 CHANT 4174.

gods (*tianshen* 天神) "call forth the myriad things," with one of its commentaries suggesting that there is a correlation between the event of thunder and rain and the fertility, life, and growth that follows in its wake. One meaning of *shen* then is the numinous associated with natural phenomena such as the sky, sun, moon, stars, rivers, mountains, forests, valleys, and so on.

Importantly, *shen* does not simply reference the numinous; it can also refer to human beings. It first refers specifically to human ancestors on the bronze inscriptions, and also comes to meaning "life" and "spirit." When *qi* 氣 takes form, *shen*—life and spirit—is born. At this level, it is associated with the moral conduct, the wisdom, and the influence of exemplary human beings. The *Huainanzi* 15 says 知人所不知謂之神 "knowing what others do not know is *shen*," and again in 2: 神者智之淵也 "*shen* is a reservoir full of wisdom." And it is frequently associated with human sagacity. The *Mencius* 7B25 says 大而化之之謂聖,聖而不可知之之謂神 "when great persons exercise a transforming influence they are called sages, and when they are sagacious beyond comprehension they are called *shen*." Henri Maspero, in his discussion of Confucius, comments on the ascent of the Master, extending from an achieved human spirituality to divinity:

> Must one go so far as to say, as certain Europeanized modern Chinese do, that he [Confucius] is not really a god? In Chinese, which has no common general term to designate beings superior to men, the question cannot even be posed, for one cannot tell what term to use. . . . Insofar as our term "god" can be applied to personages of Chinese mythology, it is thus clear that Confucius has been, at least until quite recently, a god (not of individuals, but of the State), to whom one prayed and from whom one expected "happiness."[①]

[①] Henri Maspero. *Taoism and Chinese Religion*. trans. Frank A. Kierman, Jr. Amherst: University of Massachusetts Press, 1981, pp. 136-137.

But *shen* was a contested concept in and among the various lineages of early Chinese thought, and it has been argued that the ambiguity that attends it is a significant element in its aura and semantic force.① Thus, another level of meaning of *shen* is "mysteriousness." The "Great Commentary" A5 on the *Book of Changes* states: 陰陽不測之謂神 "that which cannot be fathomed through effecting a *yinyang* contrast is what is meant by the truly mysterious," and again B4: 知幾其神乎 "understanding the incipient (*ji* 幾) gives insight into the mysteries of the world (*shen* 神)." Of significance in the nature and function of religiousness in this tradition is that the enchanted, numinous dimension of the human experience and its many mysteries (*shen* 神) does not belong to some other world. Far from it, such spirituality is the inexhaustible product of human efficacy and refinement within this world, and the boundless penumbra that emanates out from it.

Medical anthropologist Zhang Yanhua explains the intimate relationship that obtains among the aspectual cluster of terms that have been formulated to express the vital aspects of life itself from a physiological perspective, with *jing* 精 as the concentrated "life-force," *qi* 氣 as this same life-force in its activated and dispersed form, and *shen* 神 as the vigor and vitality of life itself:

> When it [life-giving energy] is concentrated, it is *jing*; when it is dispersed it turns into *qi*. If *jing* is the nurturing aspect of this energy, *qi* is the active configurational aspect of the same energy.... If *jing* and *qi* are the basis of life, then *shen* 神 is the manifestation of that life.... In other words, *shen* is the phenomenon of life activity itself.②

---

① Roel Sterckx. "Searching for Spirit: Shen and Sacrifice in Warring Staes and Han Philosophy and Ritual." *Extrême-Orient Extrême-Occident* 29, p. 23.
② Zhang Yanhua, *Transforming Emotions*, pp. 37-38.

*身 **shen.** "Lived, social body." See 體 **ti.** "Lived body, discursive body, embodying." 仁 **ren.** "Consummate persons, consummate conduct."

*生 **sheng.** "Living, growing, birthing." See also 氣 **qi.** "Vital energy, *qi*," and 勢 **shi.** "Purchase, momentum, configuration."

On the oracle bones, this character *sheng* 生 appears as 屮, and is explained by commentators as plant growth breaking through the earth.[①] There is an interesting and obvious contrast between the horticultural associations for "birth" and "life" suggested here, and the immediate human associations of mother and child. Such procreating is "derivation" in the sense of one thing being the source or origin of another as it gives birth to an independent existent. Indeed, to call the phenomenon of a plant breaking ground "birthing" in English sounds figurative and metaphorical rather than descriptive.

Sheng is conventionally translated in its noun form as "birth, life, and growth," verbally as "giving birth to, bearing, living, growing, producing," and adjectivally as "raw, unworked, fresh, strange," with the implication being that it is a new, unprecedented, and thus unfamiliar quantum of life. Thinking gerundively and thus eventfully, *sheng* as "living" takes us both generatively and qualitatively through the process from birth, through growth, to a life lived well. *Sheng* as "doing" takes us from the beginnings of an activity to its consummate fruition, and as "making" from raw, unworked ore to the refined product of an exquisite ceremonial *gu* 觚 drinking vessel. The *Shuowen* lexicon defines *sheng* as "advancing, extending, and spreading out" (*jin* 進), and as "growth breaking through the earth."

---

① Kwan, "Database," 甲骨文合集 CHANT 1381.

We might posit a contrast between a classical Greek ontological conception of human "beings" and a classical *Yijing* 易經 or *Book of Changes* process conception of what I will call human "becomings," a contrast between "*on*-tology" as "the science of being *per se*" and what I will call "*zoe*-tology" (*shengshenglun* 生生論) as "the way of living." The classical Greeks give us a substance ontology grounded in "being *qua* being" or "being *per se*" (*to on he on*) that guarantees a permanent and unchanging subject as the substratum for the human experience. With its combination of *eidos* and *telos* as the formal and final cause of independent things, this "sub-stance" necessarily persists through change. In this ontology, "to exist" and "to be" are implicated in one term. The same copula verb answers the twofold questions of first *why* something exists, that is, its origins and goal, and then *what* it is, its substance. This substratum or essence includes its purpose for being, and is defining of the "what-it-means-to-be-a-thing-of-this-kind" of any particular thing in setting a closed, exclusive boundary and the strict identity necessary for it to be this and not that.

The question of *why* something exists is answered by an appeal to determinative, originative, and undemonstrable first principles (Gk. *arche*, L. *principium*), and provides the metaphysical separation between creator and its independent creature. The question of *what* something is, is answered by its limitation and definition, and provides the ontological distinction between substance and accident, between essence and its contingent attributes. In expressing the necessity, self-sufficiency, and independence of things, this substance or essence as the subject of predication is the object of knowledge. It tells us, as a matter of logical necessity, what is what, and is the source of truth in revealing to us with certainty, what is real and what is not. As Zhao Tingyang 趙汀陽 avers, this kind of substance ontology defining the real things that constitute the content of an orderly and structured cosmos

... provides a "dictionary" kind of explanation of the world, seeking to set up an accurate understanding of the limits of all things. In simple terms, it determines "what is what" and all concepts are footnotes to "being" or "is."[①]

In the *Book of Changes* we find a vocabulary that makes explicit cosmological assumptions that are an alternative to this substance ontology and provides the interpretive context for the Confucian canons by locating them within a holistic, organic, and ecological worldview. This cosmology begins from "living" itself (*sheng* 生) as the motive force behind change, and gives us a world of boundless "becomings:" not "things" that *are*, but "events" that are *happening*. The ontological intuition that "only Being is" is at the core of Parmenides's treatise *The Way of Truth*. To provide a meaningful contrast with this fundamental assumption of "being," I have borrowed the Greek notion of "life" (*zoe*) and created the neologism "*zoe*-tology" as "the way of living." Zoetology as distinct from Greek "ontology," can be translated into Chinese as 生生論 *shengshenglun*. The *Book of Changes* B1 states that 天地之大德曰生 "the greatest capacity of the cosmos is its life-force." Again, in A5 in describing the unfolding confluence of vital "way-making" (*dao* 道) it observes that 生生之謂易 "it is the ceaseless generating and procreating that is meant by 'change'" (*yi* 易): change is defined denotatively as procreative life itself.

Seeing that the complex and ambiguous concept of "change" (*yi* 易) is thus defined in the *Changes* as a generic "ceaseless generating and procreating," we can still search the commentaries for the more specific implications of this process. The early commentaries

---

[①] 趙汀陽:《惠此中國》, 北京: 中信出版社, 2016, 引言: ……是對世界的"字典式"解釋, 試圖建立界定萬物的決定理解, 簡單的說, 就是斷定"什麼是什麼", 一切觀念皆為"在/是"(being/is)的注腳。

define the term *yi* 易 paronomastically with the homophonous *yi* 益 as "increasing, gaining, profiting, adding to." Consistent with this sense of gaining, Guo Moruo suggests we might understand *yi* 易 as an abbreviated form of *ci* 賜 or "gifting, transacting, exchanging" that leads to such increase. We can thus infer that in this *Book of Changes* ecological cosmology, such autopoietic, transactional change occurs synchronically *in situ* and diachronically *in medias res* as expansive and advantageous growth in the vital, situated relations that constitute experience. The mutual interest expressed among things in their constitutive relations grows and "appreciates" them in the sense of adding value to both themselves and their worlds. Just as human flourishing arises from positive growth in the relations of family and community, the isomorphic cosmic flourishing is an extension of this same kind of transactional growth but on a more expansive scale. Indeed, human values and a moral cosmic order are both grounded in life and its productive growth, and are thus continuous with each other as complementaries. In canonical texts such as *Focusing the Familiar* (*Zhongyong* 中庸) and the *Classic of Family Reverence* (*Xiaojing* 孝經), human feeling such as "sincerity, resolution" (*cheng* 誠) and "family reverence" (*xiao* 孝) give human beings cosmic force as co-creators, while cosmic ideas such as "way-making" (*dao* 道) and "coherence" (*li* 理) have their decidedly human aspect.

The starting point in this zoetological cosmology then is that nothing does anything by itself; association is a fact. Since the very nature of life itself is associative and transactional, the vocabulary appealed to in defining Confucian cosmology is irreducibly dyadic and collateral: always multiple, never one. Everything is at once what it is for itself, for its specific context, and for the unsummed totality. Thus there are always correlative *yinyang* 陰陽 aspects within any process of change, describing the focus and resolution that makes something uniquely what it is, and what by virtue of its vital relations, it is becoming. Important to an understanding of this vocabulary is the gestalt shift from the Greek noun-dominated thinking with its world of human beings and essential things, to the Confucian gerundive assumptions about the always eventful nature of humans "living" their lives within their natural ecology.

Turning to the human experience specifically, persons are not defined in terms of limitation, self-sufficiency, and independence, but ecologically by the growth they experience in their intercourse with other persons and their worlds. Since any one thing exists at the pleasure of everything else, the question of why things exist is explained by how they exist and what they mean for each other. And the necessity of defining what is what, is replaced by the possibilities each thing affords everything else for growth, revision, and redefinition. Zhao Tingyang suggests that in contrast to the dictionary definition afforded by Greek ontology, the Confucian cosmology provides

> ... an explanation of the "grammar" of the world, striving for a coordinated understanding of the relationships—between heaven and humankind, humankind and things, and humans and humans—by which all doings are generated, with a special emphasis on the mutuality of relationships, and the compatibility of all things.①

"Things" are not defined in terms of limitation, self-sufficiency, and independence, but by the growth they experience in their intercourse with other things. Like words in a sentence, meaning begins from the established grammar that provides the basic ordering of these words that is necessary for them to be intelligible.

---

① 趙汀陽:《惠此中國》, 引言: ……是對世界的"語法式"解釋, 力求對萬事所生成的關係（天與人, 人與物, 人與人）的協調理解, 尤其重視關係的互相性或萬事的合宜性。

And it is the association the words come to have for each other that is the basic source of meaning. The rhetorical effectiveness of the sentence, however, is achieved as the relations among the words are cultivated and are thus grown to become increasingly meaningful. And the sentence rises to the level of poetry through the artistry of optimizing the contribution each of the inimitable words makes to the specific others.

The living world as it is constituted by the interpenetration of interdependent "things" (or better, "events") requires a doctrine of intrinsic, constitutive relations to describe them. Erstwhile "things" do not occupy a place in the sense of simple location, but as living "events" they are "taking place" with time and space being simply aspectual descriptors rather than separate dimensions. Time is a quantum of growth; space is a taking place. Referring to the contrast that Confucian cosmology has with Aristotle's doctrine of "things" and their external relations, Angus Graham opines that in Chinese thought:

> ... things appear not as independent but as interdependent ... and the questions that isolate things from each other have no primacy over those which relate them.[①]

Graham is saying here that in Confucian cosmology what something "is" and how it is related to its environing others are two first-order aspects of the same phenomenon. Said another way, the individuality of something, far from being exclusive of its relationships, is constituted by those relations, and the quality of its uniqueness is a function of the quality achieved in these relations. This is but to say that the difference between personal identities and their narratives are simply a matter of foregrounding this focus or that field.

[①] A.C. Graham, *Studies in Chinese Philosophy and Philosophical Literature*, p. 395.

In clarifying the nature of vital "relations" that is relevant to this Chinese cosmology, Graham with his own language of "concrete patterns" versus second-order abstract "relations between things" introduces the distinction between internal, constitutive relations versus external, contingent relations:

> As for "relationships," relation is no doubt an indispensable concept in exposition of Chinese thought, which generally impresses a Westerner as more concerned with the relations between things than with their qualities; but the concern is with concrete patterns rather than relations abstracted from them...①

Graham is thus invoking a distinction between a doctrine of internal relations that are actually constitutive of erstwhile "things," and those second-order external relations that would merely conjoin discrete and independent things.

Appealing to the concrete example of personal identity, Graham's understanding of growing a person's "own potentialities," far from being frontloaded by locating the latent qualities or abilities of persons as some inherent nature that is then available to them for actualization, makes such potential inclusive of and a collaboration with their evolving processual contexts. It is thus that such persons, rather than being self-standing human "beings," can best be characterized in the language of human "becomings" who are internalizing their environing conditions as they emerge in the world.

With respect to human lives, human "becomings" are vital, interpenetrating, and irreducibly social "events." Such events make

---

① A.C. Graham, "Replies," in Henry Rosemont, Jr., *Chinese Texts and Philosophical Contexts: Essays Dedicated to Angus C. Graham*. La Salle, IL: Open Court, 1991, pp. 288-289.

meaning through the continuing cultivation of their relations, and transform life into poetry through the elevation and refinement of these relations. Taken at its broadest cosmic compass, the cosmological postulate we might translate as "changing and persisting" or "persistence in change" (*biantong* 變通) and its later echo in "forming and functioning" (*tiyong* 體用) gives us a summary language for how the notion of "life" (*sheng* 生) is explained in the *Book of Changes*. Instead of referencing discrete and self-sufficient "things," the notion of life-force and the events it inspires is given expression through an aspectual vocabulary that provides insight into both the determinate and the vital nature of these happenings. This language speaks to the different modalities of interaction and intercourse such events have in the flux and persistence of this world (*biantong* 變通), the symbiotic relationship between their forming and functioning (*tiyong* 體用), their presencing within a world characterized by both determinacy and indeterminacy (*dao* 道), the manifesting of a patterned configuration among these events (*xiang* 象), their assuming and then shedding of phenomenal forms (*qi* 器), and the unfathomable "more" that honeycombs these events and goes beyond our capacities of perception (*shen* 神). It is the confluence of the narratives of these events—the way-making (*dao* 道) and transactional coalescing (*de* 得) of each focal event (*de* 德) as it grows its relations with its environing others—that as an unsummed totality, is the cosmic *dao*. Importantly, the continuity between human life and the living cosmos is captured in the mantra: "the inseparability of human beings and their world" (*tianrenheyi* 天人合一).

The purpose of life and the form it takes is explained by the disposition of the natural world to an optimizing symbiosis in the relations that obtains among things, a proclivity to make the most of things captured in the prescriptive language of "balance and equilibrium" (*zhong* 中) and "superlative harmony (*he* 和). Human "becomings" as co-creators with this natural world have the capacity to participate fully in this living process, making the human life experience integral to the flourishing of the cosmic order. To human beings as cosmic meaning-makers falls the responsibility for the cultivation and the aestheticization of the human experience, rising above our natural animality to bring elegance and refinement to cosmic life through a contrapuntal, expansive relationship with the heavens and the earth.

Cosmic meaning is emergent in the vital transactions and exchanges among the unique events that constitute our world of experience. And the life experience thus understood is continuous, is genealogical, and is naturalistic in the sense of making no appeal to any external metaphysical or supernatural source. The phenomenal world in classical China is an endless flow, evidencing its formal character only as "trans-*form*-ation" in which the formal aspect, always attended by temporality, is the rhythmic cadence of life, and when properly cultivated, its musicality. In fact, the *Book of Changes* A4 says explicitly if rather obliquely that "the mysteries of the world exhibit no squareness and change is without shape" (*shenwufang er yiwuti* 神無方而易無體). The meaning of course is that insight into the mysteries of the world must go beyond all rationalizations because the process of change can never be contained or arrested by any formal structure. Putative "things" are in fact a processive and hence always provisional horizon of "events."[①]

The contemporary philosopher, Pang Pu 龐樸, makes an illuminating distinction in explaining two modalities of life as "procreating" (*sheng* 生). He contrasts procreating as "derivation"

[①] In fact, at least as early as the Ming dynasty, the Chinese expression for "thing," *dongxi* 東西, is literally "east-west," referencing the location of town markets and underscoring the relational and contextual understanding that attends Chinese phenomenological perceptions.

(*paisheng* 派生) in the sense of one thing being the source or origin in giving birth to an independent existent, like a hen producing an egg or an oak tree producing an acorn, with procreating as "transmutation" (*huasheng* 化生) in which one thing continuously transforms into something else, like summer becoming autumn, and autumn becoming winter. Although an important distinction, these two senses of "procreating" are profoundly asymmetrical. In the *paisheng* "derivative of" modality of growth, it is only the rare egg that is incubated to become another hen, and it is only the rare acorn that takes seed to become another oak tree. In the predominant *huasheng* "transmutating into" modality of change, most eggs in fact become omelets and most acorns, squirrels. And even in the rare cases where a hen's egg actually becomes another chicken, the erstwhile discreteness of this "independent existent" is qualified by the genealogical continuity that obtains between both its progenitor and its progeny.[①]

Both of these senses of the procreation of life—derivation and transmutation—have immediate relevance to Chinese cosmology as complements rather than severe distinctions. Importantly, as we have seen with the hen and her egg, the erstwhile discreteness and independence entailed by *paisheng* is necessarily qualified by the processual and contextual assumptions of *huasheng*. And the processual continuity of *huasheng* must be punctuated as unique "events" by the consummatory nature of life captured in the idea of *paisheng*. Neither uniqueness nor continuity will yield to the other; both are implicated in each other. The doctrine of internal relations that allows for the uniqueness and distinctiveness of particular things on the one hand, and for the continuity that obtains among them

---

① Pang Pu 龐樸, "Yizhong Youjide Yuzhou Shengcheng Tushi: Jieshao Chujian *Taiyi Shengshui*" 一種有機的宇宙生成圖式:介紹楚简《太一生水》, *Daojia Wenhua Yanjiu* 道家文化研究 17 (1999), p. 303.

on the other, disqualifies part-whole analysis and requires instead a gestalt shift to focus-field thinking in which this "part" and this "totality" are two non-analytic foregrounding and backgrounding perspectives on the same phenomenon.

In pursuing this distinction between "derivation" and "transmutation," Pang Pu is alerting us to a further refinement in our understanding of the relationship between what comes before and what follows from it, in the ongoing cosmological process. Taking human genealogy specifically as a concrete example, while we might be inclined to understand the progenitor and progeny as a derivative series in which there is an independence of the latter from the former, early Chinese cosmology on reflection sees genealogy as clearly a combination of both *paisheng* as "derivative of" and *huasheng* as "transmutating into." While *this* progenitor gives way to *this* unique progeny, at the same time, *this* progenitor as integral to a continuing family lineage lives on within the same progeny. The child has a certain "independence" from the parents, and yet the parents in so many ways that only begin with their physicality, live on in their child, and in their children's children too.

And the process of transmutation works in both directions. The progeny as heirs to the tradition embody what has come before. But at the same time, the histories through which progeny narrate their own origins and development are not solely or even primarily aimed at accurately depicting a closed past, but rather at disclosing arcs of change projected into open and yet more or less distinctly anticipated futures. At some level, change is inseparable from the process of both valorizing and actualizing new (or at least alternative) interpretations of the changes that have occurred. We must be self-conscious of the fact that our redescriptions of our histories while certainly being informed by past events, are also being reformulated to serve our own contemporary needs and interests.

We might also want to recall that the early associations for birth, life, and growth in the Chinese literature is plant life breaking ground rather than human beings giving birth, providing some explanation for the asymmetry favoring transmutation (*huasheng* 化生) over derivation (*paisheng* 派生). Indeed, one final reflection on life (*sheng* 生) that follows from the complementarity of the *paisheng* and *huasheng* distinction is to distinguish it from our familiar, commonsense understanding of "birthing" as simply "derivation." That is, mother gives birth to child, and one becomes two. As noted above with progenitor and progeny, each participates in defining the same, always evolving family lineage. Indeed, taken at a cosmic level, *dao* 道 is often characterized as the "mother" and thus the erstwhile fetal "source" (*shi* 始) of the myriad things (*wanwu* 萬物). *Daodejing* 1 for example, says:

> 無名天地之始；有名萬物之母……此兩者，同出而異名，同謂之玄。
> Indeterminacy names the fetal beginnings of the world, and determinacy names the mother of all things... These two emerge from the same source and yet have different names; together we call them the obscure and mysterious.

And yet *dao* and the myriad things, far from fitting the model of some independent creator and its creatures, are simply two aspectual ways of looking at the same phenomenon.

We encounter this alternative understanding of what *sheng* means in *Daodejing* 42: 道生一，一生二，二生三，三生萬物. D.C. Lau's translation of this passage is standard and ubiquitous in the literature: "The way [*dao*] begets one; one begets two; two begets three; three begets the myriad creatures."[1] "Begets" in this translation is the term *sheng* 生 that is usually translated as "birthing, living, growing." With such a conventional rendering,

---

[1] *Lao Tzu: Tao Te Ching.* trans. D.C. Lau. London: Penguin Books, 1963, p. 49.

it reinforces our sense of priority and sequencing—after all, the mother must precede the progeny. This uncritical "derivation" reading of *sheng* as simply "birthing" makes *dao* into some ultimate source that produces everything that is, and in so doing, overwrites Chinese cosmology with a familiar model of cosmogony not its own. If we read *sheng* here in a holographic way consistent with early Chinese cosmology, it will not allow for any exclusive separation between creator and creature, or between focus and field, or between derivation and transmutation. We must translate the text as describing the synchronic and diachronic "presencing" of the world around us as it is experienced from our perspective: "Way-making (*dao* 道) gives rise to continuity, continuity to difference, difference to plurality, and plurality to the manifold of all that is happening." *Dao* and all that is happening are simply two ways of entertaining the same phenomenon. *Dao* is both continuity and proliferation, both oneness and difference; what Tang Junyi characterizes as "the inseparability of one and many" (*yiduobufenguan* 一多不分觀). Many is one, one many.

This holographic way of understanding *sheng* as "presencing" is captured in the term "self-so-ing" or "such-ing" (*ziran* 自然). We must ask the question, what does *sheng* mean in a cosmogony in which *dao* 道 and the myriad things (*wanwu* 萬物) do not have the creator and creature relationship that is commonsense in metaphysical cosmogonies, but are instead two "aspectual" and nonanalytic ways of looking at the same phenomenon? The source whence they arise is *ziran* 自然: the "self-so-ing" of the cosmos. Certainly 道法自然 "*dao* models itself on self-so-ing" (*ziran* 自然), but 百姓皆謂我自然 "the people all say of themselves we are *ziran*" as well. Both *dao* and *wanwu* are explained through the vital interface between the indeterminate and the determinate, and the holography in this focus-field cosmology means that the totality is implicated in each of the foci. Which comes first, focus or field? They come together. What comes first, mother or child? They happen at the same time.

Said simply, our world, always experienced from one perspective or another, is autogenerative without appeal to some external source. In *ziran* as "self-so-ing," the "self-" (*zi* 自) is derivative in referencing the uniqueness of any particular perspective (what something is for itself), and is transmutative in referencing how this same perspective is constantly transforming in response to all of the constitutive relations it has with everything else, and that in sum makes it what it is (what something is for everything else). *Ziran* gives us a holistic, holographic model of everything being the "source" of anything, and thus anything having implicated within it the totality of all things.

With its emphasis on intergenerational transmission, on ancestor reverence, and on a continuing cultural identity, there has traditionally been a powerful sense of genealogical continuity in Confucianism, where the progeny is to be understood as a holographic foregrounding of a particular person within a continuing family lineage, and within an evolving cultural identity. One's family surname (*xing* 姓) is the first and continuing source of identity, while one's given name (*ming* 名) within the course of one's lifetime is complemented by a proliferation of assumed style names (*zi* 字), sobriquets (*hao* 號), and a web of specific family designations such as "uncle number two" (*ershu* 二叔) and "auntie number three" (*sanshen* 三婶), with a series of professional titles such as "teacher" (*laoshi* 老師) and "director" (*zhuren* 主任), and then when all is done, with a usually celebratory posthumous title (*shi* 謚). Each one of these different names as the many roles a particular person lives within a complex narrative, is a reflection of this person's unique contribution to the meaning of family and community, where the entire story is present within each ensuing episode of the life as it is lived.

*聖（人） *sheng* or *shengren*. "Sage, sagacity."

The graph for "sage" (*sheng* 聖) found on the oracle bones ![graph] is composed of the "ear" (*er* 耳) and the "mouth" (*kou* 口), and even as late as the Mawangdui archaeological find that dates from 168 BCE there are examples of this same graphic form ![graph].[①] The character is cognate with if not the same character as "listening" (*ting* 聽) ![graph], having the basic meaning of "listening to what is being said."[②] This character is also cognate with that for "sound" (*sheng* 聲). The suggestion is that sages are perceived as virtuosic communicators. The *Shuowen* lexicon defines *sheng* as *tong* 通, a term that has a range of meanings immediately relevant to sageliness: "penetrating, pervasive, connecting, communicating, understanding, expert." Sages "hear" what is valuable to hear and understand thoroughly what needs to be understood, and on this basis, give voice on behalf of the community to the shared vision of what will come to be. Their effectiveness as sages is measured by their capacity to draw the hearts and the hands of the people together to realize the shared project of shaping what it means to become human. The sage as virtuoso sings the songs that enchant the world.

Using the Confucian vocabulary itself, we might describe the ascent of human beings towards this sagely ideal from beginning as mere persons (*ren* 人) to achieving a relational virtuosity in their roles and relations (*ren* 仁). Again, personal cultivation pursued through social and political responsibility provides the possibility of becoming exemplary as a person (*junzi* 君子). For only a very few, by embodying in themselves the values and meaning that distinguishes some historical epoch of human flourishing, they have the ultimate

---

① Kwan, "Database," 甲骨文合集 CHANT H10478A and 馬王堆老子乙本卷前古佚書 89.
② Kwan, "Database," 甲骨文續存一，四五六.

distinction of becoming sages (*shengren* 聖人), and as such, sources of enduring cosmic meaning.

What the *shengren* or "sages" share in common with the "exemplary persons" (*junzi* 君子) is that both categories of conduct entail effective communication. For classical Confucianism, the flourishing community is necessarily a communicating community. The character for *jun* 君 of *junzi* is composed of "overseeing" (*yin* 尹) and "mouth" (*kou* 口); exemplary persons are those who oversee and bring order to the community through effective communication. Sages are likewise virtuosic communicators, but rise above the level of exemplary persons by virtue of the cosmic proportions of their reach and influence. Indeed, exemplary persons themselves stand in awe of the words of the sages (*Analects* 16.8).

In addition to possessing all of the qualities of exemplary persons, sages come to embody the substance of the traditional legacy, and in so doing, bring continuity to the human experience broadly, including those communities of the past, and those of the future. The continuing culture that finds its own definition in these rare persons is a resource for elevating the human experience to heights of profound aesthetic and religious refinement. The metaphors used to describe the sages are cosmic and celestial, raising the human being up to be a worthy partner with the heavens and the earth. The model of the sages shines across the centuries and across geographical boundaries as a beacon that not only anchors the human world, but that also serves succeeding generations as a source of cultural inspiration. It is these sages who lead the way of becoming human (*rendao* 人道) into its more certain future.

The *White Tiger Pavilion* (*Baihutong*《白虎通・聖人》), a text that purportedly records a series of discussions on socio-political matters held in Luoyang in 79 CA, defines what it means to be a sage paronomastically by rehearsing a series of terms frequently associated with sagacity in the philosophical literature. Again, it is the conduct of these sages described as being integral to the grand operations of nature itself that reflects the cosmic stature of these exemplars.

> 聖人者何? 聖者, 通也, 道也, 聲也。道無所不通, 明無所不照, 聞聲知情, 與天地合德, 日月合明, 四時合序, 鬼神合吉凶。
> What is it to be a sage? Sages are penetrating, are proponents of the proper way, and are listeners. There is nothing they do not understand about the proper way, there is nothing that is not illumined by their perspicacity, and on the basis of what is heard they are fully cognizant of any situation. They share in the virtuosity of the heavens and the earth, in the illumination of the sun and moon, in the turning of the four seasons, and in the fortune of the ghosts and spirits.

Much is to be learned from the frequent references to sages in the Confucian texts. In one passage in the *Analects*, Confucius dares not rank himself as a sage (7.33), and in another he laments that he never has, and probably never will, meet one (7.25). Indeed, according to *Focusing the Familiar* 29, the sage appears only once in a hundred generations. And yet the model is there.

Mencius uses the example of Confucius to define what it means to be the highest among the sages (see 2A2 and 5B1), placing him above the hoary sage-rulers of the past. Although Confucius died barely a century before the birth of Mencius, the Master is not only included in the pantheon of ancient sages, but is by virtue of his flexibility and accommodation singled out as being qualitatively far above everyone else. Mencius is picking up on a tradition that begins earlier in the *Analects* when the ever-modest Confucius gently chastises Zigong for likening him to a sage (9.6). Confucius's stature grows when in the last five books of the *Analects* that are devoted primarily to recording the observations of his now mature protégés, the metaphors used to celebrate Confucius are positively celestial. For example, in *Analects* 19.24:

> 他人之賢者，丘陵也，猶可踰也；仲尼，日月也，無得而踰焉。
> The superior character of other people is like a mound or a hill that can still be scaled, but Confucius is the sun and moon that no one can climb beyond.

This passage is representative of a number places in the *Analects* that pay tribute to the cosmic stature of the sage in general, and of Confucius in particular. This feature is repeated in *Focusing the Familiar* 31, for example, where those of the utmost sagacity are elevated to be the counterpart of *tian*. It is only of the most sagacious in the world that we can say

> 唯天下至聖……舟車所至，人力所通，天之所覆，地之所載，日月所照，霜露所隊；凡有血氣者，莫不尊親，故曰配天。
> … everywhere that boats and carriages ply, everywhere that human strength penetrates, everywhere that is sheltered by the heavens and is borne up by the earth, everywhere that is illumined by sun and moon, everywhere that the frosts and dew settle—all creatures that have breath and blood revere and love them. Thus it is said that they are the complement of *tian* 天.

Again, in *Focusing the Familiar* 30 it is the person of Confucius who is singled out in an unqualified celebration of the continuing human contribution to cosmic meaning:

> 仲尼……上律天時，下襲水土。辟如天地之無不持載，無不覆幬，辟如四時之錯行，如日月之代明。
> Confucius… modeled himself above on the rhythm of the turning seasons and below, he was attuned to the patterns of water and

earth. He is comparable to the heavens and the earth, sheltering and supporting everything that is. He is comparable to the progress of the four seasons, and the alternating brightnesses of the sun and moon.

The mantra usually invoked to capture Confucian human- and family-centered religiousness is "the continuity and inseparability of the human and the numinous" (*tianrenheyi* 天人合一). There is much textual evidence that human sagacity is the ultimate degree of coalescence in this first-order *tianren* relationship. As we witness throughout the canonical Confucian texts, the vague notion of *tian* takes on the visage of a particular human face as the texts repeatedly correlate these always unique sages with *tian* by characterizing the sages metaphorically in grand, celestial terms. Moral virtuosity (*de* 德), far from being described as the exclusive quality of *tian*, stands and is expressed as a collaboration between *tian* and the way-making of the sages who stand as the highest order of humanity. Given that the sages are the paramount exemplars of what is humanly possible, this moral virtuosity is manifested in the world as the consummate expression of the operations of both sagacious human beings and the contextualizing *tian* as their relationship is deepened in their collaborative activities. Not only is such sagacity to be understood as the human being achieving the reach and the influence of *tian*, but moreover we must allow that *tian* itself is deepened and extended by this accumulating human sagacity. This shared virtuosic conduct not only underscores the primacy of the *tianren* relationship over the secondary distinction between *tian* and human beings, but also makes the important point that human beings in their role as sages can continue and extend the work of *tian*. The highest order of human beings are nothing less than a co-creative and transformative moral force in the cosmos.

In these classical Confucian canons, human sagacity is understood not only as having the capacity to introduce epochal changes in the human experience, but also as having a transformative influence on the quality of *tian* and an amplificatory effect on the moral meaning of the cosmos broadly. Said another way, the relatively vague notion of *tian* as it is expressed in these early texts is brought into focus and made explicit through the specific lives of our human sages. If Confucius can elevate the worth of human "becomings" by insisting that they "are able to broaden the way," (*ren neng hongdao* 人能弘道), we can extend this celebration of humanity by joining Zhu Xi in proclaiming that "the sages can continue and carry out the workings of *tian*" (*shengren neng jitian liji* 聖人能繼天立極).① The ultimate expression of human stature in the Confucian world is nothing less than the aspiration of its sages to achieve a human virtuosity that would enable them to collaborate fully in guiding a flourishing cosmic order. And given the holographic nature of this cosmology, implicated within the persons of the sages are the worlds they have carried to this higher level. Their majesty comes not from a contrast between themselves and those less distinguished, but from how they have come to embody the heights that people under their sway have attained. Sages such as Confucius are not solitary and original. Rather they have evolving corporate identities that have implicated within them patterns of communal deference and meaning constitutive of the ethnic and national character inherited from the distant past. And a vital, living Confucius, expanding in significance with every passing generation, is alive and well in the twenty-first century.

Even with this cosmic stature, however, sages are not portrayed as grand, heroic figures who are proud, intrepid, audacious, and who as solitary exemplars stand apart in accomplishing superhuman

---

① See Zhu Xi's 朱熹 preface to his commentary on the *Zhongyong* 中庸章句 in his *Commentary on the Four Books* 四書集注.

feats. Rather, they are ordinary persons who become sages by doing what is ordinary in extraordinary ways. Although the conduct of the sages is of cosmic consequence, it is ultimately grounded like everything else in the prime moral imperative of family reverence (*xiao* 孝). When in the *Classic of Family Reverence*, Master Zeng asks Confucius explicitly "if there is anything in the virtuosity of the sages that is of higher value than familial reverence (*xiao* 孝)," Confucius's answer is simple:

天地之性，人為貴。人之行，莫大於孝。
Of all the creatures in the world, the human being is the most noble. And there is nothing done by human beings that outweighs family reverence.

Confucius then goes on to make the direct connection between the high human value of family reverence and the isomorphic cosmic order that is effected and galvanized through the proper regimen of sacrifices:

孝莫大於嚴父。嚴父莫大於配天，則周公其人也。昔者，周公郊祀後稷以配天，宗祀文王於明堂，以配上帝。是以四海之內，各以其職來祭。夫聖人之德，又何以加於孝乎？

In family reverence there is nothing that outweighs venerating one's father; in venerating one's father, there is nothing that outweighs placing him on a par with *tian*. And the Duke of Zhou was able to do this. Of old the Duke of Zhou performed the *jiao* sacrifice on the outskirts of the capital to the first ancestor of the Zhou, Hou Ji in order to place him on a par with *tian*. In the Hall of Brilliance, he performed the ancestral sacrifice to his father, King Wen, in order to place him on a par with *tian*. It was for this reason that all of the nobility within the four seas came each according to his office to assist in the sacrifices. How then could there be something in the virtuosity of the sages that surpasses family reverence?

The Eastern Han dynasty philosopher, Wang Chong 王充, summarizes the value that this Confucian tradition has traditionally invested in the institution of family as its singular strategy for the pursuit of optimal harmony:

聖人以天下為家，不別遠近，不殊內外……聖人舉事，求其宜適也……賢聖家天下。

Sages take the whole world as their family without distinction of near or far, of domestic or foreign . . . In their undertakings, the sages seek what is optimally appropriate. . . The most sagacious among us would "family" the whole world.

This "ordinariness" of the sages in their enchantment of the everyday is made explicit when Mencius and Xunzi both insist that everyone can become a sage. This claim is often read essentialistically as an assertion that the sage is some universally given potential in human nature that, if actualized, provides a person with those extraordinary talents through which to affect the world in some incomparable way. For Mencius, and for Xunzi too, it is important to understand that human beings are not "potentially" sages by virtue of some self-same, innate trait defining of all members of humankind who then, by virtue of it, reduplicatively become sages.

This claim that "everyone can become a sage" is an assertion that the spontaneous emergence of real significance in the ordinary business of the day is itself the meaning and content of sagely virtuosity. Those ordinary persons who in their own lives achieve *real* significance are sages. And given our initial conditions and our cultural resources, all of us have the opportunity to live such significant lives. There is an important difference between saying that everyone has some inherent potential for becoming a sage, and that everyone who behaves like a sage is a sage. The potential for sagehood lies not *within* individuals exclusive of their worlds, but when sages do appear, they have emerged *pari passu* in the collaborative and transactional careers of human becomings that constitute the substance of a human life.

The potential to become a sage emerges over time within the successful narratives of those persons who become most authoritatively human. That is, when the best among us behave habitually and consistently with sagacity in their conduct, they are then sages. Said simply, sages are what sages do. And *Mencius* 6B2 makes this point explicitly in saying that it is sagacious conduct alone that makes someone a sage:

> 曹交問曰："人皆可以為堯舜，有諸？" ……曰："……堯舜之道，孝弟而已矣。子服堯之服，誦堯之言，行堯之行，是堯而已矣。"
> Cao Jiao inquired: "Is it the case that we can all become Yaos and Shuns?" ...
> Mencius replied: "... The way-making of Yao and Shun was nothing but family reverence and deference to elders. If you wear Yao's clothes, speak his words, and do what he does, then you *are* a Yao."

*慎其獨　**shenqidu.** "Internalizing and consolidating virtuosic conduct as one's habituated disposition for action, being circumspect when dwelling alone."

This expression appears many times in several of the early Confucian canons, and the standard dictionaries have come to interpret it as "being circumspect when dwelling alone." This reading can be traced back to Zheng Xuan's 鄭玄 commentary on the term as it occurs in *Focusing the Familiar* (*Zhongyong* 中庸):

慎獨者，慎其閑居之所為。小人于隱者，動作言語，自以為不見睹，不見聞，則必肆盡其情也。

The exemplary person is circumspect in what he does when at leisure and dwelling alone. When petty persons are in seclusion and think their words and actions being out of the public gaze cannot be seen or heard, they give way to the most wanton feelings with no sense of restraint.

The rationale is that the ultimate demonstration of the virtuosity of exemplary persons who have fully internalized a sense of shame is that they conduct themselves in the one and the same way, regardless of whether they are in full public view or dwelling at home alone. While this interpretation is certainly consistent with the spirit of Confucian philosophy, in our reading of these same texts, we have chosen to translate it in a way that expresses the ultimate goal of personal cultivation: "internalizing and consolidating virtuosic conduct as one's habituated disposition for action."

The first chapter of *Focusing the Familiar* offers a succinct and explicit summary of the main thesis of this canonical text. *Focusing the Familiar* is, from beginning to end, a celebration of the continuing contributions of those human beings who embrace and take responsibility for their co-creative role in shaping the cosmic order captured in the mantra, "the continuity and inseparability of the human and the numinous worlds" (*tianrenheyi* 天人合一):

是故君子戒慎乎其所不睹，恐懼乎其所不聞。莫見乎隱，莫顯乎微。故君子慎其獨也。

It is for this reason that exemplary persons are so concerned about what is not seen, and so anxious about what is not heard. There is nothing more present than what is imminent, and nothing more manifest than what is inchoate. Thus, exemplary persons are ever concerned to internalize and consolidate virtuosic conduct as their habituated disposition for action.

The opening chapter of *Five Modes of Virtuosic Conduct* 五行篇explains how a person's conduct becomes habituated as characteristic, identity-forming patterns of moral virtuosity, and how this continuing cultivation first produces efficacy (*shan* 善) in human relations and then culminates in a world-changing moral virtuosity (*de* 德). This is the same distinction we find in *Mencius* between simply doing something that is prompted by the anticipated approbation of others, and acting consistently and instinctively out of a cultivated moral virtuosity (*de* 德) that in having been self-consciously habituated, has become who you actually are. In *Mencius* 4B19 we read:

> 舜明於庶物，察於人倫，由仁義行，非行仁義也。
> Shun was wise to the way of all things and had real insight into human roles and relationships. He acted upon his moral habit of being consummatory and optimally appropriate in his conduct rather than merely doing what was deemed consummatory and appropriate by others.

There are persons who merely follow conventional values in acting in a way deemed proper by the community, and there are those who through an assiduous personal regimen have been able to establish and consolidate consummatory habits of conduct in their roles and relations, and who act out of this moral virtuosity.[①]

[①] The processual nature of education introduces some complexity into this distinction. One begins importantly in understanding what one's significant others deem virtuosic, and then modeling one's own conduct on what they do. It is only in the fullness of time that one is able to internalize and habituate such conduct.

Contemporary scholar Liang Tao on the basis of recently recovered archaeological texts has argued convincingly that the meaning of *shenqidu* 慎其獨 is to internalize and consolidate the five modes of conduct as a habitual disposition for acting with moral virtuosity.[①] The commentary included in the Mawangdui version of *Five Modes of Virtuosic Conduct* (*Wuxingpian* 五行篇) provides an explicit definition of this familiar phrase:

慎其獨也者，言舍夫五而慎其心之謂也。獨然後一，一也者，夫五為［一］心也，然後得之。

The expression *"shenqidu"* means getting rid of the distinction among the five modes and bringing focus to one's heartminding. Having consolidated these five modes of conduct, they become one. And this "one" then refers to the five modes of virtuosic conduct that, having been consolidated as the [one] heartminding, is then taken to be who one is.

This commentary is explicit in referencing *xin* or "heartminding" as the personal identity that is produced when these five patterns are set as the root of virtuosic conduct.

How then does this cultivated moral virtuosity "take shape within" to become habituated conduct? The meaning *shenqidu* as it is found in the *Expansive Learning* (*Daxue* 大學) has much the same import as when it occurs in *Five Modes of Virtuosic Conduct*. It is defined as "becoming resolute in one's thoughts and feelings" (*chengqiyi* 誠其意): that is, internalizing and consolidating a habitual disposition of conduct to be expressed consistently in one's conduct as moral virtuosity.

[①] See Liang Tao 梁涛, "Zhu Xi dui 'Shendu' de Wudu jiqi zai Jingxue Quanshi zhong de Yiyi" 朱熹對"慎獨"的誤讀及其在經學詮釋中的意義, *Zhexue Yanjiu* 哲学研究 (2004), 第 3 期, pp. 48-54.

*士　shi. "Warrior, retainer, knight, scholar-official."

The notion of *shi* evolves over time. On the bronze inscriptions, the character appears as the head of an axe , immediately associating this category of persons in the earliest times with the military.[①] In the *Book of Songs*, for example, the term *shi* is used sometimes as a person of middle social status, at other times as a retainer, and yet again to designate a servant. It also appears to be a term for a lower-level functionary of a lord, perhaps a man of arms, somewhat akin to the old English knight (and Arthur Waley translates the term as such). In time, it was generalized as simply meaning "male person," and was used for scholars, staff members, counselors, and civil officials. The *Shuowen* lexicon defines it paronomastically with the homophone "affairs, service" (*shi* 事), noting that the graph *shi* 士 combines "one" (*yi* 一) and "ten" (*shi* 十), meaning that numbers commence from one and finish with ten. Making clear what is implied, the lexicon cites Confucius as stating that the person who is able to deduce one from ten can become a scholar-official.

Confucius appropriates *shi* for his own use, giving it (as well as other terms such as *junzi*) connotations that shift the sense and reference of the term away from position, rank, birth, or duties toward what we would describe as aesthetic, moral, and spiritual growth, the interrelatedness of these qualities being self-evident to Confucius. Most of the twelve passages in the *Analects* that refer to *shi* suggest they are civil service apprentices of some kind. The *shi* are to be precise and formal, punctilious perhaps. They have already extended themselves beyond the family, for in no passage in the *Analects* is *xiao* as "family reverence" associated with the *shi*. While these passages referring to the *shi* have suggested to many commentators that they are descriptions of the qualities of the *shi*,

---

[①] Kwan, "Database," 西周早期 CHANT 9454.

we believe they are better construed as providing instructions for what the *shi* should do. They have set out on a path, their own road, but they still have a long way to go, and there is much yet to be done. As Master Zeng instructs them in *Analects* 8.7:

曾子曰："士不可以不弘毅，任重而道遠。仁以為己任，不亦重乎？死而後已，不亦遠乎？"

Master Zeng said, "Scholar-officials (*shi* 士) cannot but be strong and resolved, for their duties are heavy and their way (*dao* 道) is long. Where they take becoming consummate in their conduct (*ren* 仁) as their duty, is it not a heavy one? And where their way ends only with their death, is it not indeed a long one?"

In the *Analects*, the *shi* are described as having assumed the burden of cultivating themselves to become consummate in their conduct (*ren* 仁), hinting strongly that this is a commitment to a moral and spiritual apprenticeship, for *ren* is, again, the highest virtuosity for Confucius. Further evidence that the *shi* are those who have set out on a spiritual path is found elsewhere in which they are exhorted to eschew material well-being on account of it (4.9 and 14.2).

There are, of course, numerous positive instructions the Master proffers not only for the *shi*, but for others as well: become steeped in poetry and in history; study and practice ritual propriety (*li* 禮) in all that you do: listen to, play, become absorbed in music; perform public service when it is appropriate to do so; and above all, by so engaging in these efforts, learn to extend empathy beyond the family, clan, and village, to become both benefactor and beneficiary within a much larger circle. Again, the *shi* are never instructed in the proper behavior and demeanor due one's parents, children, or other relatives. If this reading of early Confucianism is warranted, it will follow that the major goal toward which the *shi* are striving is to become exemplary persons, or *junzi* who are defined in terms of their service to effecting the proper social and political order. The *shi does*, while the *junzi* more nearly *is*.

*勢 **shi.** "Purchase, momentum, configuration." See also 氣 **qi.** "Vital energy, *qi*," and 生 **sheng.** "Living, growing, birthing."

Shi is in summary all of the conditions that constitute the propensity of circumstances. *Shi* is not a given; it must be cultivated and shaped. This developmental aspect of *shi* is made explicit in its etymological root, *yi* 執, "sowing, planting, cultivating," and the cognate, *yi* 藝, "the arts." *Shi* is the key and defining idea in the militarist text, *Sunzi: The Art of Warfare* 孫子兵法, and continues to be an important image in its sequel, *Sun Bin: The Art of Warfare* 孫臏兵法. Basically, in the militarist literature, *shi* is calibrating and manipulating circumstances to create a strategic advantage as the intelligent alternative to deploying brute force.

The images used to express *shi* in these militarist texts are many, each of them focused in such a way as to suggest some specific area in its broad spectrum of meaning. Round boulders and logs avalanching down a precipitous ravine and cascading water sending huge rocks bobbing about underscores its sense of the overwhelming momentum. The taut trigger on the drawn crossbow emphasizes timing and precision. That this same crossbow is able to dispatch the enemy who has been rendered vulnerable by its disadvantageous circumstances while keeping the bowman free from harm's way illustrates strategic advantage. The bird of prey swooping down to knock its victim out of the air stresses the agility that gives full control over one's own movement and the coordination of this movement with that of the target.

Shi refers to the differentials on the field of battle (numbers, terrain, logistics, morale, weaponry, and so on) that in sum gives one side an advantage over the other. *Shi* is both the shape and the momentum that the military encounter assumes: the tide of battle as it advances. *Shi* is the superior purchase that gives troops the will to join a downhill battle and the leverage that enables them to crush the enemy. In this military philosophy, all determinate situations can be turned to advantage. The able commander can create opportunities by manipulating his position relative to the position of the enemy. By reconnoitering and developing a full understanding of those factors that define one's relationship with the enemy, and by actively controlling and shaping the situation so that the weaknesses of the enemy are exposed, one is able to ride the force of circumstances to certain victory.

The distinction between "straightforward, regular, expected operations" (*zheng* 正) and "surprise operations" (*qi* 奇) is a key dyadic distinction in these militarist texts. *Zheng* is not simply a head-on assault; it is rather what the enemy expects you to do. And *qi* is the unexpected. As in the Tet Offensive in the Vietnam War, insurgency is a *zheng* tactic for insurgents, while a coordinated all-out frontal assault on multiple allied bases and urban centers for them was *qi*. In the *Sunzi* 5, the alternation of *zheng* and *qi* operations already receive important notice as essential to securing strategic advantage (*shi* 勢):

> 可使必受敵而無敗者，奇正是也……凡戰者，以正合，以奇勝。
> It is "surprise (*qi* 奇) and "expected (*zheng* 正)" operations that enable one's army to withstand the full assault of the enemy force and remain undefeated.... Generally in battle use the "expected" to engage the enemy and the "surprise" to win the victory.

The *Sun Bin* 31 further elaborates on *zhengqi*, liking its application to the cadence and rhythm of nature. A vital element in battle is preventing the enemy from accruing the information necessary to develop a complete picture of one's deployment and logistics. The "surprise" attack takes advantage of this opaqueness and impenetrability:

故有形之徒，莫不可名；有名之徒，莫不可勝……形以應形，正也；無形而制形，奇也。

All things or events that have a distinguishing shape or form can be named, and all things that can be named can be prevailed over.... To respond to the determinate (*xing* 形) by means of the determinate is the "expected" operation; to control the determinate with the indeterminate is a "surprise" operation.

The clarification that the *Sun Bin* brings to the *Sunzi*'s claim that the surprise operation will "win the victory" is to underscore the interdependence and complementarity of *zheng* and *qi*. This positive attitude toward the ability of the commander to recognize, manipulate, and capitalize upon the indeterminate element in warfare is what distinguishes the able soldier from the gambler. A corollary to this cultivation of purchase is that the best commander far from being celebrated for heroically snatching victory from defeat, is the one who in having the expertise to acquire overwhelming force, goes unnoticed as only presiding over an inevitable outcome.

Having acquired these military associations, *shi* at a later stage in its development was taken over by the Legalist theorists and given a political application in many ways analogous to its militarist usage. Whereas the ruler as an individual is limited in his capacity to regulate the conduct of others, from the strategically advantageous position of the throne he can use his political status as ruler and the techniques derived therefrom to amplify his influence over others. It is this political status and its application as a fulcrum for increasing the ruler's ability to control others that is political as opposed to military *shi*.

In response to both the Militarist and Legalist development of this term, the Confucian-oriented texts such as the *Xunzi* appropriated *shi* and reshaped it to have a moral as well as a political compass. Indeed, the *Xunzi* contests the Militarist emphasis on the primacy of *shi* as strategic advantage in military engagements, and subordinates it to considerations such as winning over the people and gaining popular support, suggesting that *shi* on the battlefield is best understood as a by-product of moral government. The ultimate outcome of war is not determined by temporary military advantages such as deployment of troops and favorable terrain. Rather, *shi* is the victory made possible by the popular support of the people who the ruler has won to his side by his moral government. Thus, from the perspective of Xunzi, *shi* is the popular support enjoyed by the ruler as a *result* of the ruler's first concern: moral government.

In addition to setting aside the Militarist emphasis on the primacy of *shi* in the use of arms, the *Xunzi* also argues against the primacy given *shi* in the Legalist conception of effective government. Legalist political philosophy rejects the Confucian reliance upon moral suasion and the loyalty it engenders in favor of the manipulation of *shi* and rule by intimidation. It repudiates the fundamental Confucian precept of exalting the worthy and employing the able. Where the Confucians placed their faith in the transforming influence of the ruler as a consummate *person*, the Legalists stressed the objective conditions of his *position*.

Given the general impetus of the *Xunzi* toward a syncretic reworking of Confucian doctrine, and given Xunzi's historical position as the standard-bearer of Confucian ideas at a time when Legalist thought and institutions were approaching their apogee, it is not surprising that he would take it on himself to defend an evolving Confucian philosophy against the Legalist conception of *shi*. To a certain extent, Xunzi does accept the Legalist insistence

勢 shi. 229

on the importance of *shi* in maintaining political control. In fact, he even credits the enlightened sages of antiquity with the innovative introduction of this notion of political purchase, accepting its function of reinforcing social and political order. In *Xunzi* 23:

故古者聖人以人之性惡，以為偏險而不正，悖亂而不治，故為之立君上之埶以臨之，明禮義以化之，起法正以治之，重刑罰以禁之，使天下皆出於治，合於善也。

The sages of antiquity regarded human tendencies to be brutish. They saw it to be prejudiced, unruly, perverse, and erratic, making the people rebellious and disorderly. They established the political purchase of the ruler in order to oversee them, clarified ritual practices and moral principle in order to transform them, introduced social standards and norms to bring order to them, emphasized penal law and punishments in order to restrain them. The people of the world as a consequence all conducted themselves with decorum and in conformity to what is good.

While maintaining certain reservations, Xunzi does acknowledge the effectiveness of the state of Qin's program for political domination of the empire. At the same time, true to his Confucian commitment, he asserts that in the attainment and preservation of political control, moral and intellectual superiority in the administration of government must take precedence over the manipulation of political advantage. In *Xunzi* 16:

處勝人之埶，行勝人之道，天下莫忿，湯武是也。處勝人之埶，不以勝人之道，厚於有天下之埶，索為匹夫不可得也，桀紂是也。然則得勝人之埶者，其不如勝人之道遠矣！

If one were to exercise the political purchase of a victorious person and carry out his ways, no one in the world would object. Tang and Wu are a case in point. If a person were to exercise the political purchase of a victorious person and yet not carry out his ways, even though he has the purchase of the emperor of the entire world, in the end he would not even get away with being a commoner. Despots Jie and Zhou are a case in point. Such being the case, that acquiring the ways of a victorious person is much more important than acquiring his political purchase is all too clear.

Although the ruler is the person with access to the most political purchase in the world, if he strays from the Confucian way of the True King, he would have been better off without any authority at all. He cites the historical examples of the miscreant rulers, Jie and Zhou, who had the birthright of emperor with all of its concomitant purchase and yet lost everything because of moral deficiency and the ultimate turning away of their people. *Xunzi* 11:

> 國者，天下之制，利用也；人主者，天下之利勢也。得道以持之，則大安也，大榮也，積美之源也；不得道以持之，則大危也，大累也，有之不如無之。

The state is the most efficacious instrument in the world, and the ruler is the person in the world with the most political purchase. If he manages this instrument within the perimeters of the proper way, he will enjoy great security and honor, and will be the source of an increasing number of good deeds. But if he exercises this purchase without reference to the proper way, he will suffer great peril and ill-repute, and would have been far better off with no position at all.

Xunzi's primary objection to the Legalist conception of *shi* is that where they regard *shi* itself to be a sufficient condition for political control, Xunzi is convinced that *shi* without popular support is a sinking ship and ultimately untenable. And the people can only be won over by the actions of a morally superior ruler who is devoted to the public good—that is, the True King. While the enlightened ruler devotes himself to the welfare of his people with that knowledge that popular support also guarantees his own security, the unenlightened ruler concerns himself with *shi*. Good governance begins with employing the right people. Xunzi condemns the Legalist injunction to control his ministers and officials by exercising the purchase available to him as ruler as a decidedly inferior method, exacting their obedience rather than winning over their loyalty. In *Xunzi* 12:

> 故明主急得其人，而闇主急得其埶。急得其人，則身佚而國治，功大而名美，上可以王，下可以霸；不急得其人，而急得其埶，則身勞而國亂，功廢而名辱，社稷必危。

The enlightened ruler takes winning over the best people as his most urgent task while the benighted ruler busies himself with the acquisition of political purchase. Where the ruler exerts himself in winning over the best people, the state will be properly ordered while he personally will lead a life of ease, his accomplishment will be substantial, and he will be held in high regard. If he is of the highest quality he can become a True King, and if less so, still a hegemon. But if the ruler does not exercise himself in winning over the best people but instead busies himself with the acquisition of political purchase, the state will be disorderly in spite of him having exhausted himself, his accomplishments will be negligible, and he will be of poor repute. The altars of his state will be in grave peril.

When understood in its extended cosmological sense, this same notion of *shi* as an alternative way of thinking about causality can be used to argue the claim made by Joseph Needham that Chinese cosmology has "its own causality and its own logic:"

> A number of modern students—H. Wilhelm, Eberhard, Jablonski, and above all, Granet—have named the kind of thinking with which

we have here to do, "coordinative thinking" or "associative thinking." This intuitive-associative system has its own causality and its own logic. It is not either superstition or primitive superstition, but a characteristic thought-form of its own. H. Wilhelm contrasts it with the "subordinative" thinking characteristic of European science, which laid such emphasis on external causation.①

Needham draws heavily on Marcel Granet to provide what is a vivid description of the unfamiliar cosmological vision we need as our interpretive context for understanding the Confucian worldview, alerting us not only to what this cosmology is, but perhaps more importantly, to what it is not:

> The Tao [*dao*] was the all-inclusive name for this order, an efficacious sum-total, a reactive neural medium; it was not a creator, for nothing is created in the world, and the world was not created. The sum of wisdom consisted in adding to the number of intuited analogical correspondences in the repertory of correlations. Chinese ideals involved neither God nor Law. The uncreated universal organism, whose every part, by a compulsion internal to itself and arising out of its own nature, willingly performed its functions in the cyclical recurrences of the whole...②

Needham says in explanation of *dao*, "the universal uncreated organism" often described as the "source" of all things, that it "was not a creator, for nothing is created in the world, and the world was not created." What he means here is that this cosmology brings with it an alternative understanding of creativity. Dismissing *creatio ex nihilo* as having any relevance, Needham understands creativity

---

① Needham, *Science and Civilisation*, Vol. 2, p. 280.
② Needham, *Science and Civilisation*, Vol. 2, p. 290.

as a generative procreativity and a continuing *in situ* or "situated" increase in meaning that would defy any erstwhile separation between creator and creature. The furniture of the world is not created in the sense of emerging out of nothing, and it does not suffer annihilation in the sense of returning to nothing. *Dao* and the myriad things (*wanwu* 萬物), rather than referencing distinct and independent realities, are two aspectual ways of looking at the same always transforming phenomenal world and our continuing experience within it.

In understanding what Needham means here by "rotational responsibility" with each thing having "a compulsion internal to itself," we must invoke the doctrine of internal relations defining of this "uncreated organism" and the alternative, holistic "causality" it entails. In this classical cosmology, the animating and transforming *qi* 氣 is conceptualized in terms of what in modern parlance we might call a "vital energy field" in which "things" are sometimes more and sometimes less persistent perturbations or foci in this field. Having arisen, these intertwined "events" continue in the fullness of time to transform into other things. The vital field is not only pervasive as a condition of all things but also, consistent with Needham's description of this field as "a reactive neural medium," it is the "neural," existential medium through which all situated things emerge in their relations to constitute what they are becoming. There is neither animating *qi* without structuring form, nor form without animating *qi*. Indeed, "form" and "animating *qi*" are two nonanalytic aspects of the same transforming reality, where both are implicit ways of understanding the transformative "functioning and forming" (*tiyong* 體用) process. As such, "animating *qi*" and the various ways we have of saying "forming" are an explanatory rather than an ontological vocabulary; we need both terms to give an adequate account of what we experience.

The focus-field cosmology that Granet and Needham are

ascribing to this Chinese worldview and the aspectual language needed to give it voice are revealing of what Needham is referring to as "the universal uncreated organism" with "its own causality and its own logic." With respect to causality then, given the vital, internal, and constitutive nature of the relations that underlies the focus-field holography, causality does not reference some agency outside and temporally prior to the perceived configuration of the things happening but rather speaks to the creative, interdependent, and causal nature of the relations themselves. Chinese cosmology begins from what is happening within the autogenerative world itself (*ziran* 自然) rather than appealing to the notion of a transcendent and independent First Mover as the cause and architect of the world. If we see relationality as first order reality and all individual actors as abstracted or derived from them, then we must understand causality in a cosmos described as autogenerative (*ziran* 自然) to be the backgrounding or foregrounding of particular foci and their unbounded fields, where anything is the cause of everything, and everything is the cause of anything. This *ziran* causality means that the "self" (*zi* 自) in the "self-so-ing" process is certainly uniquely what it is, but it is also inclusive of all of the extended relations of any particular thing or event as this manifold of relations conspires and gives life to the unique conatus (*ran* 然) that makes this thing insistently so. Said simply, everything causes anything, and thus any particular thing is both the cause and the effect of everything else.

We can use this complex notion of *shi* as a concrete way of expressing this aesthetic alternative to the logic of "things" and its "external causality." As we have seen with the etymology of *shi*, it is not a given but must be cultivated. Situations do not just happen; they emerge in their complexity as a growing pattern of changing relations that are vital, and that display the possibilities of incremental design as well as an achieved, aesthetic virtuosity. Situations by definition also have a morphology or "habituated" aspect—a localized place with its insistent particularity and its own persistent yet always changing configuration. In this morphology, we must see the relationality as first order, actual reality and all individual actors within it as conventionally abstracted and derived from this pattern of relations. Putative "things" are horizons, and thus only convenient abstractions from persistent and continuous matrices of interdependent relations. And these relations do not terminate anywhere, but reach out to the furthest limits of the cosmos. Any particular "thing" or situation emerges at the pleasure of every other situation, and is thus at once a cause and an effect.

We might be initially overwhelmed when we rehearse what is in fact only a selective, non-exhaustive list of the possible English translations for this term *shi*. At the same time, we might look for an organizational logic in this glossary of terms by relegating these different translations to four rubrics selected from among them:

Relationality: leverage, differential, advantage, purchase
Vitality: potential, momentum, timing, tendency, propensity
Virtuosity: influence, power, force, style, dignity, status
Embodiment: terrain, configuration, situation, circumstances, disposition, shape, appearance

Such a range of renderings used to translate *shi* as it is found in different contexts is revealing of the extraordinarily broad compass of meaning implicated in this one term. On reflection and with imagination, we can recover a perhaps unfamiliar, alternative logic and a sense of causality from a survey of these seemingly disparate meanings. We might observe that *shi* is holistic, denoting "thing," "action," "attribute," and "modality" all at once. Hence, it is translated in different contexts as a noun, a verb, an adjective, and an adverb. In lifting coherence out of this pattern of seemingly disjunctive associations, we might begin from the matrix of relations that constitute any particular situation and register the vital and thus changing pattern or structure that emerges from them. This dynamic structure—from its first-order relationality and vitality to its achieved virtuosity as it bodies forth—can be drawn upon to answer some of our basic cosmological questions.

First, this reflection on *shi* provides an alternative vocabulary for thinking through the dynamics of our field of continuing experience and the multiplicity of its contents. *Shi* provides a centered, 'from-field-to-focus' conception of how we come to individuate "things" and set horizons on them. That is, beginning from the wholeness of experience, we divide up, conceptualize, foreground, and thus make determinate an eventful "thing" within an otherwise continuous flow of relations, by bringing focus and meaningful resolution to its horizons as it is entertained from one perspective or another. The primacy of vital relations means that situation will always have priority over agency, and that no putative agent does anything by itself.

An ostensive "thing" is first a specific focus or matrix or configuration within an expansive context of always changing, constitutive relations. Importantly, it can be cultivated and shaped to achieve insistent focus and resolution in its interdependent relations with the "other" things that are constitutive it. The dynamics of *shi* explains what it means for something that is at once unique and yet continuous with other things to act and to move, and to be acted upon and to be moved, where it's shaping and being shaped is one continuous process.

Shi as thus one and many—as unique foci within their respective fields—provides some insight into the logic of a more fluid sense of continuity within diversity, and of an internal and spontaneous *ziran* causality in which everything "causes" anything, and anything is a cause of everything. The inseparability of continuity and diversity guarantees the uniqueness of each situation, and means at the very least that there can be no single dominant order, but only many interdependent and interpenetrating sites of order.

When this term *shi* with its alternative logic and causality is used to reflect on the human condition specifically, it explains the emerging individuality of unique, potentially large-souled "persons" situated within the evolving circumstances of their extended families and communities, and within the changing conditions of their natural and cultural environments. *Shi* suggests how the persisting habits and the specific habitudes that constitute human identities are shaped from originating existential impulses into the definite and significant activities of always unique persons. Such persons are irreducibly transactional, internalizing and embodying their environs as uniquely focused fields of roles and relations. The cultivated distinctiveness of such persons far from being exclusive of their relationships, is rather the immediate product of the quality that is being achieved in them. To the extent that we are able to thrive within productive relations, we can emerge as distinctive and sometimes even distinguished persons, thereby bringing distinction to the nexus of relations to which we belong. The holographic reversibility of inner and outer means that in searching inwardly for a unique, lived identity we are in fact surveying the quality of the web of outward relations that make us who we are. And in projecting outward to register most fully the unbounded web of relations that give us context we are reflexively discovering our innermost selves.

Since the entire world is implicated within each of us as persons, it is only appropriate that we regard ourselves with the same esteem that we would extend to the world. Or said more simply, to love ourselves is to love the world. It is only those who by fully realizing this interpenetration between world and things, and by understanding the interpenetration among things themselves, can defer to their environs as a precondition for making their own distinctive contribution to it and exercising their influence within it.

*始　shi. "Fetal beginning, natal beginning, genealogical beginning."

The absence of an independent, transcendent source in Chinese cosmology must be factored into the way in which cosmic origins has been understood. Summarizing cosmological speculations from a significantly earlier period, the second century BCE "cosmology" section of the early Han dynasty text, the *Huainanzi*, contains this passage:

> 天墜未形，馮馮翼翼，洞洞灟灟，故曰太始。太始生虛霩，虛霩生宇宙，宇宙生元氣，元氣有涯垠。
> Before the heavens and the earth had yet to take shape,
> There was a soaring, gliding, plunging, sinking.
> This is known as the Great Natal Beginning.
> The empty and remote gave birth to space-time,
> Space-time gave birth to primordial *qi*,
> And primordial *qi* had its horizons.[①]

The "cosmogony" offered here is a natal and historical account that occurs within the unfolding process of "world as such" as opposed to describing a metaphysical intervention from outside of the world. It describes a birthing from an inchoate, incipient life-form that presupposes genealogy and progenitors rather than originative principles or divine design, and a pattern of always situated and cultivated growth in significance rather than the linear actualization of some predetermined potential. This is what Frederick Mote means when he argues:

[①] *A Concordance to Huainanzi* 3/18/18; compare John Major, *Heaven and Earth in Early Han Thought*, p. 62.

The genuine Chinese cosmology is that of organismic process, meaning that all parts of the entire cosmos belong to one organic whole and that they all interact as participants in one spontaneously self-generating life process.①

Benjamin Schwartz also perceives this important generative feature of Chinese cosmogony when he is prompted to ask:

Does the fact that in later Chinese high-cultural accounts of the origins of mankind or of the cosmos, the dominant metaphor is that of procreation or "giving birth," rather than that of fashioning or creating, have anything to do with the centrality of ancestor worship with its dominance on the biological metaphor?②

There is a clear contrast between metaphysical *creatio ex nihilo* assumptions defining of some Greek and Abrahamic interpretations of origins or beginnings, and the contextualized *creatio in situ* process that is characteristic of Chinese natural cosmology.

In the process cosmology of early China, continuity, particularism, change, context, and novelty are all conditions of a continuing present. This means that, in the fullness of time, whether viewing the cosmos retrospectively or prospectively, any rationalizing vocabulary that we might appeal to as an interpretive grid for explaining our experience is outrun by the never-ending generative process itself. Hence the language of interpretation offered in this *Huainanzi* passage such as "the heavens and the earth" (*tiandi* 天墬[地]), "space-time" (*yuzhou* 宇宙), "primordial *qi*" (*yuanqi* 元

---

① Frederick Mote. *Intellectual Foundations of China*. New York: McGraw-Hill, 1989, p. 15.
② Benjamin Schwartz. *The World of Thought in Ancient China*. Cambridge: Harvard University Press, 1985, p. 26.

氣), "empty and remote" (*xuguo* 虛霩), "horizons" (*yayin* 涯垠) and so on, discloses our competence in explaining cosmic order in the present moment. But these same terms of art were "born" as insights into the nature of a changing reality, and their explanatory force will necessarily, in the passage of time, expire. That is to say that the cosmogonic account is also an "epistemogonic" narrative that at once recounts an emerging interpretation of world order, and sets historical limits on this interpretation. Our relatively clear understanding of our present, always provisional situation cannot be universalized and relied upon to explain all situations. The cosmogonic narrative takes us back to an earlier set of conditions that, requiring its own terms of understanding, cannot be explained by the application of our present philosophical vocabulary. As the cosmos changes, so must the language of its explanation. The procreative process is traced back to a dark chaos that resists description in our familiar cosmological language rather than to the increasing illumination provided by uncovering some ultimate, independent source of design and cosmic meaning. Hence, unlike some traditional Western cosmogonies that usher us back to the putative origins of an intelligibility that overcomes chaos, Chinese natural cosmogonies direct us back to what, from our present perspective, is a world wherein the further back we go, the more dark, amorphous, and remote it becomes for us.

Often *dao* 道 is described in the language of a cosmological "source," the "origins" of the world as we know it. But this cosmological *dao* far from being a superordinated metaphysical principle that stands independent of its creatures is in fact the ongoing living process that includes them all. It is the generative and always contingent genealogical unfolding of the world itself as our field of experience. If order is truly inherent and emergent rather than existing as an independent principle, then the language that describes all aspects of this "world-ing" must be historicized

始 *shi*.

as a provisional, sometimes poetic and sometimes metaphorical vocabulary for the world order *as we know it*.

Again, the sense of "beginning" in such cosmogonic narratives is *shi* 始—found on the bronzes as [glyph] and defined in the *Shuowen* lexicon as a woman giving birth.[①] This notion of a natal beginning is associated with a series of cognate characters: the fetus (*tai* 胎) that comes to inherit a world "bequeathed" (*yi* 詒) to it and "passed on" (*yi* 貽) from progenitors who have come before. The language is pervasively genealogical and ancestral (*zong* 宗), including within this vocabulary rather vague expressions such as "lord" (*di* 帝) and the often-anthropomorphic *tian* 天 that straddle the human and the numinous realms—both the ancestors and the gods.

The "empty" (*xu* 虛) as it is used in this *Huainanzi* passage is to be understood contextually as a positive emptiness within shaped, determinate things that makes things functional: for example, the emptiness of a cup that anticipates the process of filling it up. In this instance, the natal is the "empty," indeterminate source that honeycombs the phenomenal world out of which a cosmos is constantly being born. This space is the fecund life-source of the as-yet unmanifested but soon to be determinant phenomena that emerge to make our next moment different from this one. *Xu* has often and unfortunately been confused with the primordial Chaos as a gaping emptiness, a dark formless void, familiar in some classical Western cosmogonies. There is no decontextualized void as such in the classical Chinese cosmology, and thus no final emptiness. Both shaped and unshaped things have, by default, only a phenomenological reference to the interface between determinacy and indeterminacy that defines our experience. The absence of transcendence in Chinese cosmology precludes an ontology of Being as what really *is*, and of Non-Being (or Not-Being) as a putative

---

[①] Kwan, "Database," 西周晚期 CHANT 4338.

absence of existing things.

Let me try to take this distinction between natal or genealogical birthings, and metaphysical beginnings a step further. Many scholars have noted that cosmogonic myths did not feature in classical Chinese cosmology, and only begin to appear in China in the literature of the Han period.① For example, Angus Graham states:

> The past to which Confucius looks back is not the beginning of things; there is no cosmogonic myth in pre-Han literature, merely a blank of pre-history before the first Emperors, who for Confucius are the pre-dynastic sages Yao and Shun.②

This position is contested by other scholars such as Paul Goldin who is confident that the appearance of cosmogonies in China is not only of an earlier provenance, but that they are pervasive, and are similar in kind to that found in our classical Western sources.③ This

---

① See for example Michael Loewe. *Chinese Ideas of Life and Death: Faith, Myth, and Reason in the Han Period (202 BC-220 AD)*. London: Allen and Unwin, 1982, p. 63; K. Schipper. "The Taoist Body." *History of Religions* 17 (1978) No. 3, 4, p. 371; Tu Wei-ming. *Centrality and Commonality: An Essay on Chung-yung*. Honolulu: University of Hawaii Press, 1976, pp.118-119.

② Angus Graham, *Disputers of the Tao*, p. 12. See also Frederick Mote. "The Cosmological Gulf Between China and the West." *Transition and Permanence: Chinese History and Culture*. ed. David C. Buxbaum and Frederick W. Mote. Hong Kong: Cathay Press, 1972, p. 7.

③ A rather complete statement of this challenge to the claim that early Chinese cosmology offers no creation myth is to be found in Paul R. Goldin, "The Myth That China Has No Creation Myth," *Monumenta Serica* 56, pp. 1-22. On his own admission Goldin is pitting himself against most of the best sinologists of the twentieth century (see not only the text itself but his footnote 6). In characterizing the position we outline in David L. Hall and Roger T. Ames, *Anticipating China*, Goldin describes us as purveyors of "an updated Orientalism" because we claim that classical Chinese "cosmology" is "acosmotic." We introduced this neologism to argue that classical Chinese cosmology posits a world that (*Continued on next page*)

ostensive debate, however, really misses the point. The crux of the matter lies not in whether or not there is cosmogony in classical Chinese cosmology. This question is easily answered. The natural cosmology pervasive in this tradition is procreative, and is cosmogonic in entailing continuing natal beginnings, whether such birthings are remembered by existing mythologies or not. The nub of the issue lies rather in distinguishing between a genealogical and a metaphysical cosmogony, the implications of this difference being profound. This fundamental distinction is not lost on Norman Girardot:

> There is no doubt that there are significant differences in the

(*Continued from previous page*) has neither a radical beginning nor constitutes a "single-ordered world," characteristics of cosmogonies that begin from a transcendentalism. Goldin then rehearses a series of Chinese canonical texts that he claims exhibit a cosmogony that has an initial beginning and that is ordered by an independent principle. For example, he analyzes a cosmogonic passage from the *Huainanzi* 7/54/26 that describes "two gods who were spontaneously born" 有二神混生, a familiar metaphor for *yinyang* that we find in several *Huainanzi* passages (cf. 1/1/10 for example) that describe such "gods" as "traveling together with transformation" 神與化游 . The Gao You 高誘 commentary observes: 二神, 陰陽之神, 混生, 俱生也. "The two spirits, far from being external to the transformative process, are numinous forces that constitute its inner *yin/yang* dynamic." But rather than interpreting these "gods" as the tension within the continuing procreative process that produces transformation, Goldin describes them as "*custodians* external to the created world" who, because "the Myriad Things could not have come to exist by *ziran*," therefore belong to "a time before the Myriad Things." We would aver that Goldin, in his attempt to find the basis for a single-ordered world in classical Chinese cosmology, misses our point, eliding as he does the distinction between what we have called a metaphysical cosmogony that entails external agency and a holistic, continuing genealogical cosmogony that has the energy of transformation within the process itself. He is right in observing that not all cosmogonies in the classical Greek tradition entail a single-ordered world, but we too argue that the notion of *kosmos* as a single-ordered world is relatively late. Early Greek philosophers such as Anaximander and Empedocles, for example, posit multiple world cosmogonies.

ancient Chinese world view in comparison with other traditions, but the notion that the cosmological gulf consists in the nonexistence of myth, creation myth, or mythological thought is an issue that deserves to be put to rest with all possible dispatch. It is not the absence of creation mythology that accounts for the cosmological differences but the manner and nature of the Chinese interpretation of traditional mythological creation tales. The real "gulf" has to do with how different early civilizations fathomed the mythological gap of chaos. . . . The Chinese twist that is given to this archetypal plot is that creation as well as cosmological and soteriological meaning, do not ordinarily involve the epic idea of a final and permanent conquest of some existential chaotic foe.①

John Major in his interpretation of the technical chapters of the *Huainanzi* discusses in some detail the various accounts of cosmogony that are to be found in this work. Indeed, we might join the conversation between Major and Hal Roth when they compare a passage that first appears in the *Zhuangzi* 2—probably of pre-Han vintage—with a similar account found in the early Han dynasty *Huainanzi* 2. Indeed, these two passages while being almost identical in content make almost antithetical philosophical points—one questioning the very possibility of initial beginnings, and the other trying to describe the several stages in the gradual process of birthing as it unfolds.② Here I will first translate the *Huainanzi* 2 version:

[有] 有始者，有未始有有始者，有未始有夫未始有有始者，有有者，有無者，有未始有有無者。

---

① N.J. Girardot, *Myth and Meaning in Early Taoism: The Theme of Chaos (huntun)*, Berkeley: University of California Press, 1983, pp. 12-15.
② See Major, *Heaven and Earth in Early Han Thought*, pp. 326-327.

There is that which had a beginning.① There is that which has not yet begun to have "that which had a beginning." And there is that which has not yet begun to have that which has not yet begun to have "that which had a beginning." There is that which is something; there is that which is nothing. And there is "that which has not yet begun to be either something or nothing."②

The earlier *Zhuangzi* version seems very similar, although unlike the *Huainanzi* that references a concrete phenomenon as "something that had a beginning," the *Zhuangzi*'s focus is on the very idea of "beginning" itself:

> 有始也者，有未始有始也者，有未始有夫未始有始也者，有有也者，有無也者，有未始有無也者，有未始有夫未始有無也者。
> There is a "beginning." There is: "not yet begun to have a beginning." There is: "not yet begun to have 'not yet begun to have a beginning.'" There is: "something." There is: "nothing." There is: "not yet begun to be nothing." There is: "not yet having begun to have 'not yet have begun to have nothing.'"③

While the intent of the author in the *Zhuangzi* passage is to reject *conceptually* and *logically* the possibility of an initial beginning by appealing to an inescapable infinite regress, the author of the *Huainanzi* version wants instead to describe *historically* the increasingly obscure stages as we move backward through the evolving birthing process of the phenomenal world that we presently know.

---

① Note that the phrase that comes before is repeatedly embedded in the phrase that follows. On this basis, the character *you* 有 is added to the first phrase.
② *A Concordance to Huainanzi* 2/10/14.
③ *Chuang Tzu [Zhuangzi]* 5/2/49.

While the point being made in these two passages is clearly different, the *Zhuangzi* and the *Huainanzi* still share an important assumption that would distinguish both of them from what might be taken to be seemingly similar cosmogonic descriptions in classical Western sources, for example, the cosmogonies to be found in *Genesis*, the *Timaeus*, and the *Theogony*. That is, we must resist the eliding of the distinction between genealogical cosmogonies on the one hand, and metaphysical cosmogonies in which chaos is overcome by some external principle on the other. In the latter case, chaos as formlessness, as confusion, and as separation, is overcome by command (will) (*Genesis*), by reason (*Timaeus*), or by unity (passion) (*Theogony*) respectively. "Etiological tales"—stories of origins—introduce notions of agency and construal that give rise to causal thinking and rationality. To reason is to construe or uncover order; it is to think *causally*.

In a transcendental or metaphysical cosmogony, the originative and determinative principle—the Abrahamic God or Plato's Forms—stands independent of its creature and, as an external source, imposes a preassigned design on chaos. Even Aristotle's attempt to make form "immanent" does not alter its transcendental status as immutable in its relationship to matter. And his self-sufficient Prime Mover contemplating itself as the content of its own thought secures its independence from anything beyond it. Natural change is then driven by a linear teleology that takes us from origination to the realization of the given design. There is a plan, a beginning, and an end. Some ahistorical, acultural Agent—some Being behind the beings, some Creator behind the creatures—must be posited in order to explain why things *are* rather than *are not*, and *why* they are *what* they are. Metaphysical cosmogony is very ambitious: It promises us that if we are able to trace "the many" back to the ordering One, all will be known.

Both the *Zhuangzi* and the *Huainanzi*, as different as they are, come down on the genealogical side. We must distinguish between a transforming world that *emerges* historically and genealogically in the classical Chinese texts where the generative energy of its birthing comes from within the world itself, and a world *derived* from some transcendent principle familiar in some classical Western accounts. Consistent with this historical cosmogony, we find that *tian* and *di* on the oracle bones and in the early canons often have an anthropomorphic reference, prompting some of the early interpreters of Chinese culture (and some contemporary scholars as well) to assume a correspondence between the sometimes anthropomorphic Abrahamic God and these Chinese terms.[1] But on the Chinese side, anthropomorphism is a natural extension of a human-centered religiousness, where the object of reverence is usually genealogical and ancestral. Indeed, the historicist anthropomorphism we find in Chinese cosmology that allows for the intervention of ancestors on behalf of their progeny is profoundly different in kind from a transcendentalism that depends upon divine intervention as its source of meaning, and revelation as its source of knowledge.

---

[1] See Huang Yong. "Confucian Theology: Three Models." *Religion Compass* 1 No. 4, pp. 455-478 in which he gives a nuanced account of the interpretations of early missionaries such as Matteo Ricci. *The True Meaning of the Lord of Heaven.* Taipei: Ricci Institute, 1985, and more contemporary scholars such as Benjamin Schwartz. *The World of Thought in Ancient China*; Julia Ching. *Confucianism and Christianity: A Comparative Study.* Tokyo: Kodansha International, 1977; and Kelly James Clark. "Tradition and Transcendence in Masters Kong and Rorty." *Morality, Human Nature, and Metaphysics: Rorty Responds to Confucian Critics.* ed. Huang Yong. Albany: State University of New York Press, 2007; and "The God of Abraham, Isaiah, and Confucius." *Dao: A Journal of Comparative Philosophy*, Vol. 1 (2005), pp. 109-136. These scholars would claim that *tian* and *di* as discussed in the Chinese sources reference a transcendent deity comparable to the Christian God in many crucial aspects.

*恕 **shu.** "Putting oneself in the other's place, deference, empathy, dramatic rehearsal."

The commitment in Confucian role ethics to a radical empiricism is in clear evidence in its appeal to the method of *shu* 恕 as the pathway to consummate conduct (*ren* 仁). *Shu* is a critical and experimental strategy in which, with imagination, we rehearse the different possible dramatic scenarios for action in our roles and relations in our attempt to find the best one among them. There have been different interpretations of this term *shu* in the commentarial literature as scholars have puzzled over its import for ethical decision-making and its many implications. This perplexity is reflected in the various ways in which *shu* has been translated: as "altruism" (Wing-tsit Chan), as "reciprocity" (Tu Wei-ming, Raymond Dawson, and Ni Peimin), as "consideration" (Waley), as "mutuality in human relations" (Fingarette), and as "understanding" (Slingerland). I think at the end of the day, it is D. C. Lau who has the best grasp on the meaning and function of *shu* when he interprets it as the method of "using oneself as a measure in gauging the wishes of others" and thereby determining how to become consummatory in one's conduct (*ren* 仁).[1] To use the term "method" rather than "methodology" is purposeful, resisting as it does the separation of the theoretical from the practical and ends from means. Ni Peimin

---

[1] Wing-tsit Chan, *A Source Book in Chinese Philosophy* p. 44; Tu Wei-ming. *Centrality and Commonality: An Essay on Confucian Religiousness*. Albany: State University of New York Press, 1989, pp. 34–36; Raymond Dawson. *Confucius*. New York: Hill and Wang, 1981, p. 41; Arthur Waley. *The Analects of Confucius*. London: George Allen and Unwin, 1938, p. 105; Herbert Fingarette. *Confucius: The Secular as Sacred*. New York: Harper and Row, 1972, p. 55; *Confucius: Analects with Selections from Traditional Commentaries*. trans. Edward Slingerland. Indianapolis: Hackett, 2003, p. 242; and *Confucius: The Analects (Lunyu)*. trans. D.C. Lau. pp. xv–xvi.

insists that *shu* as a productive method must be distinguished from any simple application of rules:

> A method is different from a rule in that a method is *recommended* to *enable* a person to live better, whereas a rule is *imposed* on a person to *limit* what one can do.①

Shu requires imaginative analogical projection in the service to an inclusive moral generosity. Put simply, *shu* is a kind of deference. This understanding is borne out by the etymology of the graph, constituted as it is by the combination of the cognate character, *ru* 如, that means "as to, like, as if, resembling, can be compared with, supposing, the same as" and *xin* 心, "heartminding." This character *ru* 如 occurs in the oracle bones as 㘝, interpreted by commentators as one person inquiring of another.② Indeed, this notion of analogical deference is also suggested by the cognate character *ru* 汝 that means "you"—that is, paying attention to and taking the "other" into full account in what we do. Putting these ideas together, *shu* is activating the moral imagination of our thoughts and feelings necessary to conjure forth the most productive possible actions available that register fully the needs and interests of everyone, and to then arrive at and act upon one's best moral judgments. That is, *shu* is consideration: a thoughtful and heartfelt deference to others as we determine what it is best to do.

Inspired by Lau's reading, I will argue it is "deference" and the "deferring" that is entailed by "dramatic rehearsal" that is the best way of understanding this key term. *Shu* resonates with *yi* (義), "appropriateness." *Shu* like *yi* can also be thought of as discerning

---

① Ni Peimin. *Understanding the* Analects *of Confucius: A New Translation of* Lunyu *with Annotations*. Albany: State University of New York Press, 2017, 67.
② Kwan, "Database," 甲骨文合集 CHANT 0470.

and then acting upon what is judged most appropriate. The emphasis is on a careful consideration of the needs and concerns of others in determining what the best course of action might be, and how one might best dispose oneself in relationship to them in order to accomplish it. It entails "other-directed" deference in the sense that the action is prompted by the needs of someone else. *Yi*, on the other hand is doing what is appropriate, where the emphasis is on following one's own best sense of what is right in being responsive to the concerns of others. Both *yi* and *shu* entail a reflexive or "self-including" sense of how to interact with others, and both are at play in most situations that require ethical consideration.

There can be no question of the central importance this *shu* method of "putting yourself in the other's place" has in the Confucian moral vocabulary. When in *Analects* 4.15, Confucius insists 吾道一以貫之 "his proper way" (*dao* 道)—his moral vision—is bound together with a single, continuous thread," one of his senior protégés, Master Zeng, explains to the other students what Confucius means by such a declaration: 曾子曰："夫子之道，忠恕而已矣。""The moral vision of the Master is simply putting yourself in the other's place (*shu* 恕) and then doing your utmost (*zhong* 忠), nothing more." Lau makes the compelling argument that *zhong* and *shu* can be fairly described as "one" continuous thread because they are in fact two aspects integral to the same decision-making process. *Shu* is the imaginative reflection within a process of scenario rehearsal whereby one tries to determine the best thing to do, and *zhong* is then the commitment to do one's best in ensuring its successful outcome.

On another occasion, Confucius again makes *shu* a primary strategy for determining conduct when he responds to Zigong's question: "Is there one term that can be acted upon until the end of one's days?" Confucius says categorically: 其恕乎 "indeed, it is shu."[①] The process of *shu* begins from moral perplexity, requires a critical self-awareness and the imagination necessary for a creative search for the most appropriate response by rehearsing alternative scenarios and their outcomes, and then culminates in investing the assiduous effort necessary to realize what has been determined to be the best course of action. It is not surprising that *shu* in the classical texts and in the *Shuowen* lexicon is frequently associated with *ren* 仁 as the desired consequence of this method of deliberation; that is, *shu* is the method whereby one achieves what is consummate in one's roles and relations.

Just as *shu* is a matter of reflectively coordinating one's own conduct with the behavior of others to optimum effect, *ren* is also the product of such analogical deliberation and growth. Importantly, *shu* as a method of deliberation and *ren* as consummate conduct are each means and end. One deliberates in order to be deliberate, and one aspires to act consummately in order to be consummate. We have seen this process captured in the *Analects* 6.30 when this *shu* method of deliberation is explained more elaborately: 能近取譬，可謂仁之方也已 "Correlating one's conduct with those near at hand can be said to be the way of becoming consummate in one's conduct (*ren* 仁)."

Herbert Fingarette in his reflection of the use of *shu* in the *Analects* rejects a Kantian interpretation of *shu* as universalizing one's conduct because of the impossibility of arriving at universal maxims that are not themselves thwarted by the problem of "relevantly similar circumstances." That is, the application of the categorical imperative would require the moral equivalent of a legislator to formulate an inexhaustible code that would cover all possible situations. As an alternative explanation of *shu*, Fingarette

---

[①] *Analects* 15.24: 子貢問曰："有一言而可以終身行之者乎？"子曰："其恕乎！己所不欲，勿施於人。" Compare *Analects* 5.12 and 12.2.

suggests that for Confucius it functions as analogy:

> One key word here is *p'i* [*pi*] 譬, a word used with some frequency in the *Analects*. Although it is rendered in bi-lingual dictionaries by the English "to compare," the important features of its use in the *Analects* to which I would direct attention are these: First, *p'i* in the *Analects* is always a "comparison" of likenesses, not differences. Hence, "analogy" is an appropriate term. Second, the comparison is expressed in terms of imagery, of persons, situations or activities, not in terms of abstract traits. Hence, *p'i* is in the *Analects* typically metaphorical . . . The use of *p'i* is characteristic of Confucius' way of teaching. . . . It contrasts sharply with the method of abstract analysis, theory building, universalizing. *Shu*, in turn, is a specific kind of *p'i*. To be able from what is close—i.e., oneself—to grasp analogy with the other person, and in that light to treat him as you would be treated—that is *shu*.①

Another revealing discussion of this term in the classical canons that reinforces Fingarette's about analogizing the specific differences rather than Kantian universalizing is the *Focusing the Familiar* 13 commentary on *shu*'s meaning as it is used in the *Analects*:

> 子曰："道不遠人。人之為道而遠人，不可以為道。《詩》云：'伐柯伐柯，其則不遠。'執柯以伐柯，睨而視之，猶以為遠。故君子以人治人，改而止。忠恕違道不遠，施諸己而不願，亦勿施於人……"
>
> The Master said, "The proper way (*dao* 道) is not at all remote from people. If someone takes as the way that which distances them from others, it should not be considered the proper way. In the *Book of*

---

① Herbert Fingarette. "Following the 'One Thread' of the *Analects*." *Journal of the American Academy of Religion*. Thematic Issue 47, No. 3S (1979), pp. 382-383.

Songs it says:
> In hewing an axe-handle, in hewing an axe-handle—
> The model is not far away.

In grasping one axe handle to hew another, if one looks obliquely at the axe handles, they seem far apart. Thus, exemplary persons (*junzi* 君子) use one person to shape others properly, and having thus improved upon them, leave off. Putting oneself in the place of others (*shu* 恕) and doing one's best on their behalf (*zhong* 忠) does not stray far from the proper way. "Do not treat others as you yourself would not wish to be treated."

The proper way of conducting oneself always emerges out of what is close at hand—out of the particular, concrete circumstances. Although the pattern of the axe-handle is close, there is always a critical distance between the template and the product, between the established pattern and the particular axe-handle that is presently being fashioned. The new and always unique axe-handle is not only hewn on the model of the existing one, but further, the existing axe-handle itself is actually the instrument that is used to shape the emerging product. Similarly, in the human world, the conduct of one person serves as a model to inform and bring proper form to others.

Perhaps the most telling phrase in this passage is "and having thus improved upon them, leaves off." That is, just as the hewing of the axe-handle results in something similar yet discernibly different, so the shaping of one person in relation to another is directed at harmony, not sameness. The dynamics of this analogizing between the existing pattern and the newly fashioned article, when applied to the proper way of being human, is captured conceptually in *zhong* and *shu*.

We can say that *shu* is the moral application of correlative or analogical thinking. The centrality given to *shu* respects the unparalleled importance that self-awareness and imagination play in correlating one's conduct with others and in refining our moral judgment through deliberation. Moral imagination is not invoked as supplemental, subsidiary, or remedial to a critical self-awareness but as necessary for the continuous education and refinement of our empathetic capacity for understanding and responding effectively to the interests of others. As in any aesthetic judgment, imagination is the motive effort to correlate each of the specific details within the entire picture of what is occurring, and in so doing, to broaden the context of moral consideration and the quality of one's response.

Shu is a fundamentally aesthetic disposition initially shaped within family bonds where one's "person" emerges in the process of striving to optimize the concrete roles and relations one lives. *Shu* is this grandson responding to this grandmother, taking her both as an object of his deference and as a resource for his own personal growth in his relations to others. Of course, the deference runs both ways as the grandmother must determine what is best for this grandson as opposed to that one. In the fullness of time, *shu* is then extended as a quality of responsiveness in shaping and deepening relations outside of the home.

"Putting yourself in the other's place" (*shu* 恕) is thus an omnipresent and indispensable disposition for living life deliberately and responsively. It requires a critical self-awareness, a keen memory that recalls analogous situations, a creative imagination that can provide a serial rehearsal of possible scenarios in anticipation of their consequences, an empathetic understanding of the other, a penetrating intelligence that can discern the best course forward, and an assiduous resolve that is able to make the most of felicitous correlations.

And *shu* contrasts sharply with the assumption that more abstract and calculative analytic or theoretical strategies are sufficient in themselves for determining moral conduct. Understood as "putting yourself in the other's place," it is the most fundamental gesture of a concrete, contextualizing moral disposition. It entails a recognition of the importance of "deference" both in the sense of fully considering the interests of others and in the sense of deferring action until we can overcome uncertainty through sound deliberation in our moral inquiry. There is certainly a significant role for cognition and deliberation in *shu*, but we do not want to overly rationalize this process. *Shu* requires a holistic responsiveness. With *shu* there is perhaps an even more central role for affective inquiry to complement the cognitive in an epistemology of feeling that weighs up the circumstances with full empathy and concern. Just as a critical skepticism can become a matter of intelligent habit, so too an empathetic responsiveness to others can become a routinized disposition for compassionate concern. In fact, the evolution of a *shu* habitude lies in its growth from what is at first a more deliberative exercise to become a kind of extemporaneous, unselfconscious moral artistry in one's interpersonal activities. As Ni Peimin argues, such refinement in one's dispositions is not only morally empowering but liberating by expanding one's range of options for intervention:

> Once a person becomes a master artist, he or she would be able to use discretion and respond appropriately even when the situation demands deviation from well-established protocols.[1]

There is a further point with regard to deference that can be inferred from the *Analects*, where *shu* as "putting yourself in the other's place" is given an alternative characterization. *Shu* in this text is also defined negatively as "do not impose on others what you

---

[1] Ni Peimin, *Understanding the* Analects, p. 67. Ni refers the reader to *Analects* 9.30.

yourself do not want."

This Silver Rule is a "negative" version of the Golden Rule because it does not begin from the assumption that there is some objective and universal standard that can serve as warrant for "doing unto others as you would have them do to you." Indeed, to begin from the presumption that there is such a standard and that one has privileged access to it, and furthermore on that basis to assume one knows the right thing to do to someone else, is at the very least condescending if not disrespectful. Instead, by assuming the negative version of the Golden Rule, the task remains open and provisional, allowing that deliberation on how to best grow the relationship with this person can only be pursued through a careful consideration of the needs of this specific person within the possibilities of these specific circumstances.

Further, in using the critically reflective and reflexive process of scenario rehearsal as the basis for determining what would be the best course of action, an obvious principle of exclusion is to avoid doing to others what we ourselves do not like. In our reflections on what is best to do, doing to someone else what we ourselves do not want done to us would at the very least contaminate our motives. Indeed, the starting point for "putting yourself in the other's place" is the awareness that there are indeed other places. A good beginning in the inquiry, then, would be to discount those actions that we find undesirable. But more important, beyond this rather obvious beginning, we must be fully cognizant that there is a world of contingencies that require thoughtful and imaginative exploration.

In fact, it is because *shu* must be understood as the evolving patterns of deference necessary for a flourishing community that Confucius invests such singular importance in it. In a world constituted by unique individuals located within a dynamic matrix of roles and relationships, the performance of these roles and relationships can only be effectively driven by the giving and the receiving of deference. When students in the classroom defer to the wisdom of their teacher, it activates the possibilities of their learning. When the teacher defers to the potential and the important interventions of each of the very different students, the class is further motivated, and everyone including the teacher become avid learners.

*術　*shu.* "Techniques of rulership."

Inasmuch as the Legalist (or *fajia* 法家) policies were new and revolutionary for their own time, they could not count on the authority or sanction of history. On the contrary, the traditional attitudes and the political precepts of the old order for them represented alternatives to their concept of unified rule under one standard—alternatives that could not be safely entertained. In the construction and operation of their political machine, the possible interference of traditional standards and values was intolerable and had to be contained. In disposing of these old attitudes, the Legalist theorists, rather than arguing against their validity, quite cleverly devised a rational and very persuasive argument. In the *Book of Lord Shang* 《商君書・開塞》 we read:

> 聖人不法古，不修今。法古則後於時，修今則塞於勢。周不法商，夏不法虞，三代異勢，而皆可以王。
> The sage neither imitates antiquity nor follows the status quo. To imitate antiquity is to be behind the times; to follow the status quo is to be bogged down in the face of changing circumstances. The Zhou dynasty did not imitate the Shang and the Xia did not imitate the ways of Yu. These three ages lived under different circumstances and yet they were all able to rule the world.

The assertion that the intelligent ruler must make his political measures appropriate to the changing times is really the essence of the Legalist's conception of history. Different periods have different problems, and different problems require new and innovative solutions. Old principles of government, even when proven effective in their own historical moment, are now more than likely obsolete. The primary concern of the ruler when carrying new political measures into effect has to be their successful implementation and efficacy. In other words, the end served by this kind of government is first and foremost the interests of the ruler and his absolute control. While such interests may seem rather mundane, one must bear in mind the historical context of the Warring States period, and the domestic and international strife that gave rise to this extreme form of totalitarianism. It is in service to this end that the Legalist "techniques" (*shu* 術) were developed.

With the rise of the Legalists came their four cardinal precepts: penal law (*fa* 法), the "two levers" of rewards and punishments (*erbing* 二柄), political purchase (*shi* 勢), and the techniques of rulership (*shu* 術). The Legalist theorists conceived of an administration structured on self-regulating "systems" as the most effective means of achieving the purposes of the ruler. The first of these systems is the codification and promulgation of an objective and universally applicable body of laws. From the ruler's perspective, the reduction of litigation to a machinelike process through the elimination of the human element guarantees order within his borders. Once established and set in motion, the laws arrest social and political irregularity and function automatically to ensure swift and severe punishment for anyone foolish enough to challenge the system. As a complement to the rule of law, the *shu* as a generic technical term for the various techniques of rulership were developed and implemented.

The ruler, having structured the empire's administration on the basis of these systems, controls the state rather than administers it.

That is, the ruler whose absolute authority is guaranteed by the very operation of these systems simply reclines in confidence, overseeing the routine and efficient operation of his governmental machinery. His *shi* 勢, the political purchase due him by virtue of his unassailable position coupled with strict adherence to the techniques (*shu* 術) are sufficient to ensure his continuing control.

Of these techniques of rulership, one of the most important is the Legalist variant on *wuwei* 無爲, its own aberrant version of the Daoist notion of "noncoercive actions." In the Legalist conception of state, the positions and occupations of ruler and minister are clearly defined. The ministers are integral, functioning, and active components in the bureaucratic system; the ruler is not. Rather, he is the human embodiment of the government machinery as a whole. As such, any activity on his part violently disrupts the structure of the individual systems. Any intervention on his part with respect to law, for example, introduces an arbitrary element into an otherwise automatically functioning system, seriously threatening if not undermining public conviction in the absoluteness of law.

By maintaining his attitude of *wuwei*, the ruler cannot be deceived by clever people who are able to anticipate his reactions. Rather than trying to second-guess the ruler, these people are directed to look to the laws and to their responsibilities of office as their sole standards of conduct. Further, the *wuwei* ruler can avoid personal competition with his subjects who, collectively, surpass him in virtually all respects. This means that even a ruler of very common parts—not an altogether uncommon phenomenon—can maintain political control.

A corollary to *wuwei* is *wuxian* 無見, the technique of "showing nothing:" The ruler does not reveal his likes and dislikes, does not proffer an opinion on any given subject, does not announce his ambitions or personal desires. The images of this technique are the high dais of the throne, the screen that covers the throne from public view, the strings of pearls that hang down from the ruler's headdress covering his face, and the kowtow with its prohibition of lifting one's eyes in the presence of the ruler. The ruler in maintaining this posture of "showing nothing" shields the contours of his character and intellect from public sight. In keeping his own counsel and encouraging a personal mystique, the ruler becomes an ideal invested with a superlative degree of all things worthwhile. Because his subordinates have no knowledge of his actual limitations, they attribute powers to him far beyond his real capacities.

Yet another prominent technique was called *xingming* 形名 or "accountability" where the bureaucracy like the society at large is regulated by constantly and unconditionally being held responsible for its conduct. The theory behind accountability is straightforward. The duties and obligations of each office are clearly defined (hence they are "named" *ming*). At given intervals, the performance of officeholders (hence their "per-*form*-ance" *xing*) is compared with their prescribed duties. Where performance is wholly congruent with the objective definition of the office, rewards and promotions are both generous and constant; where discrepancies occur, however, the axe falls swiftly and decisively. The important point is that the officeholder, before embarking on any course of action, be wholly aware of the consequences of that action.

The same notion of accountability is applied in a less formal way to those who would approach the throne with sundry propositions. When such persons are engaged, a careful record is made of their claims. And if a gap is found between claim and services rendered, again the axe falls with speed and decision. The ruler for his part can avoid censure for any failures while basking in the praise of all for any successes.

*思 ***si.*** "Thinking, reflecting."

Philosophy as one kind of thinking has been characterized as having a significant degree of self-consciousness with regard to its theoretical assumptions. For the philosopher, clear thinking almost always leads to the reflexivity of thinking about thinking itself. It is the dialectical character of thinking that in Greek philosophy from earliest times has shaped the history of Anglo-European culture. Dialectic has the character of dialogue (*dia-logos*) as a "talking through" or "thinking through" that requires the reflective engagement we associate with the Socratic dialogues, and their openness to continual clarification. Further, the association of thinking with a historical process of measurable progress in the aggregation of knowledge might be understood best by reflecting on the contrast between "thinking" and "reasoning" in the Western narrative. The relative openness of thinking as an activity aimed at clarity can be contrasted with the exercise of reason that searches for ideal values or ends and for the methods that promote their recognition and understanding.

The fact that in this philosophical tradition the concept of thinking has gradually come to be construed in narrowly cognitive terms has two very important consequences. First, it has both ramified and reified the disjunction of theory and practice, leading to the construing of practice in terms that cannot easily be associated with the putative kind of ontological ground presupposed with respect to cognition. Second, forms of experiencing our world that stand in contrast to cognition such as appreciating, imagining, evaluating, participating in, empathizing with, embodying, and so forth, have not been given entirely respectable status as aspects of thinking *per se*.

Nathan Sivin makes an important distinction between the exclusive dialectical expectations of philosophical engagement in the classical Greek tradition, and the pursuit of a shared consensus in the Chinese world:

> Greek culture in the period that concerns us encouraged disagreement and disputation in natural philosophy and science as in every other field; in China the emphasis remained on consensus.①

The contrast being made here is between Greek dialogue and its assumption that rational analysis will provide access to some exclusive *logos* on the one hand, and a Chinese conversation that requires the ongoing negotiation of an inclusive consensus on the other. While the pursuit of apodictic truth drove the Greek dialogue, the continuing need to negotiate order within the assumed processual experience of Chinese cosmology had its own far-reaching ramifications. Such ongoing inclusive negotiation would explain why an achieved consensus in its many forms was regarded as having such high value in the classical Chinese world. That is, importance was invested in the continuing reauthorization of a moral orthodoxy, the persistent, intergenerational commentarial tradition on a shared canonical core, "the art of accommodation" (*jianshu* 兼術) in philosophical deliberation, and so on.②

In his summary reflections on the comparison between Greek and Chinese philosophy, Sivin registers the importance of semantics and the relative absence of logic in China. This contrast is another way of saying that the Chinese tradition does not privilege some fixed formal aspect—that is, logic as the "form" of thinking—as

---

① Nathan Sivin. *Medicine, Philosophy and Religion in Ancient China: Researches and Reflections.* Aldershot: Variorum, 1995, p. 8.
② Angus Graham develops this same kind of contrast between dialectic and consensus when he observes that dialectical dispute is characteristic of people who would ask, "What is the Truth?" as opposed to those who would ask "Where is the Way?" *Disputers of the Tao*, p. 3. See also Hall and Ames, *Anticipating China*, part II.

being more "real" than what is otherwise in flux (that is, semantics). Relatedly, Sivin's observation regarding the ubiquitousness in the Chinese tradition of variations on the *zhengming* 正名 theme—"using names properly"—suggests that the function of language used in a processual cosmology must reflect the flux and flow of that cosmos. That is, Chinese cosmology accepts the processual, changing, and hence provisional character of language without appeal to a literal ground guaranteed by some putative "reality."[1]

It would be an interpretive misstep to understand *zhengming* 正名 as a search for univocity, as it so often is in the translation as "rectification of names." For the attempt to properly order names is a functional and pragmatic rather than a logical or strictly semantic, procedure. This means that the pragmatics of ordering names involves establishing coherence between roles as they have already been spelled out by tradition (*li* 禮), and the specific actions of always unique persons (husbands and fathers, mothers and ministers) as they go about their prospective lives.

The distinction between rhetorical and logical uses of language is reflected in the distinction between objective and subjective connotations. In logic, connotation refers to those properties held in common by all members of a class. In rhetoric, connotation means the emotional association evoked by a word. Literal language depends upon only objective modes of connotation. In the absence of any severe rhetorical and logical distinction that allows for the privileging of logical discourse (*logos*), the Confucian may be said to employ discourse in ways that recall the languages of *ethos* and *pathos*. We must not assume that rhetorical language as employed by the Confucians simply means "persuasive communication." As employed by Confucian philosophers, analogical procedures are rhetorical in that they appeal to the authority of the tradition and

---

[1] Sivin, *Medicine, Philosophy and Religion in Ancient China*, p.3.

to the exemplars, sages, and cultural heroes of that tradition. And though this appeal to authority might seem to shape the arguments into those of the *ethos* variety, the institutionalization of ritual behavior insures that *pathos* is involved as well.

Enter Confucius. Perhaps this most prominent of all thinkers in the classical Confucian tradition may serve us as an alternative model of the activity of thinking itself. But when we turn to Confucius as a concrete exemplar of classical Confucian "thinking," we are confronted with a stubborn irony. We cannot expect to understand Confucius on "thinking" unless we have some insight into his process of thinking *per se*, and it is precisely this concept of thinking *per se* that we have been attempting to reconceptualize through our understanding of Confucius. It was precisely this problem that inspired the double entendre in the title of our book, *Thinking Through Confucius*. We sought in an analysis of Confucius to find an alternative way of thinking about thinking that would redefine the meaning of thinking itself and thus allow us to reformulate the character and the responsibilities of the philosopher in a way different from the Western experience.

For Confucius, thinking (*si* 思) has an inseparable relationship to learning (*xue* 學). To the extent that learning is strictly the appropriating of meaning—deferring to the excellence of one's cultural legacy—it does not engage scholars themselves in either the exercise of transforming the appropriated culture or in the activity of generating novel meanings. It is in this spirit that Confucius says of himself 述而不作 "Following the proper way, I do not forge new paths." There are other similar references in the *Analects* that can support this same kind of conservative reading of Confucius:

子曰:"吾嘗終日不食,終夜不寢,以思,無益,不如學也。"
The Master said, "I once went a whole day without eating and a whole night without sleeping, lost in my thoughts (*si* 思). I got

nothing out of it, and would have been better off devoting the time to learning." (15.31)

In this passage, Confucius certainly gives priority to "learning" (*xue* 學) over "thinking" (*si* 思). There can be no doubt Confucius believes that the learning of traditional culture is a necessary condition for the effective development of the moral person (17.8). And to the extent that thinking is reflecting critically on something given, the learning of the given would certainly have logical priority. But even though Confucius does emphasize the personal embodiment of the cultural tradition, it can be fairly argued he held thinking to involve both the acquisition of existing meaning and the creative adaptation and extension of this meaning to optimize the possibilities of one's own, always unique circumstances. In the dynamics of Confucian thinking, learning and reflecting are interdependent correlatives having a polar relationship, with neither one of them being adequate in itself.

The term "thinking" (*si* 思) appears on the bronze inscriptions as ▆, and is composed of an abbreviated form of the graph for "head, brain" (*nao* 腦) and "aorta" (*xin* 心), reflecting the perception of the ancients that "thinking" was an activity that involved both heart and mind.[①] The *Shuowen* lexicon defines it as "inclusiveness and accommodation" (*rong* 容), and the *Shuowen* commentaries appeal paronomastically to its homophone "silk" (*si* 絲), explaining that "thinking" as an activity is fine and delicate. *Si* has several characteristics. It is generic in covering various modes of thinking that are made explicit in the spoken language by binomial pairing: reflecting (*sikao* 思考), pondering (*sisuo* 思索), rehearsing (*fansi* 反思), meditating (*chensi* 沉思), deliberating (*silü* 思慮), pining (*xiangsi* 相思), recalling (*zhuisi* 追思), racking one's brain (*kusi* 苦

---

① Kwan, "Database," 戰國 CHANT 11348.

思), and so on. Further, *si* is not exhausted by its psychical dimension, but instead includes both affect and the physiological apparatus involved in the process of reflecting. To reduce classical Chinese discussions of the thinking person to mere cognition or assertions about the psyche that would exclude the physical and emotional person would seriously impoverish this concept.

In Confucius, the dynamic and holistic nature of the thinking process is apparent in the interdependence of the broad categories of learning and reflecting. The *locus classicus* for this symbiotic relationship is *Analects* 2.15:

子曰："學而不思則罔，思而不學則殆。"
The Master said, "Learning (*xue* 學) without due reflection (*si* 思) leads to perplexity; reflection without learning leads to perilous circumstances."

The point here is that if persons simply learn without reflecting critically upon what they are learning, they will fail to act "properly," that is, to personalize what is learned in such a manner as to make it appropriate and meaningful for their own unique circumstances. They will simply be repeating what others have said or done. Since all novel situations will require persons to go beyond any specific quantum of received learning, they will be unprepared and hence, bewildered. Said another way, the prospective vision of life to which Confucius is committed requires that each event be understood as the consequence of a unique set of conditions, precluding the mere repetition of what one already knows as a matter of historical record. In real degree then, for Confucius the pedant is condemned to move through life in a state of bewilderment.

The interplay between learning and reflecting—between appropriating widely from the cultural tradition and elaborating upon it through an investment of one's own creativity—is a recurring theme in the *Analects* (e.g. 19.6, 2.11, 13.5). The acknowledgment that each event is *sui generis* requires that whatever is learned be creatively adapted and rendered appropriate to the new set of circumstances. Persons must be creative in taking advantage of the received tradition, both in adapting it for their own place and time, and in using it as a structure through which to realize their own possibilities. They must labor assiduously in acquiring the cultural legacy intact as it has been transmitted from ancient times, but at the same time, they must also be able to extend it in building the connector for their own generation. The weight that Confucius places on critical reflection is fully illustrated in his exhortation to his students to go beyond the instruction of even their best teachers in finding their own way:

子曰："當仁，不讓於師。"
The Master said, "In striving to be consummate in your conduct (*ren* 仁) do not defer even to your teachers."

Conversely, even though learning without reflection is an undesirable source of confusion, the imbalance in the thinking process that would favor reflecting at the expense of learning is in fact even more dangerous. If persons reflect without having full benefit of the contributions made by those who have come before, they will not have the shared culture necessary to integrate into and communicate effectively with their own communities. Persons who thus live in their own separate worlds are quite literally "idiots" (Gk. *idios*, private), and are generally perceived with general suspicion as being mad, and a threat to prevailing social values. In their applications, such aberrantly individuated persons instead of sharing the middle of the road with others, will be going off on their own tangents and will pursue often fruitless and even dangerous pathways.

The Confucian value of recognizing the symbiotic relationship between thinking and learning is everywhere in the literature. Xunzi follows Confucius in decrying the failure to benefit from the received wisdom:

吾嘗終日而思矣，不如須臾之所學也。吾嘗跂而望矣，不如登高之博見也。

I once spent an entire day lost in thought (*si* 思); I would have been better off with a few moments of learning (*xue* 學). I once stood on my tiptoes to get a good view; I would have been better off climbing a hill for the panoramic vista it provides. (1/1/6)

Focusing the Familiar 20 again underscores Confucius's commitment to "reflection informed by learning; learning advanced through refection:"

博學之，審問之，慎思之，明辨之，篤行之。

Learn of the way broadly, ask after it in detail, reflect upon it carefully, analyze it clearly, and advance upon it with earnestness.

Thinking for Confucius is an undertaking that engages the whole person. Just as dualistic categories such as mind and body have little relevance for Confucius, the theory and practice dichotomy too has little meaning. Throughout the *Analects*, exemplary persons are described as those whose words do not outstrip their deeds, and those whose words are thus authenticated in practice (2.13, 14.27, 17.13). Ideas and their articulation in language are not simply academic and theoretical. They have real performative weight as promptings to act. Confucius is often critical of students who are pedantic, and rejects the description of himself that he is someone who 多學而識之者 "learns a great deal and remembers it all" (15.3), preferring instead to gauge the value of what is learned by the extent to which it has practical application in his service to others.

Does Confucius then give us a different way of thinking and thus a different definition of the philosophical enterprise? Perhaps in some ways he takes us back to the beginnings of philosophy as it was recorded in classical Greece. For the eloquent Pythagoras, his holistic, practical, and intelligent way of life was aptly described as *philosophia*—"the love of wisdom." While certainly celebrating the contemplation of abstract, theoretical science, Pythagoras as a person was devoted even more importantly to religious practices based upon assumptions about the immortality of the human soul. Indeed, he was committed to periodical ascetic observances, to a complex program of social and political reform, to sustained ethical reflection, to oratory and the making of music, to a physical regimen, and even to rigorous dietary prescriptions and prohibitions.

But Pythagoras's holistic vision of the good life as the highest aspiration of *philosophia* faded in time, and what had been a truly "philosophical" journey—that is, a quest for both practical wisdom as well as theoretical knowledge—gave way to quite a different pilgrimage, that is, to the search for abstract, apodictic knowledge and its promise of certainty. With the melding of Greek metaphysics and the Christian tradition, increasing reverence for the theoretically and spiritually abstract meant that in the fullness of time, practical wisdom, rhetoric, and the aesthetic were relegated to the down-side of a prevailing dualism. *Philosophia*, "the love of wisdom," had for all intents and purposes, become *philoepisteme*, "the love of apodictic knowledge." "Knowledge" and "truth" became the vocabulary of systematic philosophy, and "wisdom" became and still remains a largely obsolete term in the corridors of Western philosophy. While most departments teach their courses on epistemology and logic, "sophiology" does not make it into the curriculum and "wisdom" is seldom stipulated as a student learning outcome.

Richard Rorty is persuaded that this turn away from personal cultivation and the pursuit of wisdom has been a desirable advance in the Western philosophical narrative:

> Philosophy in the West started off its career as an answer to the question "What is the good life for the human being?" To gain wisdom was to have learned the answer to that question. . . . Most Western philosophers no longer try to be sages, and they are quite rightly suspicious of Eastern philosophers who suggest that wisdom is still the goal of philosophical study.[①]

Alfred North Whitehead on the other hand is not so sure that wisdom is expendable. He diagnoses what he calls the "fallacy of misplaced concreteness" as that error in reasoning committed when the formally abstracted is taken to be what is real and concrete.[②] Whitehead rehearses the history and the consequences of this "fatal virus" that has come to inhibit our understanding of the intrinsic, constitutive, and productive nature of relatedness. He accuses Epicurus, Plato, and Aristotle of being "unaware of the perils of abstraction" that render knowledge closed and complete, and that in fact precludes the possibility of attaining wisdom. According to Whitehead, "the history of thought" that he associates with these great men

> . . . is a tragic mixture of vibrant disclosure and of deadening closure. The sense of penetration is lost in the certainty of completed knowledge. This dogmatism is the antichrist of learning. In the full concrete connection of things, the characters of the things

---

[①] Richard Rorty. "Philosophy and the Hybridization of Culture." *Educations and Their Purposes: A Conversation Among Cultures*. edit. Roger T. Ames and Peter D. Hershock, Honolulu: University of Hawaii Press, 2007, p. 48.

[②] See A.N. Whitehead, *Process and Reality*, p. 10.

connected enter into the character of the connectivity which joins them.[1]

What Whitehead means here by "the sense of penetration" that is compromised by assumptions about certain knowledge is the creative advance made possible by achieving productive relations among unique particulars. Indeed, it is this cultivated, creative application of our understanding of how things can best relate to each other that is the real meaning of wisdom.

四端 **siduan.** "The four inclinations." See also 心 ***xin.*** "Heartmind, bodyheartminding, thinking and feeling," and 性 ***xing.*** "Natural human propensities."

Siduan or the "four inclinations" is introduced in the *Mencius* as a technical term used to summarize the generic native conditions from which the human experience begins. In its noun form the term *duan* 端 means variously "beginning, tip, first appearing point," "extremity," "cause," "first symptom, sign, indication," "the main threads (of an affair)." Heartmind (*xin* 心) as the stipulated locus of the "four inclinations" (*siduan* 四端) references the native physical, social, and cultural conditions of human "becomings" at their incipience. We must understand the generative force of *siduan* within the *ziran* 自然 cosmology that serves as the interpretive context. It is an unbounded and yet focal matrix of shared bonds that locate persons within family and community, and that incline them toward positive moral growth (*shan* 善) in the discursive roles and relations that constitute them. These native conditions are not only a generic description of the pattern of relations of persons as they are born into, live, and grow within the continuing narrative

---

[1] A.N. Whitehead. *Modes of Thought.* New York: Macmillan, 1938, p. 58.

of a mature culture, they are also normative as a resource for our moral growth in the specific roles that we live. That is, although it is possible through inattention and a lack of effort to lose this capacity for normative growth in our relations, such a native predilection inclines us otherwise. If in fact we commit ourselves with increasing self-awareness to living according to the promptings of these native moral propensities that animate the inchoate pattern of our relations, we grow and acquire increasing moral influence within our families and communities.

  Xin 心 in its referencing of the initial conditions and propensities of human "becomings" acknowledges that in loving families and communicating communities, infants are born into roles informed by "consummatory conduct" (*ren* 仁), "appropriateness and meaning" (*yi* 義), "an achieved sense of propriety" (*li* 禮), and "intelligence and wisdom" (*zhi* 智). Radically situated within these fecund and discursive associations, such infants through participating in the various discourses of life are inclined to efficacious growth (*shan* 善). This nonanalytic *renyilizhi* 仁義禮智 language of "the four inclinations" is "aspectual" in that each term provides a particular perspective on the same relationally-constituted, vital phenomenon, and anticipates how this incipient, socially-embedded infant, located within a grammar of familial and cultural conditions, will be inclined to grow and mature discursively as a source of communal and ultimately cosmic meaning.[①]

  In our understanding of these "four inclinations," we have to resist the popular uncritical assumption that they are in sum

---

[①] In *Just Babies,* New York: Random House, 2014, Paul Bloom argues that humans rather than being blank slates are hardwired with a sense of morality. The problem with this understanding of morality is that it locates such feelings exclusively in the babies themselves rather than in the relationally informed narrative of the baby, babies that are inchoate narratives emerging within larger continuing narratives.

referencing some essential, universal, and reduplicative "human nature." Michael Sandel, underscoring the weight and persistence of early Greek idealism and teleology as it shapes our commonsense, has observed that:

> To speak of human nature is often to suggest a classical teleological conception, associated with the notion of a universal human essence, invariant in all times and places.[①]

To distinguish *siduan* from such a conception of human nature, we might take the roles of the infant as they are informed by intelligence and wisdom (*zhi* 智) as an example of one of these prosocial inclinations. Such an attribution is not a claim that infants have some internal and innate repository of *apriori* knowledge that they then apply to the situations of their lives. Rather, wisdom is a quality of conduct that arises gradually within the social activities of which infants are a part, informed as these activities are by the persistent yet changing values of their families, their communities, and the mature culture into which they are born. Reading "conduct" etymologically as *con-* ("together," "with") and *duct* ("leading"), such wisdom (or maybe "wise-ing") is a profoundly participatory activity manifested in the ongoing transactions infants have with their environing others, and the interactions their environing others have with them. Indeed, without ready access to a mature wisdom, the lives of these same infants would be perilous and probably short.

---

① Michael Sandel. *Liberalism and the Limits of Justice*. Cambridge: Cambridge University Press, 1998, p. 50. In order to preclude such uncritical assumptions, Sandel suggests that we must be self-conscious about how we parse the notion of self or person even when moving among the various philosophical positions as they are formulated within our own academy. I would only add that of course this is even more the case when we traverse the borders of our own philosophical narrative and venture into other cultural ecologies.

Again, *xin* as "four inclinations" is no more an essential and inborn "given" than is the tendency that infants have toward prosocial "consummate conduct in their roles and relations" (*ren* 仁). Such consummate conduct is initially no more than an incipient relational disposition, an inclination, a tendency, but with assiduous effort within this matrix of relations, this inclination for infants gradually evolves to become a cultivated self-awareness and an acquired virtuosity in their roles as they unfold within the personal narratives of family and community. All of these "four inclinations" are fairly described as native conditions that, in the fullness of time and with the continuing growth of what are initially only tentative dispositions, gradually thicken to become those qualitatively achieved habits of conduct in the roles and relations that constitute our identities as persons.

We might glean some further insight from a close reading of a few passages of the *Mencius* that describe the incipient "four inclinations" (*siduan* 四端) as they stir us to moral conduct. In *Mencius* 2A6:

惻隱之心，仁之端也；羞惡之心，義之端也；辭讓之心，禮之端也；是非之心，智之端也。人之有是四端也，猶其有四體也。

Our heartmind in feeling pity at perceived suffering disposes it toward consummate conduct in our roles and relations; our heartmind in feeling shame at perceived crudeness disposes it toward appropriate conduct in our roles and relations; our heartmind in its feelings of modesty and deference disposes it toward propriety in our roles and relations; our heartmind in feeling a sense of approval and disapproval disposes it toward wisdom in our roles and relations. Persons have these four inclinations (*siduan* 四端) just as they have their four limbs.

Commenting on this passage, Angus Graham observes that the

analogy between cultivating our four inclinations and nourishing our bodies is an apposite one:

> It is essential to Mencius' case that although moral education is indispensable it is, like the feeding of the body, the nourishing of a spontaneous process. . . . A man becomes bad, not because the incipient impulses are missing from his constitution, but because he neglects and starves them.[①]

Graham underscores the analogy here between physical and moral growth. In both cases such growth occurs because of the natural conditions of the organism and the effort at nourishment that must be invested in their development. And the terms "constitution" and "incipient impulses" used to describe these natural conditions are important because *Mencius* 4B12 is referencing the native inclinations we have within our relations as human beings:

> 孟子曰:"大人者,不失其赤子之心者也。"
> Mencius said: "Great persons are those who do not lose the heartmind of the newborn babe."

We must resist an expository reading of this passage that might essentialize and reify heartmind as some "original mind." It is perhaps better to understand Mencius here as simply making a point. And the point being made is that activating the native inclinations of the relationally-constituted infant is a necessary condition upon which the project of ultimately becoming exemplary in our persons depends. Mencius's description of incipient "inclinations" not only introduces the radically-embedded newborn babe as the locus of the growth of these "inclinations," but further defines the "constitution"

---

① A.C. Graham. *Disputers of the Tao*, pp. 126, 129.

of this infant in terms of these same organic relations. That is, the newborn babe emerges *in medias res* as an inchoate narrative nested within the larger pattern of the more mature narratives of family, community, and culture.

The growth of infants born into the concrete matrix of the family and communal relations of a mature culture can be captured both descriptively and prescriptively by an appeal to the intense socializing impulses of these constitutive bonds. The *Mencius* 2A6 uses the metaphors of a run-away fire and surging water to emphasize the precipitous nature of this moral growth:

凡有四端於我者，知皆擴而充之矣，若火之始然，泉之始達。苟能充之，足以保四海；苟不充之，不足以事父母。

Now acknowledging that these four inclinations are defining of us, the process of realizing the development and fruition of them is like a fire beginning to blaze or a spring of water beginning to gush forth. Persons who are able to bring them fully to fruition can vouchsafe everyone within the four seas, while persons unable to do so cannot even be of service to their own parents.

Graham comments here that this inexorable progression of moral growth is motivated by the agreeable feelings we derive from it:

The process once launched accelerates, like fire catching, because we discover the pleasure of it.[1]

For such infants, the four inclinations that anticipate moral growth are the thick, irreducibly biological, familial, social, and cultural conditions that are defining of them. These discursive bonds are thus by nature resolutely relational and inclusive, and in their

---

[1] A.C. Graham. *Disputers of the Tao*, p. 126.

activation, a source of rapid moral growth (*shan* 善). *Shan* as "good" in describing this moral growth begins with, to use Charles Taylor's felicitous expression, the "webs of interlocution" within the continuing narrative. It is only from this continuing discursive process that "good" can be abstracted as a retroactive summary description of persons or their actions. Said simply, newborns as concrete facts are constituted by the relations that define them, and as they follow the prosocial, discursive promptings of the matrix of these relations, they grow their various roles into emerging personal identities. Infants in these relations are animated and projective, and develop their inflected and reflexively-aware sense of themselves within the expansive intrasubjective roles and relations that come to constitute them.

Importantly, it is the radial, constitutive, and transactional nature of relations themselves and their propensity to produce meaning that first locates newborns within an inchoate habitude, and thus disposes them to positive moral growth. Given its irreducibly relational nature, an infant conceived of as a discrete and separate "individual" is nothing more than a retrospective abstraction from this same manifold of relations. And further, the erstwhile "goodness" (*shan* 善) of infants, far from being some innate and isolatable endowment, is the compounding dividend produced as they activate the vital disposition they have toward social growth. *Shan* refers to the outcome of the semiotic processes and symbolic competencies that come to shape them as human "becomings."

Graham has consistently warned us that serious equivocations emerge when we elide the distinction between classical Greek ontological commitments and those assumptions grounding a classical Chinese processive, procreative cosmology. Ontology privileges "being *per se*" and a substance language with its "essence" and "attribute" dualism—that is, substances as property-bearers, and properties that are borne respectively. The Confucian "zoetological" process cosmology, on the other hand, begins from "life" (*sheng* 生) itself rather than "being," and thus gives privilege to an irreducibly relationally process of "becoming" with the vital, interdependent, correlative categories needed to "speak" process and its eventful content.

Graham is quite explicit about the nature of these philosophical differences and their linguistic entailments:

> In the Chinese cosmos all things are interdependent, without transcendent principles by which to explain them or a transcendent origin from which they derive ... A novelty in this position which greatly impresses me is that it exposes a preconception of Western interpreters that such concepts as *Tian* "Heaven" and *Dao* "the Way" must have the transcendence of our own ultimate principles; it is hard for us to grasp that even the Way is interdependent with man.[①]

Indeed Graham sees this problem of equivocation as so formidable that he worries over the very possibility of translating Chinese philosophy into English:

> Every Western sinologist knows that there is no exact equivalent in his own language for such a word as *jen* [*ren*] 仁 or *te* [*de*] 德, and that as long as he thinks of it as synonymous with "benevolence" or "virtue" he will impose Western preconceptions on the thought he is studying. He is bound to suspect that there are also deeper structural differences which mislead him in the same way, and which it is much harder to identify.[②]

[①] A.C. Graham, "Replies," p. 287.
[②] A.C. Graham, *Studies in Chinese Philosophy and Philosophical Literature*, p. 322.

These "deeper structural differences" include the enormous disparity in metaphysical and cosmological assumptions between the Indo-European family of cultures on the one hand, and the rich philosophical tradition of China that developed almost entirely independent of Europe, on the other. Such differences are embedded in the very grammar of our languages, and are so overwhelming that Graham concludes his reflection with the humbling yet undoubtedly true assertion: "None of us yet knows classical Chinese."

What then does Graham's wariness about importing teleology and formal causes into Chinese cosmology amount to when the investigation is directed specifically at how classical Confucians understood an erstwhile "human nature" and the human experience informed by it? Graham in insisting on distinguishing between Greek substance ontology and Chinese process cosmology, insists that the familiar translation of the term *xing* 性 as "human nature" that projects foreign teleological assumptions onto the Mencian conception of "persons" has led to a profound and persistent misreading of Mencius. Allowing Graham to speak for himself, he says that when we ascribe a theory of "human nature" to Mencius, the very "translation of *xing* 性 by 'nature' predisposes us to mistake it for a transcendent origin, which in Mencian doctrine would also be a transcendent end."[①] With teleology and idealism having had a profound influence in shaping our own commonsense, reading *xing* as "nature" suggests to us that human "beings" have "a universal human essence, invariant in all times and places" including a human *telos* or end as their erstwhile final cause. Indeed, it is precisely this kind of essentialism that has now become the standard reading of Mencius in both the European and Asian language literature, a persistent teleological misreading that Graham over his long career first endorsed, returned to repeatedly for further reflection, and

---

① A.C. Graham, "Replies," p. 287.

then ultimately rejected.[1]

*太極　*taiji*. "The furthest reach."

Taiji is conventionally translated as the "Supreme Ultimate." But because Chinese natural cosmology is processual and provisional, it does not appeal to "ultimates" in the etymological sense of "arriving at an end" in some basic or foundational fact, element, or principle. Literally, *taiji* means "the greatest or furthest reach, the utmost limit, the highest point." The earliest occurrence of this expression *taiji* is in "The Great Commentary A11" of the *Book of Changes* where it is used to characterize the boundless process of change itself:

是故，易有太極，是生兩儀，兩儀生四象，四象生八卦，八卦定吉凶，吉凶生大業。

Thus, in the process of change described in the *Book of Changes* there is the *taiji*. It produces the two modes (the *yin* and *yang* lines), they produce the four images, and these images again produce the eight hexagrams. The eight hexagrams determine fortune and misfortune, and fortune and misfortune give rise to the great enterprise.

Ji 極 means "pole" literally as the ridgepole or main beam (*dongliang* 棟梁) in the structure of a building, and then by way of metaphor, the utmost, highest, furthest, most extreme point. In this sense, *ji* means "one" as the distance between two points:

---

[1] For the history of this revisionist reading, see my "Reconstructing A.C. Graham's Reading of *Mencius* on *xing* 性: A Coda to 'The Background of the Mencian Theory of Human Nature' (1967)," in *Having a Word with Angus Graham: At Twenty-five Years into His Immortality*, edited by Carine Defoort and Roger T. Ames, Albany: State University of New York Press, 2018.

a relationship of polarity with the two points being relative in orientation and direction to each other. Again literally, it is the ridgepole that divides the roof into two halves, and thus means both the pivotal null point at which the halves divide (*shu* 樞), and the differentiation into the two halves themselves. The key idea here not to be overlooked is "in the process of change" (*yi* 易). The *Book of Changes* is the first among the classics because it makes explicit the process cosmology that gives classical Chinese philosophy its interpretive context. Rather than thinking of this ridgepole in a static way as the main beam within the formal structure of a building that then separates two halves of its roof, we must understand it within this "process of ceaseless change" (*shengshengbuyi* 生生不已). Located within change, the thus animated ridgepole becomes the cadence of "continuity in change," and the two halves of the roof become the vital alternations of *yin* and *yang* expressed through their two complementary and yet oppositional tendencies. *Ji* is the symbiotic process of "forming and functioning" (*tiyong* 體用) and of "continuity within change" (*biantong* 變通). The definition of *ji* as continuity and differentiation within change can be summarized with Tang Junyi's cosmological postulate, "the inseparability of one and many" (*yiduobufenguan* 一多不分觀). Within the dynamic life experience, this postulate can be translated as the inseparability of continuity and multiplicity, of uniqueness and context, of particular and totality.

Taiji does not become an important philosophical term of art until it is appropriated and developed in the work of the neo-Confucian thinkers, particularly Zhou Dunyi and Zhu Xi, and later Wang Fuzhi. The cosmogonic interpretations of some philosophers would give *taiji* a kind of primordial and generative status as the originating "one" that precedes diversity. Other more cosmological interpretations would construe *taiji* normatively as the oneness or continuity among things that is achieved in the harmony of *yin* and *yang*. But these two interpretations need not be exclusive.

Certainly, it must be understood that *taiji* is not some originative source that generates a process of change standing independent of itself, an archic model of genesis familiar in many early Western cosmogonies. But with this caveat in mind, there is no contradiction in regarding *taiji* as a characterization of the entire process of transformation that is both diachronic and synchronic—that is, that is at once historical and yet still descriptive of the process of change in a continuing present. As we look to the utmost limits of our understanding, temporal as well as spatial, the complexity of determinate experience gives way to indeterminacy. At the same time, we can appreciate how both the continuity and diversity implicated in *taiji* are necessary to explain our present experience.

Taiji is sometimes associated with the *taiyi* 太一 or the "Ancestral One" that we find in recently recovered document, "The Ancestral One Gives Birth to the Waters." This text dating back to 300 BCE that was an integral part of the Guodian *Daodejing* is our earliest source of Daoist cosmology, providing a clear "collateral" rather than "unilateral" picture of genesis and creativity. In the process cosmology made explicit in the *Book of Changes*, "life" (*sheng* 生) is always relational growth and never an isolated one. Hence, if you have "the furthest reach" (*taiji* 太極), there must also be a "beyond the furthest reach" or "without limit" (*wuji* 無極).

The expression *wuji* or "limitless" that Zhou Dunyi pairs with *taiji* first occurs in the *Daodejing* 28:

為天下式，常德不忒，復歸於無極。
As a model for the world,
Your real potency will not be wanting,
And with your potency not wanting,
You return to the state of the limitless (*wuji* 無極).

Reading these terms cosmologically, if *taiji* refers to the descriptive and normative limits of the determinate in our experience (*you* 有), *wuji* would seem to reference the indeterminate aspect of the same experience (*wu* 無) that provides an opening for the spontaneous emergence of novelty and added significance.

*體　***ti.*** "Lived body, discursive body, embodying."

In Confucian role ethics, we can correlate "lived body" (*ti* 體) and its cognate character "aspiring to propriety in one's roles and relations" (*li* 禮) by arguing that they express two ways of shaping, embodying, and thus "realizing" our personal identities: that is, these two characters reference "a living body" and "embodied living" respectively. Embodying is a form of "knowing" that is carried over into the modern language in which "knowing bodily" (*tihui* 體會 and *tiyan* 體驗) means to know something through experiencing it, and in this way, "realizing" it.

In the pre-Qin documents, the graph for "embodying" (*ti* 體) appears with three alternative semantic classifiers—*shen* 身 that alludes to the lived, vital, and irreducibly social body; *rou* 肉 as the flesh and hair, carnal body; and *gu* 骨 that references the "bones" and formal, skeletal structure. We can appeal to these different ways of writing the graph as a heuristic for attempting to give full value to the notion of how each succeeding generation has the responsibility of coming to know and to thus embody the cultural corpus that has come before.[①]

[①]　For a fuller discussion of this sense of embodiment, see Roger T. Ames, *Confucian Role Ethics: A Vocabulary*, Honolulu and Hong Kong, University of Hawaii Press and Chinese University Press joint publication, 2011, pp. 102-113. For more on the *ti* body, see Deborah Sommer, "Boundaries of the *Ti Body*" in Michael Nylan, Henry Rosemont, Jr. and Li Waiyee, *Star Gazing, Fire Phasing, and Healing in China: Essays in Honor of Nathan Sivin,* Special issue of *Asia Major,* 3rd Series, Vol. XXI, Part I (2008).

Ti with the "lived body" classifier (*shen* 身) 𢓱 is the earliest form of this character that is found on the early Warring States bronzes (c. 400 BCE), and references the vital and existentially aware dimension of the embodied experience in its dynamic social relations with others.① The body depicted in the pre-stylized *shen* graph is that of a pregnant woman 𠂤,② an image of perhaps the most intimate and visceral of all human relations. The "duplicity" or "two-ness" of the pregnant body carries over with *shen* referencing the subjective and existential as well as a more objective dimension of experience, an inside as well as an outside. We come to know and express what it means to become fully human intuitively as well as more objectively, where feelings in our various social lived-body relations are first "had," and then we struggle to organize and make sense of them.

Ti with the "flesh" classifier (*rou* 肉) 體 is found pervasively on the Guodian bamboo strips (c. 300 BCE), and references the carnal body—the body as flesh, hair, and bone.③ The modalities of our experience are rooted in and are always mediated through a unique localizing physicality, and are temporally and spatially constrained by this fact. All of our thoughts and feelings are grounded in a complex physical sensorium of seeing, hearing, touching, smelling, and tasting, a sensorium that makes specific demands on our conduct, and that registers our pleasures and pain. Philosopher Richard Shusterman has made much of what he has called a "somaesthetic"—that is, the opportunity for education that this lived "flesh and bone" body provides us for aestheticizing the human experience: the developing a keen eye for art, an acute ear for music, a fine sense of touch for the piano keys, an awakened nose for

---

① Kwan, "Database," 戰國早期 CHANT 9735.3b.
② Kwan, "Database," 西周晚期 CHANT 63.
③ Kwan, "Database," 郭店簡窮達以時 10.

good wine, and a discriminating palate for haute cuisine.[①]

The familiar, traditional form of the character *ti* 體 with the "bones" classifier (*gu* 骨) still in use today in places where simplified characters have been resisted does not occur in our current records until the Mawangdui bamboo strips (168 BCE), and references our persons as "discursive bodies" that engage in "structuring," "configuring," and "embodying" our experience not only cognitively and affectively, but also viscerally.[②] We might reflect on the difference implied by "seeing" versus "knowing" the world as a distinction between experience as immediately *had*, and reflective and deliberate experience that has been mediated through human epistemic structures. Each of us inherits a worldview and a cultural commonsense, and collaborates with the world to discriminate, conceptualize, and theorize the human experience, embodying and giving Apollonian form to the contents of our culture, our language, our habitat. And in this continuing process, our various environments speak us, as much as we relate to them.

An abbreviated form of this character that is now used as the simplified version in Chinese and Japanese is *ti* 体, combining "person (*ren* 人)" and "root, trunk" (*ben* 本), also provides us with a useful heuristic. The first and hugely significant factor we must consider in the process of focusing a persisting, personal identity and its coherent horizons of relevance is the extent to which the structure of our understanding and our habitude is "rooted" (*ti* 体) in and shaped by the fact of our embodied experience with its visceral connection to the world—the ongoing "embodying" (*ti* 體) processes of our always "discursive" bodies. Given the correlative

---

[①] See as a representative example, Richard Shusterman. *Body Consciousness: A Philosophy of Mindfulness and Somaesthetics*. Cambridge: Cambridge University Press, 2008.
[②] Kwan, "Database," 馬王堆五十二病方 376.

relationship between "heartmind" and "body" (*xinshen* 心身) in this process cosmology, it should not be surprising that Deborah Sommer in summarizing her analysis of the uses of the *ti* body in the classical literature uses language immediately reminiscent of the holography we find explicitly in the *Book of Changes* process cosmology. When for example the *Mencius* 7A4 says, 萬物皆備於我矣 "the myriad things of the world are all implicated here in me," he is averring that the cosmic totality is implicated in each vital impulse of the embodied lives lived by always unique persons. In similar language, Sommer concludes that the *ti* body is

> ... a polysemous corpus of indeterminate extent that can be partitioned into subtler units, each of which is often analogous to the whole and shares a fundamental consubstantiality and common identity with the whole... When a *ti* body is fragmented into parts (literally or conceptually), each part retains in certain aspects, a kind of wholeness or becomes a simulacra of the larger entity of which it is a constituent.[1]

At the most primordial level, the body via these three mutually entailing modalities—the vital, carnal, and discursive bodies—serves as the bond that coordinates our subjectivity with our environments, and that mediates our processes of thinking and feeling with our demonstrable patterns of conduct. If we use the vocabulary of contemporary medical anthropology to capture the nonanalytical relationship between living and embodying, we might cite medical

---

[1] Sommer, "Boundaries of the *Ti* Body," p. 294. Whereas the metaphor we associate with "body" in European languages is some form of a receptacle, the meaning in the earliest classical Chinese sources is the organic (rather than geometric) form of animal and plant bodies, where in certain contexts it has a horticultural reference as plant vegetation (roots, stalks, foliage) in general, and more specifically, as a rhizome or tuber.

anthropologist Zhang Yanhua who concludes that "*jingshen* 精神 is not perceived as opposite to *shenti* 身體 but constitutive of it"—that is, our animated life activities are not distinct from our embodiment, but are integral to and expressive of it.①

Arguing that structure and function are two aspects of the same thing, Judith Farquhar searches for an appropriate language that will provide the necessary contrast between traditional Chinese medicine's very different processual understanding of the body, and the formal anatomical assumptions of biomedicine:

> Chinese medicine most classically envisions embodiment as a dynamic complex of interwoven processes, as a physiology that must be understood in the living through analysis of signs, symptoms, and a subjective sensorium.②

This functional understanding of formal structures within the correlative cosmology is radically contextual, locating "things" such as the "lived body" or "the body as experienced" within its ever-changing circumstances—a collaboration between an existential and an external landscape. Body is understood from the inside and from the outside, as more or less subjective and more or less objective.

Zhang Yanhua analyzes the irreducibly subjective and gerundive implications of the two characters that as a binomial are usually used to denote "body" (*shenti* 身體):

> If we have to make a distinction between *shen* and *ti* as bodies, we may say that *shen* implies a socially informed body-person or

---

① Zhang Yanhua, *Transforming Emotions*, p. 38.
② Judith Farquhar. *Knowing Practice: The Clinical Encounter of Chinese Medicine*. Boulder: Westview Press, 1994, p. 162.

body-self, while *ti*, frequently used in or as a verb, emphasizes "embodying" as a process of knowing and acting. Both concepts resist dualistically positioned mind and body, subject and object.①

Farquhar cautions that if we are to overcome "our commonsense commitment to a materialism which must reduce phenomena to synchronically observable collections of objects," we must understand "things" as both existing in time, and as entailing a subjective, existential dimension. That is, the temporality and reflexivity of "things" must be considered in any and all attempts at understanding them. "Body" must be understood diachronically or "through time" wherein

> . . . it is signs and symptoms, experiences and perceptions, which are the material foundation of medical perception. They are not less concrete than anatomical organs, but they are not conceivable outside of lived time.②

Thus, any tendency to treat "body" as simply a physical object would violate the vital, contextual, and processional sensibilities of the correlative cosmology in which traditional Chinese medicine is grounded. Unsurprisingly, the personal narrative as the reflexive aspect of corporality is of enormous importance in traditional Chinese medical practices:

> The evidence here suggests . . . that Chinese medicine accords a certain importance to quotidian self-perception; while never denying the object-nature of bodies, it privileges processes of

---

① Zhang Yanhua, *Transforming Emotions*, p. 36.
② Farquhar, *Knowing Practice*, p. 386.

change that take place in personal time, which can only be entered into medical consideration via the patient's own narrative.①

The inseparability of the subjective "lived body" and the more objective "body for others" in traditional Chinese medicine provides one way of making sense of ourselves as organisms. The body—at once the self-conscious "I" as the existential experience and the embedded "me" as "my living body for other subjects"—is an indissoluble continuity between self and world.

At a genealogical level, our bodies and the process of human procreativity provide the birthing of distinctive and unique persons from those who have come before. At the same time, within this ongoing, ceaseless, and overlapping process of intergenerational embodiment, the earlier progenitors persist in this continuing process as they are transformed into their progeny. That is, while persons emerge to become specifically who they are as unique individuals, the parents, grandparents, and ancestors of such persons continue to live on in them most obviously in their physicality, but also in terms of how they think, feel, and live their lives. And the eventful process continues as these progenies too, in their turn, live on in their own descendants. The focus-field language we have proposed as a way of thinking about the relationship between particulars and the totality seems immediately relevant to this kind of holography in which the entire field of the physical and cultural experience is implicated in the moment-by-moment narrative of each person. And this "embodied knowing" and "living on" is not meant merely rhetorically. Even more obvious and significant than the transmission of physical likenesses are the continuities of the cultural tradition itself—its language, its institutions, and its

---

① Farquhar, *Knowing Practice*, p. 386.

values.①

As noted above, in this Confucian tradition we can correlate "lived body" (*ti* 體) and its cognate character "realizing propriety in one's roles and relations" (*li* 禮) by arguing that they express two ways of looking at the same phenomenon: that is, these two characters reference "a living body" and "embodied living" respectively. The notion of *li* 禮 denotes a continuing, complex, and always novel pattern of invested institutions and significant behaviors that is embodied, authored, and reauthorized by succeeding generations as the persistent cultural authority serving to unify the family lineages (*shizu* 氏族) and clans (*jiazu* 家族) as a specific yet extended body of people (*minzu* 民族). For this holistic Confucian philosophy, our unique persons in their entirety penetrate so deeply into the human experience in all of its complexity that it would be a nonsense to try to separate out some reality that stands independent of them. Said another way, for Confucianism, our reality is our lived, embodied experience, and nothing else.

It should be clear that what we are referencing here by "lived body" is not simply the transmission of a physical lineage, although it is that too. The living body and our embodied living is the conveyance of the cultural corpus of knowledge through which a living civilization itself is preserved and extended: linguistic facility and proficiency, religious doctrines and mythologies, the aesthetics of refined living, the modeling of mores and values, instruction and apprenticeship in cognitive technologies, and so on. Our bodies are certainly our physicality, but they are also conduits through which

---

① The sense of immortality implied by the expression "living on" is difficult to see if the body is taken as "belonging" only to an individual. The opening chapter of the *Chinese Classic of Family Reverence* makes clear that for Confucius, the body is an inheritance and on loan from one's family lineage, and that the first obligation we have to this lineage is to maintain its integrity by avoiding any kind of desecration or disgrace.

the entire body of culture is inherited, interpreted, elaborated upon, and reauthorized across the ages.

*天 **tian.** "*Tian*, conventionally 'Heaven.'" See also 聖(人) **sheng** or **shengren** . "Sage, sagacity," and 上帝 **shangdi.** "High god(s)."

There are two specific Chinese terms that were appropriated from the classical Chinese language by Western missionaries to denote the Christian conception of a transcendent deity: *tian* 天 (or *tianzhu* 天主) and *di* 帝 (or *shangdi* 上帝). In the subsequent centuries, especially following the encounter between indigenous Chinese religiousness and Western "God-centered" Abrahamic religion, scholars who have sought to understand Chinese religiousness better have spilled much ink in trying to bring these notions of *tian* 天 and *di* 帝 into sharper focus. But perhaps this effort to stipulate *what* precisely these terms mean is asking something from the Chinese tradition that runs contrary to its own sensibilities.

The notion of *tian* that we generally associate with Zhou dynasty religiousness occurs in the oracle bones as the graphs 奀 and 呆.[①] Scholars have read this character as an ideogram depicting a large human form and what is "above" the head, certainly referencing the pedestrian sky, but also perhaps pointing to the sublime splendor of that same sky writ large as the humbling and unfathomable firmament. On the bronze inscriptions *tian* is somewhat more stylized and closer to the modern character 天: 天.[②] The *Shuowen* lexicon bears out speculations that would define *tian* in relationship to the human world by glossing *tian* paronomastically as *dian* 顛 meaning "top of the head." It then goes on to define *tian* in terms

---

① Kwan, "Database," 甲骨文合集 CHANT 0198A and CHANT 0198.
② Kwan, "Database," 西周晚期 CHANT 2829.

of the graphic components from which the character is constructed. The number 'one' (*yi* 一) and the character for 'greatest' (*da* 大) combine to mean "the highest, the most grand." Importantly, the fact that *tian* is to be understood in its relationship to life as it unfolds in the human world has produced the mantra, "the inseparability of *tian* and the human world" as defining of a Confucian religiousness.

Tian has conventionally been translated as capital "H" "Heaven." We have chosen not to translate it, leaving it in its romanized form as *tian*. This strategy is because its rendering as "Heaven" is a metonym for "God" and is a carry-over from the introduction of Chinese culture into the Western academy by missionaries. This equivocation has been a source of real confusion in making Chinese cosmology familiar by inadvertently asserting a congruency between it and our own theistic sensibilities. Such a translation cannot but conjure up in the reader a world of misleading associations drawn from the Judeo-Christian tradition. These theological associations are largely irrelevant to the Chinese experience but have, nonetheless, often overwritten Chinese cultural practices with presuppositions that are alien to them. In any case, we must try to explain *tian* in a way free of these misleading assumptions if we are to take it on its own terms.

This insinuation of a Judeo-Christian conception of God into the early cosmology becomes immediately apparent when we compare the definitions for *tian* that we find in the Chinese-English dictionary versus the Chinese-Chinese dictionary. The standard Chinese-English dictionary entry for *tian* has 1) the material heavens, the firmament, the sky, 2) the weather, 3) a day, 4) Heaven, Providence, God, Nature, 5) husband, 6) indispensable. In spite of some overlap, these equivalencies contrast rather starkly with those provided by the Chinese-Chinese dictionary: 1) the sky, 2) *qi* 氣, 3) the movement and pattern of the heavens, 4) the sun, 5) spirituality/divinity/mystery *shen* 神, 6) nature, what is self-so-ing *ziran* 自然, 7) ruler *jun* 君, 8) father, 9) indispensable, 10) a period of time, 11) a day,

12) *yang* 陽 (as opposed to *yin* 陰), 13) one's lot, 14) one's natural tendencies *xing* 性, one's person *shen* 身, 15) great.

The most significant gap in these two definitions of *tian* is the clear absence of "Heaven, Providence, God, Nature" in the Chinese-Chinese dictionary. Interestingly, in this early process cosmology *tian* is defined in terms of other correlative categories: the sun (as opposed to the moon), ruler (as opposed to minister), *yang* (as opposed to *yin*), the heavens (as opposed to the earth). In fact, the implicit dualism in the Chinese-English definition that requires appeal to a transcendent deity has little relevance for Chinese cosmology. What has happened is that the purveyors of a Judeo-Christian vocabulary first appropriated *tian* to try to communicate their notion of a transcendent deity to their Chinese interlocutors, and then subsequently insinuated this definition into the dictionary itself.

Our understanding of *tian* is painfully vague precisely because it is vague within the Chinese tradition itself. The question asked by the classical thinkers has been not so much "What is *tian*?" but rather, "What is the most productive relationship we can nurture between human beings and their social, cultural, and natural environments?" Historically, and in the earliest canonical literature such as the *Book of Documents* and the *Book of Songs*, *tian* is often anthropomorphized, suggesting its intimate relationship with the process of a specifically Chinese version of "euhemerism" that grounds Chinese ancestor reverence, "euhemerism" being the ascent of what were in fact historical heroes to the status of gods. The qualification that has to be made with the use of the Greek term "euhemerism" to describe this process as it unfolded in early China is that in Greece "b" becomes "A" in the sense that the human being is being elevated to an alternative, exclusive category: from human to god. By way of contrast, in China "a" becomes "A." That is, given the porous boundary between human beings and gods, there are good yet not uncontested reasons to assume that Chinese gods are, by and large, primarily dead people such as ancestors and cultural heroes, and that *tian* is no exception. Witness the early form of the character as a large human being. At the least we can say that, in the absence of some transcendent creator Deity, *tian* in this earliest conceptualization would seem to stand for a cumulative cultural legacy largely focused on the continuing inspiration of those cultural heroes who have come before.

It was probably this common foundation in ancestor reverence that allowed for the conflation of the culturally sophisticated Shang dynasty's *di* 帝 (gods, ancestral spirits) with the notion of *tian* as it is associated with the militant and Romanesque Zhou federation of tribes who conquered the Yellow River Valley at the turn of the first millennium BCE. The Zhou appealed to *tianming* 天命—"the mandate of *tian*"—as a strategy for political legitimization, claiming that *tian* commands a lineage to rule only if that lineage through its own virtuosity commands first the people's and then *tian's* respect. That is, *tian's* judgment on the mandate was to be known through the response of the people to those who would govern.

The conventional translation of *tian* as "Heaven" conjures up the familiar notion of a transcendent Deity, concealing precisely those aspects of the term most essential to a robust appreciation of its meaning. We can make several observations that reinstate aspects of *tian* that tend to be overwritten by this familiar translation. First, the association between *tian* and the sky encourages proper notice of the profound temporality and historicity that attends this idea, frustrating any analogy one might want to find between "*tian*" as "sky" on the one hand and "Heaven" as "the heavens" on the other. While the perfection and aseity (or self-sufficiency) of the transcendent God locates this independent source outside of time and space, *tian* is inextricably linked to the pervasive processes of change, and is thus always provisional in its relationship to the human world.

Tian further is not only "the sky," but an articulated and patterned sky. *Tian* is thus understood as the "skies" under which culture accumulates rather than as some more disjunctive, atemporal, and aspatial "Other," some ontologically higher order of Being. Significantly, there is a continuity between the articulation of nature generally, and the inscription of human culture. The nature-nurture dualism familiar in Greek-derived cultural sensibilities is not operative; instead, the natural world and human culture are both vigorous and continuous with one another. A corollary to this notion of an invigorated world is the absence of any final boundary between the sentient and insentient, animate and inanimate, living and lifeless.

Spirituality is itself a distilled variant of life itself. And since spirituality and life go hand in hand, spirituality, like life itself, pervades all things. To say that spirituality and life are all-pervasive has two immediate implications. First, there is no value-neutral nature that can stand as encouragement for the pathetic fallacy. Humanity does not occupy a privileged link along a Chain of Being that is ordered on the basis of given ontological disparities. Instead, humankind achieves its hierarchical cosmic role through its cultivation of a complex spirituality, where this spirituality is understood in terms of extension, influence, and inclusion. In fact, it is evident from the connotations of the character *shen* 神, conventionally translated as both "human spirituality" and "divinity," and from entrenched ritualized practices such as the reverence for ancestors and cultural heroes, that gods in the Chinese tradition are generally "extended human beings" in terms of their reach and influence. *Tian* itself is the aggregate spirituality generated by a continuous culture.

But spirituality does not stand independent of materiality. Indeed, there is also a strong association between *tian* and the natural, physical environment. *Tian* does not speak, but communicates effectively although not always clearly through human-generated oracles, through perturbations in the climate, and through alterations in the natural conditions that contextualize the human world. *Tian* participates in a discourse with the most worthy persons in the human community. It is assumed that a failure of order in the human world will be reflected in ominous happenings in the natural environment.

There is a significant transition that occurs during the Zhou dynasty. In some of the earliest literature, *tian* is often portrayed in anthropomorphic terms in ways reminiscent of the sometimes angry God of the Old Testament. But in the Chinese case, anthropomorphism is a natural extension of a human-centered religiousness, where the object of reverence is usually genealogical and ancestral. Although *tian* is not a "personal" deity responsive to individual needs as found in the Judeo-Christian worldview, as the aggregate ancestor it would seem that *tian* functions impartially on behalf of its progeny to maximize the possibilities of an emergent harmony as it is registered at all levels. Given the interrelatedness and interdependency of the orders defining the early Chinese cosmos, what affects one, affects all. Indeed, a failure in the human world will automatically be reflected in the natural environment, making natural disasters a sure sign that there are problems in human governance that require immediate attention.

But in the fullness of time, with this assumed mutuality between the human and the natural order, in late Zhou China there was a growing sense that proper conduct in the human world can guarantee stability in the natural world. In some of the earlier texts, the more spiritual dimension of *tian* continues to be emphasized. But as human beings develop a sense of control over their own environment through moral cultivation, the emphasis seems to shift to a *tian* that takes on an increasingly impersonal character as the operations of nature, albeit a nature that is still suffused with a sense of spirituality.

Tian is not only culturally specific, but geographical as well. It is one and many at the same time. We might speculate that the discovery of a new and sophisticated culture would anticipate the discovery of a *tian* representative of that culture. Just as there are many skies, one would expect other traditions to have accumulated a *tian* out of their own cultural experience. When China was first introduced to the Christian God by well-intended missionaries, the inclination far from being exclusive was to move their own pantheon of gods over to make room for some more.

With the strong connotation that *tian* references the natural environment, it often occurs as an abbreviation for the binomial *tiandi* 天地—"the heavens and the earth"—underscoring the perception that *tian* and the world are inseparable, denoting the unbounded world as it turns around us, *tian* is bottomless, ever advancing, and always novel. The God of the Hebrew bible, often referred to metonymically as "Heaven," *created* a world independent of Himself, but *tian* in classical Chinese *is* the world. That is, *tian* is both *what* our world is and *how* it is. The "ten thousand processes and events" (*wanwu* 萬物)—an expression for "everything that is happening"—are not the creatures of a *tian* that stand independent of what it has ordered; rather, they are constitutive of *tian*. This absence of superordination is a condition made familiar in related notions of the Daoist *dao* and the Buddhist *dharma* that also refer to concrete phenomena and the immanent order that obtains among them. On this basis, *tian* can be described as the most refined aspect of the emergent orders negotiated out of the dispositions of the many particulars that are presently constitutive of it.

The question arises: how is *tian* and *tiandi* to be distinguished from *dao*—a generic name for the field of experience as construed from each perspective? First, it should be noted that this cluster of terms are all simply explanatory categories that are organic and reflexive, where one overlaps with and leads into the next. This being said, one distinction between *dao* and *tian* lies in the intimate *yinyang* relationship between *tian* and *ren* 人, that is, between *tian* and the human world. While *daode* 道德 is a correlative category that stipulates a relationship between any particular thing or event and its field of experience, and is thus more inclusive, the correlative *tianren* is a first order relation within *daode* that tends to highlight more specifically the mutuality of human beings and their natural, social, and cultural context.

On occasion, the Daoist texts contrast the "ways" of *tian* and *ren*, where human beings would do well to take the operations of *tian* as a model for their own conduct. In the expression *tiandao* 天道—"the way of *tian*" the texts generalize about this mode of natural activity. Even so, "nature" would be an inadequate translation here because *tian* as a correlative category will not accommodate any kind of severe "nature/nurture" dualism. *Tian*, far from being mechanistic laws or an impersonal force, still retains a strong sense of a numinous spirituality. The ruler brings order to the people and in so doing, "serves" *tian* as the progeny and surrogate of *tian*: literally the "son of *tian*" (*tianzi* 天子).

This inseparability of *tian* and the human world is often expressed in the characterization of Chinese cosmology as "the continuity between *tian* and human beings" (*tianrenheyi* 天人合一). What is important and different from the Judeo-Christian model is that it is a collateral relationship in which *tian* and human beings are defining of each other. One way in which the Confucian canons do invest the notion of *tian* with meaning and do make it determinate in degree for their readers is by putting a human face on what would otherwise remain a recondite concept. Just as persons of stature and accomplishment in traditional Chinese paintings are depicted as proportionately larger than their retinue, so in the canonical description of consummate persons there is a tendency to present them hyperbolically in celestial terms.

In the literature, culturally significant human beings—persons such as the Duke of Zhou and Confucius—are analogized as the sun and moon, and thus ascend to become the visage of *tian*, where *tian* itself is made determinate in their persons. As we have noted, not only does *tian* entail anthropomorphism, making gods human-like. *Tian* is also a euhemeristic "theomorphism" wherein exemplary persons are god-like. Worthiness in the human world contributes to the meaning of *tian*. As a narrative constituted by cultural heroes, *tian* is thus itself genealogical and biographical. *Tianren* is a correlative category that entails a symbiotic yet hierarchical relationship: *tian* is shaped and extended by the human experience, and what it means to be human is constantly being reshaped by *tian*. That is to say, *tian* is a living, cumulative and normative regularity, inclusive of nature and nurture, that is not only inseparable from the human experience, but is in important degree expressive of it. The project, then, is not to integrate two aspects of our experience that are originally independent of each other, but rather to optimize the correlative and interdependent possibilities of what is shared experience. Persons are born into a world informed by the language and values of a particular cultural legacy, and in this context, have the opportunity to enculturate themselves and enchant the human experience. The sages as the most successful among these cultivated human beings in turn contribute new meaning to *tian* as the aggregating cultural legacy, and the intimate relationship between the human and this world-centered sense of the divine continues to evolve.

*天命   ***tianming.*** See 命 ***ming***.

*天志   ***tianzhi.*** "The purposes or intent of *tian*." See also 天 ***tian***. "*Tian*, conventionally 'Heaven.'"

The Confucian ethic of roles as an alternative to principle- and rule-based ethics begins from its recognition of the native human capacity to collaborate creatively with our environments in pursuit of a consummatory, aesthetic end. As the *locus classicus* among the Confucian canons in celebrating human beings as having both the office and the responsibility to be full co-creators with the heavens and the earth, *Focusing the Familiar*, opens with the oft-cited passage:

天命之謂性，率性之謂道，修道之謂教。
What *tian* commands is called our native human propensities; acting upon these propensities is called way-making; advancing this way is called education.①

One possible reading of this opening line that immediately comes to mind when the text is located within its own interpretive context would be to read it dialectically as a Confucian argument against the Mohist camp, a philosophical lineage that constituted a pervasive

---

① An alternative translation of this same passage by Scottish "commonsense" missionary James Legge reads: "What Heaven has conferred is called The Nature; an accordance with this nature is called The Path of Duty; the regulation of this path is called Instruction." While Legge thought that his own theistically inspired reading of this opening passage gave it a good beginning, he wrote a scathing indictment of the hubris he found in rest of the document, and condemned the entire work with utter derision:
> It begins sufficiently well, but the author has hardly enunciated his preliminary apothegms, when he conducts into an obscurity where we can hardly grope our way, and when we emerge from that, it is to be bewildered by his gorgeous but unsubstantial pictures of sagely perfection. He has eminently contributed to nourish the pride of his countrymen. He has exalted their sages above all that is called God or is worshipped, and taught the masses of the people that with them they have need of nothing from without. In the meantime it is antagonistic to Christianity. By-and-by, when Christianity has prevailed in China, men will refer to it as a striking proof how their fathers by their wisdom knew neither God nor themselves. (Legge, *The Chinese Classics*, Vol. 1, p. 55)

and powerful polemical force during this pre-Qin period.[1] A Mohist interpretation of this line would have construed the relationship between *tian* and the human being in a decidedly conservative, "theistic" direction by suggesting that "Heaven" (*tian* 天) largely imposes its natural and moral order on the human world from without (*wai* 外).[2] Chris Fraser provides a summary description of this Mohist understanding of the intentions or "the purposes of 'Heaven'" (*tianzhi* 天志) as constituting and making available to human beings an externally grounded, objective standard:

> The Mohists justify their consequentialist ethics by appeal to the intention of Heaven (*Tian* 天), which they believe provides an objective criterion of morality.... The crux of the Mohists' appeal to Heaven is that as the highest, wisest moral agent, Heaven conducts itself in a way (*dao* 道) that unfailingly sets an example of correct ethical norms. Its intentions are consistently or reliably humane and right. To obtain an objective criterion of moral right and wrong, then, we can observe Heaven's conduct and notice the norms it is committed to and enforces.[3]

To be clear, I would argue that the "external" standard of

---

[1] A good example of how the interpretive context makes a difference in readings of these early texts is the recent work by scholars such as Chris Fraser, Carine Defoort, Nicolas Standaert, David Wong, James Behuniak, Dan Robbins, Hui-chieh Loy, Ben Wong, and so on, who have done much to reinstate the *Mozi* as integral to the intellectual debates that flourished during the pre-Qin period.

[2] This Mohist claim that moral order is ultimately derived from an "external" source is the basis of a frequently encountered debate in the Confucian texts, with the *Mencius* being perhaps the clearest case in point. See for example, the *Mencius* 6A chapter.

[3] Chris Fraser. "Mohism." *The Stanford Encyclopedia of Philosophy* (Fall 2012 Edition). ed. Edward N. Zalta. URL = http://plato.stanford.edu/archives/fall2012/entries/mohism/.

the Mohist is a publicly determined and implemented objective norm, and while certainly conservative and impositional, it still remains as one possible extreme within the assumed framework of a correlative relationship between *tian* and the human world. That is, the "purposes of *tian*" are negotiated and function within the parameters of "the continuity and inseparability of the human and the cosmic orders" (*tianrenheyi* 天人合一). In the Mohist context, however, the purposes or intent of *tian* would seem to be an example of cosmological postulate, "the many are one, the one many" (*yiduobufen* 一多不分). That is, the various doctrines advanced by the Mohists such as "identifying upwards" (*shangtong* 尚同), inclusive concern (*jian'ai* 兼愛), promoting the worthy (*shangxian* 尚賢), and so on, are all ultimately summary and inclusive, with the intent of *tian* emerging from below as that norm which would guarantee the welfare of the entire world. As such, as a putatively objective standard, it is of a fundamentally different quality of "objectivity" than that derived from the dualistic, two-world order we would associate with the conventional Abrahamic notion of the perfection, and thus the aseity or self-sufficiency, of an independent, transcendent God. To be clear on this point, the aseity of the Abrahamic God rationalizes the human experience by making its standard exclusive. Righteousness is to comport yourself according to the Will of a God independent of the world.

A.C. Graham seems to conflate these two importantly different senses of objectivity when he claims that the Mohists are

> ... driven in the same direction as the great Middle-Eastern religions, with their universal moralities ordained by a personal God who will judge the mighty as they deserve.[1]

---

[1] A.C. Graham, *Disputers of the Tao*, p. 48.

The Confucians in arguing here against the Mohist assertion that cosmic order is divinely imposed upon the human world, are not simply advancing a thin claim that human beings have some active role to play in the production of cosmic order. I do not think the Mohists would object to this. But in fact the Confucians go on to insist that, in this aspiration to live inspired lives, human beings contribute in an intense and inimitable way to the refulgent spirituality of the cosmos. Moreover, this spirituality far from being singular and summary in purpose as is implied by the Mohist notion of "the purposes of 'Heaven,'" (*tianzhi* 天志), is heavily weighted on the human side as multivalent, pluralistic, and inclusive. The myriad things obey no single unifying principle, but achieve their harmony and their diversity through resourcing the interpenetrating differences that obtain among them to make a difference for each one of them. Stated more simply, according to this text, the Confucian vision of the moral life is enhanced and all things in the world flourish when powerful human feelings achieve coalescence in their relations with their environing others, and are orchestrated together with them into a productive, optimal harmony.

*體用   *tiyong.* "Reforming and functioning, trans-*form*-ing."

"Emergence" is a *creatio in situ* assumption about creative advance in the Confucian cosmology characterized by "continuity in change" or "change in continuity" (*biantong* 變通) , and is captured in this related expression *tiyong*: "the mutuality of reforming and functioning." The earliest extant occurrence of this *tiyong* binomial is by the commentator (and philosopher) Wang Bi 王弼 (226-249) in his interpretation of Chapter 38 of the *Daodejing*, and it thereafter becomes ubiquitous in subsequent Confucian, Daoist, and Buddhist philosophical reflection.

"Reforming" and "functioning" is an explanatory, nonanalytical vocabulary for describing the dramatic and ceaseless unfolding of our experience. *How* we think, for example, and *what* we think about, are two coterminous aspects of the same continuing process. The determinate aspects of the embodiment of experience and the vital, creative, and as yet indeterminate life-force that fuels this continuing process are again two aspects of the same phenomenon. There is no ontological disparity between the phenomenal world as the furniture of our experience and its underlying animating source. Simply put, in Confucian cosmology, *all* creativity is construed as a situated and radically embedded, collaborative co-creativity that emerges in the relationship between phenomena and their indeterminate penumbra. Creating oneself and creating one's world is a symbiotic and mutually entailing process.

To take a more concrete example, we can use the aspectual language of "reforming and functioning" (*tiyong* 體用) to describe different ways of thinking about the human narrative, where the persistently formal and determinate aspects (body, language, ritual, life patterns, institutions, roles) can be distinguished from the vital, informal, and indeterminate ones (growth, creativity, passion, shame, skill, taste, insight, spirit). Such differences can be readily observed and experienced, but as different perspectives on the same phenomenon—this particular person—they cannot be separated analytically and isolated. Human persons are at once determinate and vital. At the same time, however, although these aspects cannot be separated out, the very different perspectives are integral to the meaning of the phenomenon itself, providing complexity and intensity to the same unique and continuous quantum of human experience.

Again, we might take different ways of conceptualizing the notion of "concept" itself as an example that illustrates this notion of "forming and functioning." Angus Graham has counseled us to acknowledge some fundamental equivocations commentators must avoid in their understandings of the terms available for theorizing classical Chinese cosmology. Early Chinese concepts, says Graham, often "tend to be more dynamic than their closest Western equivalents, and that English translation freezes them into immobility."[1]

It is only recently over the past century with the insights of contemporaries such as Ludwig Wittgenstein and more recently George Lakoff and Mark Johnson, that we have called into question the assumption that concepts can serve us as a univocal currency to guarantee the cogency of our arguments. Indeed, we have now largely abandoned the expectation that concepts can be a source of univocity, and along with this univocity, certainty. Instead, given the perceived inseparability of language and action in our "language games," we have come to understand language as being irreducibly interdependent with an always evolving practical context that at best offers us "family resemblances" among the categories we might appeal to in our attempts to best theorize our experience. Graham remarks on this recent transition:

> We are losing the faith, except in logic and mathematics, that a concept can be established by precise definitions which free the word from the analogies which guide its ordinary usage.[2]

In our search for cultural equivalencies in comparative philosophy, we might speculate that our earlier essentialist assumptions about the univocal nature of concepts themselves might have arisen from a substance ontology that naturalizes form and stasis and thus favors the more stable, decontextualizing noun as making available to us

---

[1] A.C. Graham, *Studies in Chinese Philosophy and Philosophical Literature*, p. 8.
[2] A.C. Graham, *Disputers of the Tao*, p. 120.

the unchanging object of knowledge. Formal causes and formal definitions set fixed boundaries in our understanding of the world. Such assumptions contrast rather clearly with any attempt to theorize a dynamic process cosmology that is committed to the inseparability of a rhythmic, contrapuntal reforming and functioning (*tiyong* 體用) and thus favors the contextualizing gerund (or verbal noun) not as the object of knowledge *per se*, but as the source from which we can draw the best reconnoitering information we will require to advance most expeditiously on our always prospective journey.

Another concrete example of this *tiyong* dynamic is the practical application of this cosmology in the assumptions that ground Traditional Chinese Medicine (TCM). We must acknowledge that in TCM, there is an inseparability of physiology and anatomy, and thus of function and structure. Such mutual implication precludes the formalism and the reification of the anatomical elements that introduces a doctrine of external relations. Indeed, TCM has a symbiotic understanding of the coterminous relationship between the dynamics of structure and function captured in this expression "reforming and functioning" (*tiyong* 體用) that can perhaps be translated more simply and holistically as "trans-*form*-ing." In TCM, systemic physiological functions within an ecology of relations have parity if not privilege over the more persistent, localized anatomical structures, requiring that diagnostics be holistic and inclusive rather than being overly specific, and then by extension, analytical and exclusive.

Cosmologically, this proposition "reforming and functioning" (*tiyong* 體用) is another way of expressing Tang Junyi's postulate, "the inseparability of one and many" (*yiduobufenguan* 一多不分觀), the mutuality of determinate things and their changing contexts. As such, *tiyong* provides an alternative principle of individuation that stands in contrast to classical Greek essentialism, the Platonic one-behind-the-many idealism that presupposes some self-same, reduplicated, identical characteristic (*eidos*) to be defining of all members of a particular class.

Individuation in Confucian cosmology is effected in a different way. All unique events or foci—particular persons, as an example—are constituted by an unbounded field of more or less relevant relations that collaborate to sponsor them, and they achieve their individuated identities as a function of the quality of coalescence they are able to achieve within these unique fields of relations. That is, moving from description to prescription, a dynamic reading of *yiduobufen* is a summary statement of the opportunity that is available for each of us to optimize the boundless possibilities that honeycomb the relationships between ourselves as particular persons and our environing conditions. Tang Junyi's postulate asserts not only that any phenomenon in our field of experience has implicated within it the contextualizing, unbounded "many," but further that as a unique "one" it can find self-conscious resolution and purpose, and be focused in many different ways according to the multiplicity of roles that come to be defining of its narrative. Importantly, any claim to uniqueness and individuality, far from excluding a person's relations with others, is a function of the quality that this person has been able to achieve within the unique configuration of these same relations.

A version of this same situated and situational dynamic of "individuating" through the one and the many is given expression in the language the Mohists appeal to as their explanation of the process of individuation. In the later Mohist canons, there is reference to the "unit" or "one" (*ti* 體), and the "complex" or "many" (*jian* 兼) to which it belongs, or stated more concretely, some exclusive "thing" and its inclusive context.[①] But this distinction, far

---

[①] See A.C. Graham. *Later Mohist Logic, Ethics and Science.* Hong Kong: The Chinese University Press, 1978, p. 265.

from producing simples, makes the point that any fixed and final sense of individuation—of "thing"—is problematic. According to the early *Shuowen* lexicon, *ti* as a "bodily" unit is again divided into the four subcategories of head, trunk, arms, and legs, and each again of these units is then divided into three more subcategories for a total of twelve. This fluidity between one and many is consistent with the observations of Deborah Sommer who in reporting on the occurrence of the tuber or rhizome as a "subterranean body" (*xiati* 下體) in the early literature, observes that:

> ... when a *ti* body is fragmented into parts (literally or conceptually), each part retains in certain aspects, a kind of wholeness or becomes a simulacra of the larger entity of which it is a constituent."①

In this cosmology, there are no assumed ultimate elements or simples. Instead, the formal aspect of *ti* or "unit" emerges according to the functional situation: that is, through the inseparable processes of "reforming and functioning" (*tiyong* 體用).

Again, on the bronzes, the character *jian* 兼 appears as two sheaves of grain 𩰲, an ideogram that expresses the idea of "inclusion," "in combination," "together," "simultaneously connected."② In this Mohist terminology, the particular unit—that is, what makes the *ti* a "one"—is always a function of how we choose to locate and foreground it. This thumb is a *ti* to this hand that serves as its *jian*; the hand is a *ti* to this arm as its *jian*; this arm is a *ti* to this body as its *jian*, and so on. Something or someone is not "one" in itself, but becomes uniquely one by virtue of how it becomes focused in its relations within the dynamic field of others. This thumb is only this thumb by virtue of its location within this hand, and by the self-

---

① Sommer, "Boundaries of the *Ti* Body," p. 294.
② Kwan, "Database," 戰國 CHANT 11379.

conscious process of extending its context to include this arm, this body, this hitchhiking situation, and so on.

The most familiar way of looking at this thumb is to foreground it as an individuated unit, but a more important observation is to see it as being "aspectual" and "functional" by situating it within its relational *and eventful* context not only as an integral feature of this hand, but as being integral to the experience of *what this hand is doing*. Corollary to the primacy of relationality and its doctrine of internal, constitutive relations, is the fact that the field of any particular thing—the thumb in this case—is necessarily unbounded; its web of relations does not terminate anywhere, but keeps on going. Hence, all correlations we make between thumb and hand are abstractive rather than final, functional rather than absolute, and narrative rather than essential. This being the case, the thumb is "one" as an always fluid center of relationships where, as an aspectual center, it can be self-consciously focused and reconceptualized in many different ways: as a necessary collaborator in finger-snaps or shakas, as a main actor in the familiar gesture of an emphatic "yes," or when turned downwards, of an equally emphatic "no," or as the responsible digital member for manipulating the spacebar when it is resting on the computer keyboard. And of course, the thumb so described is a simulacrum for persons who are conventionally conceived of as individuals, where such discrete individuality is also abstractive, functional, and ultimately narrative.

*同 **tong.** "Sameness, similarity." See also 聖(人) ***sheng*** or ***shengren.*** "Sage, sagacity."

The uniqueness of the particular in the Confucian relational cosmology precludes the kind of identity that informs our usual thinking about "sameness" as "strict identity" or "essential equality." Indeed, this term *tong* is most often defined in the philosophical literature as a similarity that obtains between two things (*xiangsi* 相似). The *Mencius* 6A7, for example, observes:

> 故凡同類者，舉相似也，何獨至於人而疑之？聖人與我同類者。
>
> Generally speaking, things of the same kind (*tonglei* 同類) are all similar to each other (*xiangsi* 相似). Why would we have doubts only when it comes to human beings? The sages are of the same kind as me.

Like the expression "kind" or "grouping" (*lei* 類), *tong* is not only descriptive in associating two things, but is further prescriptive in suggesting that such resonance has the potential for a responsive relationship between the two items: if Mencius in aspiring to behave as a sage, does so, he can become one.

Given how essentialism in ontological thinking has become a commonsense, this Mencius passage is often read as a claim about the essential nature of all human beings. However, the Mencian claim is not that each human being has some innate potential that can be actualized to make every one of us a sage, but rather that the collaboration between our initial inclinations and our world can produce sagacious conduct. There is an important difference between saying that everyone has some inherent potential for becoming a sage, and that everyone who behaves like a sage is a sage. The potential for becoming a sage only emerges *pari passu* in the transactional events that constitute the substance of a human life. *Mencius* 6B2 makes this point explicitly:

> 曹交問曰："人皆可以為堯舜，有諸？"曰："……堯舜之道，孝弟而已矣。子服堯之服，誦堯之言，行堯之行，是堯而已矣。"
>
> Cao Jiao inquired: "Is it the case that we can all become Yao's and Shun's?"
>
> Mencius replied: "... The way-making of Yao and Shun was nothing but family reverence and fraternal deference. If you wear Yao's

clothes, speak his words, and do what he does, then you *are* a Yao."

Mencius's point here is that it is sagacious conduct that makes someone a sage.

*王 *wang.* "King, True King."

On the oracle bones, this character for "king" appears as the head of an axe 王, with this military weapon standing as a symbol of the military power wielded by the king. On the bronzes, it is even more clearly depicted as an axe head 王, and is identical with the original character for 士 *shi* in its early meaning of "warrior, retainer, knight," again with this military reference. In the *Shuowen* lexicon, it defines "king" (*wang* 王) paronomastically as 天下所歸往也 "he to whom the people of the empire repair (*wang* 往)." It again cites Han dynasty philosopher Dong Zhongshu 董仲舒 who says that 古之造文者，三畫而連其中謂之王。三者，天地人也。而參通之者，王也。 "the ancients who created the script took three strokes with one more joining them in the middle and called it 'king.' The 'three' are the heavens, the earth, and humankind, and the one who joins them together is the king." The same term can be descriptive as simply "king," but can also be normative as "the rule of the True King."

Perhaps the most striking feature of the classical Confucians on rulership, and the attitudes of Mencius and Xunzi in particular, is the extent to which they echo the sentiments of Confucius himself in advocating for what Mencius calls "consummate governance" (*renzheng* 仁政). The common thread that binds the Confucians together in their political philosophy is the advocacy of rule by exemplary person as opposed to rule by law. Importance is invested in the consummate ruler as the innovator, interpreter, and executor of the laws, and the laws themselves are given only an ancillary role.

Xunzi in the opening passage of "The Way of the Ruler" 君道

provides a clear statement of this priority of person over law:

有亂君，無亂國；有治人，無治法。羿之法非亡也，而羿不世中；禹之法猶存，而夏不世王。故法不能獨立，類不能自行；得其人則存，失其人則亡。法者，治之端也；君子者，法之原也。故有君子，則法雖省，足以遍矣；無君子，則法雖具，失先後之施，不能應事之變，足以亂矣。

There are rulers who are the source of disorder, but no such thing as a disorderly state. There are persons who effect proper governance, but no such things as laws that can do it. The methods (*fa* 法) of Archer Yi have not been lost, but the generations that follow cannot hit the mark. The laws of Emperor Yu survive, and yet the House of Xia does not produce kings in the generations that have followed. Thus laws do not stand on their own, and cases cannot determine themselves. Where there is the right person, the laws survive; where there isn't, they are lost. Laws are the beginnings of proper order, but consummate rulers are the origin of the laws themselves. Where there is the consummate ruler, even if the laws have been whittled away, they will still suffice to meet all contingencies. But where there is no consummate ruler, even where there is a full complement of laws, they will not be applied at the right time, will not be responsive to changing circumstances, and will only bring about disorder.

The Confucians are all committed to the ideal of a political administration grounded in the moral quality of those who would rule. Implicit in this model of government is the basic Confucian principle that the ruler and his high officials exert themselves in a regimen of personal cultivation. An important aspect of this regimen is the refinement achieved through the process of carrying out the social and political responsibilities of their offices in service to the well-being of their people. The ultimate objective of this model of

Confucian governance is the self-ordering of the people effected through two avenues of moral education: the role models provided by the rulers, and the social order that emerges through achieving a ritual propriety (*li* 禮) in the roles and relations of the people. The ordinary people, naturally sympathetic to the virtuosic modeling of their political leaders, emulate these rulers and respond to them with moral conduct. And by fully embracing and embodying the family-based ritualized order, the people develop a sense of shame that integrates them as a self-governing community (*Analects* 2.3).

The closer the rulers can come to the ideal of "consummate governance," the less they have to rely upon external constraints to achieve civil obedience. While hegemonic government sustains itself through severe punishments, consummate governance wins popular support without recourse to coercion or material incentives.

*萬物 **wanwu.*** "The ten thousand things, the ten thousand processes or events, the myriad things or happenings."

This expression *wanwu* is conventionally translated as "the ten thousand things" or "the myriad things." But in the *qi* 氣 cosmology, substance is qualified by process, and discreteness by continuity. Thus, *wu* is more appropriately understood not as static "things," but as fluid processes and the always transitory disclosure within these processes of more or less consummatory events. We must understand that "things" (*wu* 物) as environing processes (happenings) and events (happenings that have achieved some relative consummation) have no final boundaries among them. As *Zhuangzi* 2 observes,

古之人，其知有所至矣。惡乎至？有以為未始有物者，至矣盡矣，
不可以加矣。其次以為有物矣，而未始有封也。其次以為有封焉，
而未始有是非也。

With the ancients, wisdom had really gotten somewhere. Where was that? At its height, at its extreme, indeed an understanding to which no more could be added was this: some of them thought that there had never begun to be "things." The next lot thought that there are things, but that there had never begun to be boundaries among them. And then the next, that although there are boundaries, they have never begun to be "this's" and "not-this's."

Wu suggests the notion of things as particular processes with a career of growth, maturation, and consummation. It is the punctuation of the ongoing fluid process into particular events that makes the world determinate and intelligible. This eventful usage of "thing" is not unknown in English when we say, "I have a million things to do."

The expression *wanwu* or "the ten thousand processes or events" refers to the "cosmos" as an unsummed totality of all particular processes and events as they constitute this world. *Wanwu* is everything that is happening. The *Zhuangzi*'s expression *wuhua* 物化—"transforming together with other things"—suggests the mutuality and interpenetration of all forms of process, as one "thing" transforms together with other things to become something else. The furniture of the world is not created in the sense of emerging out of nothing, and it does not suffer annihilation in the sense of returning to nothing. *Dao* 道 and the myriad things (*wanwu* 萬物), rather than referencing distinct, separate realities, are two aspectual ways of looking at the same always transforming phenomenal world and our continuing experience within it.

文 **wen.** "The written word, patterns, culture, refinement, King Wen." See also 文化 **wenhua**. "Culture, enculturation."

Wen occurs frequently in the ancient documents. On the oracle bones, it appears as 🔣, on the bronze inscriptions as 🔣, and on the bamboo strips as 🔣.① Traditional commentaries have interpreted this as a pictograph of a tattooed human body with the most common tattooed designs being the heart as the aorta, and a crisscrossed "X." Paradoxically, most references to tattooed bodies in the canonical literature reference what are taken to be uncultured peoples—the Yue people and the Eastern Yi.② On the bronzes, *wen* occurs in the context of sacrifices as a term of respect for the ancestors as "the noble and virtuous." As a proper name, it refers to King Wen of the Zhou dynasty whose name is then used ubiquitously in the canonical literature to allude to the responsibility for intergenerational transmission of "this culture of ours" (*siwen* 斯文).③ The *Shuowen* lexicon defines *wen* as a complex pattern: a design with intersecting lines. Abstractly, *wen* refers to the mosaic of patterns, images, and symbols as they are expressed naturally on things, such as tortoise shells and animal fur. In its noun form, it means symbols, markings, designs, and by extension, the written word, documents, writings. Verbally it means "inscribing," "embellishing," and then

---

① Kwan, "Database," 甲骨文合集 CHANT 3237B, 商代 CHANT 5362, and 上博竹書—孔子詩論 7.
② 《莊子・逍遙游》："越人斷髮文身。"《禮記・王制》："東方曰夷，被髮文身。"
③ A good example is *Analects* 9.5: 子畏於匡。曰："文王既沒，文不在茲乎？天之將喪斯文也，後死者不得與於斯文也；天之未喪斯文也，匡人其如予何？" When the Master was surrounded in Kuang, he said, "With King Wen long dead, does not our cultural heritage reside here in us? If *tian* were going to destroy this legacy, we latecomers would not have had access to it. If *tian* is not going to destroy this culture, what can the people of Kuang do to me!"

by extension, "civilizing," "enculturating" and the intergenerational transmission of that culture. It is closely related to the complex Confucian understanding of situated "creativity."

What is interesting about *wen* is that, given the absence of any severe *phusis/nomos* (nature/nurture) distinction in the classical Chinese world, this term like *dao* 道 and *li* 理 is used to characterize the patterned regularity that defines both nature and human culture. For example, *tianwen* 天文 (the natural pattern of the heavens) is astronomy while as the product of human hand there are *wenzi* 文字 as written characters, *wenxue* 文學 as literature, *wenming* 文明 as civilization, and *wenhua* 文化 as culture. In the classical written language, the single character *wen* does much of the work of these various binomial expressions. This assumed continuity between nature and the human world is another indication of the inseparability of situation and agency and the radical embeddedness of the human experience in this tradition. The aestheticization of the cosmos is a contrapuntal collaboration between human beings and their world.

*文化   ***wenhua.*** "Culture, enculturation." See also 文 ***wen.*** "The written word, patterns, culture, refinement, King Wen."

The word "culture" in European languages has important metaphorical associations: the occupations of agriculture, horticulture, and husbanding are implicated in our term "culture," and there are strong teleological assumptions that have attended this idea as its use has evolved within our own narrative. More specifically, such teleological assumptions are wont to persuade us uncritically that the "cultivation" of human "culture" by analogy with horticulture and the rearing of stock has to do with conserving, nurturing, and actualizing a specific set of inborn potentialities that are driven by a given goal (*telos*) or inherent design (*eidos*).

For the Confucian tradition, we find a much more open-ended, aesthetic rather than a horticultural metaphor that lies behind the production of *wenhua* 文化 as culture. As in Europe, there was no single term in the languages of the premodern Sinitic cultures, Chinese, Japanese, Korean, or Vietnamese, that had a conceptual reach comparable to that of our modern, now extended uses of the word "culture." But the term that emerged in the nineteenth century throughout this geographical region as an equivalency to translate and appropriate this modern Western concept differs markedly in its metaphorical implications from those assumed with the English word "culture." The languages of these traditionally agrarian Asian societies abound with terms that, like "culture," are rooted in instrumental physical processes of cultivation and nourishing: for example, *yang* 養 (providing for, keeping, growing), *xu/chu* 畜 (raising domestic animals), *pei* 培 (cultivating, training), *xiu* 修 (cultivating, trimming, pruning), *yu* 育 (rearing, raising, bringing up), *zai* 栽 (planting and growing) and so many more. But such agricultural terms are bypassed as points of metaphorical departure in favor of 文化 (*wenhua*), a compound expression that combines the characters for the "transforming" (*hua* 化) of the human experience effected by "the inscribing and embellishing processes undertaken by literary, civil, and artistic traditions" (*wen* 文).

This modern expression *wenhua* 文化 created to synchronize Chinese with modernity's word "culture" is an allusion to the *Book of Changes*, where it states:

觀乎天文，以察時變；觀乎人文，以化成天下。
Through observing carefully the heavenly patterns we can gain insight into the changing seasons; through observing carefully the embellishments made by human beings, we can transform the world.

In a word, *wenhua* is the civilization and aestheticization of the human experience in all of its parts. Human culture is understood as emerging from close attention to the changing patterns and designs of the world around us, and then correlating these images with the establishment of the human technologies and institutions needed to regulate the human experience to optimal effect.

Whereas metaphorically rooting "culture" in the agricultural practices of plant and animal domestication invites us to see cultural norms as having a transcendent disciplinary force with respect to that which is being "cultured," *wen* was understood (with significant political implications) as the disclosing processes of civilization: that is, of *collaborating* with nature's beauty, *elaborating* upon it, *elevating* it, and *achieving* a decidedly aesthetic if not spiritual product, rather than as merely regulating its spontaneous growth. In this contrast between culture driven by teleology and culture as *wenhua*, we have an important distinction between rationalized closure and aesthetic disclosure, between retrospective necessity as what is predetermined and then actualized, and prospective possibility as what is imagined and then realized.

As is demonstrated by the provenance of *wenhua* in texts dating to the Han dynasty (202 BCE-220 CE), this term is an ancient one. The modern Japanese *kanji* term that translates "culture" is pronounced *bunka*, and is derived from classical Chinese use of *wenhua* that first appears explicitly as early as the court bibliographer Liu Xiang's 劉向 (77-6 BCE) *Garden of Stories* (*Shuoyuan* 說苑). In this text we read that 文化不改，然後加誅 "it is only when our civilizing efforts (*wenhua*) fail to bring the people up to the appropriate standards that punishments are to be imposed." And, by at least the fifth century CE, Chinese literary theorists such as Liu Xie 劉勰 (465?-522?) associated human *wen* practices explicitly with the "self-so-ing" (*ziran* 自然) and ceaselessly creative dynamics (*shengsheng buxi* 生生不息) of the human and natural worlds (*dao* 道), affirming that nature and nurture far from being in opposition, together constitute a coevolving, contrapuntal process at the heart of realizing a symbiotic and mutually entailing, natural and societal harmony.

Reflecting further on the genealogy of the term *wen*, dating back more than a millennium earlier than the passage cited above from the Han dynasty *Garden of Stories*, *wen* has consistently been contrasted explicitly with the coercive, destructive, and dehumanizing use of martial force (*wu* 武) as it arises in the human experience. *Wen* so understood, in a sharp departure from our contemporary use of "culture wars" as a metaphor for cultural tensions, is indeed the antithesis of war. *Wen* denotes the expansively civil and civilizing dimension of the lettered classes of each succeeding generation as they respond to the pressing issues of their day. *Wen* is the refinement of the human experience that emerges when the life of a community is guided by an aesthetically- and critically-enriching counterpoint between persistent canonical texts and the interlinear commentaries that are continuously being written on them. And in the sharpest of contrasts, martial force far from being celebrated as a source of glory and honor as found in the classical Greek and Roman cultures respectively, is regarded even in the militarist *Sunzi* literature as a sometimes necessary but always losing proposition that should only be appealed to as a very last resort (*budeyi* 不得已), and then managed carefully to maintain minimum loss.

In sum, the conceptual genealogy of the Chinese term *wenhua* implies that culture emerges through an *intrinsic* relationship between continuity and change (*biantong* 變通), a symbiotic relationship described at great length in the *Book of Changes* between a determinate and enduring tradition and the ambient forces of transformation. Cultural conservation and prospective change, far from opposing each other, are complementary and mutually enhancing.

The disparity between European and Asian languages in the cultural metaphors in which the term "culture" itself is embedded—

that is, teleologically-informed design in the former case, and a fundamentally open-ended, aesthetic metaphor in the latter—is certainly related to an indelibly skewed understanding of "creativity" in the Abrahamic traditions. A brief excursus in this direction can provide us insight into how the important notion of "creativity" was understood in an importantly different way in Confucian cosmology.

In the evolution of our commonsense, *ex nihilo* creativity—"creativity from nothing"—properly belongs to a self-sufficient Creator God. As *Psalms* insists: "The earth is the Lord's and the fulness thereof", "It is He that has made us and not we ourselves." And when such *ex nihilo* creativity is usurped and then exercised by the idiosyncratic and audacious human genius—by eccentrics such as Goethe's Faust, Shelley's Frankenstein, Milton's Satan, and Nietzsche's Übermensch, for example—it is dark, dangerous, and deliciously depraved: a Promethean offense against God's natural and moral order. We might be inclined (although with our children at a safe distance) to admire the rakish charms of someone deemed "morally creative." We might be attracted (although with enormous caution) by the offer of "creative financial instruments." Scientists who have been "creative" in recording their data might have difficulty getting further support from the National Institute of Health. We might find ourselves curious about (although embarrassed by) the bizarre ritual performances of "new" religions. And we can only imagine what the very serious Aristotle would have thought about Gadamer's notion of "philosophy as play." Even in our contemporary times of radical innovation and entrepreneurship, our commonsense understanding of the core human occupations of morality, economy, science, religion, and philosophy still have a strong teleological cast that seems resistant to the idea of "creativity." Instead, this term "creativity" usually prompts for us an association with more marginalized aesthetic interests such as the creative arts and the writing of entertaining "fiction."

Indeed, A.N. Whitehead criticizes orthodox theism for depriving human beings of any important role in creative arts of making culture, challenging its belief in "an entirely static God with eminent reality, in relation to an entirely fluent world with deficient reality."[①] This asymmetry between God and world with respect to creativity is the consequence of radical transcendence that assigns creativity wholly to God. Whitehead points out one of the many incoherent implications of a Christian worldview grounded in such transcendence, and seeks to overcome such a problematic vision by offering a model of God and His relationship to the world that allows real contingency to be introduced into the Divine Nature, thus rendering creativity more primordial than God Himself. Whitehead's strategy is to characterize God in terms of dual natures, the primordial and the consequent. The primordial nature of God is constituted by his entertainment of eternal ideas, those pure possibilities that exist as candidates for actualization by the temporal events (the "actual occasions") that comprise the world. The consequent nature of God is constituted by God's reception into himself of the realized actualities of the world. Thus, in one sense God transcends the world; in another the world is becoming immanent within God. In this latter sense, God is contingent upon the world, just as in the former sense the world is contingent on God.

On the one hand, the Whitehead revisionist understanding of creativity is in obvious conflict with Judeo-Christian orthodoxy that embraces the notion of the aseity or perfection and self-sufficiency of God. Philosophically, the problem is simply relocated to the possible incoherence in the dual natures of God. Indeed, the early attempts by the Fathers of the Christian church to reconcile the two natures of Jesus Christ by appeal to the formula "Very God and Very Man"

[①] A.N. Whitehead. *Process and Reality* (corrected edition). ed. D. Griffin and D. Sherburne. New York: The Free Press, 1978, p. 346.

are perhaps reflected in Whitehead's formulation of the primordial and consequent nature of God. It seems that Whitehead while aware of the theistic incoherence of transcendence in its radical form, is himself far from giving it up. Eternal Objects as pure possibilities are independent of and unaffected by either God or the world. Likewise, the primordial nature of God transcends the world absolutely. And further, there is an ultimate in creativity that altogether transcends God. In Whitehead's own words, "In the philosophy of organism this ultimate is termed 'creativity;' and God is its primordial non-temporal accident."①

That Whitehead has identified and attempted to address a serious incoherence in the relationship between world, God, and creativity by making creativity itself more fundamental than God is perhaps acknowledged by the fact that the *Oxford English Dictionary* introduces a new entry for "creativity" into its pages in a 1978 supplement with two of its three references to Whitehead's own *Religion in the Making*. Again, while Whitehead's efforts at reconciliation have inspired his flourishing following among what have come to be called process theologians, concerns about his own incoherences have in some important degree relegated him to the margins in the hallways of professional philosophy. Although Whitehead has tried valiantly to address the incoherence that attends the notion of "creativity" within the Western philosophical narrative, the influence on our commonsense understanding of the strong role of a linear teleology in the evolution of the mainstream occupations of human culture still seems to persist in ethics, in religion, in science, in economics, and so on.

By contrast with the problematic status of "creativity" within the Western philosophical and theological narratives, and the boundaries it imposes on human culture, we find that in the Confucian worldview

---

① Whitehead, *Process and Reality*, p. 7.

as evidenced in Confucian role ethics, singular value is invested in the quality of the moral imagination needed to inspire real artistry in our moral lives. In the Confucian way of deference (*zhongshuzhidao* 忠恕之道) we are exhorted to be morally creative in the project of becoming consummate human beings. And in the absence of idealism, the consummation of each human becoming is one of a kind. Indeed, the Confucian project as it is defined in the cosmology of the core canonical texts such as the *Book of Changes* (*Yijing* 易經) and *Focusing the Familiar* (*Zhongyong* 中庸) requires of human beings as "the heartminding of the cosmos" (*tiandizhixin* 天地之心) nothing less than both the imagination and the refinement needed to stand together with the heavens and the earth as co-creators of the cosmos. Human "beings" are in fact human "becomings" because of our capacity and responsibility for making culture.

In terms of its religious sensibilities, Confucianism offers an alternative "family-centered" rather than "God-centered" religiousness that unlike the competing Abrahamic traditions, is not grounded in a transcendence that brings with it the singular, exclusive, and absolute power of its creator God. Confucianism is at once a-theistic, and profoundly religious.[①] It does not appeal to an independent, retrospective, and substantive Divine Agency as the reality behind appearance and as the source of all cosmic significance. Indeed, it is a religious tradition without a God; a religious sensibility affirming a spirituality that emerges out of the inspired human experience itself. For Confucianism, the world is an autogenerative, "self-so-ing" process—*ziran er ran* 自然而然—that

---

[①] See Roger T. Ames. "*Li* 禮 and the A-theistic Religiousness of Classical Confucianism." *Confucian Spirituality*, Volume One, ed. Tu Wei-ming and Mary Evelyn Tucker. New York: Crossroads Press, 2003. A more sustained argument for the profundity and legitimacy of this alternative religiousness is found in Henry Rosemont, Jr.'s *Rationality and Religious Experience*, La Salle, IL: Open Court, 2002.

includes the energy of its ongoing transformation as residing within the continuing narrative itself. Its world is an inside without an outside. And human feelings themselves are the motor of religious meaning, understood both retrospectively and prospectively as an unfolding and inclusive spirituality achieved within the qualitatively inspired activities of the family, the community, and the natural world. Human beings are both inspired by and contributors to the numinosity that elevates and refines the human experience within the world in which we live. There is no church (except for the extended family), no altars (except perhaps for the dining room table), and no clergy (except for the exemplary models both past and present who are deferred to as the living center of the community). Confucianism celebrates the way in which the process of human growth and extension is shaped by, and contributes to, the meaning of the totality—a notion of *creatio in situ* that stands in stark contrast to the theology of the *creatio ex nihilo* traditions in which the creator Godhead is everything and His creatures are nothing.

*無　*wu*. See 有無 *youwu*.

*無極　*wuji*. See 太極 *taiji*.

*無爲　*wuwei*. "Noncoercive acting."

Wuwei is usually associated with Daoist philosophy, and has most often been translated as "no action" or "non-action." But *wuwei* is in fact itself a mode of conduct, a kind of action. In fact, it is an achieved disposition in acting that seeks to optimize the human experience. The negative *wu* aspect of *wuwei* is the absence of any coercive actions that would interfere with the insistent particularity (*de* 德) of those things contained within one's field of influence. As such, *wuwei* is "noncoercive acting that is in accordance with the *de* of things." Such actions are unmediated in the sense that, in an effort to take other things on their own terms, transactions are not compromised by one's ingrained habits and prejudices. Instead, such actions are underdetermined and spontaneous in that there is no necessary grid of understanding that filters them or overwrites them with importances not their own. The productive quality of such actions are the result of deferential responses to the item or the event in accordance with which, or in relation to which, one is acting.

We begin from the observation that persons or "things" are constituted by their relations. Personal dispositions expressed as noncoercive action (*wuwei* 無爲), "unprincipled knowing" (*wuzhi* 無知), and "objectless desire" (*wuyu* 無欲) then enrich the world by allowing the life-experience to unfold spontaneously on its own terms, while at the same time, allowing persons to contribute themselves utterly to this productive process. We may say that the embodiment of these *wu*-forms in the way in which persons conduct themselves allows them to leave the world as it is. But we can make this claim only if we recognize that "world" for persons in this context means a myriad of spontaneous transactions that are characterized by emerging patterns of deference to the acknowledged excellence of other things.

In Daoism the self/other distinction is forgotten to the extent that discriminated "objects" no longer constitute the environs of the self. These three *wu*-forms—*wuwei, wuzhi, wuyu*—all provide a mode of entertaining and deferring to things in one's web of relations, allowing them to become conditions of one's own growth and transformation. Thus, in their governing of the people the sages are concerned with embodying and promoting that sort of acting, knowing, and desiring that treats other people as inclusive relations rather than excluded objects, recognizing that other people properly "object" if treated as objects.

The key to understanding all these *wu*-forms that comprise the Daoist disposition lies in the contrast between "objects" and "objectivity." Beyond the mediating confusions introduced by language, and by layers of our own distorted perceptions and tendentious categorizations, there is nevertheless, with properly Daoist qualifications, an "objectively" real world. And our task is to experience that world as "objectively" as possible.

From the Daoist perspective, the problem begins when we insist that the "objective world" is a world made up of objects—namely, concrete, unchangeable things that we encounter as over against us; things which announce themselves to us by asserting "I object!" For the Daoist, the objective world cannot be objective in this sense because it is a constantly transforming flow of events or processes that belie the sorts of discriminations that would permit any final inventory of the furniture of the world. Seemingly paradoxically, for the Daoist the objective world is thus objectless.

Sages, however, mirror the world, and 聖若鏡不將不迎 "neither see things off nor go out to meet them." As such, they 應而不藏 "respond to everything without storing anything up."[①] They mirror the world *at each moment* in a way that is undetermined by the shape of a world that has passed away, or by anticipations of a world yet to come. Importantly, the Daoist project is neither passive nor quietistic. Water is the source of nourishment; the mirror is a source of light; the heart-and-mind is a source of transformative energy. To "know" as the mirror "knows" is not representational, but is to cast the world in a certain light. Such performative "knowing" is for one to actively interpret and realize a world with healthy, productive effect. These mirroring metaphors for the heart-and-mind (*xin* 心) entail a presentation rather than a representation, a coordination rather than a correspondence. "Mirroring" then is best seen as synergistic and responsive, where all of the elements are in the stream and constitute a fluid interdependent and yet unsummed totality.

---

① *A Concordance to Huainanzi* 6/51/15.

Sages envision a world of changing events that they can, for whatever reason, choose to freeze momentarily into a distinct pattern of discrimination, but that they recognize, when they see clearly, as being beyond such distinctions. For the Daoist, the consequence of this transformed vision is that knowing, acting, and desiring in the world are no longer based upon construal. To feel ourselves in tension with objectified others can lead us to act in an aggressive or defensive manner in order to effect our will. Principles and fixed standards can lead us to construe the object of our knowledge by recourse to such principles. In this way, an item becomes one of a *kind* (rather than *one-of-a-kind*) and an instrument for the achievement of an end (as opposed to an end in itself). Desire motivated by an object of desire leads us to seek possession of that which is desired, allowing it significance only insofar as it meets our needs. A self that is consumed by objects of desire narrows, truncates, and obfuscates the world as it is.

In fact, when these *wu*-forms are understood as the optimum dispositions of the Daoist self, whether in the persons of the sage or the people, they provide us with a way of interpreting Daoism as recommending a broad social and political anarchism. Such an "anarchism" is not the absence of governance, but given the self-ordering of the people themselves, it is the difference between ruling and simply reigning, between regulating and simply overseeing.

There are also important resonances between the Daoist negative statement of optimal relationality that is captured in the *wu*-forms, and the Confucian notion of optimal relationality expressed as the term *ren* 仁, consummate conduct. The method of achieving consummate conduct is also deferring to others by putting oneself in their place (*shu* 恕), and once having identified the most productive mode of conduct for optimizing relations with them, acting conscientiously upon this judgment (*zhong* 忠).

This sense of *wuwei* as a political ideal is also a desired posture in the Confucian canons. In the *Analects* 15.5, we read:

子曰:"無為而治者,其舜也與?夫何為哉,恭己正南面而已矣。"
The Master said, "If anyone could be said to have effected proper order while remaining non-coercive in his actions (*wuwei* 無為), surely it was Shun. What did he do? He simply assumed an air of reverence and faced due south."

A passage in the *Analects* 2.3 that perhaps best expresses this Confucian political philosophy of *wuwei* statecraft claims that

道之以政,齊之以刑,民免而無恥;道之以德,齊之以禮,有恥且格。
... if you lead the people with policy and effect social order with punishments, they will avoid wrongdoing, but will not develop an appropriate sense of shame. If you lead the people by modeling virtuosity in your conduct (*de* 德) and effect social order by encouraging propriety in roles and relations (*li* 禮), the people will not only develop a sense of shame (*chi* 恥), but will also order themselves.

The ideal of such proper governing is an achieved synergy among several interpenetrating factors that serves constitutionally to effect social and political order: the moral virtuosity displayed in the role modeling of rulers, the proper functioning of familial and social roles, and the commensurate sense of shame that develops within ritually choreographed family and community relations. We can argue these Confucian texts give primacy to the thick notion of "achieving propriety in one's lived roles and relations" (*li* 禮) as its main criteria for effecting social and political order, and as such, must take the relevant, specific interests of all parties into account (*yi* 義), ruled as well as rulers. While the dynamics of *li*-structured family lineages provide a concrete normative pattern of relations for a thriving community, abstract precepts such as the application of laws or policies, or the attendant threat of punishment, are at best only secondary injunctions that serve as a clear admission of communal failure.

An appreciation of how *li* works constitutionally in effecting social and political order has a compensatory explanatory force in our own time to counterbalance the still persistent Hegelian caricature of Confucian China as an oriental despotism. In trying to fathom how a constitutional *li* works, there is the often unannounced but omnipresent Confucian assumption of an isomorphism between family and state (*jiaguotonggou* 家國同構). The great Qing scholar and translator Yan Fu 嚴復, looking back to survey two thousand years of Chinese imperial history, remarked that the social and political order was 30% emperor and 70% family lineage (*jiazu* 家族).[①] I would extend Yan Fu's insight to suggest that it is because governance is heavily invested in moral education directed at transforming the people (*huamin* 化民), we should understand such governance as a synergy between governor and governed. And as this synergy approaches an optimal symbiosis (*du* 度), the result is a kind of self-ordering that defines ideal rulership as a "non-coercive ordering" (*wuwei* 無為). The ideal of Confucian governing, far from being the unilateral exercise of sovereign control over the people, means a collateral albeit asymmetrical effecting of social and political order through promoting a self-ordering society. Such a focus and field account of the social and political "family" would mean that the differences between rulers and ruled are implicated in each other, and that the quality of each is dependent upon the quality of their relationship with the other. In what we might call a Confucian "role politics," virtuosic constitutionalism and its achieved civility allows rulers and ruled to live their different roles symbiotically and

---

① Yiqun Zhou. *Festival, Feasts, and Gender Relations in Ancient China and Greece*. New York: Cambridge University Press, 2010, p. 19, n55.

without coercion.

*五行 **wuxing.** "Five modes of virtuosic conduct, the five phases." See also 氣 **qi.** "Vital energy, *qi*," 體用 **tiyong.** "Reforming and functioning, *trans-form*-ing," and 陰陽 **yinyang.** "*Yin* and *yang*."

The connection between Mencius, Zisi, and this *wuxing* ethical doctrine has become somewhat clearer with the recent archaeological recovery of a *Five Modes of Virtuosic Conduct* 五行篇 text attributed to Zisi. Over the past generation, two different versions of this text have been found buried in two separate archaeological sites at significantly different times. The two versions of this text belonging to the Zisizi-Mengzi lineage (SiMengpai 思孟派) have been recovered, first on a silk text at Mawangdui (1973) dating to 168 BCE, and then the Guodian manuscript (1993) written on bamboo strips dating from c. 300 BCE. The fact that redactions of the same text have been found at such a physical and temporal distance from each other speaks to the perceived importance of the document in its own time. This text is in the same lineage as *Focusing the Familiar* that argues human beings through personal cultivation have both the capacity and the responsibility to serve as co-creators with the heavens and the earth.

Mencius's well-known list of the "four inclinations" (*siduan* 四端)— "conducting oneself consummately" (*ren* 仁), "acting with optimal appropriateness" (*yi* 義), "achieving propriety in one's roles and relations" (*li* 禮), "acting wisely" (*zhi* 知), in this specific order—is in fact an abbreviated version of the "five modes of virtuosic conduct," with the fifth mode, "sagacity" (*sheng* 聖), being the fruit of growing these other four "shoots." These are five acquired habits of conduct that need to be cultivated for interacting most productively in family and community, aggregating over time to become a unified moral excellence that informs future action.

The *Xunzi* associates the names of both Zisi and Mencius with the ethical doctrine of "five modes of virtuosic conduct" in his rather severe indictment of it:

略法先王而不知其統……聞見雜博。案往舊造說，謂之五行，甚僻違而無類，幽隱而無說，閉約而無解。案飾其辭，而祇敬之，曰：此真先君子之言也。子思唱之，孟軻和之。世俗之溝猶瞀儒、嚾嚾然不知其所非也，遂受而傳之，以為仲尼子弓為茲厚於後世：是則子思孟軻之罪也。

There are those who, only superficially emulating the way of the former kings, do not understand its real substance. . . . What they have seen and learned is indeed extensive and varied. Basing their ideas on ancient lore, they concoct their new theory and call it *wuxing*. In fact, this theory is perverse and bizarre. It is a lot of obscure and impenetrable nonsense. They dress it up in eloquent language, and with great reverence say: "These are truly the words of the exemplary persons of old." Zisi sang this song, and Mencius chimed in with it. The deluded and foolish Confucians of our present day are thrilled with this theory and are wholly oblivious to where it goes wrong. They have inherited it and passed it on, believing that Confucius and Zigong because of it will be held in high regard by later generations. This then is the crime of Zisi and Mencius.

There are at least two explanations for Xunzi's stinging polemic against Zisi and Mencius. The first one is that the ever-practical Xunzi takes exception to a perceived connection between the moral doctrine of *wuxing* and the increasingly popular "five phases" conjectures about cosmic operations that has emerged under the same rubric, and that he believes ought not to concern the human world. In full accord with Confucius's refusal to pronounce of speculative questions (*Analects* 9.4), Xunzi is adamant that human beings should invest their efforts in personal and communal cultivation, and should not waste their time conjecturing about things they cannot and should not hope to understand.

It has been claimed that this passage in the *Xunzi* is somewhat ambiguous. It is not immediately clear from the language whether Xunzi is criticizing Zisi and Mencius themselves, or rather criticizing the inappropriate co-opting and contaminating of their moral doctrine by those latter-day Confucians who are given to speculating on cosmic mysteries. In an attempt to resolve this ambiguity, John Knoblock points out that Xunzi himself applies the expression *wuxing* to appropriate human deportment elsewhere in his writings in a positive sense, albeit with a content clearly different from the specific five modes of virtuosic conduct of Zisi and Mencius.① Indeed, for Xunzi, apart from the passage condemning Zisi and Mencius, the expression only occurs once, where *wuxing* are five patterns of conduct governing the village wine drinking ceremony.② Given the almost total absence of the term *wuxing* in the *Xunzi* together with this casual use of it, it might also be argued that Xunzi wants to avoid any association with the technical term, whatever its reference. In any case, on this first explanation it is most probable that Xunzi's complaint was directed at the misappropriation of the term *wuxing* as a cosmological theory by his contemporaries and, even more harshly, was aimed at the complicity of his fellow Confucians in promoting this equivocation.

There is an alternative explanation of Xunzi's complaint against the moral doctrine of *wuxing* associated with Zisi and Mencius that might be more plausible. To begin with, we have no corroborating evidence that the *wuxing* cosmological theory that emerges in the

---

① John Knoblock. *Xunzi: A Translation and Study of the Complete Works*, Vol. I. Stanford: Stanford University Press, 1988, pp. 214-219.
② Knoblock, *Xunzi*, Vol. III, p. 85.

Han dynasty was current as early as Xunzi. Given Xunzi's antipathy to such speculations and his willingness to speak out against heterodox philosophical ideas, the absence of any clear reference to this development would suggest that the target of Xunzi's ire is probably the moral doctrine associated with Zisi and Mencius.

Secondly, in other contexts, Xunzi is anything but shy about voicing loud and sustained objections to the ideas of Mencius, especially Mencius's attempt to define the natural human tendencies (*xing* 性) as the prosocial "four inclinations" (*siduan* 四端). And the recovery of the *Five Modes of Virtuosic Conduct* in recent archaeological finds establishes an immediate and incontrovertible link between the *wuxing* moral doctrine and Mencius's "four inclinations," where the "four inclinations" in the same order are nothing other than the first four of the five modes of conduct.

Thirdly, given Xunzi's practical bent, the fifth of the five modes of virtuosic conduct—the celebration of the role of human "sagacity" (*sheng* 聖) as a profoundly creative cosmic force—would have surely been received by him as "a lot of obscure and impenetrable nonsense."

Finally, the passage from Xunzi condemning Zisi and Mencius is anything but ambiguous. It describes the *wuxing* doctrine as a gross distortion of historical antecedents, denounces the hyperbolic language that gives it expression, deplores the popularity it has garnered among contemporary Confucians, and blames Zisi and Mencius by name and in unequivocal terms for their role in promoting what he takes to be a heretical Confucianism.

Xunzi's rejection of the *wuxing* moral doctrine would appear to be an opening volley in what becomes a contest between two importantly distinct interpretations of Confucian philosophy: the Xunzi lineage that had some real prominence in the first centuries of the Han dynasty, and the Mencian lineage that in the fullness of time was to supersede it. The conclusion we might draw is that *wuxing* as a prescription for moral behavior is initially separate from, but is either developed into or is merged with, the later Han dynasty cosmological theories of the "five phases" (*wuxing*) first associated with Zou Yan 鄒衍 (305-240? BCE) that go by the same name.

Elemental theory is a prominent theme in classical Greek thought paradigmatic of substance ontology in privileging both discreteness and quantity. According to Nathan Sivin, such elemental theories "claim that things are made up of minute ultimate parts that usually do not look like the parts that are big enough for us to see."[①] Early on, the Chinese *wuxing* 五行 were in fact translated as "the five elements," associating this process cosmology with the various Greek elemental theories. But several prominent scholars such as Sivin himself, Angus Graham, and John Major have, in their interpretive studies, sought to correct this earlier misunderstanding of the *wuxing* 五行 cosmology. According to Major:

> The problem with "five elements" is that the Chinese concept of *wu-hsing* [*wuxing*] ... has none of the sense of "basic ingredient" or "irreducible essence" of the Latin *elementum* nor of that term's various Greek conceptual ancestors.... In contrast, the translation Five Phases, which now is rapidly gaining acceptance, clearly has connotations of change consistent with the Chinese concept of cyclical transformation.[②]

[①] Sivin, *Medicine, Philosophy and Religion in Ancient China*, pp. 2-3.
[②] John Major. "A Note on the Translation of Two Technical Terms in Chinese Science: *wu-hsing* and *hsiu*." *Early China* 2 (1976). pp. 1-2. I would, however, disassociate myself from Major's initial claim that "the Chinese concept *wu-hsing* is one of function rather than constituent matter." Major in a subsequent exchange with Richard Kunst then clarifies what he means by "function" as "categories of relations." See his "Reply to Richard Kunst's Comments on *hsiu* and *wu hsing*," *Early China* 3, pp. 69-70. My understanding is that *wuxing*, like *qi* or *dao* or *yinyang*, would resist any severe function-structure distinction, and that the relations are themselves are first order and constitutive.

Wang Aihe has provided a cogent summary of this sinological debate about the proper translation of this term, *wuxing*:

> The traditional translation is "Five Elements," a term most convenient for comparative studies of Chinese thought and thought in other civilizations. Yet "elements" does not fully represent the Chinese term *Wuxing*, which literally means five "goings," "conducts," or "doings," nor does it convey the basic nature of *Wuxing* as a cosmology of interaction and change. Many scholars have proposed alternatives, including five forces, agents, entities, activities, or stages of change. Of these, "Five Phases" has acquired a wide acceptance among specialists.[①]

These recent elucidations of *wuxing* as "five phases" have permitted a much more productive approach to the important and pervasive notion of *qi* 氣 that becomes explicit among cosmologists in the late fourth and early third centuries BCE.

The Greek elemental theories are one familiar version of the reality-appearance distinction that is markedly absent in Chinese cosmological explanations. That is, in the Chinese sensibility, there is no putative Being behind the beings, no unchanging formal aspect behind the changing world, no One behind the many, no atomic level where unchanging "real" atoms rearrange themselves to constitute an apparent world. The Chinese counterpart to Greek "elemental" theories that was initially confused with them is the phasal understanding of the animated, autogenerative process of *qi* transformation: the *yinyang* 陰陽 variations that occur in *qi* and the "five phases" (*wuxing* 五行). *Qi* is both *what* experience is and *how* it is, as it persists and yet is constantly changing in its formal

---

[①] Wang Aihe. *Cosmology and Political Culture in Early China*. Cambridge: Cambridge University Press, 2000, p. 3.

aspect. The five phases are quite literally a "functional" equivalent of the Greek elements in that, rather than referring to ultimate "parts," they reference both the functioning and the reforming of the various phases of the changing world itself as such transformation is captured in the metaphorical language of "shade and light" (*yinyang* 陰陽) and of metal, wood, water, fire, and earth (*jinmushuihuotu* 金木水火土). The bipolar opposition symbolized by *yinyang* generates a dynamic tension that drives the ongoing processes of change. These creative processes are parsed into the distinct though continuous, transitional five phases that provide an account of both continuity and flux, persistence and change, similarities and differences, associations and contrasts. Just as spring becomes summer, and summer, autumn, so wood "becomes" water, and water, fire. It is the application of the notion of "phases" to the manifold of processes that allows for these processes to be punctuated into distinctive, consummatory "events." Even though summer is a transition between spring and autumn, we can still treat it in a consummatory way as a distinctive period of time in any given year. And although persons are transitional between progenitor and progeny, they are also uniquely particular persons. Such distinct "events"—narratives nested within narratives—then serve conceptually as the functional and structural equivalent of the quantitatively discrete "things" that we find in a substance ontology.

When we ask the question: What ultimately is the perceived relationship between the seemingly disparate ethical understanding of *wuxing* and its cosmological application? we must take into consideration the interpretive context. In Wang Aihe's work on the relationship between this evolving cosmology and political change, she cautions us that such *wuxing* "theorizing" has to be understood within the holistic process cosmology. This cosmology begins from the primacy of practice and takes theorizing as an intrinsic feature of practical activity that tries to make practices more productive and intelligent within the context of the practices themselves. Such theorizing is an effort to influence the always evolving circumstances to their best advantage:

> *Wuxing* is not simply a set of concepts, a school of philosophy, a mode of thinking, or a commonly agreed-upon representation; instead, it is a cultural phenomenon that changes through history, a discourse for political argument and power struggle, and above all, an art of action in a world of conflict and change.[①]

This inseparability of the theoretical and the practical, the functional and the structural that is defining of this cosmology reflects a profoundly different way of thinking about what things are, and how they arise in the human experience.

Han dynasty speculations led to the creation of vast and complex tables of correspondences that organized the psychological, physiological, social, and "natural" ambiance of the human experience. When we look at these charts of correlations from the Han dynasty, the welter of associations seems at first random, and even bizarre. The correlated items include things (trees), actions (sounds), attributes (colors), and modalities (flavors), as well as time (seasons), space (directions), and material categories (five phases). Such classifications include body parts, psycho-physical and affective states, styles of government, weather, tastes, domestic animals, technological instruments, heavenly bodies, and much more, depending upon the main subject under scrutiny. A related consideration would be to take account of different grammatical expectations. The parts of speech inherent in our Indo-European languages encourage us to divide up the world in a culturally specific manner that has little relevance for Han dynasty China.

[①] Wang Aihe, *Cosmology and Political Culture in Early China*, p. 3.

The cosmological theories are employed in conjunction with these correspondences to organize and explain the transformations and interrelations within the system.

Given that these lists offend against our most fundamental categories, how would someone have to think about the world for these correlations to have explanatory force? Or put another way, how can we suspend our own worldview in order to entertain the Han dynasty commonsense on its own terms? These correlated categories are apt to appear as "pseudoscience" to persons who subscribe to a linear and teleological notion of causality. But we have to take account of a different, more organic and systemic understanding of causal relations. The underlying assumption of Confucian natural cosmology is that each phenomenon is embedded in a context, and that its explanation is a function of mapping out all of its associated environing conditions in order to track down their relative degrees of causal influence. The kind of correlative thinking represented by these Han dynasty charts is contextual, complex and inclusive. Given such assumptions, the notion of linear causality would appear to be simple and randomly exclusionary.

The items in these correlations are evocative only to the degree that one shares the cultural competence of the Han dynasty world they propose to interpret. When we can find a perspective internal to the everyday ways of living and thinking in Han China, the motivation behind these specific correlations and their resonances become increasingly apparent. The correlations are mutually ramifying, with each reflecting into, alluding to, and enriching the others.

象** **xiang. "Figuring, figuring out, configuring, figure, imaging, imagining, image." See also 理 ***li.*** "Patterning, coherence," 類 ***lei.*** "Categories, groupings," 倫 ***lun.*** "Order, relation, category, class."

The character *xiang* 象 appears on the oracle bones as 𧰼, and is clearly a pictograph of an elephant. The *Shuowen* defines *xiang* in the same terms: a large animal found in the southern reaches of China and Southeast Asia with trunk, tusks, and ears that has a three year gestation period (actually 22 months).[①] Although we have archaeological evidence that elephants once existed in northern China and that ivory carving as a contemporary Chinese art form was already highly developed as far back as the Shang dynasty, an analysis of this evidence suggests that the elephant, like the whale and the rhinoceros, were rare species imported from outside of China, which because of their novelty, were used primarily for display. Thus, a creature known but rarely seen came to be used to denote the presentational act of "conjuring" or "imaging."

The *Hanfeizi* provides an explanation for how this term has come to mean "imaging, conjuring, image:"

> 人希見生象也，而得死象之骨，案其圖以想其生也，故諸人之所以意想者皆謂之"象"也。
>
> People have rarely seen live elephants, but have found the skeleton of the dead animal. On the basis of this image, they have been able to conjure up its living form. It is for this reason that what people are able to conjure forth are all called "images."

The elephant as an unfamiliar image requires us actively and

---

① See J. Norman and T. Mei. "The Austroasiatics in Ancient South China: Some Lexical Evidence." *Monumenta Serica* 1976 (32), pp. 274-301.

with imagination to "imagine" it and "conjure" it up. Thus, *xiang* comes to mean "figuring out, configuring, imaging, imagining," and by extension, the outcome of the process: "a figure, an image, a presentation" that reveals both the process and the product of our conjuring. Just as we must resist objectifying the active process of "way-making" (*dao* 道) into "*the* way," we must resist reducing the process of *xiang* into the recovery of antecedent images. We have a dynamic role both in retrospectively analogizing and in prospectively configuring the world around us, a world that through our vision of its possibilities, reveals itself to us.

The images associated with the hexagrams of the *Book of Changes* are efficacious because they are particularistic, and have a communally experienceable character. That is, the image of "fire" might bring to mind particular experiences of the phenomenon of fire that are housed in an individual consulting the *Changes* through recourse to social memory and communal experiences (traditions, institutions, ritual practices, music, literature, and so on). In the classical Confucian cosmology, image is the presentation of a configured world at the concrete and historical levels. The constructed image assumes considerably more explanatory force than would a logical account. We need only to remember Plato's ultimate recourse to images, similes, and analogies when he had exhausted the power of rational explanation.

Willard Peterson in fact argues that the term *xiang*, conventionally translated as "image" or "model" as used in the *Changes*, ought to be rendered "figure" in the sense of "giving or bringing into shape."① This is what is meant by the *Changes* A8 when it reports:

聖人有以見天下之賾，而擬諸其形容，象其物宜，是故謂之象。

---

① Willard Peterson. "Making Connections: 'Commentary on the Attached Verbalizations' of the *Book of Changes*. Harvard Journal of Asiatic Studies 42 No. 1 (1982), pp. 80-81.

象 xiang.

The sages, having the capacity to survey the complexities of the world, found correlations among the vital shapes and the appearances of things, and thus conjured up suitable images for them. It is for this reason they are called "images."

There is a reported conversation in the *Changes* A12 between Confucius and his disciples that is an encouragement to read the *Analects* itself and its didactic function as a sustained image:

子曰："書不盡言，言不盡意。然則聖人之意，其不可見乎。"子曰："聖人立象以盡意，設卦以盡情偽，繫辭以盡其言，變而通之以盡利，鼓之舞之以盡神。"

The Master said, "The written word cannot do justice to speech, and speech cannot do justice to meaning."[①]
"If this is the case, then is the meaning of the sages beyond our grasp?"
The Master replied: "The sages constructed 'images' to give a full account of their meaning, set up the hexagrams to give a full account of what is natural and what is contrived, wrote their judgments on the images and hexagrams in order to say completely what they had to say, introduced the presumption of change and continuity as a way to take full advantage of any situation, and elaborated upon and embellished all this to do justice to its profundity."

The invention and ramification of images or metaphors is one of the fundamental ways through which a culture interprets its world. A third century statement of this insight is to be found in the Wang Bi 王弼 commentary on the *Changes*. In this discussion,

---

① The character *yi* 意 is translated variously as "concept," "thought/s," and "ideas." *Yi* is glossed in the *Shuowen* lexicon as "intended meaning, purpose" (*zhi* 志), reflecting its performative connotation. It is in this sense of "designing" that I understand it.

there is his attempt to sort out the relationship obtaining among image (*xiang* 象), word (*yan* 言), and meaning (*yi* 意) that provides an alternative to the notion of the literal and referential nature of language. Wang Bi begins by reflecting upon the role of word and image in constituting meaning:

夫象者，出意者也。言者，明象者也。盡意莫若象，盡象莫若言。言生於象，故可尋言以觀象。象生於意，故可尋象以觀意。意以象盡，象以言著。故言者所以明象，得象而忘言。象者所以存意，得意而忘象。猶蹄者所以在兔，得兔而忘蹄；筌者所以在魚，得魚而忘筌也。然則，言者，象之蹄也；象者，意之筌也。是故存言者，非得象者也；存象者，非得意者也。

An image expresses meaning; words clarify the image. To do full justice to meaning, nothing is as good as an image; to do full justice to an image, nothing is as good as words. Because words arise from images, we can explore the words as a window on the image. And because the image arises from meaning, we can explore the image as a window on meaning. Meaning is given full account with an image, and the image is articulated in words. Hence, words are whereby we clarify the image. In getting the image, we forget the words. The image is whereby we hold on to meaning. In getting the meaning, we forget the image. It is like the snare serving to capture the rabbit; in snaring the rabbit, we forget the snare. Or like the fishtrap serving to catch the fish; in catching the fish, we forget the trap. As such, words are the "snare" for the image. And the image is the "trap" for meaning. For this reason, holding onto the words is not getting the image; holding on to the image is not getting the meaning.[1]

---

[1] Wang Bi, "Mingxiang 明象" (Elucidating the Image), *Zhouyi Lüeli* 周易略例 (A Summary Introduction to the *Book of Changes*) in the *Baibucongshu Jicheng* 百部叢書集成, 1965, 10b-11b.

Wang Bi ends here by indicating both the heuristic function and the limitations of words and images. We cannot catch rabbits and fish without snares and traps, and cannot capture meaning without the effective deployment of words and images. Word and image are triggers as well as repositories of meaning, but if they are interpreted as mere repositories, they can hinder the holistic process of meaning-making. This is what the *Zhuangzi* 26 means when it insists on having a further word with the person who has forgotten words:

> 荃者所以在魚，得魚而忘荃；蹄者所以在兔，得兔而忘蹄；言者所以在意，得意而忘言。吾安得忘言之人而與之言哉？
>
> The reason for fishtraps is to catch fish, but having caught the fish, you forget the fishtrap. The reason for rabbit snares is to snare rabbits, but having caught the rabbit, you forget the snare. The reason for words is to capture meaning, but having grasped the meaning, you forget the words. Where can I find a person who has forgotten the words so that I can have a word with him?①

Imaging is analogical in the sense that it requires a movement between a generalized situation made intelligible in word and image, and the meaning-productive detail of one's own particular circumstances. Imaging as such has performative force. Meaning is not simply given; it is reflexively appropriated and then projected and concretized. As such, while it is retrospectively appropriated, it is also "made up" and "made one's own."

In the *Changes*, the meaning of a general situation is captured in an image, and the image is explained in words. The words constitute the most abstract level of discourse and, as such, have the least degree of meaning for one's own particular situation. Words,

---

① Chuang Tzu [*Zhuangzi*] 75/26/48-49.

however, have the power to evoke an image, which in stirring one's imagination, enables one to bring one's particular situation into meaningful focus. What was general becomes increasingly particular; what was abstract becomes increasingly concrete; what was vague becomes increasingly focused and meaningful. By virtue of its relative explicitness, the image displaces the words, and as the image is explored as a repository and stimulus of significance for one's own circumstances, the lines of the image begin to fade. The image gives way to meaning. In being deepened and made more determinate, more meaningful for oneself, the image loses its more general character and becomes increasingly indistinct. The image retreats as the particular situation is suffused with meaning.

Wang Bi's most important insight here is the fluidity and aspectual nature of the continuous and cyclical process of meaning-making that requires imaging and articulation, but that resists any foundational claims among its several aspects. There is an inexhaustibly isomorphic relationship obtaining among these levels of discourse that allows us to privilege each level in turn. Words and images in their stipulated forms are reasonably clear, but are equivocal in their application to particular situations. The meaning of a particular event, on the other hand, is clear as an immediate experience, and yet in its particular detail, is resistant to conceptual and explanatory clarity. Hence, in moving from words to meaning, the impoverished vagueness of generality which we often term "clarity," gives way to the rich vagueness of particularity.

Wang Bi's next step is to then turn the circle in the alternative direction. Now, instead of images and words expressing meaning, they inscribe it. Meaning gives rise to new images and words, which in turn give rise to new meaning:

象生於意而存象焉，則所存者乃非其象也。言生於象而存言焉，則所存者乃非其言也。然則，忘象者，乃得意者也；忘言者，乃得象者也。得意在忘象，得象在忘言。

Given that an image arises from the meaning, in holding on to the image, what you are holding on to is not really the image. Given that words arise from the image, in holding onto the words, what you are holding on to is not really the words. As such, to forget the image is to get the meaning; to forget the words is to get the image. Getting the meaning lies in forgetting the image; getting the image lies in forgetting the words.[1]

The intimacy of word, image, and meaning challenges any severe disjunction between reality and appearance, between reasoning and imagination, between determinacy and indeterminacy. There is a porous line between meaning as what is real, image as the presentation and inscription of what is real, and words as the constitutive articulation of what is real. Words as articulations of images do not identify and describe an independent reality, but both inscribe and participate in realizing it. That which is known, and the act of realizing it, come into being together. It is because the cycle is continuous that the epistemic vocabulary of the canonical texts broadly conceived is a mapping of the way forward, tracing and "unraveling" (*jie* 解) relations, shedding light upon them (*liao* 瞭), and thus getting through (*da* 達 and *tong* 通) without obstruction.

Although Wang Bi is describing the content and structure of the *Changes* here, his insights really have a much broader compass in understanding the classical corpus. We might clarify his more theoretical commentary by looking at the way in which meaning is generated by the "turning" of productive images. In the case of the *Analects*, for example, the central "image" around which the text is constructed is the life of Confucius treading a path until at age

---

[1] Wang Bi, "Mingxiang 明象" (Elucidating the Image).

seventy he 從心所欲，不踰矩 "could give heart-and-mind free rein without overstepping the boundaries."

It would be an oversight as well not to appreciate the middle chapters of the *Analects* as an album of snapshots that depict in detail an image of Confucius as one particular human being living an exemplary life. The meaning resident in an established image is revealed through the reflexive act of appropriating and then recreating the image itself. Contrary to naïve expectations, just as with a piece of music, what we finally come to see in appreciating a work of art is the creative process that has produced it and what it has come to mean for us. The image as this creative process is the repository of meaning that is the bottomless stimulus for discussion and the interlinear commentaries that follow from these conversations. As the *Analects* in the fullness of time became a canonical text, generation after generation of self-confessed "Confucians" continue to appeal to this image in shaping the meaning of their own lives and their persistent cultural identity.

Images both carry meaning and continue this fluid process of meaning-making. We might take the intelligible "words" of calligraphy as an example. In calligraphy, the meaning of the words retreat, and the expression of personal style becomes the performative configuring of an image ultimately revelatory of the artist as a particular person. The mood, times, joys and pain, and singular place in the world of the artist are all resident in the shaping of the characters. In this sense calligraphy is biographical. In much the same way, biography is again corporate and transmits not only the meaningful details of one's own narrative, but one's tradition as well. This notion of imagistic artistry as self-expression—"the outside of an inside"—is taken up by Stephen Owen in the contrast he insists upon between thinking of a poem as *poiesis*, a "made artifact," and *shi* 詩 (usually translated as "poem") as personal articulation:

If we translate *shih* [*shi*] as "poem," it is merely for the sake of convenience. *Shih* is not a "poem;" *shih* is not a "thing made" like in the same way one makes a bed or a painting or a shoe. A *shih* can be worked on, polished, and crafted; but that has nothing to do with what a *shih* fundamentally "is." ... *Shih* is not the "object" of its writer; it is the writer, the outside of an inside.①

The imaging and naming of a world is non-referential in the sense that the imaginative process itself is integral to the creation of the world. The processual nature of experience also means that any rational construal of experience as an image or a name is always provisional, and will be outrun by the process itself. We are always engaged in the project of organizing and bringing coherence to the world around us.

The cosmology made explicit in the *Changes* not only provides the interpretive context for the classical Confucian texts, but for the Daoist texts as well. The *Daodejing* 21 encourages us to discriminate, make sense of, and valorize the otherwise dark and amorphous content of our experience:

道之為物，唯恍唯惚。忽兮恍兮，其中有象；恍兮忽兮，其中有物。窈兮冥兮，其中有精……

As for the process of way-making,
It is ever so indefinite and vague.
Though vague and indefinite,
There are images within it.
Though indefinite and vague,

---

① Stephen Owen. *Readings in Chinese Literary Thought*. Cambridge: Council on East Asian Studies, Harvard University Press, 1992, p. 27. The only concern I would have with Owen's reflection here on *shi* is his seeming inclination to limit his insight to poetry as opposed to other art forms, and even to the art of life more broadly construed.

There are events within it.
Though nebulous and dark,
There are seminal concentrations of *qi* within it.

Indeed, the *Daodejing* 35 recounts how through this process of imaging a world into being, our cultural heroes with their vision have not only disciplined and stabilized the human experience, but have inspired it, drawing generations to their construal of what it means to be human:

執大象，天下往。往而不害，安平大。
Seize the great image
And the world will flock to you.
Flocking to you they come to no harm,
And peace and security prevails.

At the same time, because *Daodejing* 41 大象無形 alerts us to the fact that "the greatest image has no ultimate shape," chapter 14 cautions us that any ordering of the world in the fullness of time is vulnerable to transformation, and will gradually slip away on us:

故混而為一。其上不皦，其下不昧。繩繩不可名，復歸於無物。是謂無狀之狀，無物之象。
As for this "one"—
Its surface is not dazzling
Nor is its underside dark.
Ever so tangled, it defies discrimination
And reverts again to indeterminacy.
This is what is called the form of the formless
And the image of indeterminacy.

*孝　xiao. "Family reverence, filial piety."

Xiao 孝 is the prime moral imperative in this continuing Confucian tradition. It has conventionally been rendered "filial piety" in English, but Henry Rosemont and I in our translation of the *Chinese Classic of Family Reverence* (*Xiaojing* 孝經) have chosen to translate it as "family reverence." What recommends "family reverence" as a translation is that, in degree, it disassociates *xiao* from the duty to God implied by "piety" and from the notion of unilateral obedience that would follow from it. "Family reverence" is collateral, with the elder generation receiving appropriate deference from their younger members within their family lineages, and the younger generation deriving pleasure from deferring to those who have given both meaning and substance to their lives. The term "family reverence" at the same time retains the sacred connotations that are certainly at play in the ritualized culture of ancestral sacrifices.

The collaterality of "familial reverence" (*xiao* 孝) is captured in the composition of the character itself, constituted as it is by the combination of the graph for "elders" (*lao* 老) and that for "son, daughter, child, youth" (*zi* 子). *Xiao* has immediate reference to our lived experience within the narrative of succeeding generations as we remember our own parents and grandparents, and as we attend to our own children and grandchildren. *Xiao* quite literally describes and makes normative the lived roles and relationships that constitute the communities of elders and youth across successive generations, both the thick relations that obtain between the present generation and those generations that have gone before, and the responsibility this generation has for those yet to come. It references the continuing process of physical and cultural embodiment from one generation to the next, and thus the inseparability of grandparents and grandchildren, of fathers and daughters, of progenitors and progeny, and how such familial roles can only be learned and lived together. As with terms such as *ren* 仁 that resist any formulaic understanding, *xiao* requires us to access and to build upon our own existential sense of what it means to optimize our specific and resolutely hierarchical roles within family and community.

When we examine the earliest form of the character for "elders" (*lao* 老) as it appears on the oracle bones, we find that it depicts an old person with long, disheveled hair, leaning on a walking stick 耂, bringing immediately to mind the famous photograph of Albert Einstein with his dandelion hair.① In the small seal script this same graph for "elders" becomes stylized as 耂, anticipating its present form as 老. In comparing this character for "elders" (*lao* 老) with the earliest instance of the character for "family reverence" (*xiao* 孝) found later on the bronzes 孝, we discover that the image of a "young person" (*zi* 子) has quite literally taken the place of the walking stick as the support upon which the elders can lean, thereby constituting this character as "elders" supported by their "young."② While *xiao* certainly references the aid and comfort that succeeding older generations can enjoy from the progeny that succeeds them, the complement flows in the other direction as well. That is, *xiao* is also the vital process whereby the members of the younger generation are transformed into and become an always novel yet persistent embodied variant of those elders to whom they have deferred. The older generation is a reservoir of culture from whom the succeeding generation can draw sustenance and meaning, and in so doing, this younger generation provides their progenitors with a conduit that allows them to live on both in the bodies and in the lived, cultural experience of a continuing lineage.

---

① Kwan, "Database," 甲骨文合集 CHANT 0039A.
② Kwan, "Database," 西周晚期 CHANT 3937.

The centrality of *xiao* in the Confucian project of aspiring to consummatory conduct in one's roles and relations (*ren* 仁) becomes immediately apparent on examining one familiar passage taken from the *Analects* 1.2:

君子務本，本立而道生。孝弟［悌］也者，其為仁之本與！
Exemplary persons (*junzi* 君子) concentrate their efforts on the root, for the root having been properly set, the proper path in life (*dao* 道) emerges therefrom. As for family reverence (*xiao* 孝) and fraternal deference (*ti* 悌), these are, I suspect, the root of becoming consummate in one's roles and relations (*ren* 仁).

What then does it mean to take the practical activities of revering family members (*xiao* 孝) and of deferring appropriately to elders (*ti* 悌) to be the *root* (*ben* 本) of becoming consummate in one's roles and relations (*ren* 仁)? Much commentarial ink has been spilled on trying to argue against the claim found in this passage that "family reverence" (*xiao* 孝) is the *root* of "consummate conduct" (*ren* 仁). Zhu Xi himself in his commentary on the *Analects* worries over this problem, and endorses the interpretation of his philosophical predecessors, the Cheng brothers 二程 , who go to great lengths to challenge this reading. In their commentary, the Cheng brothers argue for a distinction between "practicing *ren*" (*xingren* 行仁) and "becoming *ren*" (*weiren* 為仁), insisting that since *ren* is integral to "human nature" itself, it must be prior to *xiao*, and that *xiao* only provides us with a forum to "practice" *ren* rather than serving as a resource to actually "become" *ren*.① *Xiao* for the Cheng brothers must be the *fruit* of *ren* rather than its *root*. But the notion of *ren* being "rooted" in "family" is clear in the alternative graphic form of this character found on the bamboo strips recovered in a recent

---

① See the discussion in Ames, *Confucian Role Ethics*, pp. 88-90.

archaeological find, where the graph for *ren* is composed of a woman's pregnant body ![graph] with the graph "heartmind" (*xin* 心) beneath it.[1] Clearly, any conception of family must begin from woman with child, and any notion of consummatory moral conduct must have its entry point in family relations.

"Family reverence" (*xiao*) certainly entails deference to elders. Confucius repeatedly insists on the importance of compliance when the young are serving their elders in family and community, and on a sense of duty in carrying out official responsibilities. He makes clear the continuing weight of deferential conduct throughout one's life when in *Analects* 2.7 he says:

> 今之孝者，是謂能養。至於犬馬，皆能有養；不敬，何以別乎？
> Those today who are filial are considered so because they are able to provide for their parents. But even dogs and horses are given that much care. If you do not respect your parents, what is the difference?

While Confucius is surely claiming that such patterns of interpersonal behavior are necessary for family flourishing and societal harmony, he is equally guiding his protégés toward living a life of deference as a path of spiritual cultivation in which appropriate conduct expressed through a reverential attitude toward family elders and by extension, to political leaders, is an opportunity for personal elevation and refinement.

It is important to note that in promoting the family as the pervasive model of order, the Confucian worldview does not accept that hierarchical social institutions are necessarily pernicious, or that simple egalitarianism should have an uncritical value. But two points of clarification on the idea of deference are needed here.

---

[1] Kwan, "Database," 西周中期 CHANT 246.

First, as I have remarked above, we must resist any simplistic equation between family reverence (*xiao*) and blind obedience. Family reverence focused on the bottom-up deference children owe their elders must be distinguished clearly from *paterfamilias* that we associate with Roman law as the juridical *patria potestas* or power and privilege of the father. Indeed, there are times when being truly filial within the family, like being a loyal minister at court, requires courageous remonstrance (*jian* 諫) rather than automatic compliance. And indeed, with this doctrine of *xiao*, initiating such remonstrance is not perceived as a possibility or an option one might choose to exercise, but as a stern if not sacred obligation. On a personal level, there is also a space for "self-remonstrating." Built into the relational "two-ness" of consummate person/conduct (*ren* 仁) as it is rooted in *xiao*, the cultivation of a critical self-awareness and sense of shame provides a perspective from which to critique one's own roles as they are lived within family and community.

In the *Chinese Classic of Family Reverence* 15, Master Zeng who is to become the paragon of family reverence in the Confucian tradition, after having benefitted from a full fourteen chapters of Confucius's instruction on *xiao*, asks the Master explicitly if strict obedience is the substance of family reverence:

曾子曰:"若夫慈愛、恭敬、安親、揚名, 則聞命矣。敢問子從父之令, 可謂孝乎?"

Master Zeng said, "Parental love (*ai* 愛), reverence and respect (*jing* 敬), seeing to the well-being of one's parents, and raising one's name (*ming* 名) high for posterity—on these topics I have received your instructions. I would presume to ask whether children can be deemed filial (*xiao* 孝) by obeying every command of their father."[1]

Confucius responds to Master Zeng's query with a disappointed impatience, making the argument that such an uncritical attitude of automatic compliance with the dictates of one's elders, far from being the substance of family reverence, can on the contrary be a source of gross immorality in conduct:

子曰："是何言與！是何言與！……當不義，則子不可以不爭於父，臣不可以不爭於君。故當不義則爭之。從父之令，又焉得為孝乎！"
"What on earth are you saying? What on earth are you saying?" said the Master, ".... If confronted by reprehensible behavior on his father's part, a son has no choice but to remonstrate with his father, and if confronted by reprehensible behavior on his ruler's part, a minister has no choice but to remonstrate with his ruler. Hence, remonstrance is the only response to immorality. How could simply obeying the commands of one's father be deemed filial?"

Indeed, the *Xunzi* takes on this same issue of automatic compliance, and devotes an entire chapter to multiple stories providing examples of how blind obedience to the older generation, far from reflecting family reverence, offends against this very same value by producing consistently dire consequences.[2]

And the second point to be made here in clarifying the meaning

---

[1] Master Zeng is best remembered as a proponent of "family reverence" (*xiao*)—the devotion and service that the younger generation directs to their elders and ancestors, and the pleasure that they derive in doing so. A natural extension of this affection for one's family is friendship, and Master Zeng is portrayed in the *Analects* as being able to distinguish between the sincerity of his fellow student, Yan Hui, much celebrated by Confucius himself, and the rashness of another student, Zizhang.

[2] See *Xunzi* chapter 29.

of family reverence is that one's immediate family is only the beginning of such deference. *Xiao* must become a pattern of conduct that, with unrelenting attention, is extended out from family to include all members of the community, and polity, and ultimately, even to nature itself. Within the human experience, *xiao* is nothing less than the high value that informs and is the motive force for the intergenerational transmission of the living cultural tradition itself.

In the first chapter of the *Chinese Classic of Family Reverence*, it declares that

> 夫孝始於事親，中於事君，終於立身。
> ... family reverence begins in service to your parents, continues in service to your lord, and culminates in distinguishing yourself in the world.

Again, in chapter 7 entitled the "Three Powers," *xiao* has cosmic reference, correlating the relationships that obtain among the heavens, the earth, and the human world within this *xiao* moral imperative. It is because these three powers are mutually implicated in each other that such cosmic relations, providing as they do a context for the human experience, have themselves a moral aspect that can serve as an isomorphic model for the proper accord aspired to in our human institutions of family and state:

> 曾子曰："甚哉！孝之大也。"子曰："夫孝，天之經也，地之義也，民之行也。天地之經而民是則之，則天之明，因地之利，以順天下。是以其教不肅而成，其政不嚴而治。"
> "Incredible—the profundity of family reverence!" declared Master Zeng. "Indeed," said the Master. "Family reverence is the constancy of the heavenly cycles, the appropriate responsiveness (*yi* 義) of the earth, and the proper conduct of the people. It is the constant workings of the heavens and the earth that the people model

themselves upon. Taking the illumination (*ming* 明) of the heavens as their model and making the most of the earth's resources, they bring the empire into accord (*shun* 順). This is the reason that education can be effective without being severe, and political administration can maintain proper order without being harsh."

In the *Chinese Classic of Family Reverence*, Confucius begins by elevating *xiao* to be Confucian philosophy's highest moral imperative, declaring that this "way of family reverence" is the very substance of morality and education:

子曰：" 夫孝，德之本也，教之所由生也。"
"It is family reverence (*xiao* 孝) that is the root of moral virtuosity, and whence education (*jiao* 教) itself is born." said Confucius.

This text's emphasis upon the transformative power of education exploits the cognate relationship between the characters for "education" (*jiao* 教) and "family reverence" (*xiao* 孝). As we have seen, while the graph for "family reverence" (*xiao* 孝) itself is constituted by "elder (*lao* 老)" and "younger (*zi* 子)," the graph for "education" (*jiao* 教) adds to it the "branch" radical (*zhi* 支), suggesting that the younger generation grows from the root and trunk of the generations that have come before. Importantly the character *jiao* underscores the centrality of familial reverence in the actual content and goals of proper education, just as the cognate relationship it has with "emulating" (*xiao* 效), emphasizes the modeling role that the elder generation has for its progeny. The *Shuowen* lexicon captures these associations in defining *jiao* as 上所施下所效也 "that which those above disseminate and those below emulate."

The opening chapter of the *Chinese Classic of Family Reverence* continues in providing us with the familiar pattern of a radial progression from a determinate center to an unbounded extreme that we find consistently in the Confucian literature, expanding outward from protecting one's own immediate physicality to distinguishing oneself in the world:

> 身體髮膚，受之父母，不敢毀傷，孝之始也。立身行道，揚名於後世，以顯父母，孝之終也。夫孝，始於事親，中於事君，終於立身。《大雅》云："無念爾祖，聿脩厥德。"
>
> Your physical person with its hair and skin are received from your parents. Vigilance in not allowing anything to do injury to your person is where family reverence begins. Distinguishing yourself and walking the proper way (*dao* 道) in the world; raising your name high for posterity and thereby bringing esteem to your father and mother—it is in these things that family reverence finds its consummation. Such family reverence then begins in service to your parents, continues in service to your lord, and culminates in distinguishing yourself in the world. In the "Greater Odes" section of the *Book of Songs* it says: "How can you fail to remember your ancestor, King Wen? You must cultivate yourself and extend his virtuosity."[①]

You begin from respect shown to your own person as what is closest at hand, extend such concern to the care for your family and kin, and then culminate in dedicating your service to your ruler and to posterity. In this passage, King Wen—that is, King "Culture" (*wen* 文)—is once again singled out as the source from which the current generation draws its inspiration and to whom, with the cultural dividends it has accrued, makes appropriate return.

The first tenet of familial reverence is the accountability persons have throughout their lifetime to protect the body that has been

---

① *Book of Songs* 235.

entrusted to them by their parents and ancestors, and the solemn responsibility they have to return this body to their progenitors intact. The charge in this passage to keep the body intact certainly refers to a person's own carnal physicality, but it also lends itself to an important broader, cultural reading. That is, each succeeding generation has the responsibility of keeping the corpus of culture that it comes to embody, whole and alive. The concluding exhortation from the *Book of Songs* states:

> How can you fail to remember your ancestor, King Wen? You must cultivate yourself and extend his virtuosity.

Reading between the lines, we might offer the following translation as what is actually being advocated in this citation:

> How can you fail to embody the culture of your ancestors? You must cultivate yourself and extend the reach and influence of this virtuosity.

Confucian ethics in substance is perpetuated through family lineages that have complex political, economic, and religious functions. There are two cognate characters that are integral to the dynamics of "family reverence" (*xiao* 孝) in the intergenerational transmission of the continuities of the family lineage: *ti* 體 ("embodying," "body," "forming and shaping," "category," "class") and *li* 禮 ("achieving propriety in one's roles and relations," "ritual"). Without the formal and determinate dimension provided by embodied living (*ti* 體), and by the social grammar afforded by meaningful roles and relations (*li* 禮), there is very real question as to whether the significant refinement that is aspired to through such embodied life forms would even be possible. Put simply, determinate forms in their many different variations—body, ritual, language, the institutions of family and ancestral reverence, and so on—are a necessary condition for cultural refinement. The "lived body" (*ti* 體) and its "embodied living" (*li* 禮) is the narrative site of the conveyance and the continuing enhancement of the culture through which a living civilization is perpetuated: the persistence of its language, its mores and values, its religious rituals, its aesthetics of cooking, song, and dance, and so on.

In Confucian ethics, the assumption is that social and political order broadly construed is rooted in and emerges from personal cultivation as it is first and foremost actuated within the institution of the family, and then extended to one's family lineage and beyond. Integral to this process is the transmission of a continuing cultural legacy and its institutions. *Focusing the Familiar* 19 defines *xiao* explicitly in such terms:

夫孝者：善繼人之志，善述人之事者也。

Family reverence (*xiao* 孝) means being good at continuing the purposes of one's predecessors and at maintaining their ways.

The renowned sociologist Fei Xiaotong 費孝通 reflects upon the contemporary configuration of the Chinese kinship-based sociopolitical model of governance the roots of which can be attested to as early as the bronze inscriptions and canons of the early Zhou dynasty.[①] Fei introduces what he takes to be several distinctions that would provide a necessary contrast between Western and Chinese models of persons and their social organization. Fei identifies Western individualism with "the organizational mode of

---

[①] Yiqun Zhou, *Festival, Feasts, and Gender Relations in Ancient China and Greece*, p. 147 also argues that "the home, where one engaged in daily practices of kinship-centered moral precepts and religious ceremonies, was the site for the most fundamental education in Zhou society."

association" (*tuanti geju* 團體格局) as groups of discrete individuals with their rule-governed social organizations functioning within clearly defined boundaries. The image Fei uses for this organizational mode is of individual straws collected and bound together to form a haystack—a bundle of discrete, individual entities. He contrasts this mode of organization with the Chinese kinship model that he calls "the differential mode of association" (*chaxu geju* 差序格局).① Fei's analogy for the differential mode is "the concentric circles formed when a stone is thrown into a lake," a relational image that is reinforced by the fact that the character for "ripples" or "rippling" (*lun* 淪) is cognate and homophonous with the graph for "the relational order in human community" (*lun* 倫). One important feature in Fei's distinction between these two modes of association is the existence of a common organizing principle binding persons together in the organizational mode of association that makes them equal (some variation on the concept of "law" or as "God" in the broadest sense). This notion of being equal before the law or all children of God stands in contrast with the interrelated, hierarchical, and graduated differences in personal roles and relations—the *li* 禮—that emerge and are at play in the differential mode. This equality versus hierarchy distinction is very much in evidence in the alternative ways of thinking about the construction of personal identity: a contrast between an individual autonomy that would assert one's perceived rights and entitlements, on the one hand, and the Chinese kinship model of managing one's personal connections—one's *guanxi* 關係—on the other.

Fei Xiaotong insists that Confucian ethics must be conceived of as animating always unique "centers fanning out into a web-

---

① Fei Xiaotong. *From the Soil: The Foundations of Chinese Society*. A translation of *Xiangtu Zhongguo* 鄉土中國 by Gary G. Hamilton and Wang Zheng, Berkeley: University of California Press, 1992, p. 63.

like network,"① centers that are "composed of webs woven out of countless personal relationships."② He would further claim that this predominant pattern of Chinese kinship relations with its hierarchically-defined roles and relations produces its own distinctive kind of morality in which "no ethical concepts . . . transcend specific types of human relationships."③ That is, kinship as the root of human relations is defined by the moral imperatives of "family reverence" (*xiao* 孝) and "fraternal deference" (*ti* 悌). And friendship as the way of extending this pattern of kinship relations to include non-relatives is pursued through an ethic of "putting oneself in the place of others" (*shu* 恕), "commitment and resolve" (*cheng* 誠), "doing one's utmost" (*zhong* 忠), and "making good on one's word" (*xin* 信).④ All such ethical values are aspired to as the way of reconciling the tensions among and promoting the accommodations made within the specific personal relationships of family members and community.

There is a primacy given to vital relationality that is exemplified by the centrality given to family reverence (*xiao* 孝) as the prime moral imperative. If *religare* as the Latin root of "religious" does mean "binding tightly" (as reflected in the cognates "ligament," "obligation," "league," and "ally")—then we can see that "family reverence" (*xiao* 孝) so described has a profoundly religious import

---

① Fei Xiaotong, *From the Soil*, p. 68.
② Fei Xiaotong, *From the Soil*, p. 78.
③ Fei Xiaotong, *From the Soil*, p. 74.
④ See for example *Analects* 1.4 and 1.8. There is an ambiguity in the expression "associates and friends" (*pengyou* 朋友) as it is used in the documents of the Western Zhou and Spring and Autumn period where these texts do not distinguish non-related friends from agnatic male relatives—that is, paternal relatives such as brothers, uncles, nephews, cousins, and so on. Some scholars have argued that *pengyou* becomes a term commonly used to denote non-kin friends specifically only in the Warring States period. See Yiqun Zhou, *Festival, Feasts, and Gender Relations in Ancient China and Greece*, pp. 110-111 and 137-139.

as well, referencing as it does those familial, communal, and ancestral bonds that together constitute a resilient and enduring social fabric.① And it is this profoundly religious sense of "binding tightly"—that is, the strengthening of family and communal bonds—that we would appeal to in interpreting the Master's autobiographical response to Zilu's question in *Analects* 5.26 about what he would most like to do:

> 子曰："老者安之，朋友信之，少者懷之。"
> "I would like to bring peace and contentment to the aged, share relationships of trust and confidence with friends, and to love and protect the young."

It is because the entry point for developing moral competence in the Confucian vision of the moral life is family relations in the broadest sense that *xiao* 孝 as "family reverence" has its singularly important place in the early Confucian canons. To better understand the notion of *xiao* itself, we need to clarify the nature and the significance of the institution of family within this Confucian context. Again, Fei Xiaotong, draws a contrast between the nuclear "family" that for anthropologists takes on its major significance as the site of reproduction, and the dominant pattern of family lineages in premodern Chinese families and clans. Such Chinese families have historically been lineages of persons with the same surname (*shizu* 氏族 or *jiazu* 家族) and by extension have been extended communities made up of several lineages who have different surnames. While such extended lineages certainly have the function of reproduction, Fei insists that within the Chinese experience they have the singularly important institutional role

---

① Sarah F. Hoyt, "The Etymology of Religion," *Journal of the American Oriental Society* Vol. 32, No. 2 (1912), pp. 126-129 provides some interesting textual evidence for this very old and sometimes disputed etymology.

as "a medium through which all activities are organized."① That is, in addition to the perpetuation of the family, such lineages have complex political, economic, and religious functions that are expressed along the vertical and hierarchical axis of the father-son and mother–daughter-in-law relationships. Lineage relations are again reinforced socially and religiously through the institutions of ancestor reverence, which is a continuing practice that archaeology tells us dates back at least to the Neolithic Age.②

In the early Shang, the ancestors—at least those of the king and the noble families—were believed to be directly responsible for the good or ill fortune in the lives of their descendants, necessitating a propitiating of these progenitors through sacrifice. That this belief was persistent helps to explain Confucius's comment in *Analects* 2.24: 非其鬼而祭之，諂也 "sacrificing to ancestral spirits other than one's own is being unctuous." One of Confucius's important insights was to appreciate the fact that, whatever the status of the supernatural raison d'être for performance of these ritual sacrifices, such rituals as a sacred celebration of past generations living on in the present could still continue to provide a good deal of meaning for human lives and serve as a binding force in the family and

---

① Fei Xiaotong, *From the Soil*, p. 84.
② See David N. Keightley. "Shamanism, Death, and the Ancestors: Religious Mediation in Neolithic and Shang China, ca. 5000–1000 B.C." *Asiatische Studien* 52 (1998), 763–828. Yiqun Zhou's analysis of the dominance of kinship and the inalienable bond between ancestors and their progeny in early Zhou society points out that "nearly one-sixth of the *Odes* pertain to ancestral sacrifices, including the ceremony proper and the subsequent feast. These pieces demonstrate the central importance of the ancestral banquet for our understanding of the Zhou discourse of sociability." And Zhou states further that "ancestor worship entails not only memorial rituals that are regular, systematic, and continuous, but also, more important, incorporation of the dead into a descent group as permanent members endowed with an essential role in forging group solidarity." See Zhou, *Festival, Feasts, and Gender Relations in Ancient China and Greece*, pp. 104, 112.

community overall.

Of course, given the fact that particularly over the past century the structure of Chinese family lineages has changed dramatically, such generalizations must be qualified by time and place, as well as by regional and temporal variations. Having acknowledged this, Yiqun Zhou marshals scholarly consensus behind her claim that premodern Chinese society was "for several thousand years largely a polity organized by kinship principles."[①] In weighing the extent to which social and political order was derived from and dependent upon family relations, Zhou insists that in contrast with the Greeks, "the Chinese state was never conceived as a political community that equaled the sum of its citizens." Rather, "the relationship between the rulers and the ruled was considered analogous to the relationship between parents and children," emphasizing the perceived isomorphism between family and state (*jiaguotonggou* 家國同構).[②] This contrast between a community of individuals and an extended family immediately recalls Fei Xiaotong's suggestive distinction between "the organizational mode of association" (*tuanti geju* 團體格局) and "the differential mode of association" (*chaxu geju* 差序格局).

At a genealogical level, our bodies and the process of human procreativity lead to the birthing of distinctive and unique persons from those who have come before. And the "embodied knowing" and "living on" that is taking place in this process is not meant merely rhetorically. Even more obvious and significant than the transmission of physical likenesses are the continuities of the cultural

---

[①] Zhou, *Festival, Feasts, and Gender Relations in Ancient China and Greece*, p. 19.

[②] Zhou, *Festival, Feasts, and Gender Relations in Ancient China and Greece*, pp. 17–18, note 51.

tradition itself: its language, institutions, and values.[1] Within this ongoing, overlapping process of intergenerational embodiment, the earlier progenitors literally persist in this continuing process as they are transformed into their progeny. That is, while persons emerge to become specifically who they are as unique individuals, the parents, grandparents, and ancestors of such persons continue to live on in them, most obviously in their physicality but also in terms of how they think, feel, and live their lives. And the eventful process continues as both they and their progeny live on in their later descendants. We have proposed a focus-field language as a way of thinking about the relationship between particulars and the totality. This foregrounding and backgrounding seems immediately relevant to a genealogical holography in which the entire field of the physical and cultural experience is implicated in the moment-by-moment narrative of each person.

In the Confucian tradition, the body is understood as an inheritance from our families and as a vital current in a genealogical stream that reaches back to our remotest ancestors. The body brings with it a sense of continuity, contribution, belonging, and importantly a sense of felt worth as precisely those feelings that most immediately inspire our religious sensibilities. The *Record of Rites* gives an account of this process:

夫子曰:"天之所生,地之所養,無人為大。"父母全而生之,子全而歸之,可謂孝矣。不虧其體,不辱其身,可謂全矣。

The Master said, "Among those things born of the heavens and

---

[1] The sense of immortality implied by the expression "living on" is difficult to see if the body is taken as "belonging" only to an individual. The opening chapter of *The Chinese Classic of Family Reverence* makes it clear that for Confucius, the body is an inheritance and on loan from one's family lineage and that the first obligation we have to this lineage is to maintain its integrity by avoiding any kind of desecration or disgrace.

nurtured by the earth, nothing is grander than the human being." For the parents to give birth to one's whole person, and for one to return this person to them intact is what can be called family reverence (*xiao*). And avoiding the desecration of your body and disgrace to your person is what can be called keeping your person whole. ①

To show respect for our own bodies—both the physical body and its function as the residence of the cultural corpus that our family lineage has bequeathed to us—is to show reverence for our ancestors embodied therein and for the relationship we have with them. Alternatively, to disrespect our bodies by treating them lightly is doubly shameless: We first fail to acknowledge our debt to our family lineage, and further, we bring shame instead of honor upon those who have come before. What is significant in this reflection on our embodied persons is that physically, socially, and religiously, our bodies are a specific matrix of nested relations and functions that are a collaboration between our own persons and the extended web of our many familial, social, cultural, and natural relations. Nobody and no "body"—not the vital, the carnal, nor the discursive body—does anything by itself.

There is an important passage in the *Analects* 8.3 in which Master Zeng, the paragon of family reverence in the classical corpus, is surrounded by his students on his deathbed, and expresses to them a deep sense of relief in having come to the end of his life with his body still intact:

曾子有疾，召門弟子曰："啟予足！啟予手！《詩》云：'戰戰兢兢，如臨深淵，如履薄冰。'而今而後，吾知免夫！小子！"

Master Zeng was ill, and summoned his students to him, saying,

---

① *A Concordance to the* Liji 25.36/128/6.

"Look at my feet! Look at my hands!
The *Book of Songs* says:
Fearful! Trembling!
As if peering over a deep abyss,
As if walking across thin ice.①
It is only from this moment hence that I can at last know relief, my young friends."

This passage is usually interpreted as Master Zeng expressing profound relief that he has been able to live to a point where he can now anticipate returning his carnal body to his ancestors without issue. But the first chapter of the *Chinese Classic of Family Reverence* (*Xiaojing* 孝經) provides us with important commentary on this exchange between the dying Master Zeng and his students that might prompt us to read something more into this concern for the body. The *Classic of Family Reverence* certainly does declare that "your physical person—literally, 'your vital and discursive body' (*shenti* 身體)—with its hair and skin are received from your parents." But when the text goes on to assert that "vigilance in not allowing anything to do injury to your person is where family reverence begins," it perhaps lends itself to an understanding of "body" in a broader cultural sense. I would argue that Confucius in elaborating upon the importance of "family reverence" (*xiao* 孝) here is not simply referencing respect for the carnal body, but is also alluding to the function that the body has as the site of intergenerational cultural transmission—that is, the "vital body" and the "discursive body" too. Confucius defines the substance of education as the serious responsibility of each generation to transmit the culture in all its fullness and without diminution to the generations that follow. In so doing, he reinforces his claim in this same chapter that

---

① *Book of Songs* 195.

xiao is indeed "the root of human virtuosity, and whence education (*jiao* 教) itself is born." Thus, keeping the cultural "body" intact is the process of embodying the tradition fully, drawing upon it creatively as a resource for distinguishing oneself in the world, and adding dividends to this compounding resource by establishing a name for oneself and one's family that will be remembered by posterity. In this way, the evolving corpus of the cultural tradition— the civilization itself—is continued in each person, embodied in each succeeding generation, and is thus perpetuated for those that follow.

Ralph Waldo Emerson in his essay, "American Civilization," provides us with a rather simple physical image of a carpenter hewing wood, to make a rather profound statement about this intergenerational march of a continuing civilization:

> Civilization depends on morality. Everything good in man leans on what is higher. This rule holds in small as in great. Thus, all our strength and success in the work of our hands depend on our borrowing the aid of the elements.

Emerson remarks on the ineffectiveness of individuals striking out and "going it alone" in this world:

> You have seen a carpenter on a ladder with a broad-axe chopping upward chips and slivers from a beam. How awkward! At what disadvantage he works!

For Emerson, such aberrant individuality stands in marked contrast with the indomitable felicity of squaring civilization behind our shoulders and living lives that are propelled by the moral and cultural *gravitas* provided by the impulse of a shared and continuing cultural tradition:

But see him on the ground, dressing his timber under him. Now, not his feeble muscles, but the force of gravity brings down the axe; that is to say, the planet itself splits his stick. ①

Emerson's image of lives empowered by the weight and momentum of a common civilization recalls the key Confucian exhortation that "it is persons who are able to broaden the way" (*ren neng hong dao* 人能弘道)②—a shared way of life that each generation has the obligation to broaden and extend as it builds its own connector.

In this Confucian tradition, the intergenerational transmission of civilization is the responsibility of two different but related conceptions of "family" (*jia* 家). There is the continuing civilization of the *daotong* 道統 or "orthodox way" embodied in the elite social stratum of "the literati family lineage" or *rujia* 儒家. And then more broadly, but certainly informed by the orthodox way of the literati lineage, there is the *xiaodao* 孝道 or "way of family reverence" that guides the lives of everyone within their extended family lineages or *jiazu* 家族.

There is a textual example that underscores the singular importance of continuing the embodied culture from one generation to the next in *Mencius* 4A26:

孟子曰："不孝有三，無後為大。舜不告而娶，為無後也，君子以為猶告也。"

Mencius said, "There are three ways of failing to observe family reverence, and to be without progeny is the most serious among them. It is because Shun's taking a wife without first asking his parent's permission was done to guarantee his issue that exemplary persons interpret his case as if he had in fact gotten their approval."

---

① "American Civilization" in *Atlantic Monthly* 9 (1862), 502–11.
② *Analects* 15.29.

For a family to be without progeny is not only a failure to continue the blood lineage but also a failure to produce the human conduits necessary for the transmission of the living cultural tradition. It is an offense not only against a person's parents for whom the continuity of sacrificial offerings will be broken but also against the collective ancestors who were the distant founders and transmitters of the civilization itself. Given that Confucian morality is nothing other than continuing growth in relationships, to lack the progeny needed to attend to one's ancestors in this broadest sense is thus considered an acute moral lapse.

Again, there is a historical example that might provide us with further insight into this extended cultural meaning of "body" and "embodying." We can immediately relate the exhortation to be vigilant "in not allowing anything to do injury to your person" to the poignant story of the Grand Historian of the Han dynasty, Sima Qian 司馬遷 (145c-86BCE). When Sima Qian was in his mid-thirties, he was called back from a military expedition to the deathbed of his father, Sima Tan 司馬談, who had in his time undertaken the ambitious project of compiling a comprehensive history of the preceding two thousand years. Sima Qian in that solemn moment rose to the occasion, and promised his father he would carry on and complete this important work on behalf of their family name. Sima Qian began at once and in earnest in his efforts to fulfill his promise to complete the compilation of a grand history that would raise the name of "Sima" for all posterity.

Some ten years later an incident occurred at court that nearly brought both Sima Qian and his history project to an untimely end. General Li Ling, under the orders of Emperor Wu, had been dispatched to quell the Xiongnu tribes who were fierce and brutal adversaries forever making incursions into the western regions of Han China. The Emperor was enraged to learn that the Han army had been routed and General Li captured by the enemy, putting the blame squarely on Li's military incompetence. In his role as a court counselor, Sima Qian was the only one who dared to speak up in defense of General Li. And the livid Emperor Wu, incensed by this perhaps courageous but impolitic intervention, sentenced Sima Qian at first to death and then commuted his punishment to castration. Accepting this physical and social humiliation only because of his promise to his father, Sima Qian returned from prison several years later to live on as a disgraced and friendless outcast at the court. Working tirelessly over the next decade, he was able to bring to completion the *Records of the Grand Historian* (*Shiji* 史記), a monumental work in 130 chapters of over half a million characters. This opus, a singular model of scholarship and literary elegance, has been passed on from generation to generation and has had an enormous influence not only on China's historiography but also on the historiographies of Korea, Japan, and Vietnam as well.

Given this narrative as described here, a question might be raised as to Sima Qian's filiality in accepting the defilement of his body rather than a noble and liberating death. He clearly violated the first precept of "family reverence" (*xiao* 孝) which is "vigilance in not allowing anything to do injury to your person." But the argument on Sima Qian's behalf must begin from the assertion that true "family reverence" (*xiao* 孝) must be attended by the stern obligation a child or a minister has to remonstrate (*jian* 諫) with the parent or ruler respectively when persuaded they are straying from the proper course. Secondly, under excruciating circumstances, Sima Qian stepped up like a truly filial son, fulfilling his promise to his father to complete the comprehensive history on behalf of the Sima family. Perhaps the most compelling argument beyond the filial obligation to remonstrate and keep a promise to his father, however, would be that while Sima Qian suffered his own physical desecration at the hands of an angry emperor, by completing the *Records of the Grand Historian* he selflessly and courageously gave of himself in preserving the body of the traditional culture intact. Sima Qian himself made the following observations:

> 網羅天下放失舊聞，考之行事，綜其終始，稽其成敗興壞之理，上計軒轅，下至于茲，為十表，本紀十二，書八章，世家三十，列傳七十，凡百三十篇，亦欲以究天人之際，通古今之變，成一家之言。草創未就，適會此禍，惜其不成，是以就極刑而無慍色。僕誠已著此書，藏諸名山，傳之其人通邑大都，則僕償前辱之責，雖萬被戮，豈有悔哉！

We have netted up and gathered the old knowledge of the world that had been dispersed and lost. We have, in a total of one hundred and thirty chapters that are composed of everything from charts and letters to biographies, reflected upon the full compass of past deeds and events to fathom their patterns of success and failure, and their vicissitudes. Our desire was to get to the bottom of all that has happened between heaven and man, to understand thoroughly the changes that have occurred from the past to present, and to compile all of this as the contribution of a single family. But before even completing an initial draft, I encountered the worst calamity that could befall a person. And it was only because I felt a deep sense of regret that I had not yet been able to finish this work that I was willing to suffer this extreme punishment without acrimony. When I have at last brought this manuscript to its conclusion, I will store it up in a sacred mountain. If this work can be transmitted down to others and spread from the towns to the great cities, then were this disgrace that I have suffered be a thousand times such a mutilation, how could I possibly feel any regret?①

---

① Sima Qian. "A Letter in Reply to Ren An 報任少卿書." A monograph entitled "The Letter to Ren An and Sima Qian's Legacy (or, Why Write History?)" by Stephen Durrant, Wai-yee Li, Michael Nylan, and Hans van Ess dedicated to exploring the authenticity of this letter and its implications for our interpretation of the *Shiji* 史記 is presently at press.

We must allow that Sima Qian clearly failed in the first dictate of family reverence that requires of him to keep his physical body intact. But then he accomplished the more difficult charge of giving service to his parents and his lord, and further succeeded in the ultimate goal of "family reverence," that is, he raised his name high for posterity and brought fame to his family lineage by distinguishing himself in the world. Indeed, we must conclude that Sima Qian as a peerless figure who faced down adversity and won fame and glory for his family, was exceptional in giving definition to what family reverence (*xiao* 孝) really means.

*小人   ***xiaoren.*** "Petty and mean persons." See 君子 ***junzi.*** "Exemplary persons, ruler, prince, lord."

*孝悌   ***xiaoti.*** "Family reverence and fraternal deference." See 孝 ***xiao.*** "Family reverence, filial piety."

*心   ***xin.*** "Heartmind, bodyheartminding, thinking and feeling." See also 性 ***xing.*** "Natural human propensities," 四端 ***siduan.*** "The four inclinations," and 内外 ***neiwai.*** "Inner and outer, inside and outside."

The character *xin* as found on the oracle bones and bronzes is a stylized pictograph of the aorta, associating it quite immediately with the physical "heart" and the many connotations such as "feelings" that attend it.[①] The fact that the character *qing* 情 which we translate as "emotions" or "feelings" is a combination of this *xin* 心 and a phonetic element, *qing* 青, justifies such an understanding. In fact,

---

[①] Kwan, "Database," 甲骨文合集 CHANT 1934 and 春秋晚期 CHANT 261 respectively.

many if not most of the characters that entail "affect" or "feeling" have *xin* as a component element. However, the fact that *xin* has often been rendered "mind" as well should alert us to the inadequacy of simply translating this term as "heart" or "feeling." Most of the characters that refer to different modalities of "thinking" such as "reflecting" (*si* 思) and deliberating (*lü* 慮) are also constructed with *xin* as a semantic component. Indeed, there are many passages in these canonical texts that would not make sense in English unless the *xin* thinks as well as feels.

The point, of course, is that in this early and persistent Confucian worldview, the mind cannot be divorced from the heart, nor the cognitive function from the affective. To avoid such a dichotomy, we have translated *xin* rather inelegantly as "heartmind" and "heartminding" with the intention of reminding the reader that there are no altogether rational thoughts devoid of feelings, nor any raw feelings that are altogether lacking in cognitive content.

The interpenetration of idea, intention, and affect expressed in the notion of *xin* suggests that thinking is rarely a dispassionate, speculative enterprise. Indeed, thinking involves normative judgments that assess the relative merit of the sensations, inclinations, and appetites in our experience of the world and of ourselves. Since ideas and intentions are always colored with emotional mood or tone, they are to be understood, more often than not, as dispositions to act that are integral to the action itself.

Another implication of the unity of feeling and thinking is the practical orientation of most of Chinese thought. If ideas are dispositions to act, what might be thought of as theories are recommendations that arise out of practice to make it more productive and intelligent. Thus, it is difficult in Confucian culture to find contexts within which the separation of theoretical and practical activities would prevail. When, for example, Confucius says, "from fifteen my heart-and-mind was set upon learning," he is indicating his commitment to a practical ethical regimen aimed at personal growth and realization rather than merely some formal course of study, and a curriculum that has as much to do with human relations as with any written texts.[①] Thinking and learning are, within the Chinese tradition, oriented to the practical ends of family, community, and the moral life.

In early Confucian cosmology, process and change have priority over form and stasis in the sense that erstwhile form is always a processual cadence, and ostensive stasis is an achieved and continuing equilibrium. Corollary to this cosmological commitment to process, in the medical literature that concerns itself with the well-being of the human body, distinctions such as anatomy and physiology, and form and function are always mutually entailing. This being the case, by analogy it might well be argued that *xin* is first gerundive, meaning "thinking and feeling," and then only derivatively, abstractly, and metaphorically, the physical organ with which these functions are associated.

The absence of any dualisms in the understanding of *xin* in this Confucian cosmology is a warrant for taking it as metonymic for "person," and in taking *xin* as "thinking and feeling," as ultimately requiring a narrative explanation. To begin with, the focus-field notion of whole persons stands in stark contrast to our familiar realist-derived conception of a private inner domain and a shared outer world. If we are not externally related in standing "outside" of each other, what then is the nature of our relationship one to another? The focus-field understanding of relationally-constituted persons is one answer to this question, beginning as it does from the doctrine of internal, constitutive relations. We are cells in an organism, organisms within an ecology, and centered ecologies within an unbounded and unsummed cluster of ecologies. This focus-

---

① *Analects* 2.4: 吾十有五而志于學.

field model requires a gestalt shift in our understanding of persons in which their particular identities and the unsummed totality—their foregrounded, always unique foci and their overlapping fields—are two holographic and thus mutually entailing ways of perceiving the same phenomenon. Just as each unique note as it is played within the context of a symphony has implicated within it the entire performance and must be evaluated accordingly, so each focal event—that is the identity expressed through each moment in a person's life—has implicated within it this person's entire, unbounded, narrative field.

Indeed, in order to fully grasp this holographic understanding of persons, the following, oft-cited passage from the *Mencius* that calls into question our familiar distinction between an inner self and an outer world might require a more literal reading than it usually receives:

> Mencius said, "The myriad things of the world are all implicated here in me."[①]

To make sense of this Mencian claim, we must appreciate the background cosmological assumptions about the perceived holographic focus and field relationship between particular persons and their experienced world, and about the processual nature and the radical contextuality of the human experience. Most obviously, it is a commonplace that the Confucian *xin* as "heartmind" serving metonymically for the concept of person does the work of both cognizing and feeling in the life experience including both felt thoughts and cognitively informed feelings. But understanding *xin* is not a matter of getting past one dualism. There are no dualisms in this cosmology. There is no strict dichotomy between self and other

---

① *Mencius* 7A4: 孟子曰："萬物皆備於我矣。"

(*zita* 自他), between subject and object (*zhuke* 主客), between body and mind (*xinshen* 心身), between structure and function (*tiyong* 體用), between thinking and doing (*zhixing* 知行), between inner and outer (*neiwai* 內外), between nature and nurture (*ziran* 自然),[①] and so on. In the reconceiving of this inner-outer dynamic as a vital, nonanalytic continuity we require an alternative reading of the full range of such distinctions.

The resolutely correlative language of Confucian cosmology can perhaps offer a way forward in reconceiving what is being expressed as the conjunction, combination, and production of erstwhile separate things—body, mind and culture—to be in fact a qualitative transformation in the relational dynamics of a complexly inclusive yet continuous experience. Said another way, Confucian cosmology offers a gestalt shift from perceiving discrete "things" defined by a doctrine of external relations to living within continuous, holistic "events" defined in terms of intrinsic, constitutive relations. Specifically, *xin* 心 in this cosmology—frequently translated as "heart-and-mind" or simply as "heartmind," but better understood as an evolving process of "bodyheartminding"—is a continuous, gerundive event rather than a conjoining of nominative things that can be separated as body, heart, and mind. Bodyheartminding is a qualitative disclosure of a continuous, holistic experience of a focus within a boundless field of experience rather than the integration of disparate things. *Xin* is at once body, heart, and mind that is profoundly normative as well as descriptive: an existentially and

---

[①] The binomial term *ziran* 自然 is usually read as "nature," or more informatively as "self-so-ing" but it can also be read contrastively like these other dyadic pairs as "nature and nurture." We can understand *zi* 自 inclusively as the complete field of relationships that together conspire to sponsor any particular thing—particular persons, for example. And the *ran* 然 then is the presencing of persons or things each as a particular focus, where their quality as unique persons is a function of the achieved coalescence in their particular fields of relations.

somatically experienced process of thoughtful feelings.

What this means for heartmind (*xin* 心) is that erstwhile inner and outer domains are irreducibly reflexive, with the objective world always being experienced from one subjective perspective or another, and the subjective world always having the objective world adumbrated within it. With heartmind (*xin* 心), structure and function, nature and nurture, and all such aspectual distinctions are nonanalytic and mutually entailing. These distinctions, rather than serving to separate and isolate different components within the "bodyheartminding" experience and thereby fragmenting the activities that are defining of it, instead reflect the interdependence and interpenetration of the matrix of myriad aspects that function together to constitute the complex human narrative.

We might take our cue from traditional Chinese medicine (TCM) as one practical application of this early cosmology in which the alternative understanding of the relationship between function and structure provides us with a significantly different way of understanding the *Mencius* 7A4 claim that "The myriad things of the world are all implicated here in me." We must acknowledge in TCM there is an inseparability of physiology and anatomy, and thus of function and structure that precludes the formalism and the reification of the anatomical elements that brings with it a doctrine of external relations. Indeed, TCM has a symbiotic understanding of the coterminous relationship between the dynamics of structure and function captured in the expression "forming and functioning" (*tiyong* 體用) that can perhaps be translated more simply and holistically as "trans-*form*-ing." As medical anthropologist Judith Farquhar observes in her attempt to make sense of this Chinese *qi* 氣 cosmology:

> *Qi* is both structural and functional, a unification of material and temporal forms that loses all coherence when reduced to one or the

other "aspect."[1]

In TCM, systemic physiological functions within an ecology of relations have parity if not privilege over the more persistent, localized anatomical structures, requiring that diagnostics be holistic and inclusive rather than overly specific, and by extension, analytical and exclusive. Remembering the reflexive nature of subjective and objective (*zhuke* 主客), these life functions also have an existential as well as a more objective character. The lived-body is experienced from the inside as well as being a physical organism to be observed and examined from the outside. The term *zhenmai* 診脈, for example, is certainly localized as "taking this pulse," but more importantly it is doctor and patient together using tactile sensitivity to feel and interpret the visceral dynamics of the living body holistically—both from within and without. As such, these transactional procedures have synoptic reference not only to the organism as experienced externally, but also to the organic, lived relationship this vital organism itself has with the more objective landscape. Remembering that "patient" comes from the Latin *patiens* from *patior* meaning "to suffer or bear," the TCM patient is not a "patient" in the literal sense of being a passive sufferer. The patient under the definition of "sufferer" is passive both in the sense of having to tolerate with patience the interventions of the outside expert, and at the same time of bearing whatever suffering is necessary internally. In the case of TCM, however, the patient is an active, existentially aware voice in the collaborative process of diagnostics and treatment.

Given the holography and focus-field assumptions that ground TCM, in "taking this pulse" (*zhenmai* 診脈), the medical practitioner and the patient are by extension collaborating ultimately to

---

[1] Judith Farquhar, *Knowing Practice,* p. 34.

feel the pulse of the living cosmos as it is expressed through this specific organism. When we use this same language of focus and field to give an account of "bodyheartminding" (*xin* 心), it is first and foremost an embodied center of thinking and feeling that, in the transactions constituting its physiological, psychological, and sociological narrative, extends out radially to the furthest reaches of an unbounded cosmos. When we read *xin* simply as the "heartmind," we are isolating this one focal aspect as a metonym for the holistic and eventful functions, both physical and psychic, existential and phenomenal, that in sum constitute a continuing human life in all of its dynamic detail and particularity. Indeed, *xin* 心 can only derivatively and abstractly be taken to be the discrete physical organ that serves symbolically to represent the full complexity of the interactions and events that are the human experience.

*信 *xin.* "Making good on one's word, living up to one's word."

While *xin* 信 is conventionally rendered "trust," "trustworthy," "credible," or "credibility," I usually translate it as "making good on one's word" or "living up to one's word." It has been described by Ezra Pound, following his teacher Ernest Fenollosa, as a picture of "a man standing by his word."[1] No small number of scholars have excoriated Pound for his philological flights of fancy, but every sinologist must analyze this particular character in the same way: the character for "person" (*ren* 人) stands to the left of the character for "speaking" or "spoken words" (*yan* 言).

We need to be clear that *xin* requires more than just good intentions; it requires practical results. Simply being sincere in

---

[1] Ezra Pound. *Confucius: The Great Digest and Unwobbling Pivot.* New York, New Directions, 1951, p. 22.

what one says and does, is not enough to be deemed *xin*; one must have the circumspection and resources, human and otherwise, to follow through and make good on what one proposes to do. The "inseparability of knowing and doing" captured in the mantra *zhixingheyi* 知行合一 is a prime value in this tradition, requiring that all normative claims such as "I am a good parent," "I love my mother" be authenticated in practice. It is because of the practical demands of *xin* that there are few themes more pervasive in the classical Confucian literature and especially in the *Analects* than a reticence to speak for fear of not being able to live up to what one has said.

The *Shuowen* lexicon glosses *xin* 信 as *cheng* 誠 (acting with resolve in one's roles and relations), and also glosses *cheng* as *xin*, suggesting some considerable overlap in meaning between *xin* as "making good on one's word" and *cheng* as "acting with resolve in one's roles and relations." Indeed, for the Confucian notion of the relationally constituted person, *cheng* often translated as "sincerity" is an essential affective ground for deepening one's relations with others, and when expressed with resolve, serves as basis for real personal growth. Commitment to the "integrative" sense of integrity that follows from such personal growth is a necessary ground for the creative process of "becoming one together." And *xin* as "making good on one's word" references a specific, concrete pathway for promoting the credibility and trust needed to achieve such personal growth.

In most of the passages that describe the process of becoming persons together, the text as we might expect repeatedly invokes "making good on your word" or "living up to your word" (*xin* 信) as the fiduciary activity out of which rewarding relationships develop. In fact, all social and moral growth is fundamentally discursive. And thus, good and lasting family relations and friendships can only be "made" through effective communication that is grounded in mutual trust and credibility. If we begin from the primary appeal to exemplary models more than abstract theories or principles to guide human conduct, then in this view, morality and the truth that informs it is less an affair of understanding and applying concepts and principles, and more of understanding the concretely specific modes of conduct relevant to being true to one's particular community. The contrast, then, is between a principled way of thinking and an analogical alternative. The analogical mode of thinking as the continuing search for productive correlations eschews any assumption that there is some final truth to be attained, or for that matter, any finality about the interpretive tools we use.

It is because of this inseparability of knowing and doing that in understanding *xin*, as with many if not most classical Chinese terms, we must appreciate the priority of situation over agency. That is, *xin* in describing the situations of persons making good on their word, goes in both directions, connoting both the achieved credibility of the benefactor and the concomitant trust the beneficiary has in this benefactor. For example, when *Daodejing* 17 reports, "where there is a lack of credibility, there is a lack of trust" 信不足焉，有不信焉, *xin* has to be translated first as "credibility" and then as "trust." *Xin*, then, is the consummation of fiduciary relationships, with agency being an abstraction from this situation.

We find that throughout the *Analects*, *xin* appears repeatedly in tandem with *zhong* 忠: "conscientiousness in doing one's utmost," where this aspectual pairing reinforces the personal resolution required to really live up to one's word. For the same reason, *zhong* as "conscientiousness" again accompanies the term *shu* 恕—"deference, dramatic rehearsal"—as aspectual in that the actual realizing of one's insight into the most productive response to any particular situation requires assiduous effort. As D.C. Lau reports, for Confucius 吾道一以貫之 *zhong* and *shu* together are the single, continuous thread that runs through his moral vision of the proper way.[1]

*性 **xing.** "Natural human propensities." See also 心 **xin.** "Heartmind, bodyheartminding, thinking and feeling," 四端 **siduan.** "The four inclinations."

Xing, or more specifically, *renxing* 人性, is conventionally translated as "human nature." This character appears rather late in the Warring States literature as a specific refinement on the term *sheng* 生: "birth, life, growth" at a juncture when this topic emerges to become an issue of intense philosophical debate. Mencius and Xunzi, the two major figures in this continuing exchange, are often taken to hold opposing positions on this issue: humans are initially inclined to good conduct and are initially inclined to base conduct respectively. An important question for the contemporary philosopher Li Zehou is whether human "beings" are born with some universal moral faculty that makes them good, or instead, that "human becomings" become morally good as the product of their personal cultivation. While many contemporary interpreters of the debate between Mencius and Xunzi might ascribe the former innatist, psychological position to Mencius, and the latter appeal to personal cultivation and refinement to Xunzi, in fact Li Zehou also sees both Mencius and Xunzi as advocating for the latter position. Li Zehou insists that

> . . . Mencius and Xunzi are consistent with Confucius in both advocating for "education." The first chapter of *Xunzi* is "Encouraging Education." And Mencius says that "what distinguishes people from the brutes is ever so slight, and while the common run of people might lose this difference, exemplary persons preserve

---

[1] Confucius, *Analects* (*Lunyu*), trans. D.C. Lau, pp. xv–xvi.

and develop it." Hence this distinguishing human characteristic has to be sought after or it will be lost. Both Mencius and Xunzi emphasize *aposteriori* cultivation and learning. The distinguishing characteristic of Confucianism is that what is fundamental to the human experience is not some fixed nature, but a process of ceaseless change and growth. Learning to become human is a key precept in Confucianism.①

As Li Zehou avers, Mencius and Xunzi both follow Confucius in arguing at great length that what human beings can become follows from a life of cultivating and refining our native conditions through a regimen of assiduous effort.

On the topic of human nature, the uncritical assumption for many if not most commentators today is that for Mencius at least, *xing* references a universal, inborn, fixed, self-sufficient endowment defining of all human beings that programs us naturally as human beings to be moral in what we do. Lee Yearley in his comparison of Mencius with Thomas Aquinas questions this assumption, and looks to refine the notion of a given human nature by introducing the important distinction between an ontological or discovery model of *xing* that he would reject as a familiar yet mistaken interpretation of both Mencius and Aquinas, and a developmental or biological model that he would endorse as the better reading of them both. Of the former ontological or discovery model, Yearley says:

> In a discovery model ... human nature exists as a permanent set

---

① Li Zehou 李澤厚 in his "An Explanation of the Summary Chart on Ethics" (《關於"倫理學總覽表，中國文化學刊2018"的說明》): 所以我說孟、荀統一于孔，即"學"。荀子有《勸學》作為首篇，孟子也講"人之所以異於禽獸者幾希，庶民去之，君子存之"，所以要"求放心"，"求則得之，捨則失之"。孟荀雙方都重視後天的培養和學習。孔學的特點就是認為人的本性並不是固定的nature，而是一個總在不斷成長、變化的過程。從而"學做人"始終是孔學要義之一。

性 xing.

of dispositions that are obscured but that can be contacted or discovered. People do not cultivate inchoate capacities. Rather they discover a hidden ontological reality that defines them. The discovery model reflects, then, ontological rather than biological notions. An ontological reality, the true self, always is present no matter what specific humans, particular instances of it, are or do.①

Yearley, rejecting this conception of human nature that would take it as an ontological given as a misreading of both Mencius and Aquinas, instead advocates for the developmental or biological understanding that he describes as follows:

> What can be called a biological framework informs Mencius's ideas on human nature and its characteristic successes and failures. . . . To speak of the nature of something within such a framework is to refer to some innate constitution that manifests itself in patterns of growth and culminates in specifiable forms.②

While the developmental model of the Mencian *xing* is certainly more compelling than the discovery model, it is still strongly Aristotelian in its teleological understanding of human potential as the innate and self-defining "capacities humans possess"③ that are then manifested and actualized in determining who we will become. One association that recommends this developmental model to Yearley and others is Mencius's frequent appeal to a horticultural analogy in which, for example, seeds of barley if uninjured and nurtured will achieve the characteristic form of barley.④

---

① Lee Yearley. *Mencius and Aquinas: Theories of Virtue and Conceptions of Courage*. Albany: State University of New York Press, 1990, p. 60.
② Yearley, *Mencius and Aquinas*, pp. 58-59.
③ Yearley, *Mencius and Aquinas*, p. 60.
④ Yearley, *Mencius and Aquinas*, p. 59.

Indeed, in the *Mencius* and other canonical Confucian texts, the appeal to horticultural metaphors is often construed as reinforcing the teleological idea that plants and animals in growing to become what they essentially are, are simply actualizing the potential inherent in their "seed" or "root." James Behuniak in attempting to rescue Mencius from Greek teleological assumptions addresses this botanical question explicitly:

> Before we think of the botanical metaphor in terms of an end-driven teleology and equate *xing* 性 with a uniform, predetermined "nature" on that basis, let us briefly attempt to locate this metaphor in its own context.... When Mencius describes growth, the stress is on the irrepressible process of emergence, a process located within nourishing conditions. The seed is the beginning of an emergent process... This is a process shaped within environing conditions; it is not teleological in any strict, end-driven sense. In the Chinese tradition, the seed is not described as containing its own end; rather the process would appear to determine its end, since not all seeds come to fruition... Generally in this tradition, the mention of botanical growth in a literary context does not evoke generic traits that are simply "actualized" in the process of growth.①

The question is whether or not such classical Greek teleology and idealism are also integral to early Chinese cosmology? And if not, or at least if not in the same degree, what in fact might make these horticulture and husbanding analogies appropriate for capturing the growth of relationally constituted "human becomings" is the acute dependence in farming and the raising of livestock upon a contrived environment and upon the concentrated and continuing human effort needed to succeed in such an enterprise. Without sustained, radical

---

① Behuniak, *Mencius on Becoming Human*, pp. xiii-xiv.

human intervention, most seeds far from becoming what they "are," become anything and everything else. While we must allow that an acorn does not usually become a chicken, we must also allow that only one in a million acorns actually becomes an oak tree. And the million-minus-one acorns left over are transmuted to become a vast range of different things. Indeed, the "seed" of anything and what it will become is always and fundamentally a transactional process. The "seed" might have the initial genetic conditions from which something "begins," but what it becomes is the internalization of the possibilities made available through whatever intensive cultivation there might be, and an integration of the many other contingencies in the circumstances that attend its growth. The point here is that on reflection, even in agriculture, context really matters.

In reflecting on what *xing* means then, there are perhaps at least three rather than just two possibilities. As Yearley has pointed out, there is first the ontological or discovery interpretation. Some would read *xing* as some fixed, universal, innate essence that makes all human beings what they are. The second familiar interpretation is the developmental or biological model that suggests *xing* as "nature" is a teleologically driven "seed" or innate design that if cultivated becomes what it is supposed to be. But the third possibility would be a historicist, process, and transactional interpretation of *xing*, reading it as an achievement concept rather than as a given, either ontologically or horticulturally. The potential for human "becomings" who are born *in medias res* as narratives nested within narratives is certainly grounded in their native propensities, but then becomes available for cultivation as it emerges *pari passu* through the many associations that over time make up a life story. In what we might call a "narrative" understanding of *xing*, we find that, as is the case in the traditional Confucian understanding of "culture," person and world evolve together in a symbiotic, dynamic, and contrapuntal relationship. The identities of persons are rooted in the native beginnings of family and community, and these environing relationships need to be both nurtured and protected from loss or injury, but such identities as profoundly unique aesthetic and spiritual achievements only emerge in the process of these relationships achieving thick resolution as they are cultivated, grown, and articulated over their lifetimes. Their distinctive and unique potential as persons, far from being a given, in fact emerges in the always transactional events that in sum constitute lives lived in the world. Said another way, in the narrative understanding of *xing* 性, emphasis is placed on the "living and growing" implications of *sheng* 生 rather than on its meaning as merely "birthing."

In the contemporary world in which individualism has become an ideology with a seeming monopoly on intellectual consciousness, we have to ask whether our own default commonsense assumptions about *individual* human "beings" are consistent with the Mencian project as it was situated and developed within the natural *qi* 氣 cosmology that serves this tradition as its interpretive context. Is not in fact the narrative understanding of persons a better reading of this ancient Confucian philosopher? Angus Graham asked and over time answered this question for himself, first setting aside his own commonsense assumptions, and then ultimately formulating an understanding of persons that is consistent with the Confucian interpretive context.

In the *Mencius*, there is in fact an inordinate emphasis on the role of unremitting personal cultivation in growing and consolidating the virtuosic habits that are expressed in and are defining of an exemplary life. This process at one end begins from our initial animality with the minimalist human advantage of the incipient "four inclinations" (*siduan* 四端), and extends at the other end to the possibility of attaining the habitude of a full-blown, epoch-changing, human sagacity as our loftiest prospect. Mencius far from assuming that our natural propensities are going to produce fields of identical human "beings," exhorts us to aspire to a sageliness that is the ultimate expression of our own assiduous, always particular, regimen of personal cultivation.

Graham takes issue with the simple identification of the classical Chinese concept of *xing* with the familiar conception of "nature" as something "inborn and innate:" those qualities which a thing has to start with. Indeed, it is precisely this kind of essentialism that has now become the standard reading of Mencius in both the European and Asian language literature, a persistent teleological misreading that Graham over his long career first endorsed, returned to repeatedly for further reflection, and then ultimately rejected.① Graham's claim is that the dynamic thrust of *xing* has not been adequately noticed. As a corrective on his own earlier work, he argues that early Chinese thinkers who discuss *xing* seldom seem to be thinking of fixed qualities going back to a thing's origin, but rather are reflecting on the process of its maturation within a specific context. *Xing* thus understood covers the career of a person's existence, denoting the entire process of becoming human. Strictly speaking, a person is not a sort of being but first and foremost a doing or making and, only derivatively and retrospectively, something done.

By contrast with human "beings," the generative and open-ended conception of human "becomings" in the Confucian tradition is itself an answer that requires the posing of a rather different question. Persons are conceived of as coterminous genealogical narratives-within-narratives, invariably *in medias res* without initial beginnings or final ends. Thus, rather than asking *What* is a person? we must ask the irreducibly contextual and generative questions of *Whence*

---

① For the history of this revisionist reading, see Roger T. Ames "Reconstructing A.C. Graham's Reading of *Mencius* on *Xing* 性: A Coda to 'The Background of the Mencian Theory of Human Nature' (1967)," in *Having a Word with Angus Graham: At Twenty-five Years into His Immortality*, edited by Carine Defoort and Roger T. Ames, Albany: State University of New York Press, 2018.

and *whither* persons? We need to ask after the story of how evolving personal identities have emerged *pari passu* within their unfolding narrative contexts, and where the trajectory that such life episodes set will lead them. We must conceive of persons not as abstract "things" or "objects," but rather as generalizable, historical "events." Graham's insight is that in the Confucian context, "human nature"

> ... is conceived in terms of spontaneous development in a certain direction rather than of its origin or goal.... The *cheng* 成 "completion" of a thing's development which in man is his *cheng* 誠 "integrity," is the interdependent becoming integral rather than the realization of an end.[①]

Graham is saying here that, in our spontaneous development, our "interdependent" context is continually becoming integral to who we are becoming. Hence, neither persons in their particularity, nor humanity as a species, can be defined in terms of a discrete beginning or some ultimate end. Graham is keenly aware here of a fundamental contrast between closure and disclosure: that is, between the potential and the actualization of a teleologically-driven and substantive human "being" on the one hand, and the continuing emergence of narratively-nested human "becomings" informed by the *gravitas* of an evolving civilization on the other. After all, Confucian persons are events within a continuing transformative, genealogical process wherein their progenitors do not have discrete origins or suffer ultimate annihilation. On the contrary, these predecessors within a family lineage embody their own antique ancestors—physically, socially, and culturally—at the erstwhile beginnings of their own particular narratives, and then continue to live on in their own progeny in those succeeding generations that

---

[①] A.C. Graham, "Replies," p. 288.

carry them beyond any ostensive end.

Graham, reflecting on the evolutionary turn that has brought him to a different, more situated understanding of *xing*, offers us a novel, revisionist interpretation that begins from citing and disputing the interpretation of *xing* posited by Arthur Waley, his predecessor among London's most famous sinologists:

> Waley says that "*hsing* [*xing*] (nature) meant in ordinary parlance the qualities a thing has to start with,"① and I have myself in previous publications translated the definition 生之謂性 by "Inborn is what is meant by 'nature'." Yet early Chinese thinkers who discuss *hsing* [*xing*] seldom seem to be thinking of fixed qualities going back to a thing's origin . . . ; rather they are concerned with developments which are spontaneous but realize their own potentialities only if uninjured and adequately nourished. Mencius in particular seems never to be looking back towards birth, always forward to the maturation of a continuing growth.②

We see that Graham here clearly wants to distinguish himself from any discovery model of *xing*, and introduces language that might on first reading seem to favor the developmental alternative. But to understand his interpretation more clearly, such a prospective, processual, and developmental reading of the maturation of an "uninjured and adequately nourished" *xing* needs to be located within Graham's insights into the early Chinese process cosmology more broadly.

For Graham, proper attention to the interdependence and irreducibly contextual nature of all things will enable us to

---

① Arthur Waley. *Three Ways of Thought in Ancient China*. Stanford: Stanford University Press, 1939, p. 205.
② A.C. Graham, "Replies," p. 287.

disambiguate some of the key philosophical vocabulary of classical Chinese philosophy such as *tian* 天 and *dao* 道 by identifying equivocations that emerge when we elide the distinction between cosmological presuppositions indigenous to the classical Chinese worldview with our more familiar classical Greek ontological assumptions.

Graham cautions us about such frequent equivocations, using as his specific example the tendency commentators have had to treat the Mencian *xing* as referencing some "transcendent origin, which in Mencian doctrine would also be a transcendent end."[①] Graham, rejecting the relevance for Mencius of an essentializing Greek idealism (*eidos*) and the radical teleology (*telos*) that accompanies it, would locate his notion of *xing* within the generic features of an early Chinese process or "event" ontology in which putative "things" and their contexts are interdependent and thus inseparable. What it means to become human, far from referencing an antecedent given that takes us back to our origins or forward to some given, pre-determined end, is in fact a provisional and emergent process within the context of an evolving cosmic order. It is just such a worldview that I and my collaborators following Marcel Granet, Joseph Needham, and Graham himself have argued for at length as the most appropriate interpretive context for understanding classical Confucianism.[②]

One familiar misreading of the *Mencius* on *xing* 性 occurs when, on the analogy of default metaphysical conceptions of an essential

---

[①] A.C. Graham, "Replies," p. 287.
[②] See for example David L. Hall and Roger T. Ames. *Thinking From the Han: Self, Truth, and Transcendence in Chinese and Western Culture*. Albany: State University of New York, 1998, pp. 23-78; and Roger T. Ames and Henry Rosemont, Jr. *The Analects of Confucius: A Philosophical Translation*. pp. 20-45. See also Roger T. Ames. *Confucian Role Ethics*, especially Chapter 2, "An Interpretive Context for Understanding Confucianism."

"human nature," we decontextualize and detemporalize *xin* 心 or "heartminding," and treat such generalized features captured in this expression *siduan* as innate, internal, fixed, independent, and isolatable conditions. *Xin*, far from being some inborn and exclusive "nature" defining of discrete individuals, is the concrete pattern of vital, constitutive relations that serve as a general description of the native, prosocial inclinations of always unique yet radically situated human becomings. The "four inclinations" are the multivalent aspects of *xin* referencing our preliminary and at first inchoate pattern of roles and relations in the ambient family, community, and culture that constitute our focal identity at birth, and that are then thickened as our narratives unfold. But *xin* is more than just such "inclinations." As integral to *xing* 性 itself, these inchoate sprouts are then available for the project of further nurturance and growth (*sheng* 生) in the transactions that constitute a life: that is, what the *Mencius* refers to specifically as the process of "making the most of the *xin*" (*jinxin* 盡心).

Attributing to Mencius a notion of an essential "human nature" as a principle of individuation is a counterintuitive assertion within the context of a holistic *qi* 氣 cosmology that begins from the primacy of process and vital relationality. In this cosmology, the assumption is that change is pervasive, and as such, everything is disposed to transformation. And again, a related misreading of Mencius is to ascribe to him a kind of individualism by appealing to *xin* 心, *xing* 性, and *siduan* 四端 as a doctrine of innate and universal human nature that would serve as a principle of individuation.

While a conception of persons as discrete and isolatable individuals is an all too familiar uncritical assumption in much of our contemporary philosophical discourse, it is at the same time being repudiated as a fallacious understanding of person within the internal critique being waged by some of our most progressive thinkers: John Dewey, Michael Sandel, Charles Taylor, Mark

Johnson. Given the principle of charity, we might want to worry about imputing such an individualism to Mencius when it seems that we ourselves are trying to get past it.

For the philosopher Whitehead, for example, as a prominent spokesperson for process thinking, the notion of the discrete individual assumed in much of the liberal theorizing of person is a specific and persistent example of the philosopher's *deformation professionelle*, and is described by him as a prominent case of not one but two fallacies. First, it is a prime and powerful example of what he calls the fallacy of simple location: that is, the familiar and yet fallacious claim that isolating, decontextualizing, and analyzing things as simple particulars is the best way to understand the content of our experience. For Whitehead, such theorizing is fatally reductionistic, and suffers from what he further describes as "the fallacy of misplaced concreteness" where we equate the abstracted and independent "thing" with what is real, while at the same time ignoring the genuine connectivity and transitivity of such "things" that animate them in the transactional events of our ordinary experience. This fallacy of misplaced concreteness is to regard abstracted entities presumed to have a simple location as being what is concrete, while at the same time, ignoring the vital and processual transitivity that attends all things in our experience of them.[①] Allowing that persons experience each other within the narratives of events that in sum constitute our shared lives together, Whitehead is insisting that we treat persons as interpenetrating "events" rather than standing outside each other as discrete "things."

What is at stake here is the deliberate Mencian answer to perhaps our most basic and important philosophical question: What

---

[①] A. N. Whitehead in *Process and Reality* p. 137 observes: "This presupposition of individual independence is what I have elsewhere called, the 'fallacy of simple location.'"

does it mean to become consummately human? How do we explain the birth, life, and growth of the human "being"? Do we appeal to reduplicative causal accounts (the infant is a ready-made adult), by teleological accounts (the infant is simply preliminary to the existing ideal)? Or do we posit the notion of human "becomings" that appeals to a contextual, narrative account available to us through a phenomenology of reflective and purposeful personal action?

How do we define what it means to be a human "being"? Do we offer speculative assumptions about innate, isolatable causes that locate persons outside of the roles and relations in which they live their lives? Or alternatively, do we give explanation of them as having "become" human by taking full account of the initial, native conditions and context within in which persons are inextricably embedded, and then going on to assay the full accretion of consequent action as their life stories unfold?

We have seen that for Graham, *xing* as a dynamic, gerundive concept references a "developmental" process that is spontaneous and realizes its own potentialities when it is nourished and unimpeded. But here we also see that Graham wants to damp down any of our familiar assumptions about the antecedent beginnings and endings we associate with the teleologically driven developmental model. Graham's understanding of early Confucian cosmology assumes a doctrine of internal relations constitutive of events rather than external relations that merely conjoin discrete and independent things. Hence, his interpretation of "their own potentialities" would make such potentialities contextual, historicist, particularistic, and genealogical. Indeed, Graham in his clarification of what kind of "relation" is relevant to this Chinese cosmology, introduces precisely this distinction between the concrete patterns of relations that constitute things, and those secondary relations abstracted from otherwise independent things:

> As for "relationships," relation is no doubt an indispensable concept in exposition of Chinese thought, which generally impresses a Westerner as more concerned with the relations between things than with their qualities; but the concern is with concrete patterns rather than relations abstracted from them...①

Again, Graham has counseled us to acknowledge some fundamental equivocations commentators must avoid in their understandings of the terms available for theorizing classical Chinese cosmology. Early Chinese concepts, says Graham, often "tend to be more dynamic than their closest Western equivalents, and that English translation freezes them into immobility."② It is only recently over the past century with the insights of contemporaries such as Wittgenstein and more recently George Lakoff and Mark Johnson, that we have called into question the assumption that concepts can serve us as a univocal currency to guarantee the cogency of our arguments.

Indeed, as we have seen, Graham in developing what we are calling his narrative conception of *xing*, locates this key term *xing* as always contextualized within a process cosmology in which persons and context are mutually shaping, and in which the context becomes integral to the person. Or in Graham's own words, we find "the interdependent becoming integral rather than the realization of an end."③ In abjuring the assumed teleological assumptions that would define *xing* in terms of antecedent design and predetermined end, and in its stead invoking the more important role of deliberate, prospective action, Graham offers us an understanding of *xing* as a vital and responsive conatus that in its narrative growth is self-

---

① A.C. Graham, "Replies," pp. 288-289.
② A.C. Graham, *Studies in Chinese Philosophy and Philosophical Literature*, p. 8.
③ A.C. Graham, "Replies," p. 288.

directing and yet collaborative in shaping and being shaped by its environments. As Graham's observes:

> Still riding my own hobby-horse, might one distinguish *xin* 心 "heart" and *xing* 性 "nature" as the centres of awareness and spontaneity respectively? . . . With the exercise of the heart for thinking, spontaneous inclination shifts away from the direction in which it is pulled by the mere action of the perceived thing on the senses. . . . In unawareness you know only present inclination; it is by full exertion of the heart to understand the things which act on you that you come to know what Heaven has ordained as the spontaneous preference of your nature in full awareness of them.①

Graham's sense of a radically situated and contextualizing center of awareness and the spontaneous growth that is directed by it, would be lost if we were to understand *xing* 性 as simply referencing a "natural endowment at birth." In such a retrospective, innatist reading of *xing* 性, we would be reducing the *sheng* 生 that is constitutive of *xing* 性 to simply "birth" as opposed to its broader meaning of "birth, growth, and life." This extended meaning requires that we include along with a putative "birth" the prospective life and growth of these native conditions within their constitutive relationships.

But in making such a severe distinction between "heartminding" (*xin* 心) as the guiding center of "awareness" and *xing* as the "spontaneity" that is thus guided, Graham is perhaps overlooking the fact that *xin* is also an integral aspect of the character *xing*; that is, the graph for *xing* 性 itself is comprised of *xin* 心 + *sheng* 生. Using Graham's own language, if *xin* is a center of "awareness" then *xing* would have to be that center of "awareness" together with its

---

① A.C. Graham, "Replies," pp. 290-291.

animating "spontaneity," thus making of *xing* itself an animated and evolving center of awareness. *Xing* would seem in sum to reference the vital and intentional unfolding of the life and growth of our native conditions—the human narrative in its wholeness.

For Mencius, at least, *xin* 心 by itself at times refers to the initial native conditions that are captured in the "four inclinations" (*siduan* 四端) formula of the inchoate *xin*: that is, *xin* is our natural inclination for "conducting ourselves consummately" (*ren* 仁), for "acting with optimal appropriateness" (*yi* 義), for "achieving propriety in our roles and relations" (*li* 禮), for "acting wisely" (*zhi* 知) as these tendencies are expressed in our roles and relations. The "four inclinations" are the multivalent aspects of *xin* referencing our preliminary and at first inchoate pattern of roles and relations in the ambient family, community, and culture that constitute our focal identity at birth, and that are then thickened as our narratives unfold. It is an appreciation of this irreducibly relational and intentional understanding of *xin* together with the vital, generative import of *xing*—what Graham describes as the complementary center of "awareness" and "spontaneity"—that might save us from the common misinterpretations of Mencius.

This more interesting "narrative" understanding of "natural human propensities" (*xing* 性) is reinforced by other contemporary commentaries. When in the *Analects* 17.2 Confucius is remembered as claiming that 性相近也習相遠也 "human beings are similar in their natural propensities, but vary greatly by virtue of their habits," he is emphasizing the transformative possibility of education. As Tang Junyi observes:

> This passage does not mean Confucius is asserting that human nature is something fixed and given, but rather implies that "similar in natural propensities" is the human capacity for personal growth

and transformation without any fixed limit to its possibilities.①

Tang Junyi underscores the vital, collaborative, and emergent nature of this process of human "becoming:"

> Within Chinese natural cosmology what is held in general is not some first principle. The root pattern or coherence (*genbenzhili* 根本之理) of anything is its "life force" (*shengli* 生理), and this life force is its *xing* 性. The *xing* is expressed in the quality of its interactions with other things and events. The *xing* or "life force" then entailing spontaneity and transformation has nothing to do with necessity... The emergence of any particular phenomenon is a function of the interaction between its prior conditions and other things and events as external influences. So how something interacts with other things and events and the form of this interaction is not determined by the thing itself... Thus, the *xing* of anything itself is inclusive of this process of transformability in response to whatever it encounters.②

The opening line of *Focusing the Familiar* states: 天命之謂性 "What *tian* commands is our native human propensities." In translating *xing* as "native human propensities" I am following Tang Junyi who insists that:

---

① Tang Junyi. *Complete Works*. Vol. 13, p. 32: 此即孔子不重人性之為固定之性之旨，而隱含一相近之人性，為能自生長而變化，而具無定限之可能之旨者也。
② Tang Junyi. *Complete Works*. Vol. 4 pp. 98-100: 中國自然宇宙論中，共相非第一義之理。物之存在的根本之理為生理，此生理即物之性。物之性表現於與他物感通之德量。性或生理，乃自由原則，生化原則，而非必然原則……蓋任一事象之生起，必由以前之物與其他之交感，以為其外緣。而一物與他之如何交感或交感之形式，則非由任一物之本身所決定……因而一物之性之本身，即包含一隨所感而變化之性。

What is meant in this opening passage by such a claim is not that *tian* according to some fixed fate determines the conduct and progress of human beings. On the contrary, *tian* endows humans with our native human propensities (*xing*) that, being more or less free of the mechanical control of established habits and of external intervening forces, undergo a creative advance within their contextualizing situation that is expressive of this spontaneity.[①]

Given this processional understanding of *xing*, the relationship between *renxing* 人性, *tian* 天, and "command" (*ming* 命) must not be construed in an altogether deterministic manner. As the source of *xing, tian* is not to be construed as a transcendent "other" that would preclude any important sense of self-determination for persons. It is better to think of *tian* and *ren* as we think of *yin* and *yang*—namely, as correlative functions that articulate the changing patterns of processes and events. Human beings come from *tian* not as ready-made persons, but as persons who in learning the best of the inherited legacy are able to use it to enculturate themselves, and ultimately, to make their own contribution to *tian*. This correlative status of *tian* and *renxing* is suggested by the oft-cited mantra defining of classical Confucian religiousness, *tianrenheyi* 天人合一, "the continuity between *tian* and the human experience." Human beings, while being endowed by *tian*, also contribute to the content of *tian* through the co-creative role of our sages and exemplary models. In some degree at least, the human being has a role in continuing to negotiate what it means to become human.

If we were going to speculate on why terms such as *xing* tend

---

① Tang Junyi. *Complete Works*. Vol. 4, p. 100: 所謂天命之為性，非天以一指定命運規定人物之行動運化，而正是賦人物以多多少少不受自己過去之習慣所機械支配，亦不受外界之來感之力之機械支配，而隨境有一創造的生起而表現自由之性。

generally to be more dynamic in meaning than Western equivalencies such as "human nature" (which indeed seems to be the case), we might want to reflect on the implications of cosmogonic speculation that is made important in this analysis by its absence in classical Chinese cosmology. The concept of "God" and the putative origins of the cosmos is a signal feature of the Western philosophical and religious narrative that has no counterpart in Confucian thinking. Where human beings, for example, within a single-ordered *kosmos* are shaped and invested by an external originative principle, the most fully creative act lies in the creator's endowment of a given potential. The creature's subsequent actualization of that potential is derivative. Where persons are endowed by, and dependent upon, some externally "given" originative principle for the "nature" of their existence, the opportunity for their own creative contribution is substantially diminished. On the other hand, in the Confucian cosmology that does not appeal to some initial cosmogonic origin, the power of creativity and the responsibility for creative product resides more broadly in human beings themselves in their ongoing interactive processes of becoming.

The difference between the "nature" of a thing in a cosmogonic tradition and its *xing* in a noncosmogonic cosmology is suggested by the kinds of questions that each culture's philosophers ask. Cosmogonic concern generates metaphysical questions, a search for origins as first principles and ontological priorities. How did the cosmos begin? What are its first principles? What are the fundamental elements from out of which it was constructed? What is the origin of the existence and growth of natural phenomena? Such is the search for the One behind the many.

The genealogical *qi* 氣 cosmology, on the other hand, will generate primarily historical and rhetorical questions. Who and what are our historical antecedents that have given us our present definition? What are their achievements that we can appropriate to enculturate ourselves? How can we further cultivate ourselves so as to contribute to the continuing tradition as it is embodied in our contemporary exemplars? How can we turn this historical and cultural interdependence to maximum benefit? The philosopher's role in the noncosmogonic tradition, then, will not be as much to discover an answer to the question of origins as to create a model of humanity that is persuasive, and that others will defer to and emulate in the transmission of the cultural tradition.

There is a related implication of this distinction between a cosmogonic and noncosmogonic worldview where in the latter there is no overarching *arche* (originative beginning) as an explanation of the creative process. Under conditions that are thus "anarchic" in the philosophic sense of this term, although *xing* might indeed refer to "kinds," in fact such categories would be dependent upon generalizations made by analogy among *sui generis* phenomena rather than by appeal to some self-same, shared characteristic. Difference is prior to identified similarities. Certain things to which *xing* is applied—water and rocks, for example—are not over their respective careers marked by growth and cultivation, and hence it makes little sense to speak of them in terms of starting conditions and mature states. The *xing* of such things remains relatively constant. However, the human being—that phenomenon most given to cultivation and refinement—is a different case.

While the human *xing* might include certain generalizable conditions that define it at birth, in its more important aspects it seems to refer to what is existentially achieved. In defining the human *xing*, the relatively constant and less interesting tendencies that constrain the creative project of personal development are outweighed by the massive transformative process that occurs between the "stirring" or "germination" of the initial conditions and the full-blown creative achievement. The given in the *xing* of persons is the generalizable initial conditions of family relations as their context, and their prosocial propensity for growth, cultivation and refinement. *Xing*, then, denotes these initial conditions and the human capacity to interact with the social, natural, and cultural environments to make life meaningful. Since *xing* is realized *in situ*, it is a dynamic process conditioned by each person's particular context. Stated more explicitly, the human *xing* is a creative process that can only be understood situationally as the outcome of specific interdependent transactions and relationships. *Xing* at once refers to the continuing existence of particular persons themselves, and also to that in each person that continues the life and culture of other persons.

The idea of an invariant human nature leaves no room for the kind of creative social intelligence and moral imagination that we are able to find in a close reading of the canonical Confucian texts. It is better to think of *xing* as spontaneous process that is at once persistent and at the same time, continually emerging through changing patterns of growth and extension. Such an understanding interprets *xing* from a particularist and historicist perspective, locating *renxing* 人性 within the generic features of a process or event cosmology.

With respect to the question of whether human "beings" are born with some universal moral faculty that makes them good, or instead, that "human becomings" become morally good as the product of their personal cultivation, I have joined with Li Zehou in resisting the assumption that the former innatist, psychological position should be ascribed to Mencius, and the latter appeal to personal cultivation and refinement to Xunzi. Instead I would interpret both Mencius and Xunzi as advocating for the position that becoming morally competent is hard work. Having said this, Xunzi parses the notion of native human tendencies (*xing* 性) in an idiosyncratic way that is decidedly different from Confucius and Mencius who have come before him.

Xunzi insists that our native human tendencies are *e* 惡. Indeed, in classical Confucian philosophy, the immediate association *e* has is his doctrine that our native human tendencies are rude and ugly, and thus produce conflict. It is in this context that the main English language translations (Burton Watson, John Knoblock) have translated *e* as "evil," with the more recent translation by Eric Hutton translating it as "bad." Although Xunzi is making a distinction between what we are born with and what is deliberately acquired, we must resist translating Xunzi's naturalism into a metaphysical claim that would align Xunzi with the dualistic realism of a Plato or an Aristotle in which some self-same and immutable "form" or *eidos* that is "inherent in persons" separates human beings from their world.

Kurtis Hagen has challenged the suggested interpretation that human beings are incorrigibly bad in some detail, settling on "crude" as his translation as middle ground between "ugly" and "detestable," a condition that leads to undesirable consequences. "The word 'crude' describes a state of something prior to refinement, thus suggesting the possibility of improvement." Hagen endorses contemporary Japanese commentators such as Masayuki Sato who say "when Xunzi characterizes human instinct by the term *e* 惡, he did not mean evil as an intrinsic attribute of human nature, rather as a cause of social disorder." Again, Kodama Rokurō rejecting the "human nature is evil theory" insists that it means "human nature is plain or crude."[①]

For Xunzi, our native human tendencies (*xing* 性) stand in contrast to conscious artifice or contrivance (*wei* 偽): mechanisms such as ritual practices (*li* 禮) and "proper naming" (*zhengming* 正名) of our world allow for a rigorous regimen that can lead us to the highest standards of refinement. In this sense, although Xunzi

---

[①] Kurtis Hagen. *The Philosophy of Xunzi: A Reconstruction*. La Salle, IL: Open Court, 2007, pp. 122-123.

has a low estimate of human beginnings, he is a stern optimist when it comes to possibilities available to humankind through assiduous application.

*虛 *xu.* "Emptiness."

Xu is usually translated as "emptiness." The character is the original form of 墟 meaning "large hill or mountain." In the *Shuowen* lexicon, it states that the legendary Kunlun that commentators describe as the ultimate mountain is called "Kunlunxu" (*Kunlunxu* 崑崙虛). The meaning of "emptiness" seems to come from its contrasting relationship as the wastelands that are a necessary complement to the mountain. Similarly, it means the ruins of a walled city, a place without people. It is often found in the correlative binomials of *yingxu* 盈虛 and *shixu* 實虛 both of which mean "fullness and emptiness," where one term is defined in its relationship with the other.

This kind of "emptiness" then, should not be confused with nonbeing or the negative, dark, formless void that we might associate with the cosmogonic myths in the overcoming of chaos: that is, disorder as a yawning abyss. Rather *xu* is a positive notion: the inchoate and indeterminate as it resides *within* the determinate that makes the process of growth and self-renewal possible. Optimal harmony is achieved in Chinese cosmology not by overcoming the indeterminate, but by making the most of its generosity as a resource for growth and novelty. It is the kind of "informed" emptiness that makes functional the cup or the house or the hub or the orifice.

For example, the "emptiness" of the heartmind is its receptivity and accommodation, and its propensity for giving birth and growth. As room to entertain a boundless amount of experience, the heartmind is "emptiness-becoming-full." It is an openness to engage each new experience on its own terms without prejudice, an empty mirror ready to shed light on the next image.

*學 xue. "Teaching and learning."

The commonplace is that personal cultivation is the root (*ben* 本) of the Confucian philosophy of education (*xue* 學). But any root that has not been properly set and that is lacking a fertile context will soon wither and die. To continue this important metaphor, Confucian education must be understood as a process that is "radically" embedded in and grows within the roles and relations that constitute us as persons in the fertile context of our families and communities. The notion of "root" is an apposite metaphor for describing the coterminous and mutually entailing process of personal, familial, political, and cosmic growth. That is, within the overwhelmingly agrarian world of ancient China, growth is perceived as a holistic process in which root and tree are dependent upon what is ultimately a cosmic context for their nurturance, and in an analogous way, in which persons, families, polity, and cosmos either grow together, or not at all. The close link between education and Confucian morality lies in the fact that they are both defined in terms of setting the root and subsequent growth in our roles and relations. Education so conceived is not instrumental as a means to some desired end, but is a process that is an end in itself. We get educated to live intelligent lives, and become moral to act morally.

To be clear on this point, education far from being understood as some cognitive exercise of discrete individuals exclusive of their immediate relations, is in fact achieved and expressed only through virtuosity in those same roles and relationships that we live as family members, and ultimately as denizens of the world. Education is the situated reception, embodiment, and deliberate reauthorization of the living culture as it has been inherited by the present generation that then has the responsibility of transmitting it not only intact but with dividends to the next generation and to the subsequent generations that succeed it.

Secondly, these themes of a rooted situatedness, vital relationality, and concomitant growth carry over to define the correlative, "*yinyang*" nature of teaching and learning as two mutually-implicated and non-analytic ways of describing the same holistic process of learning. Education is holistic learning from which the erstwhile categories of "teaching" and "learning" are simply abstractions. At the end of the day, the role of teacher provides one the opportunity to be the most advanced among the learners. The character *xue* 學 as found on the oracle bones is written as [graph] and is explained quite literally as a joining of hands to construct the physical academy in which teaching and learning takes place.[①]

Thus the term *xue* 學 originally meant "the situation of teaching and learning," and then later becomes bifurcated graphically (but still close phonetically) as "teaching" (*xiao/jiao* 斅/教) and "learning" (*xue* 學). In fact, in the fascicle *On Teaching and Learning* in the *Record of Rites* (*Liji Xueji* 《禮記・學記》), it cites the "Yueming" of the *Shangshu* 《尚書・說命》that states 斅學半 "teaching and learning are but two halves of a whole." But in citing this text, the *On Teaching and Learning* fascicle unlike the original *Shangshu* passage that distinguishes between "teaching" (*xiao* 斅) and "learning" (*xue* 學) simply repeats the character *xue* 學 to mean both teaching and learning 學學半. The Qing dynasty scholar, Duan Yucai 段玉裁, and other commentators on the ancient lexicon *Shuowen* entry for *xue* add their voices to the claim that teaching and learning were originally expressed with the same character.

Although the graph *xue* 學 originally means both "teaching and learning," the evolution of this character in which "learning" (*xue* 學) is distinguished from "teaching" (*xiao* 斅 and *jiao* 教) is

---

① Kwan, "Database," 京津 4836.

ancient, and is captured in the emergence of the graph for "teaching" found on both the oracle bones 🈚 and on the bronzes 🈚 in a form that includes the "young person" (*zi* 子) signific as both the locus of and the most critical time in the human life for such teaching and learning.①

Teaching and learning are further inseparable when we think of early Confucian education under the categories of capacity, opportunity, and effort. When in *Analects* 17.2, Confucius claims that 性相近也習相遠也 "human beings are similar in their natural propensities, but vary greatly by virtue of their habits," he is emphasizing the transformative possibility of education. By "similar" (*xiangjin* 相近), he means that human beings are alike not in having some fixed, essential nature, but in having the capacity for taking the initiative and applying themselves to the project of personal cultivation. The wide-ranging variance that occurs among people by virtue of habits is a function of the complexity of their similar, unbounded natures. In this sense, productive habits (*xi* 習) are the expression and realization of the natural propensities (*xing* 性) for growth, not something that stands in contrast to it.

It is because *xue* means both "teaching" and "learning" that Confucius, ever modest, unabashedly prides himself on his personal eagerness to learn (*haoxue* 好學)② and on his love of teaching.③ At the same time he is inclined to self-deprecation when it comes to his own native capacities.④ In his expectations of students, he

---

① Kwan, "Database" 甲骨文合集 CHANT 3233 and 西周早期 CHANT 4330 respectively. On the later Warring States bamboo strips the character for "teaching" (*jiao* 教) is also written with the "speaking" (*yan* 言) radical: 🈚 as well as with the "young person" (*zi* 子) signific: 🈚. Kwan, "Database," 上博竹書一緇依 10 and 郭店簡老子甲 12.
② *Analects* 5.28, 7.3, 7.19, 7.34.
③ *Analects* 7.2.
④ *Analects* 5.9, 7.1, 7.20.

is clear that he has an unwavering commitment to provide able students with opportunity regardless of their means,[1] but also that motivation and effort stand as his highest criteria.[2] Confucius admires his favorite protégé, Yan Hui, who in his education is able to overcome the obstacle of abject poverty.[3] The Master describes Yan Hui in the same terms as himself in being singularly motivated in his commitment to learning (*haoxue* 好學),[4] but also ascribes to him a capacity for learning that goes far beyond Confucius's own ability.[5] At the end of the day, in the relationship between Confucius and Yan Hui, it is not entirely clear who is teacher and who is student, and who is learning from whom.[6]

Again, we might appeal to the etymology of the English word "education" to illuminate the interdependent and inseparable nature of teaching and learning. The word "education" has two principal Latin roots: *educare* and *educere*. The first of these, *educare*, means "cultivating, rearing, bringing up, training, molding" and resonates with the sense of education as logically and rationally ordered guidance in which the teacher provides students with the basic vocabulary, the history of, and the presuppositions defining of a particular discipline, and the students in turn make this foundational knowledge their own. This kind of education is more rote memory than flair, and is more hard work than imagination, but it is also a critical phase in the educational process. Indeed, *educare* instills the discipline and rigor necessary for sustained personal growth, and is essential for the transmission of hard won knowledge.

Educere, by way of contrast, means "evoking, leading forth,

---

[1] *Analects* 7.7.
[2] *Analects* 7.8, 8.12, 8.17, 14.24.
[3] *Analects* 6.11, 11.19.
[4] *Analects* 6.3, 9.20, 11.7.
[5] *Analects* 5.9.
[6] *Analects* 2.9, 6.11, 9.21.

drawing out, quite literally, educing." Education so construed is fundamentally aesthetic and creative, allowing for the spontaneous emergence of novelty that is enriching for both teacher and student. *Educere* is a transactional process that is always particular and specific as an opportunity for growth in both *this* able teacher and *that* able student. It is decidedly prospective in the sense that it is a process of seeking after and exploring issues that have heretofore been unknown by both. Indeed, in this phase of education, the distinction between student and teacher is blurred and sometimes reversed as both participants press on and break through the boundaries of existing knowledge through the exercise of their insight and imagination. Yan Hui provides us with a wonderful image of just such a relationship with his teacher Confucius when in *Analects* 9.11 he describes how he is being educed by the Master to forge his path forward:

> 顏淵喟然歎曰：「仰之彌高，鑽之彌堅；瞻之在前，忽焉在後。夫子循循然善誘人，博我以文，約我以禮。欲罷不能，既竭吾才，如有所立卓爾。雖欲從之，末由也已。」
>
> Yan Hui, with a deep sigh, said, "The more I look up at it, the higher it soars; the more I penetrate into it, the harder it becomes. I am looking at it in front of me, and suddenly it is behind me. The Master is good at drawing me forward a step at a time; he broadens me with culture and disciplines my behavior through the observance of ritual propriety. Even if I wanted to quit, I could not. And when I have exhausted my abilities, it is though something rises up right in front of me, and even though I want to follow it, there is no road to take."

The *Shuowen* lexicon associates the character "learning" (*xue* 學) paronomastically—that is, by phonetic and semantic association—with *jue* 覺: a cultivated and focused awareness. The *Shuowen* also defines *xue* 學 as *wu* 悟: "awakening, realizing." At the time of Confucius, this "becoming aware" is focused on the communal responsibilities of scholars engaged in family and community service as they pursue the goal of contributing to the cultural tradition and becoming distinguished as persons. We might say that the goal is more one of acquiring a practical, moral wisdom than simply of learning *per se*. Learning, in the *xue* sense, involves inheriting, reauthorizing, and transmitting one's cultural legacy through the many familial and communal discourses available that locate a person in a time and place—language, roles and relationships, patterns of ritual propriety and deference, the playing of music, body, food, and so on. Again, the commentary of Duan Yucai on this *Shuowen* definition elaborates on a passage from *On Teaching and Learning* 15 to underscore the assumption that *xue* is not exclusively either teaching or learning, but is an inclusive activity that includes both:

學記曰：學然後知不足，知不足然後能自反也。按知不足所謂覺悟也。記又曰：教然後知困，知困然後能自強也。故曰教學相長也。
On Teaching and Learning says that it is only in learning that we realize our inadequacies, and it is only in doing so that we are able to become self-critical. This is why realizing our inadequacies is called "becoming aware" (*jue* 覺) and "awakening" (*wu* 悟). The text continues in stating that it is only in teaching that we realize our limitations, and it is only in so doing that we are able to improve ourselves. Thus, it is said that teaching and learning complement each other.

We must understand that Confucius as he is portrayed in the *Analects* and the other Confucian classics takes *xue* 學 to be integral to growth in human relationships, and thus to be moral education. That is, *xue* does not mean just "learning", but more importantly, "learning as a process of personal cultivation and growth in our relations." We can say that, simply put, morality in Confucian role ethics is to behave in a way that conduces to growth in relations, while immorality is to act otherwise.

There is another cosmological warrant for reading the character *xue* 學 as the situated process of "teaching and learning." This justification derives from an appreciation of certain presuppositions sedimented into the classical Chinese language itself. That is, in this process cosmology that will not separate our vital relationality from our uniqueness as persons, the language that provides an account of the human experience reflects a commitment to the primacy of relationships and relationally-constituted situations such as "teaching and learning" rather than the actions of specific agents in either their teaching or their learning. Focus-field agency is irreducibly transactional rather than unilateral.

The term *xin* 信, for example means both "credibility" and "trust"—that is, a fiduciary, non-coercive situation that characterizes the collaborative relationship between benefactor and beneficiary. The character *shou* 受 is initially "the situation of giving and getting," and then is only later discriminated graphically (but not phonetically) to include agency as either "giving" (*shou* 授) or "getting" (*shou* 受). *Ming* 明 means "brilliance" transactionally as both the brilliance of something ("the bright moon" 明月) and the penetrating perspicacity of the person who perceives things clearly ("the perspicacious ruler" 明君). Consider *jian/xian* 見 as both *jian* "seeing" and *xian* "manifesting to be seen," and *mai* 買 as *maimai* 買賣, "the situation of buying and selling." The language is replete with just such examples.

Again the value of "family reverence" (*xiao* 孝) that serves this tradition as its governing moral imperative sets the ultimate goal of Confucian education. As it states in the *Classic of Family Reverence* 1: 子曰："夫孝，德之本也，教之所由生也。" "It is familial reverence (*xiao* 孝)," said the Master, "that is the root of excellence (*de* 德), and whence education (*jiao* 教) itself is born." The close link between education and the promotion of social order arises from the fact that the end of education is nothing less than the transformative growth of the people through the intergenerational transmission and embodiment of the living culture. Indeed, education is the internalization of culture that enables the people to make their ordinary lives extraordinary, and that ideally, enables the people to become self-ordering (*Analects* 2.3).

*易   *yi*. "Changing, exchanging, ease."

We might begin from the observation that our conventional translation of *Yijing* 易經 as the "*Book of Changes*" is ambiguous to the extent that there are many different modalities of "change" referenced in this early process cosmology. Indeed, there is a rather extensive vocabulary of terms that can and often have been translated as "change:" "transforming" (*hua* 化), "being in flux"(*bian* 變), "removing" (*qian* 遷), "replacing" (*geng* 更), "taking away" (*ti* 替), "transferring, altering" (*yi* 移), "reforming" (*gai* 改), "exchanging" (*huan* 換), "peeling away" (*ge* 革), "increasing, adding, profiting" (*yi* 益), and many more.

The early commentaries parse the specifically *yi* 易 modality of change paronomastically as a simplified version of the character *yi* 益 "increasing, adding, profiting," a kind of change that is consistent with the declared and self-conscious claim of the text to provide its sagely counsel in making the most of the human experience. The contemporary commentator Guo Moruo 郭沫若 argues that the term *yi* 易 in fact should be read as the ancient abbreviated form of the graph *ci* 賜 meaning "gifting," "transacting," "exchanging." And given that the transactional "exchanging" modality of "change" is the ultimate source of value and increased meaning in a cosmology that gives primacy to vital relationality, Guo's suggestion is compelling.① On the other hand, given the holistic nature of this *Yijing* cosmology, perhaps it is best to understand *yi* 易 as including the broadest spectrum of these different modalities of change, and this being the case, embracing the ambiguity that comes with the *Book of Changes* as an acknowledgment that change must be parsed in different ways in different cosmic contexts.

*— *yi*. "One, uniqueness, continuity."

Throughout the philosophical texts, we have frequent reference to the "oneness" of things, or becoming "one" with things, often stated as a kind of cultivated achievement. But "one" is an ambiguous term. There is the language of "uni-" such as "universe," "universal," "unity," "univocal," and so on that would subsume things under a privileged, single-ordered world: "We are all children of the one true God." This sense of "one" has little relevance for the Confucian processual cosmology. We must distinguish the Confucian cosmological understanding of "one" from the "One-behind-the-many" ontological and idealist sense of "one" familiar in metaphysical thinking, entailing as it does a strict identity among particulars: "We all have an immortal soul" or "We humans are by definition all rational creatures." Without the ontological disparity that follows from the distinction between the real and the less so, the essential and the accidental, there can be no categories or concepts or natural kinds defined by appeal to some essential, self-same identical characteristic.

While this ontological sense of "one" that would guarantee an exclusive objectivity and certainty has little relevance, there

---

① See the entry for 易 in Kwan, "Database."

is another sense of "one" that does have immediate application to Confucian process cosmology. Beginning from the radical particularism assumed in this cosmology, there is "one" in the sense of the uniqueness of each thing-event, "*one*-of-a-kind" rather than "one-of-a-*kind*." And there is "one" in the sense of the transactional continuity that obtains among these unique particulars all imbricated within an emergent cosmic ecology.

In the cosmological assumptions that emerge from processual thinking, all particular things and their unique qualities have an equal claim on reality. This notion of an ontological parity of finitude that gives all things an equal claim on being real, might alternatively be termed "a realistic pluralism." This pluralism is an affirmation of the reality of any thing as it is constituted by the convergence of its constitutive relations, whether it be each and every thing, each and every kind of thing, or the unsummed totality of things. The assumption that there is an ontological parity among things rules out Aristotle's fundamental ontological question: "What is the 'substance' or 'being' of something?" and the corollary notion of natural kinds that follows from all members of a set having a common essence. Confucius's untidy world will not yield up an Aristotelian classificatory system or the logic that will demonstrate its truth.

There is still another sense of "one" that has immediate relevance to process thinking. There is the feeling of resonance among people or things that makes of them one and two at the same time. This inseparability of one and many is captured most immediately in the notion of consummate persons or conduct (*ren* 仁). The cultivation of such relations reflects the possibility of becoming consummatorily one with others in an interdependent, fiduciary community. It is through the pursuit of such meaningful relations that cosmic significance can be extended within family and community to the extent of giving humankind the status of being co-creators with the world in which they live.

The *Book of Changes* captures the two sides of "oneness" in the expression 一陰一陽之謂道 "It is the succession and alternation of *yin* and *yang* that is called *dao*." Each thing is at once a unique existent, and a manifold of dynamic relations continuous with its context. I am uniquely who I am, and at the same time I am constituted by the dynamic field of selves in which I am embedded as a father, a teacher, a citizen, and a human being. The conjunctive *yang* side of "one" as a continuous line is the achieved harmony in my relationships; the disjunctive *yin* side of "one" as a broken line is my discontinuous uniqueness and my openness to change. The conjunctive *yang* side is my persistent identity (*tong* 通); the disjunctive *yin* side is the novelty and spontaneity made possible by the indeterminacy in these same relations (*bian* 變). Both sides of "one"—the continuity and the uniqueness, the persistence and the change—are present in the appreciative religious sensibility of "standing and transforming together with things" (*wuhua* 物化). I find satisfaction in the distinctive uniqueness I can achieve as a particular person that gives me a sense of felt worth and belonging, and am humbled and challenged by the boundless possibilities that continually emerge in the unfolding of the world around me.

By virtue of a relational virtuosity achieved in a sustained regimen of self-cultivation, persons can become exemplary for their community. Again, such distinction makes such persons "one" in the sense of becoming distinguished, outstanding beacons to which other members of the community defer and from whom they can find their bearings. At the same time, such exemplary persons achieve resolution, with their productive transactions with other members of the community making them a meaningful, holographic focus of the larger social matrix. The exemplary grandmother has the flourishing family clearly implicated in her own person.

Such a world of unique particulars is a *kosmoi* rather than a *kosmos* in the sense that construals of order are many, and the totality is not dominated by any one order among the many. There is no "God" in this pluriverse. Rather, order is the emergent harmony achieved in the contingent relationships that obtain among "the myriad things and events" (*wanwu* 萬物 or *wanyou* 萬有). Of course, such uniqueness does not preclude abstraction and generalization. In this worldview, there are only more or less apposite analogies among more or less similar things and events that allow us to associate them in general groupings, or *lei* 類. Claiming "sameness" (*tong* 同) or "inclusion" (*tonglei* 同類) is normative in that it presumes the possibility of productive relations. Inclusion in such a group is established by virtue of analogous and appropriate conduct rather than through some assumed essential identity. For example, by appeal to the functional similarities that obtain among unique persons, we have a warrant to be included in *renlei* 人類: a human grouping. The normativity arises when we all come to acknowledge and respect this special grouping as human beings, and embrace the values that enable a shared flourishing. On the other hand, for good and for bad, someone who behaves as a beast can make no claim on membership in this group on the basis of some erstwhile ontological appeal to a shared humanity.

*義 *yi*. "Optimal appropriateness, meaning."

Yi occurs on the oracle bones as 羍 and on the bronzes as ▨. Etymologically the graph is a stylized picture of a sheep (*yang* 羊) in combination with the first-person pronoun for "I, we, me, us," (*wo* 我).[1] The sheep signific, carrying an association with sacrifice, is usually understood to suggest propitiousness. It occurs in characters

---

[1] Kwan, "Multi-functional Database," 甲骨文合集 CHANT 2456 and 西周中期 CHANT 250.

such as "efficacy" (*shan* 善), "beautiful" (*mei* 美), "auspicious" (*xiang* 祥), "sacrifice" (*xi* 犧), and so on. Revealing here is that in a tradition in which person is irreducibly social, the distinction between the singular "I" and the plural "we" is not marked. Perhaps even more telling, the distinction between the more independent, nominative "I" and the socially embedded accusative "me" or the nominative "we" and the socially embedded accusative "us" is not indicated in the language.

Much has been made of "I, we, me, us," (*wo* 我) being an integral element in the character *yi* 義. Dong Zhongshu 董仲舒 in his *Luxuriant Dew of the Spring and Autumn* 春秋繁露 29 has an extended discussion on the relationship between "consummate conduct" (*ren* 仁) and "optimal appropriateness" (yi 義), playing on the paronomastic (phonetic and semantic) associations between "consummate person" (*ren* 仁) and "other people" (*ren* 人), and between "optimal appropriateness" (*yi* 義) and "me" (*wo* 我):"

> 仁之於人，義之與我者，不可不察也。眾人不察，乃反以仁自裕，而以義設人。……仁之法在愛人，不在愛我。義之法在正我，不在正人。我不自正，雖能正人，弗予為義。
>
> The relationship of consummate conduct (*ren* 仁) to other people (*ren* 人) and optimal appropriateness (*yi* 義) to oneself (*wo* 我) must be examined carefully. Most people do not do this, but instead appeal to *ren* 仁 in being self-indulgent and to *yi* 義 in demanding a certain conduct from others... The method of becoming consummate in one's person lies in loving others, not in loving oneself. And the method of being optimally appropriate lies in doing what is proper oneself, not in demanding what is proper from others. If one does not act properly oneself, even if one is able to get what is proper from others, this cannot be called doing what is appropriate (*yi* 義).

Dong Zhongshu goes on to say that "appropriateness" (*yi* 義) is a key condition of one's own personal identity and uniqueness. Hence, conduct that expresses one's sense of appropriateness is self-realizing (*zide* 自得) while conduct that does not disclose it is self-abnegating (*zishi* 自失).

But our most distinguished scholars of the classical language warn against making too much of the contemporary meanings of the elements that constitute this character. The renowned Qing dynasty philologist Duan Yucai 段玉裁 points out that the character for the first person pronoun *wo* 我 as attested in the oracle bones and bronzes depicts a dagger-axe (*ge* 戈) ⿱: a long-handled weapon with serrated, saw-like teeth.① At some point for phonological reasons, it came to be used as a loan character for its homophone, the first-person pronoun, *wo* 我. Again, the meaning of the sheep has to do with the central importance periodic sacrifices had in galvanizing the social, political, and religious order within the aristocratic culture of the pre-Qin period. When it is remembered that sheep and other animals were periodically sacrificed at large communal gatherings, we may gloss *yi* 義 as the solemn, dignified attitude assumed in sacrifice, and the proper place and stance taken by the participants according to their status when preparing the sheep for the ritual slaughter. The propriety of the participants and their deferential attitude not only makes them sacred representatives of the community in their relation to their gods and ancestors, but also purifies and consecrates the sacrificial animal as well.

This association of *wo* 我 and *yi* 義 with sacrifice is consistent with their cognate character *xi* 犧 "sacrificing, sacrificial animal" that in its original, abbreviated form on the oracle bones and bronzes was written as *xi* 羲. Again, *yi* is glossed in the *Shuowen* lexicon as "dignity, majesty" (*weiyi* 威儀), where the connotation of assuming a proper demeanor can be attested by this cognate character 儀—"an

---

① See Kwan, "Database," 春秋 CHANT 102.

yi person"—meaning specifically a person with dignity, decorum, courtesy, and graciousness.①

There is a correlation between *ren* 仁 and the quality of deferential conduct allowing for "two persons becoming one" that associates *ren* with civility and a pliant and gentle attitude. Similarly, there is a correlation between *yi* 義 as "the solemn and dignified demeanor of persons using a dagger-axe to prepare a sacrifice" with a kind of firmness and resolve. This contrast is remarked upon explicitly in the recently recovered *Five Modes of Virtuosic Conduct* (*Wuxingpian* 五行篇) 22-23:

簡，義之方也。匿，仁之方也。強，義之方。柔，仁之方也。

"Seeing the big picture" is an expression of appropriateness (*yi* 義); "making allowances," of being consummate (*ren* 仁). Being firm is an expression of appropriateness; being lenient of being consummate.

Yi has conventionally been translated into English as "righteousness" and "meaning," and less commonly as "rightness" and "morality." "Righteousness" was the choice of the missionary sinologist James Legge who based his Confucian vocabulary on the theology of Bishop Joseph Butler.② The decidedly biblical associations that attend the word "righteousness" as obedience to the will of God introduces an independent, objective, and divinely-sanctioned standard of what is right or "moral" into the equation that has little relevance for *yi*. While a sense of justice and fairness requires that one be resolved and stand firm, *yi* is still the outcome of a negotiation between self and the specific context that requires broadmindedness, flexibility, and accommodation, dispositions

---

① See the discussion under 義 in Kwan, "Database."
② See the extended footnote to Legge in the *ren* 仁 entry.

that are often associated with Confucius himself.[①] Both resolve and accommodation are integral to a cultivated disposition to always seek what is ultimately appropriate in the flux and flow of circumstances.

In looking for a tentative translation for *yi*, the contextually inclusive "appropriate" or "fitting" are perhaps the closest English equivalents. Such a translation is reinforced by the frequent paronomastic association of *yi* 義 with its near homophone *yi* 宜 that like *yi* 義 has a primary religious meaning in its reference to "sacrificing to the deity of the soil," and derivatively, to adjust to what is "right, proper, fitting." "Appropriate" as a translation for *yi* should be understood not only with its aesthetic and ethical connotations, but also with this sacred and religious import in mind. Optimally appropriate relations are not only meaningful—they are the source of the intense sense of belonging we associate with religious communion. *Yi* is an achieved sense of appropriateness that enables one to act in a proper and fitting manner, given the specifics of any particular situation. By extension, since appropriateness is the ultimate source of meaningful relations, it should not be surprising that *yi* also means "meaning" as it is expressed and comes to reside in one's personal relations and conduct. In fact, *Focusing the Familiar* 20 defines *yi* paronomastically in precisely these terms:

義者宜也，尊賢為大。

Appropriateness (*yi* 義) means doing what is fitting (*yi* 宜) wherein esteeming those who are truly worthy of it is most important.

Yi has an intimate relationship with *li* 禮 as the aspiration for propriety in ritualized roles and relations. Over time, *yi* becomes the aggregating significance invested by a living tradition in

---

[①] See *Analects* 14.32 and 9.4, for example.

the observances of propriety expressed through those roles and institutions that come to define its persistent cultural identity. *Yi* is the repository of cultural authority that can be appropriated by persons as they become enculturated in the performance of these roles and rituals. It is this invested significance persons draw from the social form that makes a salute, a handshake, and a marriage ceremony meaningful, and it is the sense of personally expressing appropriateness through the performance of these ritualized activities that makes their observance profoundly particular.

Yi is the fittingness in relations that over time produces the fiduciary community and the feelings of credibility and mutual trust that emerge to give persons a real sense of belonging in that community. Thus, Confucius in *Analects* 1.13 says:

信近於義，言可復也。

When making good on your word (*xin* 信) is done in tandem with optimal appropriateness in your conduct (*yi* 義), your words will bear repeating.

In this passage we find in *yi* that necessary combination of accommodation and resolve. The vocabulary of *shu* 恕 and *zhong* 忠—putting oneself in the other's place and then doing one's utmost—resonates immediately with *yi* 義 as a third term in this Confucian moral vocabulary. *Yi* is "achieving an optimal appropriateness in one's relations"—that is, the satisfaction of moral uncertainty through an acquired sense of what is most fitting in the situation. *Shu* can be thought of as rehearsing the possibilities for what would be most appropriate in a relationship, where the emphasis is on careful deliberation in determining what the best course of action might be. *Shu* entails "other-directed" deference in the sense that a person's actions are deferred until there is a full consideration of the needs of others through a process of dramatic rehearsal. And *zhong* then is persons giving their utmost effort to this process of moral inquiry itself and to the initiation and satisfaction of their subsequent actions.

Yi certainly requires this strong sense of deference to others, but it is also an expression of a person's own best judgment on how to dispose themselves in their relation to others in order to accomplish the deliberate action. The emphasis is on following one's own sense of what is right in being responsive to the concerns of others. It is other-directed but also requires this "self-including" sense of how to interact with others most productively. Both the searching *shu* and the consequent *yi* are at play in situations that require ethical consideration.

Yi as an "optimizing appropriateness" locates the present action both synchronically and diachronically. Synchronically *yi* action attempts to extend the context as broadly as possible, taking under consideration the sometimes competing yet still legitimate interests of all concerned, and attending to the full range of possibilities involved. Diachronically *yi* action locates the immediate circumstances within the continuities it has with both past and future activity, making a comprehensive consideration of the continuing present the best way to make full use of those resources inherited out of past experience and to identify the most productive way of anticipating what is yet to come.

Yi carries with equal weight the sense of "appropriateness" and "meaningfulness." This combination of meanings underscores the place of correlative modalities of thinking in this tradition by suggesting that meaningfulness is the consequence of efficacious dispositioning that juxtaposes things in a mutually enhancing and fruitful manner. The optimally appropriate relationship between teacher and student is the most meaningful relationship.

There are many important dimensions of the human experience that require impartiality, transparency, and more objective regulative ideals, and the Confucian tradition has always been cognizant of this need. Beginning with the distinction between "optimal appropriateness" (*yi* 義) and "personal advantage" (*li* 利) that we find as early as the *Analects* and the *Mencius*, Confucianism has struggled with the seemingly necessary relationship between ethical conduct and a sense of impartiality.① But rather than invoking some transcendental and thus reductive moral standard or some faculty of impersonal reason as a strategy for claiming such impartiality—an appeal that is always hobbled by the contingencies of circumstances—the Confucian tradition develops its holistic notion of impartiality that remains true to the family metaphor. That is, even in the distinction made between subjective and objective perspectives, impartiality is served practically by extending one's range of concern from "the master's-eye view" (*zhuguan* 主觀) that might be limited by some self-serving personal advantage (*li* 利) to "the guest's-eye view" (*keguan* 客觀) that seeks what is most appropriate for all concerned (*yi* 義). *Yi* in the master-and-guest relationship becomes meaningful hospitality and mutual fidelity. The Confucian formula of "putting oneself in the other's place" (*shu* 恕) and then "doing one's best" (*zhong* 忠) is another variation on this deferential attempt to keep one's range of concerns open in determining what is the most moral course of action. The point is that there are resources indigenous to the tradition on which to build more robust safeguards that can rein in the possible excesses of partiality.

For Confucius, the *li* as ritual propriety are meaning-invested and meaning-disclosing actions that are ultimately derived from the personal sense and expression of appropriateness (*yi* 義). It is this grounding in personal appropriateness that makes *li* irreducibly participatory and makes the achievement of social harmony a "bottom-

---

① See for example *Analects* 4.16, 14.12, 14.13, 16.10, and 19.1, and *Mencius* 1A1, 2A2, 7A33, 7A34, 7B31.

up" communal responsibility. Confucius in *Analects* 4.10 says explicitly that *yi* does not reduce to right and wrong or some generic principle:

子曰:"君子之於天下也,無適也,無莫也,義之與比。"
The Master said, "Exemplary persons (*junzi* 君子) in making their way in the world are neither bent on nor against anything; rather, they go with what is most appropriate (*yi* 義)."

Xunzi does understand the sense of *yi* as a distinctively human capacity that enables the human being to make the social and political discriminations that are fundamental to communal living:

水火有氣而無生,草木有生而無知,禽獸有知而無義,人有氣、有生、有知,亦且有義,故最為天下貴也……故序四時,裁萬物,兼利天下,無它故焉,得之分義也。
Fire and water have *qi* 氣, but no life, the grasses and trees have life but no awareness, birds and animals have awareness, but no sense of moral principle. Human beings then have *qi*, life, awareness and also a sense of moral principle, and are thus the noblest creatures in the world... The fact that they accord with the four seasons, exercise control over everything, and bring benefit to all things in the world is for no other reason than they have the capacity to discriminate and a sense of moral principle.

What is distinctively human is the capacity to make distinctions on the basis of what in Xunzi seems to mean generic moral principle (*yi* 義) more than a situational appropriateness. It is this capacity that makes human community possible and that provides it with its tensile strength. It both elevates human beings over all other creatures in the world and enables them to exercise their benign influence in benefitting all things. The question that arises is whether this description of human beings is consistent with Xunzi's assessment of the native human propensities (*xing* 性) that seem to be lacking in any inherent moral compass.

With respect to how *yi* is used throughout the text, Xunzi has departed from the Confucian understanding to an extent that has escaped the notice of few commentators. Derk Bodde, for example, with respect to Xunzi's understanding of *yi*, reports that

> ... in conjunction with the rules of proper conduct (*li*) ... it [*yi*] seems to lose its sense of "righteousness" as practiced by the individual, and to become more general and impersonal, a thing possessed by society as a whole.①

In fact, Xunzi explicitly assimilates *yi* to *li* to form a binomial expression *liyi* 禮儀 in some 85 instances, more than one third of the occurrences of *li* in the text, with the effect of subordinating *yi* to *li* and thus, in important degree, externalizing *li* as public norms. That there is this tendency for *yi* to be externalized and made generic at the expense of its specific reference to individual instances of appropriateness is reflected in the rendering of *yi* in the current *Xunzi* English translations as "justice," "just principles," "moral law," "moral principles," and "standards of righteousness."②

---

① Fung Yu-lan. *A History of Chinese Philosophy*. trans. D. Bodde. Princeton: Princeton University Press, 1952, Vol. 1, p. 287 footnote.
② See H. Dubs. *The Works of Hsüntzu*. London: Probsthain, 1928; T.T. Ch'ü. *Law and Society in Traditional China*. Paris and The Hague: Mouton & Co., 1961; Joseph Needham. *Science and Civilisation in China*. Cambridge: Cambridge University Press, Vol. 2, 1956; B. Watson (trans.), *Hsün Tzu: Basic Writings*, New York: Columbia University Press, 1963; Noah Fehl, Li. *Rites and Propriety in Literature and Life*. Hong Kong: Chinese University Press, 1971; J. Knoblock. *Xunzi: A Translation and Study of the Complete Works*. Stanford: Stanford University Press, Vol. 1-3, 1988, 1990, 1994; Eric Hutton. *Readings in Classical Chinese Philosophy*, 2nd edition. ed. P.J. Ivanhoe and Bryan Van Norden. Indianapolis: Hackett Publishing Company, 2005.

The ramifications for *li* that are introduced by these altered implications of *yi* are profound. The diminished importance of personal participation in the actual production of social harmony transforms *li* into a largely external, closed, and "top-down" set of prescriptions that dictates a regulatory order for society. Using Xunzi's own metaphors, the *li* are a plumbline, a pair of scales, a compass and set square, all of which can be applied to people to bring them to rule. Thus it is that warped wood can only be straightened by being steamed and bent into shape in a pressframe; blunt metal can only be sharpened by being whetted on a grindstone. And since the natural propensities of human beings are base, they can only be made proper through their teachers and set norms and can only be properly ordered through ritual practices and moral principles.

*陰陽　***yinyang.*** "*Yin* and *yang.*" See also 五行 ***wuxing.*** "Five modes of virtuosic conduct, the five phases," 氣 ***qi.*** "Vital energy, *qi,*" and 體用 ***tiyong.*** "Reforming and functioning, *transform*-ing."

Yin and *yang* are terms used to express a contrastive tension that obtains in the relation between two or more things, a relationship between polarities like magnetic or electrical fields that are defined in terms of the oppositional and complementary relations they have with each other, keeping them apart while also enabling them to bond. Changes within one polarity immediately stimulates change in the other. Since in Confucian cosmology, "things" as events are not separate in any final sense, the line between them is a shared horizon rather than a definition. *Yang* is attested on the oracle bones 昜, but only as a place name. In the bronze inscriptions, given China's geography in the northern hemisphere with the sun rising in the east and setting in the west, *yin* 侌 references the north side of a mountain and the southern bank of a waterway, while *yang* 陽 indicates the south side of the mountain and the north side of the waterway.[1] The contrastive dark and light image is captured in the etymology of the two characters. There is one hill, with *yin* being its shady side, and *yang* its sunny side. But with the ineluctable changing of the seasons, it is an image that will not allow for any final separation between temporality and location, producing both glimmers of light and dancing shadows.

In the *Book of Changes* A5 it states:

一陰一陽之謂道，繼之者善也，成之者性也……陰陽不測之謂神。
It is the alternating of *yin* and *yang* that is meant by way-making (*dao* 道). What continues way-making is its efficacy, and what brings it to fruition are the natural tendencies of things. . . . And what cannot be fathomed by appeal to *yin* and *yang* is what we call the mysterious (*shen* 神).

In the *Book of Changes* we find a vocabulary that makes explicit cosmological assumptions that are a stark alternative to substance ontology, and provides the interpretive context for the Confucian canons by locating them within a holistic, organic, and ecological worldview. This cosmology begins from "living" (*sheng* 生) itself as the motive force behind change, and gives us a world of boundless "becomings:" not "things" that *are*, but "events" that are *happening*. The ontological intuition that "only Being is" is at the core of Parmenides's treatise *The Way of Truth* and is the basis of the ontology that follows from it. To provide a meaningful contrast with this fundamental assumption of *on* or "being" we might borrow the Greek notion of *zoe* or "life" and create the neologism "zoe-

---

[1] Kwan, "Database," CHANT 4529A, 春秋晚期 CHANT 74 and 西周晚期 CHANT 10173.

tology" as "the art of living." Zoetology standing in contrast to Greek "ontology," might be translated into modern Chinese as 生生論 *shengshenglun*. The *Book of Changes* B1 states that 天地之大德曰生 "the greatest capacity of the cosmos is its life-force." Again, in A5 in describing the unfolding confluence of vital "way-making" (*dao* 道) it observes that 生生之謂易 "it is the ceaseless generating and procreating of life that is meant by 'change'" (*yi* 易). Change itself is defined denotatively and thus specifically as procreative living.

In the *Changes*, the phenomenon of cosmic life is described in the aspectual and processual language of symbiotic bipolar dyads such as "flux and continuity" (*biantong* 變通), "alternating succession" (*yinyang* 陰陽), and "penetration and receptivity" (*qiankun* 乾坤). The vital pathway of life is always contextual, a shaping and being shaped, a doing and an undergoing. Within the unbounded totality of the heavens and the earth (*tiandi* 天地), these transactional tensions in their complementarity, describe the processes of transformation that continue without respite—the ceaseless and always creative rhythm of *yin* and *yang* alternations.

Yinyang explains how one thing stands in relation to another, and hence expresses a correlation between them. *Yinyang* is sometimes used to describe generalized circumstances—the seasons of the year and different geographies, for example. But given that *yinyang* must always take a particular time and place into account, they are not static categories or principles. Indeed, such correlations are subject to change and are invariably unstable. Physically, this young woman is *yang* to the *yin* of this old man.

The *yinyang* contrast provides a sense of a continuous and interdependent difference, and by extension multiplicity. Since classical Chinese natural cosmology begins from the presumption of the uniqueness and the processional nature of all things, this *yinyang* vocabulary describes how particular things hang together in their dynamic and always changing relationships. Importantly, these relationships that are defining of things are intrinsic and constitutive. Persons, for example, are radically situated within their natural, cultural, and social environments; they *are* their relationships. They are spouses and parents and neighbors. As they cultivate their friendships, they become increasingly significant as persons. And when they lose a significant person, they are in their persons surgically diminished to the extent that a piece of themselves has been lost.

When this shady-sunny analogy is applied to the relationship between two particular things or persons in respect of some characteristic or attribute, one thing at this point in time and in this particular situation will necessarily "overshadow" the other, and hence will be *yang* to the other's *yin*. In some other respect or at some other time and place, however, the opposite might well be true. For example, in respect of wisdom, a young student might generally (but not always) be *yin* in relationship to an older teacher who is thus *yang* in this particular relationship. But when it comes to physical strength or virility or potential or endurance, the opposite might well be the case (although again, not always). And as the young students themselves grow older, the relationships that locate them in the world will change accordingly.

In fact, the *Book of Changes* appeals to *yinyang* as a way of articulating the process of ceaseless change within which the human experience is played out. It is this propensity of things to move through different phases across their careers that aligned *yinyang* with the "five phases" (*wuxing* 五行) cosmology that emerged in the early Han dynasty. This "*yinyang* five phases" cosmology would track the general correlations that constitute things as they make their way through their narratives in the world, with the strategy being that insight into such correlations provides the wisdom needed to optimize their meaning.

In addition to being a vocabulary of contrast within particular contexts, *yin* and *yang* suggests the interdependence of proximate things in the world. Students stand in a *yinyang* relationship with their teachers, but they are interdependent in the sense that the teacher can only be a great teacher to the extent that they have great students, and the better the students, the better the teacher. This is what *Daodejing* 42 means when it says:

萬物負陰而抱陽，沖氣以為和。
All things carry *yin* on their shoulders and *yang* in their arms and blend these vital energies (*qi* 氣) together to make them optimally harmonious (*he* 和).

In this "correlative" cosmology of classical China, *yinyang* became a pervasive way of understanding how all things are related to each other, and sets a pattern for the vocabulary used to articulate such insight. The relationship is understood as correlative rather than dualistic, and at once complementary and in opposition. The challenge is coordinating the various tensions in search of their optimal productivity.

There are two important clarifications that need to be made. First, as should be apparent from what has been said above, *yin* and *yang* are explanatory rather than ontological categories. That is, the language of "principle" and "essences" that we often find associated with *yinyang* is inappropriate and misleading. There is nothing that is "essentially" *yin* or *yang*; it depends upon what particular relationship is being expressed. That does not preclude the abstract cultural assumptions that have come to associate *yin* with female, and *yang* with male, thereby generating generalizations that reinforce these same assumptions.

Secondly, the usual pattern of classical Chinese correlative categories is that dominance is given to the first member of the pair. For example, *tianren* 天人 gives privilege to the numinous over human beings in their interdependent relationship; "knowing and doing" (*zhixing* 知行) gives privilege to "knowing" in this relationship; "master and guest" (*zhuke* 主客) gives priority to master. There have been various explanations for why *yinyang* violates this pattern, including linguistic facility (it is easier to say "*yinyang*" than "*yangyin*") and the positing of a matriarchal character to the proto-Chinese society (with little by way of evidence to support such a claim).

David Keightley argues that in early China, absent the foundational assumptions of Greek idealism, lives were lived in which human success or failure lie in making the most of the changing phenomenal world around them. He ascribes to these early Chinese divinatory sources what is today being described by interpreters of the classical period as a distinctively Chinese mode of correlative thinking through dyadic *yinyang* "aspectual" categories that stands in stark contrast to Greek rationalism and its resolutely dualistic vocabulary. According to Keightley's reading, oracle-bone divination subscribed to:

> . . . a theology and metaphysics that conceived of a world of alternating modes, pessimistic at times, optimistic at others, but with the germs of one mode always inherent in the other. Shang metaphysics, at least as revealed in the complementary forms of the Wu Ting [Ding] inscriptions, was a metaphysics of yin and yang.[1]

This "correlative" *yinyang* thinking, purported here to date back at least into the Shang dynasty, is a modality of reflection that advances in both complexity and explanatory force through the proliferation and accumulation of productive dyadic associations,

---

[1] David Keightley. "Shang Divination and Metaphysics." *Philosophy East and West* 38 No. 4 (1988), p. 377.

persistent images, and evocative metaphors, all of which are weighed, measured, and tested in ordinary experience. This correlative *qi* cosmology that is an omnipresent background in the later philosophical dialectic and cultural practices of Warring States China was evolving *pari passu* with the increasingly complex life forms of the ancient period. It is certainly the case that this correlative way of understanding relatedness and opposition that has come to be characterized as "*yinyang* thinking" predates the use of *yinyang*, with this particular binomial expression taking on this cosmological function much later.

*勇 *yong.* "Courage, bravery, vigor, vitality, boldness, fierceness."

The *Shuowen* lexicon defines *yong* as *qi* 氣: a relatively neutral "vigor, vitality." In the early bronze inscriptions it is associated with bravery and military prowess. The main point that is made repeatedly in these early Confucian texts is that the absence of timidity does not in itself rise to the level of courage. Indeed, all desirable qualities such as courage are the product of assiduous effort and personal moral refinement. *Yong* is an energy that must be mediated by proper conduct in order to become "courage." In *Analects* 8.2 we read: 勇而無禮則亂 "bravery unmediated by ritual propriety in roles and relations is just rowdiness," again in 8.10: 好勇疾貧, 亂也 "persons fond of bravery who despise poverty will be a source of trouble," and again in 14.4: 仁者必有勇, 勇者不必有仁 "consummate persons are certain to have courage, but someone who is merely brave is not necessarily a consummate person." (see also 14.12, 17.8, 17.23, 17.24) *Analects* 2.24 insists that *yong* must be put into the service of moral ends in order to become courage: 見義不為, 無勇也 "failing to act upon what is seen as being most appropriate (*yi* 義) is a want of courage."

But the distinction Confucius is inclined to make between mere boldness and courage is not simply in the abstract. The portrait we have from the *Analects* of Confucius's protégé Zilu is that he was close to Confucius in age with a military background that made him rash, impetuous, impatient, and immodest. Although Confucius has real affection for the irrepressible Zilu, he is used repeatedly by Confucius as a concrete example of how boldness without moral refinement falls short of true courage (5.7, 11.26, 17.8, 17.23). The ambiguity in how to translate *yong* arises from the fact that this same term can refer to anything from rashness and even fierceness to true courage, depending upon the person and context.

*友　*you.* "Friend, friendship."

This character *you* 友 appears on the oracle bones as 𠂇 and similarly on the bronze inscriptions as 𠬪, suggesting friends as two hands oriented in the same direction.[①] Within the web of Confucian relations, intimate friendships take on a transformative force that can only be adequately explained by understanding them as an extension and amplification of the family itself. As a dimension of a Confucian family-centered ethic, friendship serves as an expansive and sometimes compensatory source of meaning and value. These voluntarily chosen relations, as they develop, bring the friend in the door in the sense that close friends frequently become part of the extended families and are customarily referred to in family terms: brothers and sisters, uncles and aunties.

But friendship at the same time is at least initially different from family. While immediate family relations are usually non-fungible as a matter of birth and blood, developed friendships are contingent, and bring with them diversity made available through

---

① Kwan, "Database," 甲骨文合集 CHANT 1025 and 西周早期 CHANT 2706.

deliberate choice. In *Analects* 13.28, Confucius is explicit about how the difference between relatives and friends requires of us an importantly different response:

切切、偲偲、怡怡如也，可謂士矣。朋友切切、偲偲，兄弟怡怡。
Persons who are critical and demanding, yet amicable and accommodating can be called scholar-officials. They need to be critical and demanding with their friends, and amicable and accommodating with their brothers.

In proactively seeking out and developing meaningful friendships, these critical and self-conscious relations provide a latitude and a degree of freedom not usually characteristic of our relations with blood relatives. Confucius is keenly aware that freely chosen and expansive friendships bring with them significant difference that in some important degree compensates for more homogeneous family relations, and in many ways, can serve as an opportunity for quantum personal growth.

The vital importance of friendship for Confucian philosophy lies in its function as an open conduit that leads from the security and stability of one's own family out into the more uncertain and sometimes taxing social, political, and cultural realms. Confucius anticipates that friendships can in some ways be more challenging than intimate family relations. One can fairly take for granted the love and protection of one's immediate family, while successful life in the public sphere requires a higher degree of discrimination and a more critical sense of engagement. But then again the dividends to be reaped from enduring friendships over a lifetime are truly substantial, introducing into personal productivity a deeper degree of difference.

In this Confucian tradition, to "make" friends is quite literally to participate in the "making" of each other to the extent that it is the friendship that becomes first order as what is most concrete, while the "individuals" who participate in the growth of the relationship become increasingly an abstraction from it. Friendship is a relationship that is constituted by the persons involved, where the continuity of a truly meaningful friendship is a matter of vibrant disclosure in which the friends "change each other's minds" in the most literal, concrete, and transformative sense of this expression. Importantly, the realization of this vital relationship is not at the expense of their personal uniqueness. On the contrary, such friendships are both the source and the consequence of the integrity friends acquire as distinctive persons. Their personal integrity is expressed as both the persistent and always evolving uniqueness of each friend, and the integrative "becoming one together" that is the substance of real friendship. This understanding of relations among friends as intrinsic and constitutive is best described as productive of an "aesthetic order" in the sense that aesthetic achievements can be described fairly as the aspiration to realize the fullest disclosure of the particular details in the totality of the achieved effect. Such significant relations accrue dividends through the fullest "connectivity" and coalescence within the various activities of the friendship itself.

On this topic of friendship, commentators have often puzzled over what Confucius means when he cautions not once, but on two occasions, *Analects* 1.8 and 9.25: 毋友不如己者 "Do not befriend anyone who is not as good as you are." The logic that seems to follow from this advice is that while the friends of an exemplary person will be precious few, the friends of a scoundrel will be legion. The simple point Confucius is making here, however, is that since self-conscious moral growth is the outcome of our relating effectively in our relationships, it is only through a regimen of personal cultivation in the most productive of these relationships that we have the opportunity to grow from some inchoate relational beginnings into distinguished and efficacious persons (*daren* 大人 or *shanren* 善人

or *chengren* 成人). Such growth is purposeful; it starts here and goes there. As Confucius himself opines in *Analects* 12.1, this project of personal cultivation 為仁由己, 而由人乎哉? "is self-originating—how could it originate with others?" But while it is self-originating and reflects purpose, such cultivation is by no means a solitary affair; it can only be pursued by nurturing the fecund relations that locate us within our everyday roles of family and community. It is for this reason that, as we have seen above, the vocabulary of personal cultivation in Confucian philosophy is described in terms that frequently and specifically reference growth and extension from "small persons" to those who, having been nourished through moral conduct, have added consequence.

This declaration to seek friendships only among the very best of persons is a clear acknowledgment that Confucius understands both personal growth and diminution as a function of associated living. Not all erstwhile friendships are equally fertile. Indeed, our relations are not always benign. While our associations are certainly an opportunity for growth, Confucius is keenly aware that they can also be a source of personal attenuation (*Analects* 16.4). And this prompts us to ask: For Confucius, where does meaning come from in a "meaningful" friendship? For Confucius, the ultimate source of meaning is not external, but emerges through the self-conscious nurturing process of the friendship itself. It is the ways in which friends are qualitatively superior to and different from each other that provides the opportunity for a collaborative growth and advancement. Friendship is a classic illustration of the Confucian mantra in *Analects* 13.23: 君子和而不同 "exemplary persons seek harmony not uniformity" in which harmony is the activation of productive differences. Importantly, it seems that the resources for productive friendships tend to be dispersed among people rather than belonging exclusively to particular paragons. This generous appreciation of both the positive and negative possibilities that most relations with other people provide for us in our moral development is made abundantly clear when in *Analects* 7.22, Confucius famously observes:

> 三人行，必有我師焉。擇其善者而從之，其不善者而改之。
> In strolling together with just two other persons, I am bound to find a teacher in their company. Identifying their strengths, I follow them, and identifying their weaknesses, I reform myself accordingly.

Since each person is different, Confucius has something—sometimes more, sometimes less—to learn from everyone.

*有無   *youwu.* "Something and nothing, determinate and indeterminate, presence and absence."

Perhaps it is a majority of interpreters of the canonical texts who have been comfortable in using "being" and "non-being" as equivalents for *you* 有 and *wu* 無 respectively. We would follow the more philosophically astute in resisting such an equivalency. D.C. Lau has consistently opted for the non-technical language of "something" and "nothing" instead, and Jana Rosker explains them insightfully as "presence" and "absence." Indeed, we would take a step further in arguing strongly against the appropriateness of the language of "being" and "non-being" altogether. Angus Graham remarks on the difference between substance thinking that relies upon essences and the Chinese question of appropriate naming:

> In the absence of an affirmative copulative verb, there is no *being* an ox, any more than there is *being* white, and so no essence intervening between name and object; the terms closest to Aristotelian essence, *ch'ing* [*qing*] 情, covers everything in the ox without which the name 'ox' would not fit it, not everything without

which it would not *be* an ox. One begins to understand why in Chinese philosophy argumentation is conceived solely in terms of whether the name fits the object.①

Going back to Aristotle, "being" or *on* has most generally been invoked in the philosophical investigation that seeks to determine what it means to exist. Such notions of "being" are generally associated with the concept of ontological ground. Ontology is thus the science of being—the understanding of what something essentially is. Being *qua* being (*on*) is the proper object of metaphysics, and individual beings (*onta*) are the objects of the other sciences.

The proper understanding of *youwu* depends importantly upon our ability to suspend assumptions derived from such Western philosophical sources, and to think from the alternative interpretative context itself. The Chinese discussions of the *youwu* relation must not be thought to be "metaphysical" if we mean by metaphysics anything like a universal science of first principles or of "being *per se*." Rather, *youwu* as a term of art is directed at an understanding of the processual nature of experience and the interdependence of determinacy and indeterminacy that enables us to live most productively.

Early in the Western metaphysical narrative, thinking about the order of things begins with ontological questions such as "What kinds of things are there?" and "What is the essential nature (*physis*) of things?" Why would this same ultimate mystery of being *per se* not arise in classical Chinese cosmology? The profound question of why there is being rather than non-being, something rather than nothing, does not seem to occur to the early Chinese thinkers.

At least one reason for the irrelevance of such ontological questions in Confucian cosmology is reflected in the classical

---

① A.C. Graham, *Disputers of the Tao*, p. 410.

Chinese language itself. For Chinese cosmology, in the absence of the ontological "being" and "non-being" dualism that by virtue of the aseity of being *per se*—that is, existence originating from and having no source other than itself—allows for the separation of the determinate and the indeterminate aspects of things, there is only the eventful flux and flow of "becoming." "Being" and "non-being" as ontological categories are not available as possibilities that would have occurred to these early Chinese thinkers.

Said the another way around, because the determinate and indeterminate—*youwu* 有無—are always mutually entailing *yinyang* 陰陽 correlative categories required to describe the unfolding process of experience, there is no such thing as "being" as something that is independently permanent and unchanging, and no such thing as "non-being" as a gaping void or an absolute nothingness. *You* describes a persistent yet always changing determinate pattern or rhythm within the flux and flow of experience. And *wu* is language that describes an "emptiness" or "nothingness" within the bounds of determinate yet always changing form captured in the term "empty" (*zhong* 盅) as in an empty vessel. And *wu* further describes an undulating, throbbing, inchoate state of indeterminacy reflected in the term "surging" (*chong* 沖)—*wu* as the yet unformed penumbra that honeycombs each of the myriad things and that explains the emergence of an always novel determinacy in the ceaseless process of transformation.①

Since the classical Chinese language does not employ a copulative verb that predicates "existence *per* se" as essential being, the terms usually used to stand in for and translate these alien notions of "being" and "non-being" have been *you* 有 and *wu* 無. But in fact *you* means not that something "is" (*esse* in Latin) in the existential

---

① See *Daodejing* 4 in which the textual variants describe *dao* 道 itself in these terms.

sense that it exists in some essential way; it means rather "having present-to-hand." On the bronzes, *you* is depicted as the right hand holding sacrificial meat as something to be shared: 🧍, thus underscoring the social, political, and religious importance of sacrifice in this aristocratic culture.① "Being" is thus irreducibly relational: "being available," "being around, and having something to share in the relationship." In the case of having sacrificial meat in a culture that seldom has meat to eat, this would be something important to share. Likewise, *wu* as "not being" is again relational: it means "not being around, not being available for sharing." The sense of "being" as expressed in the classical Chinese language overlaps with "having," disposing those who would employ the notions of *you* and *wu* to concern themselves with the presence or absence of concrete particular things and the consequent relational effects of having or not having them at hand. *You* and *wu* thus describe the growth or diminution of eventful relations among things by virtue of their immediate proximity rather than referencing essences that individuate discrete and independent things. Even in recent centuries when the translating of Indo-European cultures required the Chinese language to designate a term to do the work of the copula, the choice was the demonstrative pronoun *shi* 是, meaning "this" that again indicates relational proximity and availability rather than "existence *per se*."

Not a little misunderstanding of classical Chinese thought has been occasioned by the fact that uses of *you* and *wu* often seem to echo the speculative understandings of classical Western metaphysics. We can illustrate this with a passage from *Daodejing* 40:

> The events of the world arise from the determinate (*you* 有)天下萬物生於有, and the determinate arises from the indeterminate

---

① Kwan, "Database," 西周早期 CHANT 9091.

(wu 無)有生於無.

The *you* and *wu* here might also be translated as "something" and "nothing" or "present" and "absent" respectively. They refer to the more determinate and indeterminate aspects of the ongoing process of experience: that which is present to hand and that which is not. Confusing this explanation of process with an existential claim that "non-being" is the source of "being" has given rise to a host of speculative and even mystical reflections inspired by the Parmenidean and Heideggerian projects.

You and *wu* are also an explanatory vocabulary for the always situated nature of growth, novelty, and creativity within this early cosmology. The history of the doctrine of *creatio ex nihilo* within the Greek, Hellenistic, and Abrahamic traditions is a complex and contested story, but to the extent that it has been a warrant for the quest for apodictic certainty and that it guarantees the independent power, the absolute sovereignty, and the aseity of God, it has been a prominent philosophical and theological theme in the Western cultural narrative. As such, the doctrine of *creatio ex nihilo* has had a profound role in shaping a persistent commonsense. Indeed, we might use the familiar conditions of this *creatio ex nihilo* notion of creativity, an act of unilateral origination, to distinguish this doctrine of creativity corollary to strict transcendence from those assumptions that ground the understanding of situated, contextualized procreation (or *creatio in situ*) characteristic of classical Chinese process cosmology.

First, *ex nihilo* is dependent upon a notion of discrete and independent agency, and is front-loaded in separating this exclusive Creator from its creature. In fact, given that the perfect and self-sufficient Creator does not "create" something that is other than itself and hence does not bring something novel into being, such "creativity" is in fact an exercise of manifest power rather than creativity in any interesting sense. In the processual cosmology of ancient China, by way of contrast, situation and context are always prior to agency. That is, the individual as agent is a conceptual abstraction from a concrete, constitutive matrix of relationships. Since creativity is radically situated and reflexive, the acts of creativity and self-creativity are inseparable. One both shapes and is shaped by one's evolving world. Since such creativity is always a transactional co-creativity, to collaborate effectively is to participate in the continuing process of reconstituting the world as its co-creator. This *in situ* creativity precludes the language of absolute Alterity familiar in the *ex nihilo* doctrine, and also the self-abnegation that attends it.

Secondly, *ex nihilo* focuses on originality as its source of value. The creature is a derivative manifestation of its single, independent, determinative source, and hence must look back retrospectively to this Otherness as the exclusive ground of its value. *In situ* creativity on the other hand, beginning from its doctrine of internal relations and an ontological parity among all things, emphasizes the continuing production of enhanced, novel significance in these constitutive relations over erstwhile "originality." Shared relationships that appreciate in meaning over time are the source of increased significance. *In situ* creativity is certainly retrospective in its resourcing of what is already present to hand, but it is also prospective in that its applications are productive as value-added in a process of creative advance.

Thirdly, *ex nihilo* entails the logical problem of supposedly bringing "some-thing" ostensibly novel into existence that is absolutely dependent upon its creative source. In itself, the putatively created "some-thing" is in fact a "no-thing." With *in situ* creativity, each particular is constituted by its contextualizing relations. And it is the growth of these constitutive relationships that is the ultimate source of meaning. In this process of growth, what is initially inchoate is transformed into "something" that is increasingly unique and distinctive. Importantly, rather than discrete "things" coming into relations, it is the concrete relations themselves that are the site of growth. The connectivity of friendships constitute friends who are then themselves second order abstractions from the first order relations.

Fourthly, since *ex nihilo* creativity entails a single, perfect source—a radical monism—we can use the bounded language of a single-ordered *logos*, a *kosmos*, a universe. Being and non-being thus give us the options of "one or none," "all or nothing." The *in situ* creativity of *youwu* by contrast, offers us a cosmological vision of *kosmoi* that together constitute the unbounded and unsummed totality or *dao* 道 as a pluralistic collaboration among particular orders (*wanwu* 萬物) in which no single order prevails. We can in the unique narratives of our experience foreground either its unbounded, inexhaustible, and fecund continuity (*dao* 道) or its rich, irreducible multiplicity (*wanwu* 萬物). *Dao* and "the myriad happenings" (*wanwu* 萬物) do not reduce to some separate and exclusive Creator and its creature, some source and its product. Nor is the multiplicity of "things" an imperfect, immanental manifestation of this same Creator that would negate its ostensive "creature." Rather *dao* and *wanwu* are an inclusive, aspectual language—two ways of foregrounding and backgrounding aspects of the same phenomenon.

Fifthly, *ex nihilo* is dualistic, with the transcendent as absolute Alterity negating particularity as the One-behind-the-many. The immanent is simply an imperfect representation of the transcendent, an imperfect reflection of a greater whole. *In situ* creativity, beginning from the primacy of vital relations, is holistic and thus holographic, making self and other simply two aspects of the same phenomenon. That is, since any particular is constituted by the matrix of relationships that give it context, and since these relationships continue radially without boundary or end, the totality is implicated within each particular. Rather than the language of part and whole, for Confucian cosmology we need a vocabulary of foci and their fields. The unsummed totality of *dao* as field is implicated in and construed from the perspective of each of the myriad happenings as a particular focus within its extended field.

Sixthly, the *ex nihilo* model appeals to a source of novelty that denies any meaningful notion of particularity, hybridity, history, process, or development. For *in situ* creativity, on the other hand, it is precisely growth in significance that is the substance of history, and tells the story of cosmic evolution through the aggregation of episodic, consummatory events. Within the process of *in situ* creativity, using the language of William James, the transitivity of relations with their transitions and conjunctions are all equally real. The dynamic nature of creative experience requires appeal to consequences as well as antecedents, to possibilities as well as precedents. It is this forward propensity of experience that gives it its consummatory possibility. This *in situ* conception of creativity accounts for both persistence (the propensity of things), and spontaneous variations that emerge and persist because of their consequent efficacy (the expanding and accumulating significance of "things" or "events" within this process of transformation).

And finally, different versions of *ex nihilo* creativity appeal to "beginnings" that are etymologically a "yawning gap" or a "gaping abyss" as a void or chaos. Some external *arche* or *principium,* be it Divine Will (*Genesis*), reasoning (*Timaeus*), or passion (*eros* in the Orphic creation myths) then exercises discipline and imposes order. Such superordinate, transcendent principles in referencing something independent of our world are, unsurprisingly, difficult to conceptualize and even more difficult to define from within our world. In negative theology, for example, God cannot be known or even described because as transcendent, He is wholly "Other," and can only be referenced in negative, apophatic language. Such principles are, therefore, often explained by the negation of those concepts readily available from our empirical experience. For example, infinite is defined as "not finite," eternity is "not temporal," absolute is "unconditioned," and so on. It is thus that apophatic definitions as "nothing" in trying to say "something" are attempting to say the unsayable. This reflexive appeal to the negative is thus a transcendental apophatism.

In situ creativity, on the other hand, is radically empirical in positing an indeterminate "nothing" (*wu* 無) as the constant and inseparable correlate of determinate "something" (*you* 有). Together the determinate and its indeterminate penumbra that describe the ongoing process of experience is needed to give expression to both its persistence and its novelty. In a tradition in which all beginnings are fetal beginnings (*shi* 始), there is no notion of "void" but only genealogical transformation at the interface between persistence and a fecund receptivity.

*樂   ***yue.*** "Music." See ***le.*** 樂. "Enjoyment, making the music of enjoyment."

*正   ***zheng.*** "Proper, acting properly."

Zheng as what is right and what ought to be done in a particular context, means proper conduct. Translating it as "proper" rather than "correct" or "right" respects the reflexive nature of judgments within a cosmology in which agent and context are mutually entailing. What is important in our understanding of this term is that *zheng* has the connotation of "proper" rather than simply "correct," as a description of what is appropriate in a particular situation rather than a claim to be objectively right. The *Shuowen* lexicon defines *zheng* as "what is to be affirmed, what is deserving of approbation (*shi* 是)." In the modern language, the binomial *zhengyi* 正義 has come to mean a decidedly holistic sense of justice that resists a reduction to abstract principle and its objectivism.

What recommends the translation of *zheng* as "proper" is that along with other words such as "appropriate," "propriety," and "property," it is derived etymologically from the Latin, *proprius* with its core meaning of "making something one's own." The substance and depth of *zheng*, beyond merely formal regulations, is dependent upon a process of personalization. The Latin *proprius*, "making something one's own," gives us a series of reflexive cognate expressions that are useful in translating key Confucian philosophical terms to capture this sense of participation and personalization: *Zheng* 正 is not merely "rectification" or "correct conduct" as an appeal to some external standard, but "proper conduct" as it can best be determined by persons within any particular situation. *Zheng* 政 is not simply "government" but "governing properly," and *li* 禮 is not just "what is ritually appropriate in one's roles and relations," but *personally knowing and doing* what is ritually appropriate in such relations. Again *yi* 義 is not "righteousness" as compliance with some external divine directive, but rather is an optimal "appropriateness" as the sense of what is most fitting for all concerned in this particular communal context. It is the necessity of personalization that prompts Confucius in *Analects* 3.12 to observe:

祭如在，祭神如神在。子曰："吾不與祭，如不祭。"
The expression "sacrifice as though present" is taken to mean "sacrifice to the spirits as though the spirits are present." But the Master said: "If I myself do not participate in the sacrifice, it is as though I have not sacrificed at all."

*政 **zheng.** "Proper governing, effecting sociopolitical order."

Peter Boodberg perceptively yet somewhat vaguely hovers about the holistic nature of *zheng* in his philological analysis, defining it as "effecting sociopolitical order."[1] First, he seeks to distinguish *zheng* from its common rendering as "government" on the grounds that "government" derives from the Greco-Latin etymon *guberno*: "to steer (as a helmsman)." *Zheng* on the other hand derives paronomastically from *zheng* 正 as "proper conduct," where "paronomasia" begins from redefining terms by appeal to phonetic and semantic associations, to alternative terms that sound alike or that have a similar meaning. Significantly, in this paronomastic process of adding to our repository of correlations, the expectation is that we are not just "discovering" definitions about an existing world. Rather, we are actively redefining and delineating an ever-expanding world of meaning, and in so doing, bringing it into being.

Such paronomastic definition is to be found everywhere in the classical Chinese literature. Making Boodberg's point about the holistic implications of *zheng* 政, we read in the *Analects* 12.17:

> 季康子問政於孔子。孔子對曰："政者，正也。子帥以正，孰敢不正？"
>
> Ji Kangzi asked Confucius about proper governing (*zheng* 政), and Confucius replied to him, "Governing properly (*zheng* 政) is doing what is proper (*zheng* 正). If you, Sir, lead by doing what is proper, who would dare do otherwise?"

The important point being made here is that the entire population is

---

[1] Peter Boodberg. "The Semasiology of Some Primary Confucian Concepts." *Philosophy East and West* 2 (1953), p. 323.

implicated in the persons of their rulers who qualify as good rulers to the extent that they are deemed to embody "proper" values of the community. Adding to this holism, the character *zheng* 政 is an earlier graphic form found on the bronze inscriptions for the cognate term, *zheng* 征, meaning "a punitive expedition to compel submission," thereby extending the notion of "effecting sociopolitical order" beyond the boundaries of the state itself.

Boodberg goes on to identify a positive and a pejorative sense of *zheng* 政. The positive sense is alluded to in this same passage above: it is "rectitude" in which "effective government was to be achieved in a happy medium between the correctness of the rulers and correction of the subjects."[①] The negative sense Boodberg associates with the cognate character *zheng* 征 which he reads as "to compel submission." In this case *zheng* 政 would mean the "compulsory enforcement of a standard." In distinguishing between the function of the rulers to model what is proper and to impose their authority, Boodberg is suggesting that it might be too narrow and restrictive to limit *zheng* 政 to the political sphere alone. These Confucian texts certainly give primacy to the thick notion of "achieving propriety in one's lived roles and relations" (*li* 禮) as its primary criteria for moral judgment that is holistic in having to take the relevant, specific interests of all parties into account (*yi* 義). But this passage is not presenting an either-or. Confucius clearly regards abstractions such as the rule of law and the application of punishments as second best, but at the same time, he respects them as social institutions that unfortunately must sometimes be imposed.

This negative impositional sense of *zheng* arises because personal cultivation requires commitment and effort. A *li*-ordered society to be self-governing requires that people as individuals exercise their capacities to be accommodating (*yi* 義) and thus conduct themselves

---

[①] Boodberg, "The Semasiology of Some Primary Confucian Concepts," p. 323.

appropriately with proper regard for each other. But even with the influence of the exemplary modeling of the rulers on the people, there will inevitably be a recalcitrant fringe that, for want of wit or refinement, will pursue their own personal advantage without concern for the social consequences of their actions. For the sake of social stability, such persons must be held to a minimum standard of orderly conduct described and enforced by the rule of law. This second ancillary sense of *zheng* is negative in the sense that it does not require the meaningful participation (*yi* 義) of those whom it most immediately affects. Although Confucius's sympathies clearly lie with participatory governance, he was practical enough to acknowledge the need for enforced compliance as a backup measure.

Thus *zheng* as Boodberg suggests is better understood as "effecting sociopolitical order" in its broadest sense rather than as the more politically specific "administering government." That Confucius understood *zheng* in this way is made clear in *Analects* 2.21 in his response to a mean-spirited interlocutor who uses *zheng* restrictively in the sense of formal government:

或謂孔子曰："子奚不為政？" 子曰："《書》云：'孝乎惟孝、友于兄弟，施於有政。'是亦為政，奚其為為政？"
Someone asked Confucius, "Why are you not employed in government?" The Master replied, "The *Book of Documents* says: 'It all lies in family reverence. Being filial to your parents and finding fraternity with your brothers is in fact carrying out the work of governing.' In doing these things I am participating in governing. Why must I be employed in government?"

Confucius himself is making an astute observation when he asserts that within this cultural tradition, the proper functioning of the institution of family is integral to the production of the sociopolitical order of the state. Indeed, it is this persistent family-based sociopolitical organization of Chinese society that has within this antique culture, late and soon, elevated the specific family values and obligations circumscribed by the term *xiao* 孝 to serve as its governing moral imperative.

Perhaps the most distinctive characteristic of the Confucian understanding of *zheng* is the isomorphic relationship between family and polity. The opening section of the *Classic of Family Reverence* (*Xiaojing* 孝經) that sets the theme for the entire document extols the virtue of family reverence (*xiao* 孝) in both its personal and sociopolitical dimensions. *Xiao* is whereby one lives a moral and productive life and equally the basis of governmental legitimacy and hence authority:

身體髮膚，受之父母，不敢毀傷，孝之始也。立身行道，揚名於後世，以顯父母，孝之終也。夫孝，始於事親，中於事君，終於立身。

Vigilance in not allowing anything to do injury to your person is where family reverence begins. Distinguishing yourself and walking the proper way (*dao* 道) in the world; raising your name high for posterity and thereby bringing esteem to your father and mother— it is in these things that family reverence finds its consummation. Such family reverence then begins in service to your parents, continues in service to your lord, and culminates in distinguishing yourself in the world.

For Confucius, neither person nor family nor society is subordinated as an instrumental means to serve the realization of the others. Rather, they stand as mutually implicatory ends. Any and all semblance of order in society and the state is ultimately traceable to and is an integral feature of the personal cultivation of constituents. On the other hand, personal cultivation would not be possible except for the context provided by the flourishing social and political life of the people.

Just as the character *zheng* 政 as "effecting sociopolitical order" is derived from *zheng* 正 used frequently by Confucius as persons themselves "acting properly," so sociopolitical order itself is traceable to the concerted achievement of personal cultivation among the people. Confucius on numerous occasions moves to underscore the symbiotic relationship between sociopolitical order and the proper conduct of each person:

> 子曰："其身正，不令而行；其身不正，雖令不從。"
> The Master said, "Where someone is proper (*zheng* 正) in their own person, others will accord with them without need of command. But where they are not proper, even when they issue commands, others will not obey."

It is for this reason that social and political order must always begin from personal cultivation. As observed in *Analects* 14.42:

> 子路問君子。子曰："脩己以敬。"曰："如斯而已乎？"曰："脩己以安人。"曰："如斯而已乎？"曰："脩己以安百姓。脩己以安百姓，堯舜其猶病諸！"
> Zilu asked about exemplary persons (*junzi* 君子). The Master replied, "Cultivating themselves they earn respect."
> "Is that all there is to it?" asked Zilu.
> "Cultivating themselves they bring accord to their peers."
> "Is that all there is to it?" asked Zilu.
> "Cultivating themselves they bring accord to the people broadly. Even a Yao or a Shun would find such a task daunting."

The symbiotic relationship that obtains among the various dimensions of personal, social, and political order makes problematic some of the familiar "us and them" distinctions that would separate them. Confucius with his irreducibly social understanding of person-making would not be inclined to invoke clear lines between private and public interests, between ethical and political concerns, or between social and political institutions.

*正名　zhengming. "Using names properly." See also 名 **ming**. "Naming, making a name for yourself, reputation."

 The prevailing translation and interpretation of *zhengming* is the "rectification of names." It assumes that there is some established and stipulated definition of things—ritual vessels, titles, roles, and rulers—and that any breach between theoretical definition and actual performance is a source of disorder. Such an understanding tends to treat names as some theoretical grid that has been inherited out of the tradition, and that can rectified by comporting ourselves in a way consistent with this persistent construct.

 It is certainly the case that in the literature, Confucius has a strong commitment to such conventions, and to this extent, the idea of "rectification" does part of the job. Simply put, established conventions provide stability and reinforce the hard-won values that are defining of a cultural identity. The past is importantly with us prospectively as guidance for new experience. But this exclusively retrospective understanding of *zhengming* fails to take the dynamic, prospective function of language into account. Since prospective, novel experience is always underdetermined and must quite literally be taken on its own terms, the translation of this expression as "rectification of names" is inadequate at best, and misleading at worst.

 Unquestionably Confucius evidences a profound respect for the institutions of the past, but this respect is by no means equitable to a simple reconstruction of early Zhou institutions and culture.

Confucius tempers his deference to antiquity with the practical consideration that inherited wisdom must be constantly reauthorized to accommodate the shifting circumstances of an always unique world. In short, he believes that human culture is cumulative and generally progressive. In *Focusing the Familiar* 28, Confucius states explicitly:

> 愚而好自用，賤而好自專，生乎今之世，反古之道。如此者，災及其身者也。
>
> Being obtuse and yet insisting on depending on themselves, being base and yet insisting on taking charge of themselves, being born into the present generation and yet insisting on returning to the ways of old—such people as these will bring down calamity on their own heads.

This *zhengming* doctrine of attending carefully to first the spoken and then the written word is thus more appropriately understood as "using names properly." The sage is a master communicator. Confucius is remembered by the tradition as the editor of the classics and is associated with the commentaries on the *Book of Changes*. There was a central branch of learning (*jingxue* 經學) in early China that continues today dedicated to a decoding of the classics by astute readers to reveal Confucius's hidden meanings.

In the emergent and processual cosmos of Confucius, a correlative complementarity obtains between idea and action, reason and experience, theory and praxis. Further, Confucian philosophy begins from an irreducibly interpersonal and transactional conception of the human being in which person, community, and polity are radial correlates determined through effective communication. If persons and personal relationships require a constant attuning to be optimally meaningful, it would follow that the media or forms through which these persons are composed, related, and performed—

mediums such as language, body, ritual actions, food, and music—also require unrelenting attention. In this worldview, "naming" for Confucius cannot simply be a process of attaching appropriately corresponding labels to an already existing reality. The performative and perlocutionary force of language—that is, the ability of language to actually do things and to alter the feelings of its audience—means that to interpret the world through language is to impel it towards a certain realization, to make it known in a certain way. And the extent to which one is able to influence the world is a function of the extent to which one can articulate one's meaning, value, and purpose in such a manner as to evoke deferential responses from one's community.

For Confucius, this doctrine of "using names properly" is the starting point of sociopolitical order. The pragmatic aspect of naming and its relationship to meaning is evidenced in the fact that "name" (*ming* 名) has a paronomastic relationship with "commanding" (*ming* 命), being similar in pronunciation and occasionally used as loan words. In fact, the *Shuowen* lexicon defines "naming" (*ming* 名) as "declaring oneself" (*ziming* 自命). There is a very real sense in which to name a world is to command it into being.

A full explanation of Confucius's doctrine of "using language properly," in addition to reflecting his appreciation for the way in which language conveys past realizations of the world, must provide some account of how language can be used creatively to realize the new worlds appropriate to emerging circumstances. Language, ritual action, and other mediums of communication can be viewed as formal structures used to capture and transmit meaning (*yi* 義). In fact, "using names properly" (*zhengming* 正名) functions in a way similar to "deferring to others" (*shu* 恕). To use a name or perform ritual actions meaningfully entails drawing an analogy between past and present circumstances to evoke invested significance and then redefine it to accommodate new conditions. The fertility of language, like the fecundity of *dao* 道 that means both "way-making" and "speaking," lies in activating the indeterminacy that attends it, allowing as it does for *ars contextualis*: that is, the omnipresent need for artful recontextualizing.

This process can perhaps best be understood as "paronomasia"—a prospective reconstruing of the contextualizing conditions of any situation that would allow us to call something by "another name" and in so doing, to produce additional meaning. This liquid called "water" certainly irrigates plants and produces life, and as hydropower has been used as a traditional source of energy. But might we not anticipate that with further ingenuity, we can transform it through controlled fusion into a resource that will drive our cars and fly our planes? This amplificatory process certainly begins from a careful mapping out of names as they have been used—that is, a retrospective "rectification of names"—but it also requires the imagination to find those productive correlations through language to effect novel meaning in an ever-changing world.

Language and ritual actions are always context-specific, qualified by a unique set of circumstances. That is, their meaning cannot be exhausted generically. A given name or ritual action, although describable at an abstract level, is truly meaningful only as a particular and personal disclosure of meaning. Just as ritual actions exist only to the extent that they are considered, embodied, reformulated, and extended via the peculiar conditions of the present moment, so the use of language is a dynamic enterprise in which the existing structure and definition is qualified by the understanding that names and their achieved significance are always fluid within the parameters of a context, and are in continual need of attunement.

This fluidity of names and their patternings represents a challenge to any purely logical, referential explanation of *zhengming*. Ritual actions are not only performed *by* people but, because they actively evoke a certain kind of response, in an important sense they also "perform" people. Similarly, not only do names describe, they also act in that they impel a person towards a certain kind of experience. Not only are names used to name a determinate structure, they are also used for effecting order in what is to be named.

This interpretation of *zhengming* argues against the priority and recalcitrance of formal constructions by questioning the assumption that Confucius simply uses language reductionistically to organize the process of human experience into some preestablished pattern that is perceived as defining the meaning, value, and purpose of life. It argues for the priority of aesthetic order by insisting that Confucius regarded the particular person in a specific context as a contributing source of signification. Confucius, in giving this priority to the persons as particular foci, regards the network of names to serve a sense of continuity and coherence and, at the same time, to be a malleable framework through which novelty and uniqueness can be disclosed.

Zhengming thus understood is another way of giving primacy to vital relationality. The primary gerundive meaning of "relations" is "relating," "reciting," "rehearsing," "telling," "giving a detailed account of a situation or series of events." Such "relatings" are not only discursive, but also become constitutive of who we are becoming. We are, by virtue of the wholeness of our experience, inextricably embedded within a pattern of genealogical, social, and cultural DNA that in sum constitutes our unique genomes. Our incipient relations then grow in value through various modes of associative discourse such as language, music, ritualized conduct, body, gifting, food, and so on as they serve to make us at once distinctive and yet like-minded. Increasingly resolute self-conscious individuals are constituted as distinctive persons through the expanding patterns of deference that locate them in a communicating community, while at the same time the shared communal mind itself is produced through effective "relatings" by the consociation of its members.

Confucius is himself keenly aware of the performative and perlocutionary "ontology" of "relatings" or discourse—that is, the power that language (*ming* 名) in the broadest sense has to shape the community and to command a desired world into being (*ming* 命). For Confucius, "knowing" a world, far from being just cognitive, is to realize it in the sense of "making it real." Confucius is expounding upon precisely this point when he explains to his student Zilu what he means by the central Confucian precept, "using language properly" (*zhengming* 正名). In this exposition, Confucius uses "names" as "pragmatics" to do the work of an expanding range of different yet organically related modes of discourse, from language itself to the functioning of the institutions of law and governance. Most importantly, for Confucius, the function of "naming," far from being primarily abstract, theoretical, and referential, has immediate, practical consequences for the quality achieved in the always changing life of the community. The classic statement of the doctrine of *zhengming* is given in *Analects* 13.3:

子路曰："衛君待子而為政，子將奚先？"子曰："必也正名乎！"子路曰："有是哉，子之迂也！奚其正？"子曰："野哉由也！君子於其所不知，蓋闕如也。名不正，則言不順；言不順，則事不成；事不成，則禮樂不興；禮樂不興，則刑罰不中；刑罰不中，則民無所措手足。故君子名之必可言也，言之必可行也。君子於其言，無所苟而已矣。"

"Were the Lord of Wey to turn the administration of his state over to you, what would be your first priority?" asked Zilu.

"Without question it would be to ensure that names are used properly (*zhengming* 正名)," replied the Master.

"Really? That is so pedantic." responded Zilu. "What does it mean to use names properly anyway?"

"How can you be so obtuse!" replied Confucius. "Exemplary persons defer on matters they do not understand. When names are not used properly, language will not be used effectively; when language is not used effectively, matters will not be taken care of; when matters are not taken care of, propriety in roles and relations and in the playing of music will not be achieved; when propriety in roles and relations and in the playing of music is not achieved, the application of laws and punishments will not be on the mark; when the application of laws and punishments is not on the mark, the people will not know what to do with themselves. Thus, when exemplary persons put a name to something, it can certainly be spoken, and when spoken it can certainly be acted upon. There is nothing careless in the attitude of exemplary persons toward what is said."

Zhengming as it is explained in this passage should certainly be understood as remembering and applying standards inherited from the past. But for Confucius, a thriving community must continuously reform, reconfigure, and reauthorize its institutions. The proper use of language is a continuing redefining of our terms of understanding, explanation, and performance through those semantic and phonetic associations that would enable us to make the most of our always changing world.

Confucius is trying to make several points in defining *zhengming* that in degree confound our expectations. As we have seen, Confucius does not begin from assumptions about discrete agency and agent-centered, productive activity. Rather, his starting point is the importance of the proper and productive use of language within the human community as it provides ambience for the ordinary affairs of the day. In this respect, Xunzi carries on this same assumption. Xunzi uses the same expression *zhengming* in a chapter that takes it as its title with the same "constructivist" or "pragmatic" meaning as Confucius. In a way that distinguishes him from a realist understanding of naming, Xunzi insists that

名無固宜，約之以命，約定俗成謂之宜，異於約則謂之不宜。名無固實，約之以命實，約定俗成，謂之實名。名有固善，徑易而不拂，謂之善名。

... names are not fixed in their appropriateness, but become so by mutual agreement. When there is mutual agreement and the name becomes customary in its usage then it is said to be appropriate. When used in a way different from what has been agreed upon, it is said to be used inappropriately. Names are not fixed in their reference, but become so by mutual agreement. When there is mutual agreement and the reference becomes customary, it is said to be the referent. Names are not fixed in their efficacy, but when direct, easy to use, and not at odds with the phenomenon, they are efficacious names.

These same insights about what language does have become familiar to us in the work of Ludwig Wittgenstein. Indeed, Wittgenstein has an understanding of how language functions that resonates with the prospective expectations expressed by Confucius and Xunzi. Introducing his notions of "language games" and "family resemblances," Wittgenstein is keenly aware that language and life are two aspects of the same experience. He challenges realist assumptions that language is somehow separate, and that by mapping it onto the world, it comes to "correspond" to reality in some referential and representational way. Wittgenstein uses the term "language-games" to highlight "the fact that the speaking of language is part of an activity, or a form of life," (PI 23), where such games consist of "language and the actions into which it is woven" (PI 7). Wittgenstein has a keen awareness of the underdeterminedness of language, allowing room for the prospective activation of the ambiguities and equivocations that are always present to increase its meaning and effect. He argues that concepts do not need to be clearly defined to be meaningful and to precipitate change in the world. Wittgenstein uses the analogy of "family resemblances" to describe how the same word is used in many different ways without any ultimately final or essential meaning, and to underscore the lack of any formal boundaries or precision in the different application of one and the same concept. Such an understanding of language highlights the allusiveness and the productive ambiguity that attend the imaginative use of language.

John Dewey too invests enormously in the centrality of language and other modes of communicative discourse (including signs, symbols, gestures, and social institutions) in explaining how the community grows its persons:

> Through speech a person dramatically identifies himself with potential acts and deeds; he plays many roles, not in successive stages of life but in a contemporaneously enacted drama. Thus mind emerges.[1]

For Dewey, mind is "an added property assumed by a feeling creature, when it reaches that organized interaction with other living creatures which is language, communication."[2] For Dewey, then, what we might call "heartminding" is self-consciously being created in the process of realizing a world. Heartminding, like the world, is *becoming* rather than *being*, and the challenge before us is always how much shared meaning and enjoyment can be generated in its operations. The way in which heartminding and world are changed is not simply in terms of human perception, but in their substantial growth and productivity, and in the efficiency and pleasure that attends this process. The alternative—that is, for a community to fail

---

[1] Dewey, *Later Works*, Vol. 1, p. 135.
[2] Dewey, *Later Works*, Vol. 1, p. 198.

to communicate effectively—is for the community to wither, leaving it vulnerable to the "mindless" violence and "heartless" atrocities of shameless creatures who have failed to become human.

This understanding of the generative function of language is further developed in the work of Charles Taylor who, taking discourse as one of the necessary sources of our personal identities, says:

> One cannot be a self on one's own. I can only be a self in my relation to certain interlocutors.... A self only exists within what I call "webs of interlocutions."[1]

The range of meaning-making activities described in this *Analects* passage are irreducibly social and situational; persons, families, and communities become who we are discursively through what we say and do in our roles and relations, through what Taylor is calling "our webs of interlocutions."

In this Confucian model of constitutive "correlatings," then, we are not individuals who associate in community, but rather because we associate effectively in community we become distinguished as unique individuals; we do not have minds and therefore speak with one another, but rather because we speak effectively with one another, we become like-minded with shared life-forms and values; we do not have hearts and therefore are empathetic with one another, but rather because we feel effective empathy with one another we become whole-hearted as a community. Indeed, paronomasia understood as defining a world through associated living within a communicating community is the Confucian way of making meaning.

---

[1] Taylor, *Sources of the Self*, p. 36.

*知/智 **zhi.** "Living wisely, realizing, wisdom, knowing."
See also 體 **ti.** "Lived body, discursive body, embodying."

The character *zhi* 知, with or without the "speaking" (*yue* 曰) signific beneath it as *zhi* 智, is usually translated nominally and as a verb as "knowledge, wisdom, knowing." In analyzing the etymology of *zhi* 知 as it appears on the bronzes, it is composed of "an arrow" (*shi* 矢) and "a mouth" (*kou* 口) ![]. ①The *Shuowen* lexicon infers meaning from the "mouth" radical in defining *zhi* 知 as *ci* 詞: "something said, or expressed." The Qing commentator on the *Shuowen*, Duan Yucai 段玉裁, also ascribes semantic reference to the arrow, suggesting that it 識敏，故出於口者疾如矢也 "alludes to a nimbleness in wit that makes anything said as quick as an arrow." It is interesting that erstwhile "knowing," far from being associated with the passive, intellectual cognition of some pre-existing reality, seems to include both the social and discursive aspects necessary for living wisely. This "mouth" element and other related ways of indicating communicating such as "mouth" (*kou* 口), "speaking" (*yan* 言)," "showing" (*shi* 示), "listening" (*er* 耳), and "thinking and feeling" (*xin* 心) appear in many if not most of the key philosophical terminologies in classical Chinese philosophy. Together with the "speaking" (*yue* 曰) semantic indicator in "wisdom" (*zhi* 智), this association with speaking reflects the importance of the social, communicative aspect of knowing. In fact, the distinguished philologist, Bernhard Karlgren, had his reasons for speculating that the "arrow" element in the character *zhi* was originally "persons" (*ren* 人) which if true reinforces the sense that *zhi* entails a sociology of knowledge: a shared knowing by a community rather than

---

① Kwan, "Database," 春秋早期 CHANT 2766.

"knowing" on the part of any solitary knower.① Given the irreducibly social character of the Confucian person, the locus of knowing is not the individual knower, but a knowing community wherein knowledge as an applied wisdom is perceived as an immediate resource for communal flourishing.

Consistent with this sociology of knowing that enables the community to live wisely together, zhi 知 also means "an intimate or friend," thus putting a human face on what it means to know as "a pattern of fiduciary relations." This social aspect of zhi leads to a second observation: zhi is meliorative—it seeks to make the world better. *Analects* 6.20 observes:

> 子曰: "知之者不如好之者，好之者不如樂之者。"
> The Master said, "Cherishing it is better than just knowing it, and finding enjoyment in it is better than just cherishing it."

As suggested here, zhi certainly has a cognitive dimension. In fact, in *Mencius*, zhi as an initial capacity for making productive distinctions is one of the "four inclinations" (*siduan* 四端) that distinguishes the human being from the beast: 是非之心，智也 "it is this sense of discrimination that enables persons to act wisely." But the expectation is any cognitive capacity must prompt a quality of understanding and the purposeful actions that follow from it that is productive of human flourishing. It states rather clearly that the kind of knowing that is directed and purposeful is superior to simple cognition. And again that the kind of knowing that actually conduces to communal enjoyment is better yet. To know in this classical Confucian world is indeed a source of a joyful wisdom. If we were to take liberties with the last proposition of Spinoza's *Ethics* that reads

---

① Bernhard Karlgren. *Grammata Serica Recensa*. Taipei: SMC Publishing Inc., 1996, p. 228.

"Blessedness is not the reward of virtue, but is virtue itself," we might say that enjoyment is not the reward of living wisely, but is wisdom itself. Said perhaps more clearly, rather than taking enjoyment to be the goal of living wisely, we might say that enjoyment is the affective character of wise living.

Ren 仁 understood as the relational virtuosity that enables consummate conduct has an immediate correlation with living wisely (*zhi* 知), and so it ought to come as no surprise that these two terms, like the water that shapes the mountains and the mountains that occasion the waters, are never far apart in the Confucian vocabulary. In *Analects* 6.23, for example:

子曰: "知者樂水, 仁者樂山; 知者動, 仁者靜; 知者樂, 仁者壽。"
The Master said, "The wise enjoy water; those consummate in their conduct enjoy mountains. The wise are active; consummate persons are still. The wise find enjoyment; consummate persons are long-enduring."

And *Analects* 4.2, 仁者安仁, 知者利仁 "Consummate (*ren* 仁) persons find satisfaction in acting consummately; wise (*zhi* 知) persons flourish in it."

Dong Zhongshu 董仲舒 in his *Luxuriant Dew of the Spring and Autumn Annals* 春秋繁露 30 has a chapter entitled 必仁且智 "Where consummate conduct (*ren* 仁) then wise living (*zhi* 知) for sure." In his explanation of wisdom (*zhi* 智), Dong's emphasis is upon the inseparability of speaking and knowing, and the discursive implications that make such knowing a "realizing" of what is to be done:

何謂之智? 先言而後當……智者見禍福遠, 其知利害蚤, 物動而知其化, 事同而知其歸, 見始而知其終, 言之而無敢嘩, 立之而不可廢, 取之而不可舍, 前後不相悖, 終始有類, 思之而有複,及之而不可厭。其言寡而足，約而喻，簡而達，省而具，少而不可益，多而不可損。其動中倫，其言當務。如是者謂之智。

What does *zhi* mean? It means that once something has been said things happen accordingly . . . Those who live wisely can see calamity and good fortune a long way off, and early on anticipate benefit and injury. When things happen, they anticipate how they will unfold; when affairs arise, they anticipate the outcome. In seeing the beginning, they know the end. When they say something none would dare dispute it; when they set something up none can take it down; when they take something up none can put it aside. They are consistent in their actions, and there is a logic to what they do. They consider something and then think again, and when they get to it, it cannot be undone. Their words are few but sufficient. They are brief yet clear, simple yet explicit, terse yet ample. When of few words, there is no embellishing them; when the words are many, none are superfluous. There is method in what they do, and efficacy in what they say. Such persons can be said to be acting wisely.

There is an important passage in the *Analects* itself that provides a rather succinct statement of the isomorphic relationship between "consummate conduct" (*ren* 仁), "aspiring to ritual propriety" (*li* 禮) and "living wisely" (*zhi* 知):

子曰："知及之，仁不能守之；雖得之，必失之。知及之，仁能守之；不莊以涖之，則民不敬。知及之，仁能守之，莊以涖之；動之不以禮，未善也。"

The Master said, "Where in their wisdom they are up to effecting social and political order and yet in their persons are not sufficiently consummate to sustain it, even though they have succeeded, they are sure to ultimately fail. Where in their wisdom they are up to it and are sufficiently consummate to sustain it, and yet they fail to oversee it with proper dignity, the common people will not be respectful. Where in their wisdom they are up to it, are sufficiently consummate to sustain it, and are able to oversee it with proper dignity, and yet they fail to inspire the common people by aspiring to ritual propriety, they will still not make good on it."

In Arthur Waley's translation, he despairs: "This paragraph with its highly literary, somewhat empty elaboration, and its placing ritual on a pinnacle far above Goodness, is certainly one of the later additions to the book."[①] But in fact it makes good sense. It is clear from the reference to the common people at the end that this passage provides an inventory of what is needed by those who would rule if they want to succeed not only in establishing sociopolitical order, but in sustaining it. Without taking account of the performative force of "living wisely" (*zhi* 知) only as it is complemented by "achieving consummate conduct" (*ren* 仁) and "aspiring to ritual propriety" (*li* 禮), this passage is difficult to interpret. Perhaps the best way of understanding it is to acknowledge that "living wisely," "achieving consummate conduct," and "aspiring to ritual propriety" in themselves, while each being necessary, is not sufficient to the task. These three aspects of effecting social and political order complement each other, and all three must be coordinated to a common end.

The classical Chinese language does not distinguish between "knowledge" and "wisdom," and there is a question as to whether "knowledge" is itself an appropriate translation. Although the mantra "the inseparability of knowing and doing" (*zhixingheyi* 知行合一) is usually associated with the Ming dynasty philosopher Wang Yangming 王陽明, this assumption has deep roots in the Confucian classics. An argument could be made that in the absence of any severe theory/praxis and self/other dichotomy, the assumption is that since erstwhile "knowledge" must be authenticated in communal action, it

---

① Arthur Waley, *The Analects of Confucius*, p. 200, n. 1.

must in fact be wisdom. It must be practically efficacious. Since *zhi* has this important pragmatic entailment, we might understand the translation as "wisdom," not so much as "practical intelligence" but more as "acting intelligently." And since *zhi* involves practice, it is always a localized knowledge, a situated wisdom belonging to a time and place.

Said another way, there is no putative "view from nowhere," no "*God's* eye view" that would provide a strictly "objective" perspective. This being the case, knowing a world is reflexive and evaluative: It is to recommend *this* world from *this* point of view. *Zhi* certainly has a factual "knowing-that" aspect that can be judged as being correct or otherwise. A keen knowledge of existing conditions is presupposed in acting effectively in the world. But even here, such "knowing" rather than having an either/or finality, is qualitatively transformed in moving from mere cognition to thick perception. To merely recognize someone is different in significant degree from knowing them as a dear friend. In the knowing process, the language is not one of closure—"I know"—but of the disclosure that comes with a qualitative advance, an intensifying and expanding "knowing" that is also a "doing." Hence, *zhi* references a prospective and qualitatively cumulative "knowing-how" to do things in the world—how to ride a wave, how to perform an organ transplant, and perhaps most importantly, how to be an intimate.

We can say that "knowing" thus understood as intelligent social practice not only informs conduct, but also has performative force. "Knowing" changes the world. In order to highlight this sense of "making the desired outcome real"—that is, bringing a particular world into being—*zhi* might also be translated as "realizing." Thus, such "knowing" or "realizing" is to be cognizant of prevailing conditions, to have the imagination to see the unrealized possibilities of these conditions, and to have won the respect of one's own community that then rallies around one to aspire to this chosen future. *Zhi* is not only the application of a moral epistemology; it is the pursuit of an intelligent morality. Such knowing is a normative world-making. Cultural avatars late and soon—Gandhi, Mandela, Martin Luther King (MLK), and Confucius himself—who in conjuring up and then prompting alternative futures for their constituents, were just such world-makers. MLK challenged and changed America with "I have a dream," and Confucius had a dream too that gave him the company of the Duke of Zhou as his source of wisdom and inspiration (*Analects* 7.5).

Again, *zhi* has a perlocutionary force: It entails an epistemology of feeling. "Knowing" has a direct and significant affect on the feelings, beliefs, and the moods of those who come to know each other empathetically. Such knowledge quite literally changes their hearts as well as their minds. In this classical Confucian world, persons and their shared mind are both irreducibly social. There is a priority of situation over individual agency, where discrete persons are always an abstraction from a natural, social, and cultural context. The locus of knowing is a knowing community, where such knowing can serve as an immediate resource for elevating communal happiness.

Turning to the extraordinarily important somatic aspect of "knowing" in this Confucian tradition, we can correlate "lived body" (*ti* 體) and its cognate character "aspiring to propriety in one's roles and relations" (*li* 禮) by arguing that they express two ways of shaping, embodying, and thus "realizing" our personal identities: that is, these two characters reference "a living body" and "embodied living" respectively. This relationship between "knowing" and "body" is carried over into the modern language in which "knowing bodily" (*tihui* 體會 and *tiyan* 體驗) means to know something through experiencing it, and in this way, "realizing" it.

In the pre-Qin documents, the graph for "embodying" (*ti* 體) appears with three alternative semantic classifiers—*shen* 身 that alludes to the lived, vital, and irreducibly social body; *rou* 肉 as the flesh and hair, carnal body; and *gu* 骨 that references the "bones" and formal, skeletal structure. At a personal level, the body is the intermediary through which we coordinate our subjectivity with our environments, and that mediates the quality of our thinking and feeling with our demonstrable patterns of conduct. We can appeal to these different ways of writing the graph as a heuristic for attempting to give full value to the notion of how each succeeding generation has the capacity and the responsibility of embodying fully the cultural "corpus" as it has been passed on to them.[1] At the most primordial level, the body via these three mutually entailing modalities—the vital, carnal, and discursive bodies—serves as the conduit through which a living civilization is being transmitted.

The English vocabulary of knowing reflects the primarily cognitive sense of discerning ontological distinction between the real world and mere appearances. "To grasp, to get, to comprehend, to understand" is to seize upon some formal, unchanging reality behind the passing shades. This correspondence model of a subjective, mental idea mirroring an external reality and thus promising the spectator an unconditional, apodictic knowledge has been an important theme in classical Greek epistemology. The Greek truth (*aletheia*) is linked closely to the distinction between mere opinion (*doxa*) and true knowledge (*episteme*) that affirms its properly real object. The equation between knowledge, reality, and truth reflects the two-world ontological distinction between reality and appearance, with reality as the object of knowledge belonging to those high abstract principles available to the intellect. When the Greek philosophical vocabulary becomes the language of Christianity, it is Jesus as the only path to the highest abstraction called God who declares that

---

[1] For a fuller discussion of this sense of embodiment, see Roger T. Ames, *Confucian Role Ethics*, pp. 102-113. For more on the *ti* body, see Deborah Sommer, "Boundaries of the *Ti* Body."

he is the Way, the Truth, and the Life (John 14:1). In the absence of the Greek ontological distinction between reality and appearance, for Confucianism, the equation between knowledge, reality, and truth has little relevance for Confucianism. All experience is equally real: A dream is a fact, a mistaken opinion is as real as the right answer. This has led Angus Graham to say repeatedly that "Chinese philosophizing centres on the Way rather than on Truth."[①]

Perhaps the pragmatic turn in the Western philosophical narrative that is a rejection of this kind of Greek ontological thinking might provide a bridge in our attempt to better understand "knowledge, reality, and truth" in the Confucian tradition. There are three aspects of pragmatism that prepare us to access Confucian modes of thinking. First, there is the pragmatist's rejection of both realist and idealist ontologies (that is effectively an abandonment of the Greek metaphysical tradition); second, the consequent rejection of representational understandings of knowing (that is in effect an abandonment of Greek epistemology); and third, the appeal to "experience" as the starting point of all philosophical reflection and discussion (that is an affirmation of a radical empiricism).

The functional equivalent of reflections concerning truth in the Confucian tradition might become clearer if we can see how the pragmatists turned away from being "Truth-seekers" to join the Confucian philosophers in becoming "Way-seekers." To begin with, the pragmatic "theory" of truth drawn from C.S. Peirce, William James, and John Dewey is itself less of a "theory" than a vision of way-making. As James says, pragmatism "is a method only," and as a method, pragmatism is merely a way, a set of means or instruments that permits the accomplishment of certain practical actions involved in "getting on with it." Again, the pragmatic understanding of truth is not strictly conformable with either correspondence or coherence

---

[①] A.C. Graham, *Disputers of the Tao*, p. 395.

theories of truth. According to James, "truth is the expedient in the way of thinking." For the pragmatist, a belief is a habit that guides action. If the belief brings persons into productive harmony with their community, it functions expediently, and is true insofar as it brings welcome outcomes. The Jamesian pragmatist explicitly denies a reality/appearance contrast and the notion of a single-ordered world, rejects any theory/praxis dichotomy, treats concepts not as essences but tools for action, and accedes to the dominance of metaphor in language, thus denying the value of any quest for literal language or univocal discourse.

Consistent with this pragmatic turn to finding a way forward, in the Confucian process cosmology, the metaphor grounding its epistemic vocabulary seems to reflect a "mapping" of a way forward in which any severe distinctions between subject and object, and between the theoretical and the practical, are moot. *Zhi* allows for a productive "forging ahead" within a particular situation, and thus promises practical efficacy (a way forward we can trust) rather than any particular truth: that is, "finding our way" (*zhidao* 知道), "unraveling the patterns within the context" (*lijie* 理解), "seeing with full clarity" (*liaojie* 瞭解), "getting through with facility" (*tongda* 通達), "being well acquainted with everything" (*baishitong* 百事通) and so on.

The language of knowing is to read the signposts as we walk together in the proper direction. This sense of mapping carries over into modern Chinese in which the expression for "I know" is quite literally "I am walking the way, I am realizing the way" (*wo zhidao* 我知道), thus suggesting both a specific bearing and how best to get there. To know is to be cognizant of prevailing conditions, to have the imagination to see their possibilities, and through virtuosic relationality (*ren* 仁) within one's own community, to have achieved the deference necessary to rally support behind and enthusiasm for a chosen future. And the assumption is that Confucian "knowing" is preemptive in the sense that such social intelligence broadly diffused will in important measure preclude the hard cases that require ethical deliberation and its attendant appeal to regulative ideals.

Importantly, in the transitive "I know the way" (*wo zhidao* 我知道), "the way" (*dao* 道) is not the "object" of knowledge as such, but has a real subjective and performative dimension as well. *Dao* is a holistic, qualitative way of conducting one's life in the world that entails both subject and object, and the attributes of the subject as well as the modality of the actions being carried out. *Dao* defies Aristotle's philosophy of grammar, having as much to do with the conditions of the subject as with the object, and having as much to do with the quality of understanding as it does with the conditions of the world as understood. Knowing tells us as much about the quality of the person who "knows" as it does about something known, as much about a particular disposition to act as it does about the modality of acting itself.①

The epistemic critique we find in many of the classical Confucian texts does not rely heavily upon the language of right and wrong or true and false that follow from a reality-appearance and essence-attribute kind of ontological assumptions. Instead, criticism often takes the form of insisting that someone has only limited knowledge—having access to only one aspect of a situation while

---

① This pragmatic association between "knowing" and finding our way productively forward is not entirely unnoticed in our own tradition. John Dewey makes a similar point:
> If ideas, meanings, conceptions, notions, theories, systems are instrumental to an active reorganization of the given environment, to a removal of some specific trouble and perplexity, then the test of their validity and value lies in accomplishing this work. . . . That which guides us truly is true—demonstrated capacity for such guidance is precisely what is meant by truth. The adverb "truly" is more fundamental than either the adjective true, or the noun, truth. An adverb expresses a way, a mode of acting.

John Dewey. *Reconstruction in Philosophy*. New York: Henry Holt and Co., 1920, pp. 156-157.

being insufficiently aware of the others. For example, the *Xunzi* has a whole chapter entitled "Dispelling Obsessions" (*jiebi* 解蔽) that opens with the charge: 凡人之患，蔽於一曲而闇於大理 "The affliction most people have is that they are obsessed with one corner and cannot see the big picture." The best kind of "knowing" must be overarching and comprehensive (*quan* 全), and must include the kind of effective application in practice that conduces to human flourishing. It means living wisely.

There is a popular proverb in modern Chinese that everyone knows: 不識廬山真面目，只緣身在此山中 "I cannot see the true face of Mount Lu because I am standing within this mountainscape." While everyone is aware of this phrase, I think people often misunderstand its meaning. This expression is usually read as asserting that an external, more objective perspective is better than one from the inside that would recommend Zhuangzi's insight that

親父不為其子媒。親父譽之，不若非其父者也。
... a father will not act as matchmaker for his son because whatever the father might say in praise of him is not as persuasive as it would be coming from someone else.

Perhaps we might offer a salutary corrective on the internal-external understanding of this proverb that begins by looking at the whole Su Shi 蘇軾 poem rather than just the last two lines. Su Shi's famous verse, "Written on the Wall of the Western Forest Temple" 題西林壁 reads:

橫看成嶺側成峰，遠近高低各不同。不識廬山真面目，只緣身在此山中。
Horizontally I see the ridges, vertically, the peaks;
Far or near, high or low, each affords a different view.
I cannot see the true face of Mount Lu

Because I am standing within this mountainscape.

Indeed, the poem begins first by asserting that there are a countless number of competing vistas within the changing landscape of Mount Lu. Further, and most profoundly, there is never an "outside" of this mountainscape, but only an inside, seeing it from one perspective or another. And again, following the same logic, the best way of looking at Mount Lu or anything else in the human experience is the most comprehensive view that includes as many perspectives as possible. This then is an argument for a holistic epistemology of "comprehensiveness" (*quan* 全) where at the end of the day, the best we can achieve is not truth or certainty, but only a continuing intelligent and edifying conversation that will provide us incrementally with the most perspectives and the most inclusive, panoramic view of things.

What is the consequence of this distinction: the distinction between a Greek assumption that knowledge is the grasp of one exclusive truth and the Chinese pursuit of a comprehensive knowing? One implication is the contrast between a tradition of systematic philosophies that follow from the Greeks, and the commentarial tradition we find in China. When we reflect on the general character of the different lineages of Chinese philosophical thinking, rather than being systematic in the sense of relying on one exclusive principle, they are broadly eclectic and hybridic, drawing upon as many perspectives as possible. Again, we remember the cosmological postulate, "the inseparability of one and many, many one" (*yiduobufenguan* 一多不分觀). Indeed this characteristic within the broad compass of Chinese philosophy has led Graham to observe:

> The final tendency of the schools was towards syncretism; philosophers settle for "I see the whole thing, you are one-sided"

rather than "I am right, you are wrong."①

In knowing the world, Aristotle gives priority to the analytic, ontological "What?" question that secures the subject necessary before the other contingent questions can be asked of it: Where? When? Having what? Doing what? and so on. One way of formulating the more holistic Confucian alternative to Aristotle is to look at the scope of the Chinese question particle, *an* 安, as it functions in the classical canons. Parsed according to specific contexts, the particle *an* seems to mean How? in the *Book of Songs*, Where? and What? in the *Zuo Commentary*, and quite famously Whence and Whither? as we try to make sense of the "happy fish" story in the *Zhuangzi*. But in fact, this same question particle, while seemingly delimited by its use in different contexts, in fact always carries with it the full range of questions simultaneously. As the particle *an* proliferates into many different questions, each of these questions provides an answer about some aspect of the same phenomenon, and in sum, they provide us with a panoramic overview of the complexities of the experience. Indeed, the fullest answer to any one of these organically related questions requires an answer to all of them.

Thinking further about priorities among the questions asked within the Confucian cosmology, given the fact that in such a fluid, process cosmology, the "What?" question is predicating "events" rather than asking after discrete "things," it in some ways provides the least satisfying answer. Far from promising us truth by revealing what is ontologically essential and thus knowable, the "What?" question in this case has the specious effect of arresting and delimiting a temporally and spatially focal event having implicated within it all of the history that has preceded it, and all of the history that would follow from it. Indeed, in this process cosmology, the

---

① A.C. Graham, *Disputers of the Tao*, p. 398.

questions of "Whence?" and "Whither?" that would allow us to assay *an event over time* become the primary and most revealing questions to be asked. Indeed, this "Whence?" question form carries over into the modern Chinese language's "Do you know?" (*ni zhidao ma*? 你知道嗎?) that asks quite literally "Are you realizing the whence and the whither on this shared way forward?" And since events are "taking place" rather than resolving to a simple spatial or temporal location, the "Where?" and "When?" questions only provide us with putative *points in place and time*. Like the "What?" question, "Where?" and "When?" give us conventional abstractions from, and indeed distortions of, what comes to us as both continuous and eventful in the flow of our experience.

Turning more specifically to the questions we might ask if we want to know particular persons, the project of coming to really know someone requires an appeal to a narrative, processual, and generative understanding of their identity with all of the transitivity and conjunctions integral to the course of who they have become, and who they are becoming. Persons thus understood are to be likened more to historical events than to marbles in a jar. And when we ask after historical events—the Civil War, for example—we are more inclined to ask, "How did it come about?" (Whence?) and "What were its consequences?" (Whither?) rather than "*What* was the Civil War?" That is, Aristotle does not need to ask the *Whence?* and *Whither?* questions because Aristotelian "things" are invested with an assumed generic *eidos* and *telos* that implicitly provide us with these answers in their evolving process of actualization. By contrast, in order to provide an adequate description of any resolutely particular event in the Chinese cosmology, the explanatory "Whence?" and the "Whither?" questions that Aristotle would abjure in describing his subjects and their predications, are immediately relevant as providing information that is not otherwise available to us. This eventful nature of persons is the first inkling of the holographic, focus-field conception of persons that inhabits Confucian role ethics.

Asking the Whence? and Whither? questions provide the most information about both the content and the nature of experience, especially with respect to the experience of becoming human. But importantly, in a holistic cosmology, we must not undervalue the "What?" "When?" and "Where?" questions. These abstracting and isolating questions when asked about the Civil War, for example, come to have increased significance when we are called upon to draw comparisons between the Civil War as one particular example of a campaign that can then be compared with others in different times and places. The importance of these analytic questions emerges from the need to register some degree of integrity, determinacy, and intelligibility in experience. These delimiting questions are functional in providing us the convenience of parsing the continuous flow of experience into eventful units having tentative beginnings and consummating endings. With these "abstracting" questions, we are provided with the felicitous distinction between the flow of process and the meaningful integrity of particular events within that continuing process, where both flow and particularity are vital to our understanding. Asking such abstracting questions serves us in the production of meaning that emerges as we parse the flow of experience and impose an intelligible order upon it. To the extent that the process of experience is eventful, the identities of these events as particular foci are a function of both unique disclosure and punctuating closure, with the most meaningful events among them exhibiting the distinctiveness of a uniquely executed work of art or a virtuosic performance of piece of music. Such closure comes along with the ostensive beginnings and endings of experiences, and allows these events to achieve their own provisional consummation even while they at the same time open out onto further stages in what is the ever-evolving process of experience.

The meaning and complexity of our experience emerges from the cadence and quality of these distinctive events. The distinctive episodes are at once mutually imbricated and yet determinate, and while sometimes ephemeral like momentary eddies in a stream, they are also sometimes persistent like the banks of the stream that produces these same eddies and give definition to the stream's ceaseless flow.

We have seen that Aristotle with the primacy of his "What?" question within his "thing" substance ontology, gives grammatical privilege to the noun. Graham finds a distinct contrast with Aristotle in Chinese process cosmology in arguing for the privileging of the verb:

> If . . . one starts from the action, then duration and direction are already inherent in the verb; action is as much *from* and *to* as *in*, and as much *to*, *from* and *in* things and persons as places. . . . We may link this asymmetry with the verb-centeredness of Chinese language and thought [*my italics added*].①

Graham is asserting that in this "eventful" Chinese cosmology, human becomings as "events," for example, are better understood as fluid and inclusive verbs rather than as static and exclusive nouns. We might take inspiration from Graham's insight here and suggest that on further reflection, it is perhaps the gerund form as the more inclusive verbal-noun that might be a better choice than the verb—that is, a notion of "person-ing" that does not separate "persons" from "what they do." In any case, Graham offers us a holographic understanding of this Confucian world in which radically situated persons cannot be extricated from the temporality and fluid locale of their continuing narratives as these stories are "taking place."

In addition to *dao* as "way-making" resonating with a pragmatic way of thinking about "truth," there are other Confucian terms that are immediately relevant to "truing" the way forward. Indeed,

---

① A.C. Graham, *Studies in Chinese Philosophy and Philosophical Literature*, p. 391.

beginning with *de* as the "virtuosity" of the insistent particular moving straight ahead, much of the modal vocabulary of Confucian role ethics are alternative ways of expressing the "trust" or "fidelity" that conduces to a flourishing fiduciary family and community. Fei Xiaotong claims that the Confucian pattern of kinship relations with its hierarchically-defined roles and relations produces its own distinctive kind of morality in which "no ethical concepts . . . transcend specific types of human relationships."[①] Kinship as the root of human relations is defined by the values of "family reverence" (*xiao* 孝) and "fraternal deference" (*ti* 悌). And friendship as the way of extending this pattern of kinship relations to include non-relatives is pursued through an ethic of "commitment and resolve" (*cheng* 誠), "doing one's utmost" (*zhong* 忠), and "making good on one's word" (*xin* 信). All such ethical values are aspired to as the way of reconciling the tensions among and promoting the accommodations made within the specific personal relationships of family members and community.

It might be salutatory to end this reflection on the Confucian preoccupation with the putative efficacy of knowledge *zhi* with a Daoist qualification if not corrective. After all, the *Daodejing*, for example, repeatedly exhorts us to be literally "without knowledge" (*wuzhi* 無知). The concern in the Daoist canons is to celebrate particularity and pursue what they take to be an alternative inclusive rather than a doctrinal understanding of "objectivity." That is, to the extent that we can, we must strive to entertain what are always novel situations without prejudice or presupposition. In order to understand a situation thoroughly, we must make every effort to take it on its own terms without imposing preexisting structures or values onto it. For the Daoist, *wuzhi* is thus better understood positively as an "unprincipled knowing"—a kind of knowing that

---

[①] Fei Xiaotong, *From the Soil*, p. 74.

abjures any final vocabulary in favor of an ironic sensibility with its readiness to relinquish this way of understanding the situation for another, better way.

*志 **zhi.** See 天志 **tianzhi.** "The purposes or intent of *tian.*"

*直 **zhi.** See 德 **de.** "Moral virtuosity, excelling morally, virtuality."

*質 **zhi.** "Native temperament, raw stuff, basic disposition." See also 文 **wen.** "The written word, patterns, culture, refinement, King Wen."

Zhi appears as a technical term in *wenzhi* 文質: "refinement and native temperament," a *yinyang* correlative pairing with *wen* 文: "refinement, culture." Confucius advances the argument that "native temperament" and "refinement" are isomorphic in the sense that each is dependent upon the other. In *Analects* 6.18 we read:

子曰："質勝文則野，文勝質則史。文質彬彬，然後君子。"
The Master said, "When one's native temperament (*zhi* 質) overwhelms refinement (*wen* 文), the person is boorish; when refinement overwhelms one's native temperament, the person has the officiousness of a scribe. It is only when native temperament and refinement are in appropriate balance that there is the exemplary person (*junzi* 君子)."

What is philosophically important here is that the Confucian understanding of the contrapuntal relationship between native conditions and refinement stands as the alternative to the Greek ontological assumption about the teleologically informed actualization of a given potential. Aristotle's subject as defined by a formal cause gives us a reduplicative account of persons where the infant as a human "being" is a ready-made adult. Again, Aristotle's subject as it is defined by a final cause gives us a teleology in which the infant is simply preliminary to the existing ideal.

The alternative as expressed in this passage is an example of how the pervasive value of optimizing symbiosis (zhonghe 中和) or "getting the most out of your ingredients" is doing the work of teleology in Confucian philosophy. Exemplary persons are not predetermined by their native stuff nor are they the attainment of some pre-existing ideal. Rather such persons are a cultural product shaped under the specific conditions of their lives. They are an open-ended aesthetic in which the quality of the native materials and the growth informed by a pattern of refinement have found their proper balance. To begin with, perhaps it is better to think of the native materials not as the "material" cause: that is, as some one thing that exists in itself at the beginning of a process. The native materials are resources that are continually changing and compounding in value as they are deployed in a continuing contextualized event. Their potential and possibilities emerge in response to how they are being used. Refinement too is not an externally imposed disciplining of given raw materials, but the creative play between imagination and the possibilities made available by the materials as the process of refinement unfolds.

Let us take the casting of an exquisite bronze vessel as an example. If the raw materials for the vessel are deficient or if there has been a lack of imagination in how to make the most of these resources as they are being used, the process of refinement will be stunted and the quality of the vessel will be left wanting. There is waste when the raw materials have been used in a way that falls short of the creative possibilities provided by the particular situation. What makes the vessel exquisite is the organic relationship between the raw materials, the imagination invested in the workmanship, and the oxygen in the environment that over time produces the incredible verdigris patina. The raw stuff, the refinement, and the environment are each the cause and the effect of the others.

Returning to the example of exemplary persons, when the regimen of refinement is insufficient, the opportunities that emerge within the continuing narrative are uniformed and underused, and there is a failure to produce the graciousness that is the real substance of morality. On the other hand, when the narrative is disciplined by too much refinement, like mere technical skill without style in a pedestrian musical performance, there can only be an anemic product.

In this Confucian tradition, native temperament (*zhi* 質) is not a neutral given; it is laden with possibilities and thus has its own intrinsic quality. The metaphors of "raw silk" (*su* 素), "unworked wood" (*pu* 樸), "the infant mind" (*chizizhixin* 赤子之心), and "the next generation" (*housheng* 後生), allude to how each thing given its best conditions has the possibility of achieving aesthetic depth (*du* 度). It is in this sense that when Mencius and Xunzi too are making the claim that everyone can become a sage, they are talking about narrative possibilities rather than some universally given, essential nature.

Relationally-constituted persons are born into the broadest swath of family, community, and cosmic relations. They cannot exist exclusive of these relations, nor can they grow without them. By locating the notion of persons within the relational ecology that serves as interpretive context for these texts, we can argue that terms such as "root," "potential," "cause," "source," and "nature" that are at times taken as disjunctive and exclusive terms to be associated with some underlying cosmic teleology, have to be reconceived as referencing always multilateral, symbiotic, and reflexive processes.

Bringing this rather abstract reflection to bear on how we are to understand "human nature" as the "source" of what we become as humans, we would have to allow that human nature is a provisional generalization made with respect to the totality of human lives as they have been lived within their natural and social relations. The contingency in the ongoing process of what humans have become is no less relevant to this notion of source than where they have come from. The source is the collaborative nature of relations themselves *and* what is produced in this collaboration. In becoming human as in making friends, there is no separation between maker and made, between means and end, between cause and effect, between source and product.

Further, we might clarify the notion of "potential" to underscore the inseparability of person and context in this Confucian conception of persons. The "potential" for becoming human is not simply the first inclinations, something inborn "within" the person exclusive of family relations. In the first place, there is no such person. Since persons are constituted by their relations, the "potential" of a person in fact emerges from the specific, contingent transactions that, in the fullness of time, eventuate in the identity of this particular person in this particular family. Thus, the best sense we can make of "potential" here is that rather than being antecedent and ready-made, it evolves *pari passu* with the ever changing circumstances; rather than being generic or universal, it is always unique to the career of the relational person; and rather than existing as an inherent and defining endowment, it can only be known *post hoc* after the unfolding of the particular narrative.①

---

① For John Dewey too, "potentialities cannot be known till after the interactions have occurred. There are at a given time unactualized potentialities in an individual because and in as far as there are in existence other things with which it has not as yet interacted." *Later Works*, Vol. 14, p. 109. Lincoln is not Lincoln independent of the circumstances of history, nor are the circumstances of history the making of Lincoln. Indeed, Lincoln is a collaboration between person and circumstances expressed as thick habits of conduct. "The idea that potentialities are inherent and fixed by relation to a predetermined end was a product of a highly restricted state of technology." *Later Works*, Vol. 14, p. 110.

*自然　**ziran.** "Self-so-ing, so-of-itself, spontaneity."
See also 勢 **shi.** "Purchase, momentum, configuration."

This term *ziran* as it is used in the modern language is conventionally translated as "nature," "naturally," and "Nature." On the oracle bones, the character "self- (*zi* 自) occurs as ![], a pictograph of the human nose.[①] The explanation in the commentaries for how this serves as a reference to the self is because persons in identifying themselves point to their nose with their index finger. It is significant that *zi* is reflexive, and means "self-" or "auto-" as in "self-critical" and "autonomous." But used as a preposition, it is also directional and like the character *you* 由 it means "from" and "going out from." If we put these meanings together, we might observe that the *zi* of *ziran* makes "so-ing" locative and projective, proceeding from a particular place.

Ran 然 occurs on the bronze inscriptions as ![] and originally means roasting dog meat, and by extension, a blazing fire.[②] As an auxiliary term, *ran* means "this" (*shi* 是) or "like this, as such" (*ruci* 如此), as in the conjunction "although like this . . ." (*suiran* 雖然 . . .). *Ran* 然 thus means "so-ing" or "such-ing" in the sense of the emergence and presencing of things, with the suggested image of rising up like fire.

Philosophically nuanced interpreters reflecting on the use of *ziran* in the canonical texts often choose to render it "self-so-ing" or "spontaneity."[③] The presencing of things and the cultivation of

---

[①]　Kwan, "Database," 甲骨文合集 CHANT0 700.
[②]　Kwan, "Database," 戰國晚期 CHANT 2840.
[③]　The problem with "spontaneity" is the paradoxical way it is used in the English language, meaning either "self-causing" (the tree grew spontaneously) or "uncaused, random" (he spontaneously threw his glass at the wall). The notion of spontaneity that has relevance here with *ziran* is the cultivated spontaneity of the calligrapher or martial artist.

harmony among them always has a particular locus and direction. In Confucian philosophy, rather than appealing to the idea of a transcendent and independent First Mover as the cause and architect of the world, the world is perceived as an autogenerative, "self-so-ing" process that includes the energy of its ongoing transformation as residing within the continuing narrative itself: *ziranerran* 自然而然. This world-ing is an inside without an outside. And analogously with respect to persons, this same cosmology begins from a phenomenology of what unfolds and compounds as moral habits within the human narrative itself rather than by appealing to an independent and reduplicative nature or soul as the source of human conduct.

If we thus see relationality as first order reality and all individual actors as abstracted or derived from them, then we must understand causality in a cosmos described as autogenerative (*ziran* 自然) to be the backgrounding or foregrounding of particular foci and their unbounded fields, where anything is the cause of everything, and everything is the cause of anything. Given that "self-" is always uniquely situated and is inclusive of its relations, persons can grow their relations and extend this "self-" through a process that includes deferring to others within a radially expanding field, and on that basis, pursue the most inclusive and productive course of action described as the method called *shu* 恕 "deference, dramatic rehearsal." Order starts here and goes there. *Zi* as "self-" indicates that the energy and trajectory of presencing is focused within and is a collaboration of being projected from what is immediate as well as being shaped from without. It is a doing and an undergoing, a shaping and being shaped.

This notion of "self-" then has three aspects. First, this *ziran* causality means that the "self" (*zi* 自) in the "self-so-ing" process is certainly uniquely what it is, one of a kind. It is a continuing specific identity. Secondly, this *zi* identity has both an objective and subjective dimension to it, perceived from the outside, but also lived from the inside. It is this existential self-awareness that is prospectively negotiating its *zi* identity from within, having a projective influence in setting and maintaining its horizons within its environing conditions. And thirdly, since this *zi* identity is constituted by an unbounded field of relations, the *zi* is what it is by virtue of the quality of coalescence it has achieved within the manifold of relations that conspire together to make it insistently so (*ran* 然). Said simply, since everything causes anything, any particular thing is both the cause and the effect of everything else.

This *ziran* causality becomes an important qualification on how we understand a term such as "birthing, living, growing" (*sheng* 生) within this Confucian cosmology. In *Analects* 17.19 it states:

> 天何言哉？四時行焉，百物生焉，天何言哉？
> What does *tian* 天 have to say? And yet the four seasons turn and the myriad things are born and grow within it. What does *tian* have to say?

Rather than reading such "birthing" as the familiar A giving birth to an independent B, we must understand that in this cosmology, each and every thing emerges out of a collaboration of the unsummed totality of things that in different contexts we might refer to as *tian* 天 or *dao* 道.

*中 *zhong*. "Center, balance, focus, equilibrium."

The character *zhong* 中 meaning "centering, equilibrium" appears on the oracle bones as 㐭 and 中, and on the bronzes as 𦀚.[1] These graphs reference perhaps the two most common ways of assembling

---

[1] Kwan, "Database," 甲骨文合集 CHANT 7375, CHANT 1063, and 商代 CHANT 6933.

the people and of rallying the troops; the first way is by sight and the second is by sound. The *zhong* character depicts a banner or standard that would be hoisted in the marketplace as a visual signal for the people or for the troops to gather together. Another way of calling assembly for the people or the military implicated within the graph is to sound a drum. The mouth of the drum 口 suspended on a stand is thus visually represented with the graph for *zhong* 中. As with the earlier form of the character "harmony" (*he* 龢) constructed with the *yue* 龠 wind instrument, *zhong* 中 also has an immediate musical association in including a visual reference to the drum.

Zhong appears frequently as an aspiration in the classical texts. *Focusing the Familiar* 1, for example, explains the symbiotic relationship between harmony and focus—the ongoing negotiation of a productive harmony (*he* 和) among things, and the cultivation necessary to bring the web of relations that constitute a thing into meaningful focus (*zhong* 中). The opening passage of this text traces cosmic flourishing back to the achieved harmony and equilibrium in human feelings:

> 喜怒哀樂之未發，謂之中；發而皆中節，謂之和；中也者，天下之大本也；和也者，天下之達道也。致中和，天地位焉，萬物育焉。
> The moment at which joy and anger, grief and pleasure, have yet to arise is called a nascent equilibrium (*zhong* 中); once the emotions have arisen, that they are all brought into proper focus (*zhong* 中) is called harmony (*he* 和). This notion of equilibrium and focus (*zhong* 中) is the great root of the world; harmony then is the advancing of the proper way (*dadao* 達道) in the world. When equilibrium and focus are sustained and harmony is fully realized, the heavens and earth maintain their proper places and all things flourish in the world.

Stated more simply, when the expression of human feelings as the ultimate resource for achieving moral competence is orchestrated into a productive harmony, the Confucian vision of the moral life is advanced, and all things in the world flourish. It is the human participation in bringing the world into meaningful focus and the human contribution to sustaining this equilibrium that establishes the human being as a full partner with the other forces shaping the natural, social, and cultural environments. Human beings share in a moral cosmos. Because a state of equilibrium and balance (*zhong* 中) precludes coercion, it is an essential condition for maximizing the creative possibilities in the pattern of relationships that constitute any particular situation. And real novelty as an indeterminate element is potentially destabilizing. Thus, the quality of creativity itself is dependent upon the capacity of the sage to orchestrate harmony in the world, and to modulate it in accordance with changing circumstances.

Focusing the Familiar 20 explains creativity in precisely these terms:

誠者，天之道也；誠之者，人之道也。誠者不勉而中，不思而得，從容中道，聖人也。誠之者，擇善而固執之者也。

Creative resolve is the way-making of *tian*; applying this creative resolve is the way-making of becoming human. Such resolve is achieving equilibrium and coalescence without coercion; it is succeeding without reflection. Freely and easily traveling at the center of way-making—this is the sage. Resolve is selecting what is most efficacious and holding on to it firmly.

*忠　*zhong.* "Conscientiousness, doing one's utmost, loyalty."

The character *zhong* 忠 as it appears on the bronze inscriptions as 忠 is constituted by the components "centering, into, interior, focus" (*zhong* 中) and "heartmind" (*xin* 心).① The character *zhong* 中 suggests ways of assembling the people visually and aurally with banners and drums respectively. The second element is the "heartmind" (*xin* 心), or perhaps better, "thinking and feeling." The character *zhong* 忠 that is constituted by components "into, interior" (*zhong* 中) and "heartmind" (*xin* 心) means "doing one's best" or "giving oneself fully" to the task at hand—quite literally putting one's heart into what one does. The indefatigable commitment to a positive outcome in growing relations, a central feature of Confucianism, brings motivation into the discussion. D.C. Lau provides us with a significant corrective for the popular understanding of *zhong* 忠 as simply "loyalty" by insisting upon its more primitive meaning as "doing one's best."

> Translators tend to use "loyal" as the sole equivalent for *chung* [*zhong*] even when translating the early texts. This is a mistake and is due to a failure to appreciate that the meaning of the word changed in the course of time.... *Chung* [*zhong*] is the doing of one's best and it is through *chung* [*zhong*] that one puts into effect what one has found out by the method of *shu*.②

Lau's interpretation of *zhong* is reinforced by the *Shuowen* lexicon that defines *zhong* as being "respectfully attentive" (*jing* 敬). Later commentary on the *Analects* defines *zhong* explicitly as "giving oneself utterly" (*jinji* 盡己) in what one does. It is when *zhong* is used in the context of the relationship between ruler and subject, "doing one's best" becomes more narrowly focused as "loyalty."

---

① Kwan, "Database," 戰國晚期 CHANT 9735.
② Confucius, *Analects* (*Lunyu*), trans. D.C. Lau, p. xvi.

We find that in the *Analects*, *zhong* as "conscientiousness in doing one's utmost" appears repeatedly in tandem with *xin* 信 "living up to one's word." This association reinforces the personal resolution required to really make good on one's word. For this same reason, *zhong* as "conscientiousness" again accompanies the term *shu* 恕—"deference, dramatic rehearsal"—in that turning one's insight into the most productive response to any particular situation requires assiduous effort.

Zhong, "doing one's utmost," is thus a conscientiousness in one's deliberations and actions. We have seen that an otherwise demurring Confucius is not shy about being described as "cherishing learning" (*haoxue* 好學). It is because the *what* of one's specific actions is a complex variable that will always need to be qualified by the uniqueness and exigencies of the circumstances that Confucius is given to emphasizing the more modal *how* to live morally. Since in Confucian ethics, moral actions that conduce to growth in relations are resistant to general prescription, optimizing modal values such as "inclusiveness" and "capaciousness" that come with "optimal appropriateness" (*yi* 義) and "assiduousness" that comes with "doing one's best" (*zhong* 忠) consistently attend the exhortation to "live up to one's word" (*xin* 信).

As the *Classic of Family Reverence* observes with respect to the political application of *zhong*, superiors and subordinates can only appreciate each other if subordinates "try to assist in promoting what is commendable in their superior's conduct while taking steps to remedy what cannot be condoned." (17) The point is that simple obedience is a counterfeit loyalty. It is only by assuming a mutuality and shared concern between superior and subordinate that one can exercise one's judgment on how to do one's best, entailing as *zhong* does both enthusiastic obedience and sincere remonstrance (*jian* 諫).

*中庸 ***zhongyong.*** "Focusing the familiar, hitting the mark in the everyday, making the ordinary extraordinary."

Zhong 中 means "center, balance, focus, equilibrium," and as a verb, "hitting the target." *Yong* 庸 appears on the oracle bones as 庸, and is used as a loan for its cognate character *yong* 用 that appears as 用 meaning "use, using."[①] Indeed, the *Shuowen* lexicon defines *yong* 庸 with this same term *yong* 用. Interestingly, there is logic in the relationship between the English "use" and "usual:" from L. *ūsuālis* "for use, fit for use, also of common use, customary, common, ordinary, usual." This same logic is apparent in the extension of the meaning of *yong* 用 from "use, using" to *yong* 庸 "familiar, usual, everyday, ordinary." Thus, the expression *zhongyong* suggests that the locus for achieving focus and equilibrium is *yong* 庸— the ordinary business of the day. This project of ritualizing the human experience and of enchanting the common, the routine, the concrete and immediate, requires an unremitting attentiveness to disciplining and making the best use of what is spontaneously novel as it emerges in our everyday experience. Ritualizing the human experience requires both an appreciation of our ordinary and persistent life forms, and the full exercise of our imagination in reauthorizing them for our own time and place.

This term *zhongyong* as the title of one of the *Four Books* has been translated in many different ways. It was first translated as "The Doctrine of the Mean" by James Legge but then as "The State of Equilibrium and Harmony" when Legge translated it a second time as a fascicle included in the *Record of Rites* (*Liji* 禮記). E.R. Hughes rendered it "The Mean-in-Action," Gu Hongming as "Central Harmony," Ezra Pound as "The Unwobbling Pivot," Tu Wei-ming as "Centrality and

---

[①] Kwan, "Database," 甲骨文合集 CHANT 12839 and CHANT 34300.

Commonality," Andrew Plaks as "On the Practice of the Mean" and Ian Johnston/Wang Ping as "Using the Centre" (Zheng Xuan) and "Central and Constant" (Zhu Xi). The Han dynasty commentator Zheng Xuan 鄭玄 defines *yong* 庸 as its homophone *yong* 用 "using, applying"—and describes the text as 記中和之為用 "a record of the application of center and harmony." Zhu Xi in his commentary concludes that *yong* means 平常之理 "the coherence of that which is ordinary and constant." Our translation as "Focusing the Familiar" is a considered choice that follows these commentators. What for Zheng Xuan is "the application of center and harmony" we would understand as "focusing" in the sense of making something more meaningful by bringing it into clearer resolution. What is brought into focus is as Zhu Xi suggests: the coherence within the ordinary and constant, the familiar affairs of the day. Our choice of "familiar" reminds us that this notion of "family" is the governing metaphor in Confucian culture, and that "familiar" and "family" from L. *familiāris* "of a household" share the same root.

*主客 **zhuke.** "Subject and object, subjectivity and objectivity." See 內外 **neiwai.** "Inner and outer, inside and outside."

Bibliography of Earlier Glossaries

The Classic of Family Reverence: A Philosophical Translation of the Xiaojing 孝經 (with Henry Rosemont, Jr.). Honolulu: University of Hawaii Press, 2009.

Daodejing: Making This Life Significant (with David L. Hall). New York: Ballantine Books, 2003.

Focusing the Familiar: A Translation and Philosophical Interpretation of the Zhongyong (with David L. Hall). Honolulu: University of Hawaii Press, 2001.

The Confucian Analects: A Philosophical Translation Based on the Dingzhou Manuscripts (with Henry Rosemont, Jr.). New York: Ballantine Books, 1998.

Tracing Dao *to Its Source* (with D.C. Lau). New York: Ballantine Books, 1998.

Sun Pin: The Art of Warfare (with D.C. Lau). New York: Ballantine Books, 1996. Reprinted as *Sun Bin: The Art of Warfare*. Albany: State University of New York Press, 2002.

Sun-tzu: The Art of Warfare. New York: Ballantine Books, 1993.

The Art of Rulership: A Study in Ancient Chinese Political Thought. Honolulu: University of Hawaii Press, 1983. Reprinted with a forward by Hal Roth. Albany: State University of New York Press, 1994.

Bibliography of Works Cited

Ames, Roger T. (2020). *Human Becomings: Theorizing Persons for Confucian Role Ethics*. Albany: State University of New York Press.

—— (2018). "Reconstructing A.C. Graham's Reading of *Mencius* on *xing* 性: A Coda to 'The Background of the Mencian Theory of Human Nature' (1967)," in *Having a Word with Angus Graham: At Twenty-five Years Into His Immortality*. ed. Carine Defoort and Roger T. Ames. Albany: State University of New York Press.

—— (2011). *Confucian Role Ethics: A Vocabulary*. Honolulu and Hong Kong: University of Hawaii Press and Chinese University Press.

—— "Paronomasia: A Confucian Way of Making Meaning," in *Confucius Now: Contemporary Encounters with Confucius*. ed. David Jones. La Salle: Open Court.

—— (2003). "*Li* 禮 and the A-theistic Religiousness of Classical Confucianism," in *Confucian Spirituality* 1. ed. Tu Wei-ming and Mary Evelyn Tucker. New York: Crossroads Press.

Ames, Roger T. and David L. Hall (trans.) (2003). *A Philosophical Translation of the Daodejing: Making This Life Significant*. New York: Ballantine Books.

—— (trans.) (2001). *Focusing the Familiar: A Translation and Philosophical Commentary on the Zhongyong*. Honolulu: University of Hawaii Press.

Ames, Roger T. and Henry Rosemont Jr. (trans.) (1998). *The

Analects of Confucius: A Philosophical Translation. New York: Ballantine Books.

App, Urs (2010). *The Birth of Orientalism*. Philadelphia: University of Pennsylvania Press.

Barrett, Tim (2005). "Chinese Religion in English Guise: The History of an Illusion," in *Modern Asian Studies* 39.3.

Behuniak, James, Jr. (2005). *Mencius on Becoming Human*. Albany: State University of New York Press.

Bloom, Paul (2014). *Just Babies*. New York: Random House.

Boodberg, Peter (1953). "The Semasiology of Some Primary Confucian Concepts," in *Philosophy East and West* 2.

Ching, Julia (1977). *Confucianism and Christianity: A Comparative Study*. Tokyo: Kodansha International.

Ch'ü, T.T. (1961). *Law and Society in Traditional China*. Paris and The Hague: Mouton & Co.

Clark, Kelly James (2007). "Tradition and Transcendence in Masters Kong and Rorty," in *Morality, Human Nature, and Metaphysics: Rorty Responds to Confucian Critics*. ed. Huang Yong. Albany: State University of New York Press.

—— (2005). "The God of Abraham, Isaiah, and Confucius," in *Dao: A Journal of Comparative Philosophy*, Vol. 1.

Cua, A.S. (1985). *Ethical Argumentation: A Study in Hsün Tzu's Moral Epistemology*. Honolulu: University of Hawaii Press.

Dalmiya, Vrinda (1998). "Linguistic Erasures," in *Peace Review* 10 (4).

Davis, John Francis (1836). *The Chinese: A General Description of the Empire of China and Its Inhabitants*. London: Charles Knight & Co.

Dawson, Raymond (1981). *Confucius*. New York: Hill and Wang.

Dewey, John (1985). *The Later Works of John Dewey* (1925-53), Vols. 1 and 14. ed. Jo Ann Boydston. Carbondale: Southern Illinois University Press.

—— (1920). *Reconstruction in Philosophy*. New York: Henry Holt and Co.

Dubs, Homer H. (1928). *The Works of Hsüntzu*. London: Probsthain.

Emerson, Ralph Waldo (1862). "American Civilization," in *Atlantic Monthly* 9.

Farquhar, Judith (1994). *Knowing Practice: The Clinical Encounter of Chinese Medicine*. Boulder: Westview Press.

Faulkner, William (1968). *The Lion in the Garden: Interviews with William Faulkner 1926-1962*. ed. James B. Meriwether and Michael Millgate. New York: Random House.

Fehl, Noah (1971). *Li, Rites and Propriety in Literature and Life*. Hong Kong: Chinese University Press.

Fingarette, Herbert (1983). "The Music of Humanity in the *Conversations of Confucius*," in *Journal of Chinese Philosophy* 10.

—— (1979). "Following the 'One Thread' of the Analects," in *Journal of the American Academy of Religion*, Thematic Issue 47.

—— (1972). *Confucius: The Secular as Sacred*. New York: Harper and Row.

Fraser, Chris (2010). "Mohism," in *The Stanford Encyclopedia of Philosophy (Fall 2012 Edition)*. ed. Edward N. Zalta. http://plato.stanford.edu/archives/fall2012/entries/mohism/

Fukunaga Mitsuji 福永光司 (trans.) (1968). *Roshi*老子. Tokyo: Asahi Shinbunsha.

Fung Yu-lan (1952). *A History of Chinese Philosophy*. trans. D. Bodde. Princeton: Princeton University Press.

Gadamer, Hans-Georg (1989). *Truth and Method* (2nd edition). London: Sheed and Ward.

Gimello, Robert M. (1972). "The Civil Status of *li* in Classical Confucianism," in *Philosophy East and West* 22.

Girardot, Norman J. (2002). *The Victorian Translation of China: James Legge's Oriental Pilgrimage*. Berkeley: University of

California Press.

―― (1983). *Myth and Meaning in Early Taoism: The Theme of Chaos (hun-tun)*. Berkeley: University of California Press.

Goldin, Paul R. (2008). "The Myth That China Has No Creation Myth," in *Monumenta Serica* 56.

Graham, A.C. (1991). "Replies," in Henry Rosemont, Jr., *Chinese Texts and Philosophical Contexts: Essays Dedicated to Angus C. Graham*. La Salle: Open Court.

―― (1990). *Studies in Chinese Philosophy and Philosophical Literature*. Albany: State University of New York Press.

―― (1989). *Disputers of the Tao: Philosophical Argument in Ancient China*. La Salle: Open Court.

―― (1978). *Later Mohist Logic, Ethics and Science*. Hong Kong: The Chinese University Press.

Gu Zhengkun 辜正坤 (trans.) (2006). *The Book of Tao and Teh*. Peking: China Translation and Publishing Corporation.

Hagen, Kurtis (2007). *The Philosophy of Xunzi: A Reconstruction*. La Salle: Open Court.

Hall, David L. and Roger T. Ames (1998). *Thinking From the Han: Self, Truth and Transcendence in Chinese and Western Culture*. Albany: State University of New York Press.

―― (1995). *Anticipating China: Thinking through the Narratives of Chinese and Western Culture*. Albany: State University of New York Press.

Hamilton, Gary G. and Wang Zheng (trans.) (1992). *From the Soil: The Foundations of Chinese Society, A translation of Fei Xiaotong's* Xiangtu Zhongguo 鄉土中國. Berkeley: University of California Press.

Hansen, Chad (1994). *A Daoist Theory of Chinese Thought*. Hong Kong: Oxford University Press.

Hartshorne, Charles (1950). *A History of Philosophical Systems*. New York: Philosophical Library.

Hershock, Peter (2012). *Valuing Diversity: Buddhist Reflection on Realizing a More Equitable Global Future*. Albany: State University of New York Press.

Hoyt, Sarah F. (1912). "The Etymology of Religion," in *Journal of the American Oriental Society* 32.

Hsiao Kung-chuan (1979). *A History of Chinese Political Thought*, Vol. 1. trans. F. Mote. Princeton: Princeton University Press.

Huang Yong (2007). "Confucian Theology: Three Models," in *Religion Compass* 1.

Hutton, Eric (2005). *Readings in Classical Chinese Philosophy* (2nd edition). ed. P.J. Ivanhoe and Bryan Van Norden. Indianapolis: Hackett Publishing Company.

Ing, Michael David Kaulana (2012). *The Dysfunction of Ritual in Early Confucianism*. Oxford: Oxford University Press.

James, William (1985). *The Varieties of Religious Experience*. Cambridge: Harvard University Press.

James, William (2000). *Pragmatism and Other Writings*. New York: Penguin.

Karlgren, Bernhard (1996). *Grammata Serica Recensa*. Taipei: SMC Publishing Inc.

—— (1950). *The Book of Odes: Chinese Text, Transcription and Translation*. Stockholm: The Museum of Far Eastern Antiquities.

Keightley, David N. (1998). "Shamanism, Death, and the Ancestors: Religious Mediation in Neolithic and Shang China, ca. 5000–1000 B.C," in *Asiatische Studien* 52.

—— (1988). "Shang Divination and Metaphysics," in *Philosophy East and West* 38.

Kim, Myeong-seok (2014). "Is There No Distinction Between Reason and Emotion in *Menzi*?" in *Philosophy East and West* 64.

Knoblock, John (1988, 1990, 1994). *Xunzi: A Translation and Study of the Complete Works*, Vols. 1-3. Stanford: Stanford

University Press.

Kwong-loi Shun (2009). "Studying Confucian and Comparative Ethics: Methodological Reflections," in *Journal of Chinese Philosophy*, 35 (3).

—— (1997). *Mencius and Early Chinese Thought*. Stanford: Stanford University Press.

Lai, Karyn (2014). "*Ren* 仁: An Exemplary Life," in *Dao Companion to the Analects*. ed. Amy Olberding. Dordrecht: Springer.

Langer, Susanne (1951). *Philosophy in a New Key*. Cambridge: Harvard University Press.

Lau, D.C. (trans.) (1983). *Confucius: The Analects (Lunyu)*. Hong Kong: Chinese University Press.

—— (trans.) (1963). *Lao Tzu: Tao Te Ching*. London: Penguin Books.

Lau, D.C. and Chen Fong Ching (1992). *A Concordance to the Huainanzi*. Hong Kong: The Commercial Press.

—— (1992). *A Concordance to the Liji*. Hong Kong: The Commercial Press.

Legge, James (trans.) (1960 rep.). *The Chinese Classics*, 5 volumes. Hong Kong: University of Hong Kong Press.

Lewis, Martin W. and Karen E. Wigen (1997). *Myth of Continents: A Critique of Metageography*. Berkeley: University of California Press.

Li Chenyang (2015). *The Confucian Philosophy of Harmony*. New York: Routledge.

—— (2006). "The Confucian Ideal of Harmony," in *Philosophy East and West* 56.

Li Zehou 李澤厚 (2018). "An Explanation of the Summary Chart on Ethics" (關於"倫理學總覽表"的說明), in 中國文化學刊.

Liang Tao 梁濤 (2004). "Zhu Xi dui 'Shendu' de Wudu jiqi zai Jingxue Quanshi zhong de Yiyi"朱熹對"慎獨"的誤讀及其在經學詮釋

中的意義, in *Zhexue Yanjiu* 哲學研究, 第 3 期.

Liu, Lydia H. (1995). *Translingual Practice: Literature, National Culture, and Translated Modernity – China, 1900-1937*. Stanford: Stanford University Press.

Lloyd, Geoffrey and Nathan Sivin (2002). *The Way and the Word: Science and Medicine in Early China and Greece*. New Haven: Yale University Press.

Loewe, Michael (1982). *Chinese Ideas of Life and Death: Faith, Myth and Reason in the Han Period (202 BC-220 AD)*. London: Allen and Unwin.

Major, John (1993). *Heaven and Earth in Early Han Thought: Chapters Three, Four, and Five of the* Huainanzi. Albany: State University of New York Press.

—— (1977). "Reply to Richard Kunst's Comments on *hsiu* and *wu hsing*," in *Early China* 3.

—— (1976). "A Note on the Translation of Two Technical Terms in Chinese Science: *wu-hsing* and *hsiu*," in *Early China* 2.

Maspero, Henri (1981). *Taoism and Chinese Religion*. trans. Frank A. Kierman, Jr. Amherst: University of Massachusetts Press.

McLeod, Alex (2012). "*Ren* as a Communal Property in the *Analects*," in *Philosophy East and West* 62.

Mote, Frederick (1989). *Intellectual Foundations of China*. New York: McGraw-Hill.

—— (1972). "The Cosmological Gulf Between China and the West," in *Transition and Permanence: Chinese History and Culture*. ed. David C. Buxbaum and Frederick W. Mote. Hong Kong: Cathay Press.

Needham, Joseph (1956). *Science and Civilisation in China*, Vol. 2. Cambridge: Cambridge University Press.

Neville, Robert Cummings (2018). "On the Importance of the Ames-Hall Collaboration," in *Appreciating the Chinese Difference: Engaging Roger T. Ames on Methods, Issues and Roles*. ed. Jim

Behuniak. Albany: State University of New York Press.

Ni Peimin (trans.) (2017). *Understanding the Analects of Confucius: A New Translation of* Lunyu *with Annotations*. Albany: State University of New York Press.

Nietzsche, Friedrich (1977). *A Nietzsche Reader*. trans. R.J. Hollingdale. Harmondsworth: Penguin.

—— (1966). *Beyond Good and Evil*. trans. W. Kaufmann. New York: Vintage.

Norman, J. and T. Mei (1976). "The Austroasiatics in Ancient South China: Some Lexical Evidence," in *Monumenta Serica* 32.

Nylan, Michael and Michael Loewe (ed.) (2010). "Administration of Family," in *Early China's Empires: A Re-appraisal*. Cambridge: Cambridge University Press.

Owen, Stephen (1992). *Readings in Chinese Literary Thought*. Cambridge: Harvard University Press.

Pang Pu 龐樸 (1999). "Yizhong Youjide Yuzhou Shengcheng Tushi: Jieshao Chujian *Taiyi Shengshui*" 一種有機的宇宙成圖式：介紹楚簡《太一生水》, in *Daojia Wenhua Yanjiu* 道家文化研究 17.

Peterson, William J. (1986). "Another Look at *Li*," in *The Bulletin of Sung-Yuan Studies* 18.

—— (1982). "Making Connections: 'Commentary on the Attached Verbalizations' of the *Book of Changes*," in *Harvard Journal of Asiatic Studies* 42.

Pound, Ezra (1951). *Confucius: The Great Digest and Unwobbling Pivot*. New York: New Directions.

Pye, Lucian W. (1998). *International Relations in Asia: Culture, Nation and State*. Sigur Center for Asian Studies.

Raphals, Lisa (2002). "A Woman Who Understood the Rites" in Bryan Van Norden (ed.), *Confucius and the Analects: New Essays*. New York: Oxford University Press.

—— (1998). *Sharing the Light: Representations of Women and Virtue in Early China*. Albany: State University of New York Press.

Ricci, Matteo (1985). *The True Meaning of the Lord of Heaven*. Taipei: Ricci Institute.

Richards, I.A. (1932). *Mencius on the Mind: Experiments in Multiple Definition*. London: Kegan Paul, Trench, Trubner & Co.; New York: Harcourt, Brace.

Rorty, Richard (2007). "Philosophy and the Hybridization of Culture," in *Educations and Their Purposes: A Conversation Among Cultures*. ed. Roger T. Ames and Peter D. Hershock. Honolulu: University of Hawaii Press.

Rosemont, Henry, Jr. (2002). *Rationality and Religious Experience*. La Salle: Open Court.

Rosemont, Henry, Jr. and Roger T. Ames (trans.) (2009). *The Classic of Family Reverence: A Philosophical Translation of the Xiaojing 孝經*. Honolulu: University of Hawaii Press.

Ryle, Gilbert (2009). *The Concept of Mind*. New York: Routledge.

Sandel, Michael (1998). *Liberalism and the Limits of Justice*. Cambridge: Cambridge University Press.

Schipper, Kristofer. (1978). "The Taoist Body," in *History of Religions* 17.

Schwartz, Benjamin (1985). *The World of Thought in Ancient China*. Cambridge: Harvard University Press.

Sellars, Wilfrid (1963). "Philosophy and the Scientific Image of Man," in *Empiricism and the Philosophy of Mind*. London: Routledge & Kegan Paul Ltd.

Shusterman, Richard (2008). *Body Consciousness: A Philosophy of Mindfulness and Somaesthetics*. Cambridge: Cambridge University Press.

Sim, May (2007). *Remastering Morals with Aristotle and Confucius*. Cambridge: Cambridge University Press.

Sivin, Nathan (1995). *Medicine, Philosophy and Religion in Ancient China: Researches and Reflections*. Aldershot: Variorum.

Slingerland, Edward (trans.) (2003). *Confucius: Analects with*

Selections from Traditional Commentaries. Indianapolis: Hackett.

Sommer, Deborah (2008). "Boundaries of the *Ti* Body," in *Star Gazing, Fire Phasing, and Healing in China: Essays in Honor of Nathan Sivin*, special issue of *Asia Major*, 3rd Series, Vol. 11. ed. Michael Nylan, Henry Rosemont, Jr. and Li Waiyee.

Standaert, Nicolas (1999). "The Jesuits did NOT Manufacture 'Confucianism'," in *East Asian Science, Technology and Medicine* 16.

Sterckx, Roel (2007). "Searching for Spirit: Shen and Sacrifice in Warring States and Han Philosophy and Ritual," in *Extrême-Orient Extrême-Occident* 29.

Tang Junyi 唐君毅 (2016). "Chang Tsai's Theory of Mind and Its Metaphysical Basis," in *The Complete Works of Tang Junyi* 唐君毅全集, Vol. 29. Beijing: Jiuzhou Press.

—— (1991). *The Complete Works of Tang Junyi* 唐君毅全集, Vols. 4, 11 and 14. Taipei: Xuesheng Shuju.

—— (1962). "The t'ien ming (heavenly ordinance) in pre-Ch'in China," in *Philosophy East and West* 11.

—— (1954). "張橫渠之心性論及其形上學之根據," in *Journal of Oriental Studies* 東方文化, I.

Taylor, Charles (1989). *Sources of the Self: The Making of the Modern Identity*. Cambridge: Harvard University Press.

Tu Wei-ming (1989). *Centrality and Commonality: An Essay on Confucian Religiousness*. Albany: State University of New York Press.

—— (1976). *Centrality and Commonality: An Essay on Chung-yung*. Honolulu: University of Hawaii Press.

Waley, Arthur (1939). *Three Ways of Thought in Ancient China*. Stanford: Stanford University Press.

—— (trans.) (1938). *The Analects of Confucius*. London: George Allen and Unwin.

Wang Aihe (2000). *Cosmology and Political Culture in Early China*. Cambridge: Cambridge University Press.

Wang Bi (1965). "Mingxiang 明象" (Elucidating the Image), *Zhouyi Lueli* 周易略例 (A Summary Introduction to the *Book of Changes*) in the *Baibucongshu Jicheng* 百部叢書集成.

Watson, Burton (1963). *Hsün Tzu: Basic Writings*. New York: Columbia University Press.

Whitehead, A.N. (1985). *Process and Reality* (corrected edition). ed. D. Griffin and D. Sherburne. New York: Free Press.

—— (1938). *Modes of Thought*. New York: Macmillan.

Wing-tsit Chan (1963). *A Source Book in Chinese Philosophy*. Princeton: Princeton University Press.

—— (1955). "The Evolution of the Concept *Jen*," in *Philosophy East and West* 4.

Wittenborn, Allen (1981). "*Li* Revisited and Other Explorations," in *The Bulletin of Sung-Yuan Studies* 17.

Wittgenstein, Ludwig (1953). *Philosophical Investigations (PI)*. ed. G.E.M. Anscombe and R. Rhees. trans. G.E.M. Anscombe. Oxford: Blackwell.

Wong, David B. (1991). "Is There a Distinction Between Reason and Emotion in Mencius?" in *Philosophy East and West* 41.

Xunzi 荀子 (1950). Harvard-Yenching Institute Sinological Index Series, Supp. 22. Peking: Harvard-Yenching Institute.

Yearley, Lee (1990). *Mencius and Aquinas: Theories of Virtue and Conceptions of Courage*. Albany: State University of New York Press.

Zhang Yanhua (2007). *Transforming Emotions with Chinese Medicine: An Ethnographic Account from Contemporary China*. Albany: State University of New York Press.

Zhao Tingyang 趙汀陽 (2016). 惠此中國. 北京: 中信出版社.

Zhou Yiqun (2010). *Festivals, Feasts and Gender Relations in Ancient China and Greece*. Cambridge: Cambridge University Press.

Zhuangzi 莊子 (1947). Harvard-Yenching Institute Sinological Index Series, Supp. 20. Peking: Harvard-Yenching Institute.

Acknowledgements

This *Conceptual Lexicon for Classical Confucian Philosophy* is a companion volume to the new *Sourcebook in Classical Confucian Philosophy*, a project that has been under construction for the past several decades. The *Lexicon* has taken as its foundation the research into and glossaries of key philosophical terms found in my collaborative translations and publications over the years with D.C. Lau, David L. Hall, and Henry Rosemont, Jr. In many ways, the compilation of this work is my tribute to them and to the proposition that the shared enjoyment of academic collaboration is itself an object lesson in Confucian values. Again, another major source of energy and inspiration for this work has been a team of scholars who have worked tirelessly under the auspices of the Master of Confucianism 儒學大家 project sponsored by the Shandong Provincial Government and the Confucius Research Institute 孔子研究院: Tian Chenshan 田辰山, Wen Haiming 溫海明, Bian Junfeng 卞俊峰, Zhang Kai 張凱, and Sun Zhihui 孫智慧. Our goal in "translating China" has always been bilingual publications that promote the continuing dialogue between the Chinese and Western academies. I have also had two research assistants during this period, Kevin J. Turner 田凱文 and Marzia Yinqi Zhou 周音琪, who have invested themselves in these projects in different ways, and who in giving their best, have demonstrated to me the inseparability of teaching and learning. I have used earlier versions of these works in my classes at Peking University over the past few years, and am indebted to my many students who have asked challenging questions and been the occasion for much revision. With collaboration being a major trope, I would also like to thank my editor at the Commercial Press 商務印書館, Liu Tong 劉彤 and my editor at State University of New York Press, James Peltz, for their professionalism and stoic patience in managing the production of this joint publication.

Book Cover: On the cover is an image of the 4500-year-old cypress tree that continues to grow in the garden of the Songyang Academy 嵩陽書院 in Henan province. This Academy was first established in 484 as a Buddhist temple and retreat under the name of 嵩陽寺, and then during the Sui dynasty, was converted into a Daoist monastery named 嵩陽觀. In 1035 during the Song dynasty it became a seat of higher learning under its current name devoted to research in and the teaching of the Confucian classics by succeeding generations of distinguished Confucian scholars, taking its place among China's four great academies.

www.ingramcontent.com/pod-product-compliance
Ingram Content Group UK Ltd.
Pitfield, Milton Keynes, MK11 3LW, UK
UKHW041920140426
5217IPUK00014B/251